NEGOTIATION

SAGE PUBLISHING: OUR STORY

At SAGE, we mean business. We believe in creating evidence-based, cutting-edge content that helps you prepare your students to succeed in today's ever-changing business world. We strive to provide you with the tools you need to develop the next generation of leaders, managers, and entrepreneurs.

- We invest in the right authors who distill research findings and industry ideas into practical applications.

- We keep our prices affordable and provide multiple format options for students.

- We remain permanently independent and fiercely committed to quality content and innovative resources.

NEGOTIATION

Moving From Conflict to Agreement

Kevin W. Rockmann

George Mason University

Claus W. Langfred

George Mason University

Matthew A. Cronin

George Mason University

Los Angeles | London | New Delhi
Singapore | Washington DC | Melbourne

SAGE

FOR INFORMATION:

SAGE Publications, Inc.
2455 Teller Road
Thousand Oaks, California 91320
E-mail: order@sagepub.com

SAGE Publications Ltd.
1 Oliver's Yard
55 City Road
London EC1Y 1SP
United Kingdom

SAGE Publications India Pvt. Ltd.
B 1/I 1 Mohan Cooperative Industrial Area
Mathura Road, New Delhi 110 044
India

SAGE Publications Asia-Pacific Pte. Ltd.
18 Cross Street #10–10/11/12
China Square Central
Singapore 048423

Printed in the United States of America

Library of Congress Cataloging-in-Publication Data

Names: Rockmann, Kevin W., author. | Langfred, Claus W., author. | Cronin, Matthew A., author.

Title: Negotiation : moving from conflict to agreement / Kevin W. Rockmann, Claus W. Langfred, Matthew A. Cronin.

Description: Los Angeles : SAGE, [2021] | Includes bibliographical references and index.

Identifiers: LCCN 2019031604 | ISBN 9781544320441 (paperback ; alk. paper) | ISBN 9781544397474 (epub) | ISBN 9781544397481 (epub) | ISBN 9781544397467 (pdf)

Subjects: LCSH: Negotiation in business. | Negotiation. | Conflict management.

Classification: LCC HD58.6 .R6325 2021 | DDC 158/.5—dc23
LC record available at https://lccn.loc.gov/2019031604

This book is printed on acid-free paper.

Certified Chain of Custody
Promoting Sustainable Forestry
www.sfiprogram.org
SFI-01268
SFI label applies to text stock

Acquisitions Editor: Maggie Stanley
Content Development Editor: Janeane Calderon
Editorial Assistant: Janeane Calderon
Marketing Manager: Sarah Panella
Production Editor: Veronica Stapleton Hooper
Copy Editor: Colleen Brennan
Typesetter: C&M Digitals (P) Ltd.
Proofreader: Sarah J. Duffy
Indexer: Molly Hall
Cover Designer: Janet Kiesel

20 21 22 23 24 10 9 8 7 6 5 4 3 2 1

BRIEF CONTENTS

SECTION III • MANAGING *YOUR* NEGOTIATION

DETAILED CONTENTS

SECTION III • MANAGING *YOUR* NEGOTIATION

PREFACE

We wrote this book because in teaching negotiation for a combined 50 years at the undergraduate, graduate, and executive levels, we have noticed that our students seem to struggle with negotiating despite learning many of the tactics utilized by "good negotiators." Although we teach negotiation one concept (or tactic) at a time, negotiations are actually comprised of a set of interdependent moves or behaviors that have to fit into a large, complex picture. Students seem to grasp the moves if discussed independently—for example, how adding an issue to the negotiation might facilitate the creation of value—but fail to understand the interrelations and larger context, such as the conditions under which adding an issue to the negotiation is more or less likely to work.

Let's take an example of that specific negotiation tactic, **adding an issue**, which is typically taught as an "integrative" tactic that can be used to create value. Adding issues "expands the pie," allowing negotiators more options to be creative in negotiations. However, this gives budding negotiators an overly simplistic, and unfortunately unrealistic, view. What is more difficult to convey to students is that, depending on the parties and the state of the negotiation, adding an issue can mean different things and lead to different outcomes. For example:

- Adding an issue can show the other side a willingness to be vulnerable via empathizing with one of their tangible or intangible interests.

- Adding an issue could be a deceptive way to take advantage of someone else's uncertainty.

- Adding an issue might make someone else uncomfortable if they are already overwhelmed by the complexity of the negotiation.

- Adding an issue can be used to help someone save face in the negotiation and ultimately say yes.

- Adding an issue that the other side believed was permanently off the table can lead to feelings of anger and distrust.

A student may not realize these possibilities when the tactic of adding an issue is confined to discussions of integrative negotiation and creating value. A similar point can be made for using BATNA, forming a coalition, asking questions, and other tactics.

We want students to wrestle with the underlying psychology of negotiation, so they can diagnose not just what a tactic is, but why it worked or why it didn't work. Our goal here, while covering the main concepts of negotiation, is to flip the discussion so that students start by analyzing *why* things happen, and then focus on understanding *what* things happen. If students can grasp these underlying concepts (*why* negotiators behave and think the way they do) in addition to the more specific negotiation tactics (*what* negotiators do), they will hopefully have a stronger conceptual base by which to understand the range of behaviors and outcomes that occur in negotiation.

HOW IS THIS BOOK DIFFERENT?

Look at the table of contents. You will notice that while the concepts in many of our chapter titles are familiar, the titles of our chapters perhaps are not. The traditional way to organize a book on negotiation is by the research on negotiation. We have purposely not taken this approach. Rather, we structure the book around the lived experience of the actual negotiator, starting with the common mistakes (Chapter 1); the fundamentals and planning (Chapters 2–3); the main ways in which negotiators obtain value, or what we call "negotiation levers" (Chapters 4–10); individual and cultural differences (Chapters 11–12); and some best practices on how to manage negotiations (Supplements and Appendices).

With the chapters on negotiation levers (Chapters 4–10), you will notice that we begin each chapter with a discussion of the *underlying concept*, separate from negotiation. We then weave in negotiation examples to show how that concept does or does not work in various situations. Before we get to logrolling, we talk about reciprocity; before we get to BATNA, we talk about opportunity costs; and so on. We've found that our students benefit from knowing why and how certain tactics work, not just whether or not they work and how to use them. This allows students to make connections between chapters as well, so they are not labeling negotiations as being *only* about creating value, or *only* about power, or *only* about BATNA. In the real world, negotiations are about all of these simultaneously.

As you look closer at the table of contents you may notice chapters or topics that are not traditionally associated with a negotiation course. We include an entire chapter on intangible interests, for example, where we delve into issues such as identity and saving face. Why? Because issues related to identity are often very much in play when negotiations are happening. Identity helps us explain why someone might say "yes" or not; thus, we felt as if we had to give it the attention it deserves.

You will also see that we use many nonwork examples in addition to work examples of negotiation. Why? Because negotiation is everywhere! Anytime someone has conflict that is interdependent with someone else, that person has the opportunity to negotiate. We purposely tried to put as many diverse examples of negotiation in the book as possible so that students come away with a broader understanding of conflict management and resolution, not just of formal business negotiations.

WAIT, DOES THIS MEAN I HAVE TO COMPLETELY RESTRUCTURE MY COURSE?

No. You will find familiar terminology in this book that you would find in any negotiation book—integrative/distributive negotiation, creating value, BATNA, logrolling, anchoring, and the like—which makes any change much easier to bear. You also do not have to use the role-plays provided here—you can easily use the current role-plays or cases you are using along with the various chapters in this book. What we are encouraging is a discussion around *why* tactics work or not so that students understand the more complex dynamics of real-world negotiations.

ARE YOU SAYING THAT THERE IS NO CHAPTER ON INTEGRATIVE AND DISTRIBUTIVE BARGAINING?

Yes, in fact. But think about these terms. In almost *every* negotiation there are both integrative and distributive elements. Our experience is that when you label negotiations "integrative" or "distributive," it puts students in the wrong mind-set. We want students to see the underlying forces at play in every negotiation and understand when and why tactics such as reciprocity or using intangible interests or leveraging formal power are likely to work or not. Being able to "label" a negotiation as integrative or distributive, while potentially helpful post hoc, is very difficult for a novice negotiator heading out to solve their own conflict. Given the previous example of adding an issue, we also hesitate to label tactics as "integrative" or "distributive"—the same tactic might create value in one negotiation and destroy value in the next depending on the mind-set of the other party.

CAN I USE THE CHAPTERS OUT OF ORDER?

Of course! We've designed and labeled the chapters so that, besides Chapters 1 and 2, they are not overly dependent on what has come previously. Some instructors will want students to read reciprocity (Chapter 4), intangible interests (Chapter 5), and relationships (Chapter 6) early in the course. Others may want to discuss formal power (Chapter 8), alternatives (Chapter 9), and persistence and goals (Chapter 10) early in the course. Some might want to start with uncertainty (Chapter 7). Others will want to discuss planning (Chapter 3) after Chapters 4–10. Still others may want to discuss individual (Chapter 11) and cultural (Chapter 12) differences early in the course. All of these uses are possible.

WHAT DO I DO WITH THE PLANNING CHAPTER (CHAPTER 3)?

This is perhaps the most significant divergence between this book and other textbooks. What we provide in Chapter 3 is a thoughtful way for any negotiator to prepare for a negotiation. This chapter comes with many examples and worksheets that students can use. We give our students Tables 3.10 and 3.11 on the first day of class. They won't know all of the terminology just yet, but it shows them where they are going. By the mid-point (depending on pace) of the class, they should be able to do most of the plan. By the end of the class, they should be able to do an entire negotiation plan. We've found that it is through planning, as a complement to the anxiety-producing doing, that the real learning of negotiation takes place. Planning gives students a structured space to think through the psychology of the negotiation and script out what they might do and say and, more importantly, *why*.

WHAT ABOUT ROLE-PLAY EXERCISES?

We have provided seven new role-play exercises that are associated with Chapters 4–10, which are yours to use if you use this book. These have been designed specifically to highlight the concepts in each chapter while also building on the previous chapters. Each one comes with its own teaching note.

WHAT ABOUT ETHICS?

While it may be tempting to have a dedicated chapter on ethics, our fear was that having a dedicated chapter on ethics would lead students to see ethics as relevant only when they are primed as such to deal with "ethical" negotiations. As we know from the work of Ann Tenbrunsel and colleagues,[1] this creates significant problems, because segmenting ethics unconsciously tells students when to put their "ethics hat" on, reducing the likelihood that other situations will be seen in terms of their ethical questions. We address this by having a dedicated section on ethics in every chapter following the introduction of ethics in Chapter 2. Our goal is to have students understand that ethical concerns (like concepts and tactics) do not exist in isolation but rather are always potentially present in negotiations.

HOW CAN I USE THE SUPPLEMENTS AND APPENDICES?

The six supplements and three appendices have a few purposes. (1) We have included the supplements because many instructors wanted, for example, dedicated sections on mediation and arbitration (Supplement D), technology (Supplement B), or "hardball" tactics (Supplement E). Although these supplements could've been entire chapters, we tried to keep these discussions as focused and useful for students as possible. (2) We have included the first two appendices with short vignettes (Appendix 1) and a long case (Elqui Terra—Appendix 2) because we wanted there to be material to aid in the integrated teaching of negotiation. That is, most negotiations involve multiple concepts, tactics, and other elements. These vignettes and the long case are designed to help emphasize that point for students. (3) We have provided tips on job negotiations (Appendix 3) because that is always the negotiation students ask about the most. So you can pair these with chapters, use them for in-class discussions, or leave for the students to explore on their own.

Structure of the Book

Section I: Introduction to Negotiation

The first two chapters represent an introduction to the study of negotiation and fundamental material basic to understanding the science of negotiation. The third chapter presents a framework to plan for negotiation.

- Chapter 1: This chapter provides an overview of how to think about negotiation, including the reasons for negotiating and some of the main mistakes negotiators make. The goal for this chapter is to understand generally why individuals should negotiate and also why individuals struggle with negotiating.

- Chapter 2: This chapter follows the traditional saying "You need to walk before you can run." We use this chapter to teach many of the fundamental terms and concepts central to all negotiations, such as interests versus positions, issues, resistance points, creating and claiming value, and so on. We also introduce the idea that some negotiation tactics are more centered on convincing others, whereas others are more centered on understanding others. This chapter contains background on negotiation ethics.

- Chapter 3: We walk through a negotiation plan in this chapter, including preference sheets, bargaining mixes, and anticipating negotiation dynamics. This chapter includes a planning worksheet (see Tables 3.10 and 3.11) for students to work through as they prepare for their own negotiations.

Section II: Negotiation Levers

Chapters 4 through 10 represent the negotiation levers, moving generally from understanding to convincing as shown in Figure 1. Specifically, Chapters 4 through 6 are focused more on how to understand others in order to obtain value, whereas Chapters 8 through 10 are focused more on how to convince others in order to obtain value. Chapter 7, on uncertainty, represents both, as to use uncertainty to convince others requires an understanding of what they know or how they are thinking about the negotiation. Following each of these chapters is a supplement on a specific practical implication of negotiation: The Stages of Negotiation, Negotiation and Technology, Negotiating With More Than One Person, Mediation and Arbitration "Hardball" Tactics of Negotiation, and Resource and Time Constraints.

- Chapter 4: This chapter focuses on reciprocity, one of the most fundamental ways to obtain value in negotiations. Many of the tactics covered in this chapter are the "tried and true" tactics of what you might think lead to integrative negotiations.

- Chapter 5: Negotiators don't care just about things; they also care about how they are treated and how they are seen. In this chapter we take this idea that negotiators have intangible interests and discuss the source of such interests. We explain why identity and saving face matters, why individuals feel threatened, and what negotiators can do to manage their own and others' egos.

- Chapter 6: In this chapter we explore the importance of relationships. Negotiations happen in the context of relationships, so we need to understand trust, liking, and other relationship dynamics that are bound to help or hinder negotiations.

Figure 1 Negotiation Levers

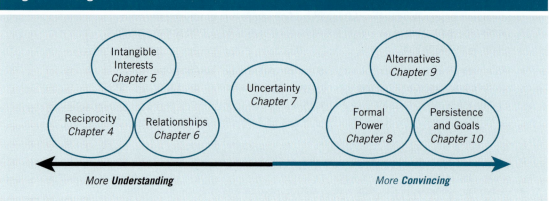

- **Chapter 7:** Negotiations are about making decisions in the context of incomplete information. We use this entire chapter to explore these ideas, such as what happens when we have uncertainty about others, about ourselves, about issues, or about anything else in the negotiation. Knowing this uncertainty dynamic in negotiations allows for many opportunities to get value from others in negotiations.

- **Chapter 8:** This chapter is a discussion of formal power. The tactics in this chapter reveal how to convince individuals to give more as a function of formal control of resources, positions, and authority.

- **Chapter 9:** One potential source of power comes from one's alternatives, typically discussed in negotiation as one's BATNA (best alternative to a negotiated agreement). Given the centrality of this concept in almost every negotiation, we devote an entire chapter to this idea.

- **Chapter 10:** The more work you put in, the more you care about your negotiated outcomes and the more likely you are to meet your goals. We devote this chapter to persistence and goals, and we provide an understanding of how negotiators might be more or less motivated to be persistent in reaching outcomes.

Section III: Managing *Your* Negotiation

Chapters 11 and 12 discuss various features of negotiations that help (or hinder) the leveraging of tactics learned from the earlier chapters.

- **Chapter 11:** This chapter covers individual characteristics such as personality, gender, ability, diversity, and emotions.

- **Chapter 12:** This chapter describes how culture impacts negotiation, including defining culture and cultural dimensions, understanding different types of culture, and exploring the implications of cultural differences, while providing general advice for dealing with cross-cultural negotiations.

It is through the knowledge of why people react and behave the way that they do that students will be able to truly understand what happens and, more importantly, why it happens in negotiation. Knowing why makes deciding what to do easier and more effective. We hope that students will use this as a basis for not only gaining knowledge and insight into negotiation but also solving the conflict in their lives more effectively.

Digital Resources

edge.sagepub.com/Rockmann $\mathbf{\$}$SAGE edge™

SAGE Edge offers a robust online environment featuring an impressive array of tools and resources for review, study, and further exploration, keeping both instructors and students on the cutting edge of teaching and learning.

SAGE Edge for Instructors supports teaching by making it easy to integrate quality content, creating a rich learning environment for students.

- **Microsoft® Word test bank**: This test bank offers a diverse set of test questions and answers for each chapter of the book. Multiple-choice, matching, and short-answer questions for every chapter help instructors assess students' progress and understanding.

- **Microsoft® PowerPoint® slides**: Chapter-specific slide presentations offer assistance with lecture and review preparation by highlighting essential content, features, and artwork from the book.

- **Instructor's manual**: The instructor's manual contains numerous resources for each chapter, including learning objectives, key concepts, suggested teaching strategies, resources, suggested exercises or projects, and answers to end-of-chapter questions, activities, and/or cases. These resources are collated in the instructor's manual files.

- **Multimedia resources**: Videos, articles, and helpful links reinforce and further engage learners.

SAGE Edge for Students provides a personalized approach to help students accomplish their coursework goals in an easy-to-use learning environment.

- Mobile-friendly **eFlashcards** strengthen understanding of key terms and concepts.

- Mobile-friendly practice **quizzes** allow for independent assessment by students of their mastery of course material.

- **Multimedia content** includes video and web resources that appeal to students with different learning styles.

ACKNOWLEDGMENTS

Kevin would like to thank Greg Northcraft, who mentored him in the art of teaching negotiation; Shalini Nambiar and Ashley Richardson, whose research assistance proved to be invaluable; Mike Pratt, who was brave enough to try out portions of the book; all of the George Mason MBA students who have commented, refined, and edited versions along the way; and, most importantly, Alison, Naomi, and Blake, whom he feels extremely fortunate to be able to negotiate with every day.

Claus would like to thank Jeanne Brett, who was the director of the Dispute Resolution Research Center and was a formative influence on him, not only introducing him to the field of negotiations but also mentoring and developing him as an instructor; and Neta Moye, who has always kept him sane and focused on what is important.

Matt would like to thank Laurie Weingart for introducing him to the skills of negotiation and conflict management, Katie Gordon for making such an introduction possible, Heather Rekeweg for helping him keep those skills sharp, and Alex Cronin for showing him the limits of those skills.

PUBLISHER'S ACKNOWLEDGMENTS

SAGE and the authors gratefully acknowledge the following reviewers.

John Baur, University of Nevada, Las Vegas

Joy E. Beatty, University of Michigan–Dearborn

Theodore Brown Sr., Oakwood University

Dan Carrison, University of La Verne

John E. Cicala, Texas A&M University–Kingsville

Melissa W. Graham, University of Central Oklahoma

Loraleigh Keashly, Wayne State University

Dale F. Kehr, University of Memphis

Mary C. Kern, Baruch College–City University of New York

Jalane Meloun, Barry University

Edward W. Miles, Georgia State University

Alexandra Mislin, Kogod School of Business, American University

Thomas Mobley, SPHR, University of Cincinnati

Silvia Ramirez, University of San Francisco

Judith Richards, California Lutheran University

Timothy L. Schauer, Sweet Briar College

John Shuford, Portland State University and Royal Roads University

M. Joseph Sirgy, Virginia Polytechnic Institute and State University

Dustin J. Sleesman, University of Delaware

Alexandra N. Sousa, Texas A&M University

Bradley S. Wesner, Sam Houston State University

Eric Albert Zimmer, University of Notre Dame

ABOUT THE AUTHORS

Kevin W. Rockmann is a professor of management at the George Mason School of Business. His primary research area is psychological attachment and relationship formation and as such is particularly interested in theories of identity, social exchange, and motivation. He enjoys studying distributed, virtual, on-demand, and other nontraditional work contexts. His research has appeared in *Academy of Management Review*, *Academy of Management Journal*, *Academy of Management Annals*, *Journal of Applied Psychology*, *Organization Behavior and Human Decision Processes*, *Academy of Management Discoveries*, and *Academy of Management Proceedings*, among other outlets. His research has also been covered by *Time*, the *New York Times*, NPR, *Forbes*, and the *Chicago Tribune*. He designed and has taught MBA and undergraduate negotiation courses for 15 years and in the process has won six separate teaching awards. He currently serves on the editorial boards of *Academy of Management Journal*, *Academy of Management Review*, and *Administrative Science Quarterly*.

Claus W. Langfred is an associate professor of management in the School of Business at George Mason University. He received his PhD in organization behavior from Northwestern University in 1998, where he worked with the Dispute Resolution Research Center. His research has appeared in the *Academy of Management Journal*, *Journal of Applied Psychology*, *Journal of Organizational Behavior*, *Journal of Management*, *Small Group Research*, and *International Journal of Conflict Management*. His work has also appeared in multiple book chapters, been selected for the Best Paper Proceedings of the Academy of Management, and been covered in the *Harvard Business Review* and the *Financial Times*. He currently serves on the editorial boards of the *Journal of Trust Research* and the *Journal of Organizational Behavior*. He has taught negotiation for over 20 years, primarily at the MBA level, but also in other graduate and undergraduate programs, as well as to executive clients. He has received numerous teaching awards at multiple universities (Northwestern University, Washington University in St. Louis, and George Mason University) for both graduate and undergraduate classes on negotiation.

Matthew A. Cronin is an associate professor of management in the School of Business at George Mason University. He received his PhD in organizational behavior from Carnegie Mellon University in 2004. His research has appeared in *Academy of Management Review*, *Organizational Behavior and Human Decision Processes*, *Journal of Organizational Behavior*, *Academy of Management Annals*, and *Management Science* and has been presented at the World Economic Forum in Davos, Switzerland. He has served on the editorial boards of *Negotiation and Conflict Management Research, Organizational Behavior and Human Decision Processes, Management Science, Academy of Management Review* and is currently an associate editor at *Organizational Psychology Review*. He has won numerous teaching awards and is the coauthor (with Jeffrey Loewenstein) of *The Craft of Creativity* (Stanford University Press, 2018).

INTRODUCTION TO NEGOTIATION

CHAPTER 1

HOW TO THINK ABOUT NEGOTIATION

Learning Objectives

1. Describe and develop examples of negotiation potential.

2. Understand that negotiators have wrong assumptions and faulty knowledge that impede the ability to negotiate effectively.

3. Provide examples of how various biases limit negotiation effectiveness.

4. Develop examples of how the common mistakes made in negotiation affect negotiations at work, at home, when shopping, and in other situations.

5. Utilize the knowledge of the common mistakes to develop a personal plan for overcoming negotiation weaknesses.

$SAGE edge™

Master the content at study .sagepub.com/rockmann

Negotiation is both art and science. It is art in that there are many different ways to accomplish the same goal, style matters, and ability increases through practice. It is a science in that much of negotiation operates systematically and with regularity, and you can formalize the process if you pay attention. These regularities provide knowledge that will enable you to explain, predict, and control how negotiations will proceed. The more adept you become in the science of negotiation, the more comfortable you will be in exploring different ways to negotiate (i.e., the art of negotiating).

To understand, access, and use scientific knowledge about negotiation, you must understand what a negotiation entails in a precise and sophisticated way. Precision comes from using terminology that is clear and specific in meaning. Learning such an analytical framework is a significant challenge because negotiation is something most people have had some experience with. Therefore, the terms we will use (e.g., a negotiation *issue*), as well as the concepts (e.g., compromise), will be things that are likely familiar to you. However, your knowledge of what these concepts are might be imprecise at this stage. Clarifying what these terms mean is central to this book. For instance, an *issue* in negotiation is a specific item that you are trading or negotiating over (e.g., salary), not just a general concern or problem. Similarly, compromise, contrary to folk wisdom, typically exemplifies poor negotiating skill, in that it describes a scenario in which all parties are at least somewhat dissatisfied.

The reason we take so much time to improve your vocabulary and understanding is because folk wisdom and imprecise terminology can work together to support false beliefs about how negotiations work. Take, for example, the dogmatic notion that, in negotiation, "information is power." This belief makes negotiators very reluctant to share information with other parties, for fear of being taken advantage of. However, in negotiations, often the only way to get what you want is by sharing some information with the other side. Sharing information builds trust, and trust sets the tone for collaboration in effective negotiations. This habit of always withholding information for fear of losing power is a bad habit that takes work to break.

WHAT IS A NEGOTIATION, AND WHY DO WE NEGOTIATE?

One of the first lessons in the study of negotiation is that there are far more negotiation opportunities around us than we realize. Negotiation knowledge should not be reserved for special occasions such as major purchases or career transitions. As we go about our lives, there are likely to be situations that come up on a daily basis that could be resolved more effectively if we applied negotiation knowledge to them. A colleague of ours at the University of Michigan, Dr. Shirli Kopelman, has told us (and shown us) that she negotiates practically everything: discounts when none are advertised, reduced admissions to clubs because "It is Thursday, there is no one at this club, and I am bringing 10 people in." She uses her knowledge in all sorts of situations where people normally do not think to negotiate, and she benefits greatly by doing so.[1]

Of course, not all situations can be negotiated. For example, you could not negotiate with the city to dump poisonous waste into the local lake because law (and common sense) forbids this. Similarly, you would probably not try to negotiate with a judge after you were issued a verdict ("OK, I am guilty of reckless driving, but how about instead of a $1,000 fine and 5 points on my record, we go with $500 and no points?"); norms and the threat of punishment make this a bad choice. You may also think it a bad idea to negotiate with a bank robber if you are a bank teller. "I know you want all the money in my drawer, but how about I just give you half and agree not to call the police for 10 minutes?" Negotiation, while potentially successful (as seen in this sidebar), in this case is quite the risky choice.

Confronted by a gunman demanding that he empty the cash register, Subway Sandwich Shop manager Ollice Nettles made a counteroffer: $10 and a meatball sandwich. "This is the first time we've seen a robbery that was negotiated," police spokesman Mike Wright said. Police said the robbery started when a slim, 6-foot, unshaven customer walked into the Subway shop Monday. He ordered a meatball sandwich and went to the bathroom. He returned a few moments later and a female clerk waited to take his money. That is when the customer turned robber and announced, "By the way, this is a holdup." The robber then pointed a black revolver at the woman. She ducked behind the counter and fell to the floor. Nettles, who apparently did not see the gun or realize what was going on, turned and asked the man what he wanted. The robber said he wanted all the money, and negotiations began. Nettles asked the robber if he would accept $10 and the sandwich. The robber replied that he would take no less than $20 and the sandwich, and the deal was done. Police said the thief fled with the money, the sandwich, and two other men who were waiting outside in a gray Pontiac.

Source: Knight-Ridder Newspapers, Spring 1991, Delray Beach, FL.

You can think of **negotiation potential** as the degree to which a conflict situation might be resolved through negotiation. Negotiation is effective when you get more or lose less than you would have if you had not negotiated, and getting more of what you want is *always* the objective when negotiating. To think about negotiation potential, let us first try to define what conditions must exist in a situation for negotiation to happen. We start with the formal definition of negotiation as "a process of potentially opportunistic interaction by which two or more parties, with some apparent conflict, seek to do better through jointly decided action than they could otherwise."[2] If we simplify this definition, we can identify three basic conditions under which negotiation can take place:

1. There is more than one person.

2. The people want, or seem to want, different things (**apparent conflict**).

3. The people have to deal with each other in order to get what they want (**joint action**).

To map this on to what is probably the most familiar negotiation scenario, the selling of a car, negotiation involves multiple parties (buyer, seller), the parties want different things (a good car for the money, to get reasonable value for the car), and the parties have to deal with each other to get what they want. For instance, the buyer can't just say, "I am paying $4,000; now give me the car," nor can the seller say, "You buy this car or else!" Both the buyer and the seller need each other to make the deal happen.

As you will see throughout this chapter and throughout the book, there are a wide variety of situations that fit these criteria, many that we typically don't see as "negotiation." Table 1.1 provides some of these examples. The bottom line is that when you think about what situations have negotiation potential, you need to include any situation that involves multiple parties, apparent conflict, and joint action or interdependence.

Although many situations have negotiation potential, some do not. Figure 1.1 presents a flowchart to help decide. This is also useful for drawing boundaries around the situations that are and are not responsive to negotiation knowledge.

Do Others Have Control Over What You Want or Need?

The factor that needs to be considered first is the nature of the interdependence among those involved in the negotiation. Interdependence means that parties require interaction to accomplish their goals. Interdependence can take many forms. Examples of social interdependence (want to be together) appear in Table 1.1 along with logistical interdependence (need to work together), which can take multiple forms. No matter the type of interdependence, what is important here is that interdependence implies a constraint that is manifest in the other parties. In its simplest form, you cannot get what you want without someone else's participation. If you could, then there would be no need to negotiate.

You may want to be paid more, but if your boss is not the person who decides salaries in your company, you have no need to negotiate with them on this matter. This is important to think about because if you spend time negotiating with someone who

Figure 1.1 Is There Negotiation Potential?

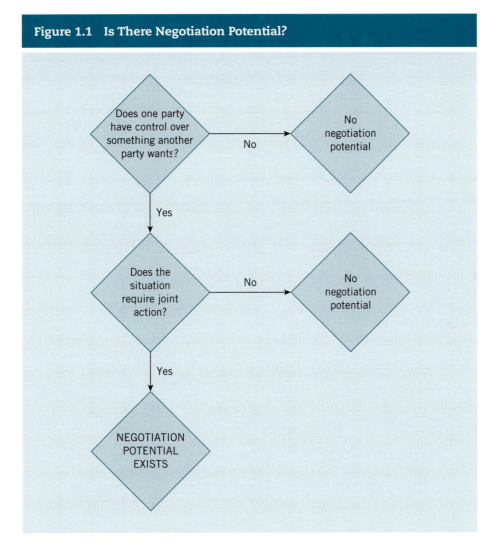

cannot change the outcome, you're wasting your time. The reverse is true as well: Involving people who do not care about a particular outcome wastes both people's time. The bottom line is that if negotiation cannot help you do better than you could have working alone, you should not do it; in other words, you can do better through joint action than you could do otherwise.

Does the Situation Involve the Need for Joint Action?

Even if one party has control over what another party wants, negotiation potential does not exist unless something is preventing the party from providing it free of cost. This

Table 1.1 Nontraditional Situations With Negotiation Potential

Situation	Parties	Apparent Conflict	Interdependence
Bill is not performing at his job	Bill, Bill's manager	Bill's manager wants high performance from Bill. Bill wants recognition from his manager.	The manager has formal authority over Bill but needs Bill to do his work for the good of the department.
Several university students are working together on a class project	Students on the team	Some students are more concerned about the grade, some more concerned about learning, others concerned about the duration of team meetings and how much effort they have to expend.	The students need to pool their work in order to produce the final product.
Driver gets a speeding ticket	Officer, driver	The officer wants the driver to accept the ticket and wants to avoid going to court. The driver doesn't want points on his or her license.	The officer has the formal power but can be influenced if he or she thinks the driver will show up in court and fight the ticket.
Friends have to decide what to do on a Saturday night	A group of friends	Some care about the location, some care about the price, some care about the music, and some care about the food.	This group may have both social interdependence (want to stay together) and logistical interdependence (only one person has a car).
Politicians need to pass laws	Constituents, legislature	The politicians want to resolve community issues, keep their jobs, and support their political party.	No one can pass legislation on their own.
Vacation with spouse	Two partners	One wants to save money and relax alone; other wants to go somewhere exclusive with friends.	If one "wins" and the other "loses," resentment will occur, hurting the vacation (and the relationship).

is why the usual hallmark of negotiation is the apparent conflict between parties. Such conflict is the impediment that warrants adjustment on the part of one or more of the parties. If Martha has been unhappy working past 5 pm on Fridays and upon asking realizes her supervisor can happily fulfill her request to leave at 5 pm, there is no need to negotiate because there is no conflict. The need for joint action was minimal as Martha didn't need to do anything beyond asking.

Summary of Why We Negotiate

Negotiation is possible in situations where there are multiple actors who want different things, but they need each other to get them. It also requires that the situation will involve adjustment of some sort so that they can resolve whatever conflict is limiting what they can get. Negotiation potential is realized depending on whether one can adjust the situation to limit or remove the conflict. This adjustment is the result of influence. So, if you know you should negotiate and you know the number of situations that could be effectively resolved via negotiation is endless, why don't you negotiate more often? And further, why might you be *uncomfortable* negotiating? This is probably a main reason you are reading this book and/or taking a negotiation class. We'll highlight a few core challenges to negotiation and summarize some of the most common negotiation mistakes.

COMMON MISTAKES MADE WHEN NEGOTIATING

In this section of the chapter we want to highlight some of the common pitfalls to effective negotiating. Mistakes are not just in what you *do* during a negotiation; mistakes are also about how you *think* about negotiation and conflict in general. Before we get to the mistakes, we want to help you understand why you might be primed to think about negotiations in certain ways that impede your ability to obtain value.

The Mental Model of a Negotiator

Mental models are explanations or thought processes about how things work in the real world.[3] These models are cognitive representations (in your mind) of situations you encounter. Think of them like a rule book: When you go into a store, meet a person, go to class, or any other situation you can think of, there are rules for behavior. Those rules regarding what to expect and how to behave are contained within your mental model of that situation. Mental models also help you organize all the information stored in your mind. As will be discussed in Chapter 7, people inherently don't like complexity and uncertainty and this is why information is organized in mental models. These cognitive structures allow you to simplify the world. Every individual has mental models, and they are different for everyone.

For a simple example of the importance of mental models, consider membership in a team. In a team discussion you may find yourself agreeing with the views expressed by Lisa. This could be because Lisa fits into your mental model of how a "competent" team member looks or behaves. If, on the other hand, Nirish shows up to a team meeting in shorts, flip-flops, and a Hawaiian shirt, you might question his ability to be a productive team member. That is because your mental model of someone who is believable includes certain characteristics. Note that these assumptions may have nothing to do with Lisa or Nirish's actual skills.

Let's do a short exercise to further expand on this idea of mental models:

- What are the first three words or phrases that come to your mind when you think of negotiating for a car?

- What are the first three words or phrases that come to your mind when you think of trying to negotiate which movie to see with your best friend, assuming you each want to see a different movie?

If you are like most people, your answers to the first question might include words such as *difficult, anxious, dishonest, nervous,* and so on. Similarly, your answers to the second question might include words such as *friendly, trade-off, compromise, trust,* or and so on.

Mental models explain why these answers diverge so drastically. Your mental model of a car negotiation is quite different from a negotiation about which movie to go see. When you negotiate for a car, dishonesty is what you are actively thinking about in that negotiation and what you expect from the salesperson. Everything that is said or done in that negotiation is filtered through this lens of dishonesty: *Is what they say true?* This mental model helps you determine what is relevant or not in that negotiation. You might be continually asking yourself: *Does this piece of information help me figure out whether the salesperson is dishonest?*

You may be thinking: car negotiation = difficult = adversary = no trust and choosing movie = easy = friend = trust. Why is choosing the movie so easy? Because you are not thinking of it as a negotiation! You and your friend have different preferences and might want different things, but you are able to navigate that conversation quite easily because you are not worried that your friend is going to take advantage of you. While the car negotiation might seem more difficult, in reality it's quite similar to the movie negotiation. Both situations involve conflict. Both involve two parties. In both negotiations there is the possibility of negotiating other issues. In the car negotiation you might negotiate a warranty, a payment plan, and a service contract. In the movie negotiation you might negotiate who pays for popcorn, who chooses the next movie, and who decides where to eat afterward. Yet our minds ignore these similarities because our mental models of these situations are so starkly different.

So what? Why does it matter that these "negotiations" have similarities? As you will learn in this book, when you negotiate with the car salesperson in a similar way to how you might negotiate with your friend, you increase your chances of getting more. Similarly, when you treat your friend like an adversary, you decrease your chances of getting more.

Now that you have an understanding of mental models, we move to the list of mistakes (Figure 1.2). We discuss these mistakes briefly here so that you can start improving your negotiation behavior immediately, even before we get to the explanation of negotiation fundamentals (Chapter 2), planning for negotiation (Chapter 3), and the negotiation levers (Chapters 4–10).

Figure 1.2   Why Is Negotiation So Difficult?

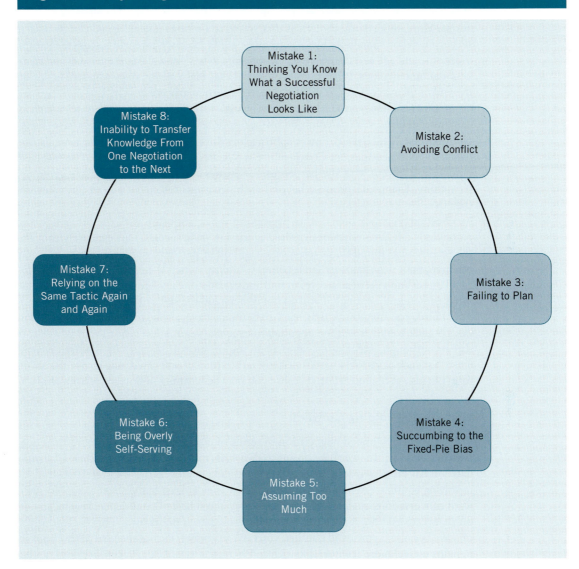

Mistake 1: Thinking You Know
What a Successful Negotiation Looks Like

You might think that you know what it means to "successfully" negotiate. Perhaps you feel like you "won" in your own past negotiations, or have witnessed hard-bargaining, or feel like you always get what you want. Unfortunately, if you are like most of the thousands of students we've taught over the past two decades, you are likely wrong in that belief. Why do you feel like this? Part of the reason is that you haven't yet taken a negotiation class, and so you do not understand the intricacies of what is involved in effective negotiations. More importantly, though, is that you have a motive to feel like you know what a successful negotiation looks like—your own ego! In Chapter 5 we will discuss the nature of identity and ego and the desire for negotiators to feel good about themselves and their negotiation outcomes. It has even been found that many negotiators who feel happy at the end of their negotiations did not negotiate particularly effectively.[4]

Unfortunately, you are likely to be using "folk wisdom" to negotiate, which is misguided. Here are a few common misperceptions that many negotiators have. First, **compromise**, which we define as splitting the difference on a negotiated issue, is not (usually) good negotiation. Compromise is a strategy by which issues can be resolved quickly and (often) with the perception of fairness, in that both sides have given up something. Using compromise beyond such situations can mean you've left value on the table.

Second, you may believe that preserving the relationship with the other side is a particularly effective indicator that the negotiation was a success. Unfortunately, though, the research has found that even spouses and other partners who deeply care for each other are poor negotiators when it comes to adding value.[5] Why? Because it takes dedicated intent and a set of strategies to find and create value in negotiations. Caring for the other person is not enough if you do not understand the skills of negotiation.

Third, you may think that hard-bargainers are great negotiators. This idea has been popularized by so-called negotiation experts. Negotiation is not about power and threats, although such factors can play an important role. Again, the research is very clear that such aggressive tactics destroy rather than create value, not just in the short term but also in the long term, because you may be harming important relationships.

Mistake 2: Avoiding Conflict

We have already defined negotiation in terms of conflict that requires more than one person to resolve. To negotiate means to deal with, rather than avoid, conflict. Unfortunately, it has long been acknowledged that avoiding conflict is often a preferred strategy to solving conflict.[6,7] Avoiding conflict, is, well, easier, at least in the short term. No awkward conversations, no fear of losing, no worry about lack of confidence. If you can put off that conversation, maybe the issue will resolve itself on its own. This is obviously a mistake because if you avoid conflict, you can't negotiate. Part of the goal of this book is to help you feel more comfortable with conflict situations. After all, conflict need not be about fighting or competition. Rather, conflict is about differences. If you can realize the nature of those differences and respond accordingly, you can get more. It's about seeing negotiation not as a tug-of-war, which we'd all like to avoid, but rather as a puzzle, which sounds like fun (See Figure 1.3).

Why do we do this? Two common reasons include differences in individual personality as well as difference in culture and the context of the negotiation. It has long been established that individual differences, especially in personality, can have effects on the process and outcomes in negotiations,[8] and the tendency to avoid conflict is one

Figure 1.3   Negotiation Doesn't Have to Be a Tug-of-War

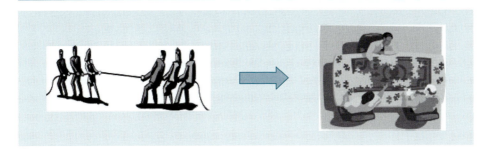

such individual difference.[9] A person with a personality characterized by high levels of conflict avoidance is going to react to negotiation situations in very different ways than a person with a personality characterized by low conflict avoidance. For example, an aggressive opponent in a contentious dispute will likely provide a very unpleasant and uncomfortable experience for the person with a relatively high conflict avoidant personality, whereas it might be seen as an exciting and invigorating challenge by the person who scores very low on measures of conflict avoidance. One of the most common things we hear from students when we ask them what they are hoping to gain from the course is a desire to be less afraid of negotiating, and to be more assertive and proactive in a negotiation. (We discuss personality in more detail in Chapter 11.)

Culture is the other possible reason some people have a tendency to avoid conflict rather than seek a negotiated solution. We discuss cultural differences extensively in Chapter 12. The ways in which conflict is viewed and appropriate methods for conflict resolution can vary greatly from culture to culture.[10] In some cultures, conflict is accepted as a natural state of affairs and consistent with individualism and even aggressiveness, whereas in other cultures there may be strong expectations that overt conflict (especially public conflict) should be avoided and minimized for the greater collective good.[11]

Mistake 3: Failing to Plan

Many people begin negotiations with no more plan than relying on their instincts and hoping for the best. This is unwise. Expert negotiators plan, and they may spend much more time planning than actually negotiating. They plan because they need to think about what they want, what the other side is likely to want, and what possible options may satisfy those needs.

When there is no negotiation plan, instinct causes negotiators to focus on nonideal outcomes. They fail to see outside of standard solutions to negotiation problems (see Mistake 8). They also fail to think about the other side other than in a stereotypical way (see Mistake 5). Earlier we talked about negotiating as a means to get what you want. While there are many ways to do this, you are not going to be able to come up with these options if you cannot use different tools to get what you want. You cannot think flexibly if you are in the middle of arguing for what you want while trying to outwit the other party. Consider the following scenario:

> Betsy was interning at AwesomeCorp in her spring semester. She was getting ready to graduate and was a little worried about finding a job. To Betsy's surprise, her boss called her in to his office and said, "We really like you and we'd like to hire you after you graduate, but we need to get your commitment now. So what salary were you thinking?" Unprepared, Betsy had no idea what to do. She blurted out a reasonable-sounding amount, $40,000, to which the boss said, "Well, that may be just a little high. How about $35,000?" They agreed on $37,500.

At first glance, this may seem like a complete success. Betsy got a job, and the salary, although not exactly what Betsy wanted, was a compromise between her and the boss's offer. Now let's look closer. First, was Betsy creative? No; the only thing they negotiated was salary, even though there are many other issues that could have been negotiated.[12] Now that she's accepted the job offer, it may be hard for her to get other things. We see that she is caught off guard and she is excited because she will have a job, but this works against her. Does she know if $40,000 is a good starting point? Odds are against it. This kind of thinking under pressure is not likely to yield good answers in people without much practice. What should she have done? She should have said, "Wow, this is great; thank you for the offer. Let's set up a time to hammer out the details." She could have had more time and mental space to research and think about what she wanted. The fact that she did not is also probably due to stereotypical thinking—Betsy assumes incorrectly they need to settle this now. Of course, they do not. If the boss wants to hire her, then it is completely reasonable to discuss the offer more formally.

When you plan, not only can you be a more creative negotiator, but you can also understand more ways to productively engage the others with whom you are negotiating. Planning also helps you anticipate problems. You cannot prepare for every contingency, but you certainly can prepare for the likely ones. For example, if you plan to ask for a raise, you are likely to think about how your manager might react. What information does he or she value? What tactics have others used in prior successful negotiations with the manager? You do this in order to manage the process to a favorable outcome. If your manager is emotional, it is better to prepare for anger rather than for silence. If the manager is no-nonsense, then you should prepare for them to want you to cut to the chase than to prepare lots of extra information. You can also prepare for countermeasures to your persuasion techniques. If your manager says, "Why don't you find another job if you think you are worth so much?" it is far better to have a prepared calm response than either shrinking in fear or saying, "Fine, I will!"

Mistake 4: Succumbing to the Fixed-Pie Bias

People use mental shortcuts to simplify thinking in real time. These mental shortcuts are called **heuristics**, which are systematic rules of thumb that we use when making decisions. Heuristics are not necessarily bad, but they can trick us into misinterpreting information that will be used in our decisions. As negotiations are fundamentally about making a large number of sequential decisions (Should I open the negotiation? What should I say? How much should I ask for?), understanding and avoiding the heuristics we use will ultimately make us more effective negotiators.

The biggest error made in decision making is thinking that anything we get in the agreement costs the other side just as much—that is, we assume there is a "fixed-pie" in the negotiation. This is called the **fixed-pie bias** or the **zero-sum bias**.[13,14,15] This bias causes us to believe that the benefits to one side are equal to the costs paid by the other side; in other words, they always equal zero. You can think about this literally as a pie. Imagine that you and your friend are each sitting at the table and are hungry for pie. Your friend's parent, who both of you know makes great pie, brings over a pie with eight precut slices. The options for divvying up the pie thus are set:

- You: 0 pieces; Friend: 8 pieces; **TOTAL: 8 pieces**

- You: 1 piece; Friend: 7 pieces; **TOTAL: 8 pieces**

- . . . and so on . . .

- You: 8 pieces; Friend: 0 pieces; **TOTAL: 8 pieces**

Notice that in each of these possibilities the total number of slices is "fixed" at 8. There are no extra pieces or more pies that can be eaten. The only negotiation here is how to split those 8 pieces between you and your friend.

While most negotiations do not have a fixed number of "pieces," we assume that they do. This is the error we make—the fixed-pie bias. In most negotiations there are other issues to negotiate and, consequently, more "pies" to be added to the table.

We can see in Table 1.2 that negotiations where we fall victim to the fixed-pie bias are very difficult; by nature, they seemingly have to have a "winner" and a "loser." Negotiators who fall victim to this bias thus are more defensive and perhaps more likely to give up quickly, attack, or compromise—none of which is an effective strategy. This is

Table 1.2   Fixed-Pie Bias

Negotiation	Fixed-Pie	Non Fixed-Pie
Job	Salary is the only issue	Salary, job start, job title, bonus, moving expenses all need to be negotiated
Car	Price is the only issue	Price, service plan, financing, trade-in all need to be negotiated
Vacation	Location is the only issue	Location, cost, activities, length all need to be negotiated

also quite prevalent, because this bias has been shown to affect upward of 80% of negotiators.[16] This bias is also notoriously difficult to overcome, even if you know it exists and have experience negotiating.[17,18]

Ian Bremmer of the *Washington Post* wrote eloquently about the dangers of politicians seeing issues in terms of the fixed-pie or zero-sum bias.

"In [the politician's] view of the world, there is a finite amount of everything—money, security, jobs, victories—and nothing can be shared. In other words, the [country], and all of its inhabitants, are in a zero-sum competition over everything, all the time. And you're either victorious or defeated. It's a universe where the strong do what they can and the weak suffer what they must, as Thucydides said. The problem is that the triumphs that [the politician] craves—strength, safety, prosperity—cannot be achieved alone. They require friends and allies, and they require [the politician] to see those people as partners, not competitors. But [the politician] doesn't know how to do that, which makes everyone suspicious; other governments don't like to be punching bags, the only role [the politician] appears to envision for them. Mutual distrust imperils the collaboration the [country] needs to succeed. Which is to say, [the politician's] determination to win could easily position the country to lose."

Source: Bremmer, I. (2018, March 4). In the zero-sum universe, you're either victorious or you're defeated. *Washington Post.*

A phenomenon closely related to the fixed-pie bias is that we assume there is conflict when there really is not any conflict. This is known as false or **illusory conflict**. Take, for example, the situation where you are negotiating with a loved one over where to go on vacation. Perhaps you want to go to Mexico and you assume that the other person wants to go somewhere else. You might approach this negotiation in a very defensive, contentious mode because you believe this is going to be a very difficult conversation. Unfortunately, due to reciprocity (Chapter 4), the other person acts in a hostile manner toward you, even though before the negotiation your loved one would have been absolutely fine with Mexico as a destination. You end up fighting about Mexico and choosing a location neither of you would have put first on your vacation destination list. This is called a **lose-lose agreement**.[19]

Mistake 5: Assuming Too Much

One of the mistakes that is particularly damaging to many of the strategies discussed in this book is when negotiators assume something about the person or people with whom they are negotiating. You value money to a certain degree, so you assume they value money in the same way. You don't like vacationing in Florida because of the heat, so you assume others don't like the heat. You think *Star Wars* is a great movie choice, so you assume others like *Star Wars*. These are all potentially damaging mistakes, as they will cause frustration due to misunderstandings. The **false-consensus effect** is this phenomenon, whereby you tend to overestimate the degree to which your own values, beliefs, and attitudes are normal and shared by others.[20] That is, you assume that others think about the world in the same way that you do. Consider the following scenario:

Peter is a relatively new manager with 10 employees in his accounting department. He has an opening for a new position and wants to hire Danya to fill that role. Danya has told some of Peter's employees and Peter himself that she wants to take the job and is very excited about joining the company. Toward the end of negotiations, Peter asks if Danya is satisfied with the offer, and Danya asks for 3 extra days to review the offer with her husband and close out negotiations with the other companies she is considering. Peter immediately gets upset, because he would never ask a potential employer for 3 extra days and feels that anyone asking for more time must not really want to join his team. He immediately suspects that Danya is using him to get a better offer from another company.

What is happening here is that Peter is assuming Danya has the same thoughts and intentions as he does. He becomes suspicious because in his mind his response (were he in Danya's shoes) is the only reasonable response. He fails to understand that Danya really wants to be 100% committed and because her husband works out of town, she needs the extra time so that she can sit down with him and make a decision together. This causes Peter to have a negative attitude toward Danya and the situation, when in reality Danya is simply making sure she is making the best decision.

Another assumption negotiators often make that may not always be correct is the expectation that others will be consistent over time in their behavior and attitudes. Clearly, the better you are at understanding and predicting another party's behavior, the more effective you may be in a negotiation with them. However, when you try to predict behavior in negotiations, you often do so based on the assumption that past observed behavior was determined by personality (which, after all, is relatively stable and consistent over time). For example, Petya assumes that Jonathan is going to be a very tough negotiator because she's seen him negotiate fiercely in the past. Petya is making the mistake assuming that Jonathan's past behavior was based on his personality, which will carry over into every future negotiation. Unfortunately, using this approach instead of trying to predict behavior based on the situational aspects of the negotiation context—such as bargaining positions, alternatives, power, and so on—turns out often to be very inaccurate.[21] Petya is setting herself up for a difficult negotiation with Jonathan when that may in fact not be the case—perhaps he was just negotiating with someone he didn't trust.

Assuming also creates problems for gaining buy-in with negotiations that involve organizational change. Consider this scenario involving Deb.

Deb was called in to completely reorganize a 60-year-old privately owned company with 75 employees. It had always been loosely run by three owners, two of which inherited the company from their parents. Due to federal regulations, Deb had to put rules into place, including creating a human resources department. Throughout the process and the daily training that was involved, Deb assumed everyone was just as excited as she was about the changes. However, when it came time to work together, she had zero support and felt nothing but resistance.

Deb failed by assuming the employees were all on board with what she was doing. In the end, nobody was willing to make it work. Had she considered their interests, she would've given herself a better chance of completing the process with them in a mutually agreeable way.

Mistake 6: Being Overly Self-Serving

There are a number of ways in which negotiators are self-serving. First, negotiators fall victim to **egocentrism**, in that we tend to be much more interested in our own interests and needs than the interests of the other party. We see this in all types of negotiations. Take, for example, the 10-month lockout in the National Hockey League (NHL) in 2004–2005. During these negotiations the NHL Players Association (NHLPA) was focused almost entirely on preventing the implementation of a salary cap and ultimately turned down multiple offers from the owners in which a salary cap was part of the package. The players were so concerned about protecting their salaries that they failed to understand the financial limitations of the owners. Collectively the owners had lost $273 million operating the league in 2003–2004. They had no incentive to give in to the players and thus were content with canceling the season. If the players had considered the interests of the owners, they could have asked for many other concessions such as changes to the rules, changes to the season, changes to the retirement plan, changes to the draft, changes to the drug-testing policy, and anything else they might have wanted. Their egocentrism prevented this, though, costing them 1,230 games and tens of millions of dollars in lost pay.

The tendency to demand more for an item than you would pay for an item is called the **endowment effect**.[22] You may not be objective about the value of your car, house, or the vacation you want to take because people become emotionally attached to things. This can hurt your ability to process information in negotiations because the other party is not going to have the same emotional attachments you do. If you are selling something, it can lead you to make arguments such as "This TV is wonderful!" which really isn't convincing anyone of anything. In the television show *American Pickers*, hosts Mike and Frank do an excellent job of managing the endowment effect. These two guys are "pickers," in that they travel around the United States to people's homes looking for antique items such as bikes, records, signs, and furniture. Their goal is to buy the items and resell them in their own shop for a profit. This is a ripe environment for the endowment effect, because the individuals selling these items often have emotional attachments to the items. That is, they value the items much more than someone off the street does. This makes them reluctant to sell, even at a profit, which is a problem Mike and Frank must work to overcome.

When we overvalue our own experiences and information that we can easily recall, we fall victim to the **availability bias**. When we enter a new negotiation, we draw on what we can remember about similar negotiations in the past. Those could be past experiences with that party or similar past experiences with other parties. If you remember having a difficult car negotiation at dealership X, you might be distrustful of sales staff at dealership Y. Is there an objective reason for this? No, but without other information to go on, we weight our own memories heavily. This anticipated difficulty becomes part of our schema of "car negotiations." The problem with relying on these memories is that it sets your own expectations for the negotiation and can change the other side's behavior. If you expect the other side not to trust you, you will behave as if they don't trust you. The other side will mimic that behavior because they won't believe they can gain your trust. This leads to your initial belief coming true, as you say to yourself: *I knew I couldn't trust them.* Thus your own bias has in effect created reality; this is a phenomenon known as the **self-fulfilling prophecy.**[23]

Finally, we protect our "self" through the **confirming evidence bias,** the tendency for people to seek out and pay attention only to information that confirms their prior beliefs. Consider a job negotiation where the applicant has "fallen in love" with a company. The impulse for the candidate will be to pay attention and overweight information that supports their "love" for the company and not objectively look at any flaws that the company might have. The confirming evidence bias shuts down the learning process, because individuals are no longer attending to information that could potentially help them make a better decision. So they may overweight "free lunches on Fridays" (something they like but which really tells them nothing new in terms of how they should evaluate the job) but will ignore the 80% turnover rate (something that may uncover why the job is not so great). The prior belief about the company being great thus has been "confirmed," but in the end once they learn more, they might regret taking the offer.

Mistake 7: Relying on the Same Tactic Again and Again

Part of learning to negotiate involves learning to use various tools, but an equally important part involves knowing which negotiation tools or behaviors, which are called **tactics,** are right for which tasks. Not only should you think about which tactics are right for the negotiation, but you also need to understand why. As usual, there are common mistakes people make when picking them.

The reason for this mistake is that people use the tactic that is most comfortable rather than the one that is likely to be most effective. For instance, we see over and over again that students in class exercises resort to compromise with their friends, even when they have just finished a lesson on how compromise leaves value on the table in the negotiation. Friends are reluctant to engage in the difficult discussions surrounding negotiation, and they end up stuck in patterns of nonoptimal solutions (and less value) because of the (incorrect) notion that negotiating means the friendship will be harmed.

Negotiators have a tendency to rely on their own past experiences rather than the best knowledge at hand when negotiating. For instance, in one study researchers found that negotiators who had previously reached an impasse were more likely to reach an impasse or an agreement of low value the next time, compared with those who had reached initial agreement.[24] We get stuck in the pattern of poor negotiation behavior and strategy and struggle to change.

This inability to adapt to various situations is called the **functional fixedness** bias. The person who uses the same inability to transfer knowledge from one negotiation to the next tactics for all negotiations may perform well in business or one-shot negotiations but is likely to make enemies or have a bad reputation in subsequent negotiations. Take again the example of the budding manager. Focusing only on what you will get as the boss and disregarding the relationship or concerns of the workers might make you appear distant, selfish, and power-hungry. The astute manager will realize that although overt power is at his or her disposal, it should be used only when the situation dictates its use.

In addition to tactics, people tend to think of objects only in the way they were designed, or to believe that an object can be used only in one way or works the same way all the time. The place where this happens most frequently is money. People think that money is a motivating factor, but they become functionally fixated when they think it is the *only* factor to motivate, or the strongest factor, or that it always works. In our university, which is by no means wealthy and has many people who do their job for love, it is disappointing to see how often the first thing used as a carrot is money. This is suboptimal because money's influence is marginal (comparatively), and the school does not have a lot of it (meaning using it to influence behavior is like trying to dig dirt with a paper plate).

Mistake 8: Inability to Transfer Knowledge From One Negotiation to the Next

Negotiations come in an infinite number of forms, so each negotiation you encounter will be unique. Luckily, they will also be extremely similar to the other negotiations you will encounter. Although negotiations look different on the surface, they all have basic commonalities that, once you realize what they are, allow you to analyze and/or act in them effectively. Seeing past the surface details can be challenging. Consider the following two situations:

Situation 1: Kai recently finished his MBA and, although he currently has a job, has just received an offer from another company. However, Kai would like to stay with his current employer. The struggle for Kai is that the new company has offered him a 20% increase in salary, an increase that is very important to him because he and his wife plan to start a family. In anticipation of his negotiation with his current boss, Kai does extensive research on what other people with MBAs in his profession are making, creates arguments about what he has done and what he could do for the company, and plans to share information about his family and his desire to stay with the company. After a few discussions, Kai's manager offers him a 17% raise, which is more than satisfactory to Kai.

Situation 2: After hearing about the raise, Kai goes home to talk with his wife, Michelle, about the good news. She shares his excitement and says that they should go on vacation, given the extra money and given the fact that, once they have a child, traveling will be more difficult. Kai agrees. Michelle immediately states that she has always wanted to go hiking in the Andes in Peru and is so excited they will finally be able to do this. Unfortunately, Kai had his heart set on Europe and has no desire to go to South America. He is completely dumbfounded at Michelle's enthusiasm and responds by saying, "Uh, yeah, that'd be great." He has totally missed his chance to get the trip of his dreams.

Why has Kai succeeded in negotiation so well at work and failed so miserably at home? Because of the **inert knowledge problem**, the difficulty in transferring details from one situation to the next. Although the inert knowledge problem was originally conceived as a problem of transferring knowledge from educational contexts to the real world,[25] we can clearly see the parallels in the two Kai examples.

Kai likely thinks of the problem at work as a "negotiation" and does not think of the conversation with Michelle about vacation in the same way. Why? Are these situations really that different? Both have two people negotiating, in both there is conflict, both are seemingly only about one issue (salary in the first, vacation location in the second), and in both Kai seems to have a good relationship with the other party. However, whereas he engages in effective negotiating in the first situation, which influences his boss, he neglects to engage in these same tactics with Michelle. He agrees too quickly and fails to present his research, explore alternative options, and share his desires. He might now be able to step back after this conversation and revisit the location with Michelle, but that may be difficult and may be something he does not want to do since he has already agreed.

The underlying problem for Kai here is that he has compartmentalized his knowledge of negotiation.[26] That is, what he thinks of as "negotiation" is defined by the context; he is failing to see the similarities between the conflict that he has at work and the conflict that he has at home. As noted by Renkl and colleagues: "The major problem with this kind of knowledge compartmentalization is that in situations where knowledge should be applied, the [negotiator] relies on old, deficient (but nevertheless in some contexts functional) misconceptions."[27] This is the challenge in becoming a competent negotiator, seeing the similarities across situations so that the knowledge you gain about negotiation can be applied in situations where it is likely to be effective. This will lead to more value than will relying on strategies and tactics that, while functional, are deficient.

The inert knowledge problem is pervasive in negotiations. Research by Loewenstein, Thompson, and Gentner showed that MBA students at a top-five business school often failed to transfer what they learned to new negotiation cases, even when the cases were given in a negotiation class one right after the other.[28] These students didn't transfer their learning simply because the surface details of what was being negotiated in later cases were different from the earlier ones. The earlier negotiations were for a computer and a job, the later for a lease. This gave the students the incorrect idea that the underlying problem—how to trade most effectively across a set of issues—was somehow different across these negotiations. Thus, to understand and analyze negotiations, you must know how to see past the surface details into the deep structure of what any particular negotiation situation is really about.

We mention the inert knowledge problem here because your goal as a student is likely to use the knowledge you are learning here. If you cannot transfer knowledge from this book to your negotiation class, and then from your negotiation class to your real-world negotiations, we have not made a difference in your negotiation style. So how do you overcome the inert knowledge problem? First, you learn by doing, not just by reading. In most negotiation classes you will have the opportunity to engage in role-play exercises where you can apply the concepts you have read about. This has the effect of cementing your knowledge in a specific domain more permanently than just reading about a concept and hoping that the concept transfers. This also suggests that, if you are reading this outside of a negotiation class, you need to start negotiating to gain experience and practice. Second, there is evidence that a critical comparison approach to cases and exercises is needed.[29] This means that situations and cases should constantly be compared, in order to break the compartmentalization of knowledge. In this book we will constantly provide examples such as the Kai (work and home) examples, so that you start to see many of the similarities that exist across all situations involving conflict between multiple parties.

To help you in this regard, we have organized the book around the possible negotiation levers you can use to obtain more value from your negotiations. By organizing it this way, we hope to help you change your mental model of negotiations, as you should start to see features that are common to most or all negotiations. Instead of defining a negotiation by the contextual details (e.g., this is a team-on-team negotiation, this is a mediation, this is a job negotiation, etc.), we hope you instead define negotiations by the negotiation lever being used or that could be used (e.g., reciprocity, power, alternatives, uncertainty, etc.) and the nature of the relationship between the negotiating parties. This will help you see the commonalities. Take the following scenario:

> Jennifer has agreed with the salesperson on a purchase for a new car. They have settled on price, and Jennifer has turned over the down payment check. However, upon final inspection of the car, she notices a very small dent in the front bumper. When she mentions this to Spencer, the salesman, he immediately goes into the back room of the dealership and disappears for 20 minutes. The dealership is about to close, and they have her check, but she is wondering whether she should try to get out of this deal or force them to fix the car or just take the car as is and take some money off the price.

If you were to assess the features of this negotiation, you might say the following:

- This is a car negotiation between Spencer and Jennifer.

- The car has a dent and Jennifer needs to figure out what to do.

- Spencer is trying to stall, for unknown reasons.

Hopefully by the end of reading this book, you will look at this negotiation differently, perhaps by saying the following:

- This is a two-party, seemingly one-issue negotiation.

- The resource power, based on money, is in the hands of Jennifer (buyer), and she has various options to attempt to influence Spencer (seller).

- The absence of Spencer suggests he is either investigating options for furthering the negotiation or attempting to increase the sunk cost (i.e., time) of Jennifer. How valuable time is to Jennifer, the deal is to Spencer, and the relationship dynamics between the two will determine the value obtained by each side.

- We lack information about Jennifer's alternatives, but it is likely that she could use this power to her advantage if left with no other recourse by Spencer.

The benefit of looking at the negotiation in this way is that you can compare these types of characteristics across negotiations. The negotiation is no longer about "a car"; rather, it is about two negotiating parties and the dynamics between them.

Summary. You might be dismayed at all of the mistakes that you have committed (or are going to commit). Do not fret! You can use the self-fulfilling prophecy to your advantage. If you accept the fact that you are susceptible to such mistakes, you can incorporate the material from this text and improve in a number of areas. You can leverage the fact that negotiators do better when they believe that negotiation skills can be learned.[30]

By this point you should have a much deeper understanding of not only what negotiation is but also the mistakes that you specifically are likely to make in negotiation. Think about the negotiations that you are likely to be in and why you might be susceptible to different mistakes. Are you taught in your company that hard-bargaining is most appropriate? Perhaps then you are likely to fall victim to Mistake 1. Do you find yourself always assuming that whatever you want is going to be the opposite of what someone else wants? Perhaps you are most likely to fall victim to Mistake 4. Use these mistakes as a resource as you work your way through the rest of the book and identify how you are going to improve as a negotiator.

CHAPTER REVIEW

Discussion Questions

1. Why are mental models so important to understand in negotiation? Take one of your in-class negotiations and compare it to a job negotiation. A car negotiation. A negotiation with a friend. Look for the similarities, and think about how you can apply what you've learned in class to your real-world negotiations.

2. List all the mistakes of negotiation, and summarize in your own words what each mistake means to you.

   a. Identify situations where you've fallen victim to these mistakes.

b. Rank which mistakes are most likely for you and state why.

c. State how you might overcome each mistake.

3. Sometimes you may want to *reduce* negotiation potential, either because you already have a good deal or simply because you are not interested in negotiation.

a. In what situations might you want to reduce negotiation potential?

b. For each situation, how will you do that?

4. For each of the five situations below, answer the following three questions:

a. Identify the parties, the nature of the interdependence, and the apparent conflict.

b. Does this scenario have negotiation potential? Why or why not?

c. Which mistakes are these negotiators likely to suffer from?

i. Monica, Joe, and Naina are creating a team contract so that they can work more effectively together. The last presentation they worked on together was a disaster and they want to avoid that in the future. Monica says, "We need to put a penalty in for people who come late or leave early, especially since Joe always seems to need to leave early." "I have soccer practice," replies Joe. Naina then adds, "Sometimes I have to get my kid from day care; I just can't commit to schedule certainty with a 2-year-old. So I am against this." Monica yells, "Well HOW are we supposed to function that way? It is not a free-for-all!" "Calm down," Naina says. "No! I am sick of this. You two always gang up on me!" Monica exclaims.

ii. Jamal and Bill are in the middle of a heated debate over who will lead when delivering the presentation to the CEO. "You just want to hog all the glory," Jamal accuses. "Oh, I do? What about you? I can barely get a word in when we meet with people before you

interrupt with some story of how great you are," Bill replies. After sitting in silence for a while, Jamal says, "Whatever. We need to figure out *something*. How about we just flip a coin? The winner leads." Bill retorts, "We are supposed to tell our presentation plan and rationale to our supervisor. You think she is going to go for 'We decided who would lead by flipping a coin'?"

iii. Animesh's boss walks into his office and says, "You have been leaving early at least two times a week for the past month. You were warned about this." Animesh replies, "But I told you, I have soccer practice two or three times a week." The boss says, "And we told you that you can't leave early per company policy regulation Article 4, Section 5. That regulation also states that a person who does this shall get one warning, and if they don't comply they can be terminated." Animesh then says, "I only have one more month in the season. Can't you just let me slide and I'll make it up somehow?" The boss looks at Animesh and says, "I was only coming in to tell you that you are fired."

iv. Consider this car-buying negotiation:

- Salesman: Well, for this car, we can give it to you for 10% below MSRP, so $38,452.

- Shawn: That is too much.

- Salesman: What were you expecting?

- Shawn: I was thinking more like $32K.

- Salesman: Are you kidding?

- Shawn: I didn't think so. I guess we are done here.

- Salesman: Wait, let me go ask my manager. [Comes back in about 15 minutes.] What if we do $38K but we throw in the extended warranty and roadside assistance for 5 years?

- Shawn: I really don't think so. Even with that I couldn't go above $35K.

- Manager: Hello, my name is Jen. I am the manager here. Maybe I can help.

Concept Application

1. Go into a situation where negotiation is uncommon and create negotiation potential. Report to the class how you did that.

2. Come to class prepared to discuss conflict situations that would not *typically* be thought of as negotiations.

3. Interview someone who engages in a lot of negotiations. Ask this person about the eight mistakes listed in this chapter and how he or she has managed these mistakes in negotiations.

$SAGE edge™   **Visit study.sagepub.com/rockmann to help you accomplish your coursework goals in an easy-to-use learning environment.**

CHAPTER 2

NEGOTIATION FUNDAMENTALS

Learning Objectives

1. Demonstrate the difference between understanding and convincing as approaches to negotiation.

2. Accurately distinguish between issues, interests, and positions when analyzing a negotiation.

3. Assemble a bargaining mix based on a set of issues to be negotiated, and understand what it means to claim value and create value among those issues.

4. Describe what a resistance point is, draw the ZOPA, and use these concepts to analyze the challenges and/or opportunities in a one-issue or multiple-issue negotiation.

5. Discern what ethical issues are likely to occur in negotiation, and think critically about what it means to become an ethical negotiator.

$SAGE edge™

Master the content at study .sagepub.com/rockmann

APPROACHES TO NEGOTIATION

When you sit down to renegotiate a contract at work, or negotiate an apartment lease, or decide what color to paint a room with your significant other, when does the negotiation actually start? Think about this for a minute. Do you think it starts when you start talking? How about when you agree to have the meeting where you are going to start talking?

While the conversation might start at one of these points, the dynamics of the negotiation begin much earlier, inside your head and the head of the person(s) you are negotiating with. Why? Because once you start anticipating the negotiation, you start making choices—choices about what you are going to say, what tactics you might use, what your opening offer might be, and so on. These conscious and unconscious choices you make before you ever utter a word have an enormous impact on negotiation, which is why we talk about them here. Unfortunately, people often rely on "instinct" or "gut" to make those choices; this results in many of the mistakes we discussed in Chapter 1.

Perhaps you have heard these negotiating strategies before (Table 2.1):[1]

- Avoid: Low assertiveness, low cooperation
- Yield: Low assertiveness, high cooperation
- Compete: High assertiveness, low cooperation
- Collaborate: High assertiveness, high cooperation
- Compromise: Moderate assertiveness, Moderate cooperation

Although often discussed, these strategies are not particularly helpful, at least to us. Why? First, avoiding and yielding can be done without negotiating at all. Second, competing and collaborating convey the idea that negotiations have winners and losers—that simply isn't the case in most negotiations. Third, these terms connote how you *view* the negotiation (e.g., competitive), rather than how you intend to *obtain value* in the negotiation.

Table 2.1 Traditional Negotiation Strategies	
COMPETE High Assertiveness, Low Cooperation	COLLABORATE High Assertiveness, High Cooperation
AVOID Low Assertiveness, Low Cooperation	YIELD Low Assertiveness, High Cooperation

For these reasons we leave these strategies behind and focus on convincing and understanding as key approaches to negotiation (Table 2.2). These terms describe how the negotiator intends to obtain value in the negotiation. When you take an **understanding** approach to negotiation, you try to comprehend what the other side is thinking as completely as possible. You go into the negotiation with the express purpose of uncovering the interests and goals of the other side so that you can use the various resources at your disposal to persuade the other party and ultimately get what you want.

We can contrast understanding with **convincing**, which is exactly as it sounds—attempting to alter the beliefs or actions of the other side in order to get something. Perhaps you want them to lower their price or settle on the negotiation today by convincing them they are not going to get any other offers. Perhaps you want to convince them you are the boss, and they should concede because of your formal position. Whatever it is, the idea here is that you are causing them to change their mind or their request without having to give up any resource. While the negotiator still must "understand" or know something about the other side, the intent is to change their mind, to move them off of some preexisting belief or stance.

Table 2.2 Convincing and Understanding: Key Approaches to Negotiation	
Understanding	**Convincing**
• *Comprehend* what the other side is thinking. • *Question* others to uncover interests. • *Give* the other side enough value so they say yes to what you want.	• *Alter* the beliefs of the other side. • *Demonstrate* to others why you are right and they are wrong. • *Force* them to give you value.

Understanding

Although negotiations are a means to satisfy **interests**—the fundamental reasons people want what they want—it can be hard to discover what people's underlying interests actually are. Typically, it requires some kind of questioning to get to the root of the interest. Once you do this, it becomes possible to find other ways to reach agreement. Consider the following example:

Employee:	I'd like a higher salary.
Manager:	Why?
Employee:	Well, because I see other people getting raises.
Manager:	OK, but why do you want a higher salary?
Employee:	Because I want to feel valued by the company. [Note: Feeling valued is the employee's interest.]
Manager:	And you think that getting a raise shows value?
Employee:	Well, I guess so, yes.
Manager:	That's important to understand because maybe there are other things I can offer that will make you feel valued. How about I recommend you to attend that special conference overseas?

We can see that the manager in this scenario is clearly taking an understanding approach to this negotiation. In this scenario, by digging down (asking questions) the manager is able to figure out what the underlying interest is on the part of the employee.

It is often hard to predict what a negotiator truly wants. Consider another scenario where it is not so obvious what the underlying interest might be:

Manager:	I need you to cc me on all of your e-mails to customer X.
Sales Employee:	Why?
Manager:	Because I need to maintain an administrative presence.

This answer does little to explain what the manager really wants. The employee needs to keep asking questions to find out:

Sales Employee:	But was there a concern?
Manager:	Yes, the customer expressed concern to our top management that they were not as valued as they once were. Cc'ing me will convey that they have the ear of upper management, which is going to keep the customer happy. [Note: Keeping the customer happy is the manager's interest.]

Knowing this is the interest, the employee might find additional ways to use resources to get more value from the manager.

Sales Employee:	OK, I'll cc you and I'll look for ways to pamper the customer more, maybe through increased visits, more frequent communications, and maybe even a golf date with our CEO.
Manager:	Great ideas, thanks.

In this scenario, we can see the benefit of the employee taking an understanding approach. In asking that second question, the employee was able to discern what was really bothering the manager. The employee also offered to take on extra work, which influences the manager because it satisfies the manager's underlying interests. Without the employee's digging for that underlying interest, those additional opportunities to take care of the customer would've been lost.

Convincing

Why do we use arguments in negotiation? To convince others. To show someone else that they are wrong and that we are right.

Let's look at the following example:

Employee:	I'd like a higher salary.
Manager:	That would cause problems.
Employee:	But I see other people getting raises.
Manager:	Yes, but those people have more experience than you.
Employee:	Then I'm going to have to look for another job.
Manager:	I can't stop you from doing that.

It is very clear in this now revised scenario that both the employee and the manager take a convincing rather than understanding approach going into this negotiation. With each statement, each person is trying to convince the other to change his or her mind. The employee uses a comparison argument ("other people getting raises") and a threat ("I'm going to have to look for another job"). The manager uses data ("Those people have more experience"). Neither individual seems interested in understanding the other's interests.

To better grasp understanding versus convincing as negotiation approaches, consider the story of Joan and Louise at the company holiday party. Joan and Louise mistakenly get raffle tickets with the same number, and they both "win" two tickets worth $100 each to go see a concert. The question now is who gets the two tickets, so they start to negotiate.

Joan:	You should let me have them because this is my favorite group and I've never seen them in concert.
Louise:	True, but I did technically win them.
Joan:	Yes, but technically I won them, too.
Joan:	Wait, aren't you a huge basketball fan?
Louise:	Yes.
Joan:	I actually have two tickets to an upcoming NBA game that were given to my husband. Neither of us are crazy about basketball. How about I give you those tickets?
Louise:	Really? That'd be great! Are you sure that's okay with you?
Joan:	Absolutely. We were just going to sell them online. I'd rather avoid that hassle anyway and give those tickets to someone I know is going to enjoy them.

There are several things we can see here about the approaches that Joan and Louise are bringing to the negotiation. Let's look at the conversation again:

Joan:	You should let me have them because this is my favorite group and I've never seen them in concert. **[Convincing]**
Louise:	True, but I did technically win them. **[Convincing]**
Joan:	Yes, but technically I won them, too. **[Convincing]**
Joan:	Wait, aren't you a huge basketball fan? **[Understanding]**
Louise:	Yes.
Joan:	I actually have two tickets to an upcoming NBA game that were given to my husband. Neither of us are crazy about basketball. How about I give you those tickets? **[Understanding]**
Louise:	Really? That'd be great! Are you sure that's okay with you? **[Understanding]**
Joan:	Absolutely. We were just going to sell them online. I'd rather avoid that hassle anyway and give those tickets to someone I know is going to enjoy them. **[Understanding]**

Notice that in each statement the goal for the statement is now highlighted. Louise starts by trying to convince Joan. Joan reciprocates (i.e., does the same thing back to her) by trying to convince Louise. This does not result in an agreement, and Joan wisely shifts to an understanding approach, whereby she asks Louise an interest-based question about wanting the basketball tickets. Louise appreciates this and reciprocates again by asking Louise if this is okay with her. Both individuals have gone from convincing to understanding and, in doing so, have found a good solution to their problem. This is very typical in negotiations, which often involve individuals changing their negotiation tactics over the course of the negotiation.

Notice, though, the danger in starting with a convincing approach. If Joan had not remembered that Louise was a huge basketball fan (even the act of remembering shows Joan is focused on *understanding* Louise), Louise might have instead just offered for Joan to pay $100 for the one ticket. While this might have closed the negotiation, it is not an optimal agreement. Table 2.3 compares these agreements.

Table 2.3 Convincing vs. Convincing → Understanding	
Outcome 1: Only Convincing	**Outcome 2: Convincing → Understanding**
Joan: Two concert tickets, $100 payment to Louise	Joan: Two concert tickets; not having to worry about basketball tickets; gratitude toward Louise
Louise: $100 payment from Joan	Louise: Two basketball tickets; gratitude toward Joan

It's pretty easy to see here why Outcome 2 is preferable to Outcome 1. The relationship is strengthened *and* they both get something tangible that they want.

As seen in the sidebar on the NBA negotiation in 2011, choosing just convincing as an approach severely limits the tools at your disposal. Further, as we will discuss at length starting with Chapter 4, you should understand the relative benefits of choosing either path. Unlike Joan and Louise, you don't want to rely on getting lucky in negotiation and thinking of something on your feet to solve the problem at hand. You want to be conscious in your approach so that you can best satisfy your interests.

My friend [Jason] Whitlock wrote earlier this week: "[David] Stern has been balling in the basketball boardroom for three decades. The players look as out of place barging into meetings and negotiating with Stern and his lawyers as Stern and his lawyers would challenge Fisher, Wade, Garnett and Pierce on the court."

From day one, the players have approached this lockout like it's a *competition*—they don't want to be beaten, they're not rolling over, they're staying strong and all that macho bullshit. It's all small-picture stuff. When's the last time you heard someone from the players' side say, "Maybe the owners are right, maybe we *should* work with them to create a better system?" Where are the Bill Russells, the Bill Bradleys, the Oscar Robertsons, the Phil Jacksons, the Bob Cousys and Tommy Heinsohns—thoughtful *stars* pushing for real change instead of just pretending to be tough at a meeting? Where are the guys who stood up before the 1964 All-Star Game in Boston and basically said, "The current system is broken and needs to change NOW, or we're not playing?" Where is this generation's Larry Fleisher, a brilliant legal mind who can successfully look out for the players while also helping to shape the league's bigger picture? Seriously, where is he?

Source: Simmons, B. (2011, October 31). Proactively mourning the NBA [Web log post]. Retrieved from https://grantland.com/features/proactively-mourning-nba/

THE BASICS OF NEGOTIATION

There are some fundamental concepts that are relevant in all negotiations. We must understand these before we can even begin to talk scientifically about negotiation. They represent concepts that you always need to think about, as opposed to some of the other concepts and principles that may only be relevant in certain situations. They also provide a language and structure for talking about negotiations. These concepts include participants, issues, interests, and positions.

Negotiating Participants

Many different types of participants are involved in negotiation. The **parties at the table** are those who actually perform the negotiation. They make the moment-to-moment decisions and conduct the negotiation conversation. They are also the ones who engage in various tactics and take actions to move the negotiation along. We often tend to think about negotiation only in terms of these people sitting at the negotiating table. The parties at the table are rarely operating in a social vacuum; what they choose to do and think is often influenced by others not at the table.

Even when you are buying some used car from a stranger that you met online, it is unlikely that you will negotiate without others influencing your decisions. If the stranger you are buying a car from is married, for instance, his or her spouse may have a problem if you get the car too cheaply. If you are thinking about your professional image, the way people will react to the giant dent in the fender may affect how you evaluate the car. In some situations the social connections that influence the negotiation are obvious. In a job negotiation, your boss (the participant at the table) is constrained by his or her boss (not at the table) in terms of what he or she can give you. But often there are other, less obvious people that, although in the background, can have a strong influence on what happens in a negotiation. For example, your boss may be worried that other employees (those not at the table) will think he or she is showing you favoritism.

We can expand our view of the people involved in the negotiation by considering two types of participants who, though not at the table, can influence what happens. These background participants and background nonparticipants affect the negotiation process in different ways.

Background participants are people with the capability to directly change or affect the progression of the negotiation via their influence on the parties at the table. Background participants are important in a negotiation because they have the power to disrupt or facilitate progress toward agreement. That is, they can start and stop a negotiation, or they can change its direction. It's all well and good to negotiate a strong job offer with a representative from the human resources department, but if the line manager is unwilling to accommodate the job offer, the negotiation either will be reopened or will fail. It is not just that background participants have the final say; background participants also can change the way a negotiation progresses. The salesperson who has to get approval from her manager to give the customer the price he wants on a specific item is under the direct influence of the manager; in this way the manager has the power to change how the negotiation is going. If the salesperson comes back and says, "Well, my manager won't let me give you that much of a discount, but how about I offer you X, Y, and Z instead," the negotiation will move in that new direction.

Changing the way the negotiation progresses can be accomplished in an overt or subtle way. Consider a union negotiation in which the union negotiator tells the company negotiator that the membership will agree to a wage cut. The membership (the background participants) will vote on this deal, and if they vote it down, the union negotiator will have to continue negotiating. This is overt control. Consider also the example of a middle manager negotiating a contract for a client. Although the CEO of the manager's company is not in the room and may not overtly tell the manager to sign or not sign the deal, the manager is thinking about the CEO when signing that deal and the guidelines the CEO has sent down from the executive suite. That CEO is thus directly affecting the negotiation but is doing so without getting involved and, possibly, without even knowing about the deal. This is a subtler form of control.

Although background participants may have varying degrees of influence, what is important is that they can actually change the course of the negotiation in real time. This may necessitate focus on the background participants, because if a negotiator is able to get the person at the table to agree to something that one of these background participants *does not* like, then they will soon be renegotiating.

Background nonparticipants are people who are watching the negotiation but have no way to directly change its course. For example, if Tim is negotiating a contract with a vendor, the other vendors will be interested to see what Tim does, even if they can't do anything to change Tim's approach. As with the background participants, the background nonparticipants influence negotiations mostly in terms of how the people at the table are thinking. Since the background nonparticipants are not going to be affected by the outcome directly, their views are not really updated with the ebb and flow of a negotiation. However, negotiations can set precedent, and because of that the parties at the table may be worried about how the background nonparticipants will construe this precedent based on what happens.

Whereas you could ostensibly bargain (albeit indirectly) with background participants by offering things they might want as part of the package, you cannot really do that with the nonparticipants. So when Debbie tries to negotiate a new chair for her office, her boss may be concerned that if she does that, it will be seen as favoritism by the other employees—the background nonparticipants. This is because Debbie's coworkers, although not participating, are watching the boss's actions. This example also illustrates how nonparticipants may not even be people but rather abstract groupings such as "customers," "constituents," or "departments." The boss is worried what "other employees" across the organization think, not necessarily about what specific people will think. It is not the background nonparticipants themselves that affect choices and behaviors in a negotiation, but rather what the parties at the table *think* the background participants might care about. Debbie's boss may think she knows how the "other employees" will view Debbie if she gets a new chair, but that might be a mistake in perception. If Debbie's boss were to actually talk to those individuals, she may find out they don't really care.

The influence of background nonparticipants is more indirect and amorphous but also more constant when they are abstractions (e.g., "the public"). You should not underestimate the power of this group. The background nonparticipants are often the "court of public opinion." This is why, in certain negotiations, seemingly absurd details are added to the agreement because the parties at the table are concerned about how the agreement is going to look to the public.

Summary. As the negotiation progresses through moves and countermoves by the parties at the table, the background participants are in the position to evaluate this progress and redirect how the negotiation is proceeding. They are typically specific individuals whose perception of the negotiation process can be influenced. Background nonparticipants may or may not be specific individuals or groups; they are just as likely to be abstractions. In either case, the background nonparticipants do not act to change the negotiation process, but rather will evaluate the negotiation outcome, which can impact future negotiations. Thinking about how these nonparticipants will react influences parties at the table in a fairly constant way.

Issues and Bargaining Mix

Issues are the items "on the table" being negotiated—days off, a bonus, a company car, warranties, discounts, favors, food, hats, *anything*. Issues are the fundamental building blocks or pieces of the puzzle used to craft an agreement. The collection of issues being negotiated is called the **bargaining mix**. We talk about bargaining mix because people typically have too small a bargaining mix (too few issues), and they typically assume those issues to be zero-sum (see Chapter 1). You will be able to negotiate more effectively if you can increase the number and types of issues included in the bargaining mix. This has benefits that we will cover later in the book.

One of the mistakes in understanding what an issue is in negotiation stems from the definition of the word *issue*. In normal lexicon, an issue can be anything that needs to be resolved or is creating discomfort. Your mistrust of another, using this definition, would be a potential issue. However, in negotiation we will use the word *issues* only to refer to things on the table for agreement; thus, in this book, we will ignore the other meaning of the word.

Some issues are obvious when we negotiate, but many others are hidden by the tendency to think about negotiations in stereotypical and narrow ways. One way to add issues to the bargaining mix is to think more broadly about why parties are at the table. Another is to see what emerges during the negotiation. This is difficult, and so we will spend a lot of time in subsequent chapters discussing effective and ineffective ways to do this. Here are examples of both **obvious issues** and **potential issues** in popular negotiations (Table 2.4).

Interests vs. Positions

What do you want? The fundamental concept here, and probably the most important one you will learn in reading this book, is the interest. An interest is the fundamental

Table 2.4 Obvious vs. Potential Issues

Negotiation	Parties at the Table	Obvious Issues to Be Negotiated	Potential Issues to Be Negotiated
Job	Employee Manager	Salary Bonus Moving expenses	Performance review date Task assignments Tuition reimbursement
Car	Customer Salesperson	Cost Financing plan	Administrative fees Oil changes, maintenance
Trade agreement	Country 1 Country 2	Tariff rates Length of time Products covered	Technology transfer between countries Immigration restrictions
Wedding	Future partner Future partner	Location Reception cost Number of guests	Location of honeymoon Structure of ceremony Choice of music

reason why you want something. This means that it is something that you want just because you do, and you will be satisfied with the negotiation based on how much of your interests are satisfied. Interests can be anything—respect, admiration, love, power, music, fun, safety, silence. Interests are rooted in needs, and they are what gives something value. If you don't have an interest in baseball, another person's season box seats at the stadium won't really hold a lot of value in the negotiation. People have different sets of interests. Some are likely to be universal: safety, shelter, food. Some are likely to be universal but vary in strength, such as the desire for power, respect, or achievement. Some are very idiosyncratic, such as a love of cuckoo clocks or a love of rainy gray days. Interests tend to persist beyond a specific negotiation. Someone who wants the respect of their peers will likely always want this. Someone who wants to be able to take long vacations will probably like doing this in the future as well. Your interests are based on your history and your personality, and those things are relatively stable. You negotiate in order to satisfy your interests.

We contrast the interest with the **position**, which is equally important to understand in negotiation. Positions are the means by which you try to achieve your interests. Perhaps an easier way to think about this is that positions are things that are asked for in negotiations. For example, Joe wants the respect of his professional colleagues (interest), so he negotiates for a big corner office (position). Nancy wants flexibility in her work schedule (interest), so she negotiates to telework 2 days a week (position). Steve is curious about Mayan history (interest), so he negotiates with his wife to take their next vacation to Mexico (position).

Take, for example, the issue of money. People ask for a certain amount of money rarely because they just love the sight and smell of it but mostly because it allows them a means to satisfy their interests, whatever they may be. While effective negotiating is a matter of satisfying your interests, more often you focus on getting whatever position you have decided you want. You want respect, but you argue for the corner office. Or worse yet, you want respect, so you argue for a raise. Why is this a problem? Because a feeling of respect comes from how others treat you. Even if you are successful in acquiring a raise, this good feeling is likely to be temporary as (a) you will still remember not getting the raise previously and that you had to ask for it and (b) others will continue to treat you in the same way you were treated before. The position has been reached, but your underlying interest may still be unfulfilled.

You should be seeing the connection between issues, interests, and positions (Table 2.5). Issues are what are on the negotiating table. Each issue has a set of one or more possible positions. Some issues (e.g., salary) have infinite positions. Positions offered, in turn, come from the desire to meet interests.

Table 2.5   Issues, Positions, Interests

Issue	Position	Interest
Telecommuting	Telecommute 3 days a week	My spouse can't pick the kids up from school on certain days.
Dinner	California Pizza Kitchen	I'm concerned about money and we have a coupon for this restaurant.
Salary	$70,000/year	I want to feel that I am valued in the new company.
Grade	An "A" in negotiation class	Impress my employer, get a good recommendation from my professor, and actually become a better negotiator!

In January 2018 the Teamsters, representing about 260,000 drivers, began their collective bargaining process with UPS, in what is one of the largest collective bargaining agreements in the United States. The current deal between the Teamsters and UPS, which was signed in 2013, was set to expire in July 2018. The Teamsters, in their initial proposal to UPS, included many issues to be discussed, such as late-night delivery, the number of future employees, and future package delivery technology. The Teamsters also provided initial *positions* on those issues: no delivery after 9 pm, 10,000 additional workers, and prohibiting UPS from using "drones, driverless vehicles, and other new technology to transport, deliver or pick up packages."

From a negotiation point of view, what is missing, at least in this initial reporting, are the *interests* of the Teamsters. Clearly the Teamsters are worried about the jobs and well-being of their members, but their initial positions may not be the best ways to satisfy those interests. For instance, if the Teamsters prohibit UPS from exploring such drone and driverless technologies, UPS could suffer in terms of brand image in comparison with FedEx, ultimately hurting the company and reducing the number of jobs available to the Teamsters in the future. Similarly, there may be drivers who prefer working at night and would be happy to do so, perhaps for extra wages.

Source: Ziobro, P. (2018, January 25). Teamsters tell UPS: No delivery drones or driverless trucks. *Wall Street Journal*, p. B6.

You can think of interests and positions as falling along a continuum, with the position or *offer* at one end of the continuum and the purest version of the underlying interest at the other end of the continuum. As shown in Figure 2.1, when you can move along the continuum (the horizontal axis) from positions to interests, you increase the number of possible outcomes that can prove satisfactory in the negotiation. Take this simple example of a teenager's request to his parent: "*Can I stay out until 11 pm on Saturday?*" How many options will satisfy this agreement? One. This is because what the teenager is offering is a position. If the parent responds, "*What is important that is going on Saturday?*" and the teenager says "*My friend is in town this weekend,*" immediately more positions become possible. Perhaps the teenager and his friend can hang out earlier on Saturday, or on Sunday, or on Friday. In this case, by asking the interest-based question, the parent has moved down the continuum (the horizontal axis) closer to interests and in doing so has increased not only the number of possible options but the potential for both sides to obtain value from the negotiation.

Figure 2.1 Using Interests vs. Positions in Negotiations

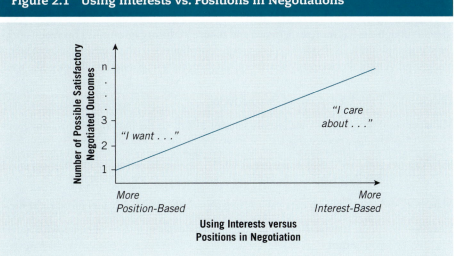

Evaluating Success

When we ask our students whether they did well in a negotiation, they almost universally discuss positions, that is, how much "stuff" (money, days off of work, etc.) they got. These are the tangible issues that can be measured at the end of a negotiation. The problem, though, is that these outcomes are positions, not interests. As interests represent root needs, wants, and desires, it is in the fulfilling of interests that we derive negotiation success.

Take, for instance, negotiating with your supervisor over a raise. You would like a 5% raise, whereas your supervisor would like to give you a 2% raise. You may think that success in this negotiation is measured by whether or not you convinced your supervisor to give you the 5% raise. While that is one measure, don't forget the relational value that you obtain from your relationship with your supervisor. If you make your supervisor angry by threatening to leave, have you really won, even if you get a bigger raise? No, because the relationship is harmed, and that supervisor, who might have been willing to open doors for you later on, now sees you in a more negative light.

This happens in our classrooms all of the time. When we engage in a negotiation role-play exercise, invariably a student does quite well as measured by the points within the role play. It becomes clear, though, that the student gained an advantage in the negotiation by lying to his or her classmates and/or by bullying them to back down from their position. Can these tactics work in a negotiation to convince someone to change his or her offer? Absolutely. But at what cost? The student has cost himself or herself significant social capital in the classroom (no one wants to work with or help him or her), and we use this performance as an example of what *not* to do.

Tangible vs. Intangible Interests

People's interests can take a lot of different forms. Suppose Yashika really likes her current job as an accounting consultant but feels that management doesn't really appreciate her. She learned that some of her newly hired coworkers are being paid almost as much as she is, even though she has more experience and tenure in the organization. This really bothers her because she feels that her expertise and contributions to the company are not being recognized. A typical position-based attempt to negotiate might end up looking like this:

Yashika: I think I deserve to be paid more.

Manager: I'm sorry, but we simply cannot afford to do that right now, since our budget is very tight.

Yashika: But I'm very competent at what I do and have lots of experience, and I feel that I am not being paid accordingly.

Manager: I hear what you are saying, but we simply cannot pay you more right now.

Yashika: Well, maybe I'm going to have to explore other options with other companies.

As both parties walk away from that exchange, there's a risk that Yashika will conclude that manager's refusal to give in to her position is proof that the company really does not appreciate her, and the manager might get the impression that Yashika is greedy and insensitive to the company's current budget problems. Even though both of those conclusions are probably incorrect, these impressions can damage the relationship going forward.

On the other hand, a more interest-based attempt might sound more like this:

Yashika: I am concerned that management doesn't appreciate me, as indicated by the salaries of my peers, even though I am very competent and have a lot of experience. I love working here and don't want to leave, but this is really bothering me.

Manager: I agree that you're a great employee, but unfortunately we don't have any money for raises in our budget right now. Is there another way for us to demonstrate that we DO appreciate you?

Yashika: I don't know. What are you thinking of?

Manager: Well, how about a title of "senior consultant" that would emphasize that you are a more experienced and valuable employee than the newer hires. We could also look for a larger office for you, which would also signal your higher status. We really do appreciate you, even if we cannot pay you more right now. Would some of these sorts of things help?

Yashika: That sounds interesting. Can we also talk about increasing my 401k contributions?

Manager: That actually might be possible. Let me see what I can do.

Now, as the parties walk away from the exchange, management is aware that Yashika feels underappreciated, and Yashika knows that her concerns have been heard and that management is trying to do something, even if they are not going to pay her more in salary.

As noted in this example, interests need not necessarily be tangible. **Tangible interests** are underlying wants that can be seen, touched, or felt (e.g., money, goods, time). Interests can also reflect, for instance, a desire to maintain a relationship or respect or trust. These are **intangible interests**, underlying wants that cannot be seen, touched, or felt (e.g., respect, love, appreciation). If the interest of the person you are negotiating with is for you to show them respect, it doesn't matter how much money you give the person; what matters is how you treat that person. Showing respect through your actions and words will mean more to the employee and will ultimately be the key to your getting what you want. Consider another example:

J.E., the buyer, was negotiating for a 1965 Mustang with a seller, David, whom he met online. There were several hurdles to the negotiation, not the least of which was that J.E. was located on the East Coast and David was located in Phoenix, Arizona. This meant that J.E. not only had to negotiate with David for the price of the car but also had to figure out how to get the car back to the East Coast in an affordable way. On top of this was the uncertainty about purchasing a used car built in 1965. Is it in good condition? How is the paint? Are there any engine troubles? David sent him pictures, but there still remained a great deal of uncertainty. J.E.'s interests thus were to lower the price to the level at which he would (a) be comfortable with a reasonable number of emergent problems and (b) have enough money to get the car back from Phoenix, by either shipping it or driving it. When discussing the price of the car with David, he noticed that David was reluctant to lower the price below $16,000, but that reluctance did not tell J.E. anything about David's interests. David assured him that the car was in great shape, but from J.E.'s perspective, he didn't have much reason to trust a stranger on the other side of the country. In fact, it gave him the impression that David was very inflexible and primarily concerned about money.

At this point in the negotiation many potential buyers would just walk away, not realizing the intangible interests at play. David's desired position is $16,000, and it's clear he wants to negotiate based on this desired position. David doesn't want to move the price, yet J.E. has a lot of concerns that need to be addressed in order to agree to the deal. What could J.E. do? What were the underlying intangible interests he didn't know about? Here's a bit of background on David.

David bought this car in 1991 and it had been his dream car for 20 years. Because he was a mechanic by trade, he had personally restored it and taken great care of it. Most of all, he enjoyed driving it and taking it to car shows. He was forced to sell it because of the recession that began in 2008; he lost his job and needed the money. Needless to say, this was painful for David. It turns out that while the money was obviously important, the most important thing to David was selling the car to someone who would respect and care for the car as much as he did. To him, selling the Mustang was like losing a member of his family, and he really did not want to see it go to someone who wouldn't be able to appreciate it as he did and who wouldn't love to drive it.

We can see here David's interests—that he is losing a "member of his family" and he desperately wants someone to love and care for the Mustang as much as he did. The sales price of $16,000 (or any amount of money) is not going to address this intangible interest of David's. What allowed David to say yes to the deal was learning about J.E.'s intangible interests:

As the negotiations went on, J.E. communicated that he had wanted this car since he was a little kid and planned to drive around in it every weekend and keep it for a long time.

Unbeknown to J.E. at the time, this was crucially important information for David and made him much more likely to be flexible on lots of issues, including helping to get the car to J.E. The eventual negotiation was resolved very positively. Once David accepted that J.E. was the kind of buyer he wanted to sell to, he was extremely helpful. Whereas before he had seemed suspicious and reserved, he now was overly generous.

In this example of David and J.E., if they had only discussed positions, there would not have been a deal. But once both parties understood the underlying interests of the other person better, not only was a deal possible, but in fact a deal that both parties were very happy with was struck.

Understanding the concept of interests and how they underlie positions and offers in negotiation will open the door to agreement, as we see in the previous example. There are two reasons that parties are motivated to collaborate when interests are on the table. First, because you are giving the other party something they value, they will reciprocate. This is what we will focus on in Chapter 4. Second, you are addressing needs that are personal to them, needs that may be tied up in their identity. You will learn more about how to manage these intangible interests in Chapter 5.

ZOPA and Resistance Points

A tool for thinking about how much value you may be able to obtain from a negotiation is the **zone of potential agreement (ZOPA)**. The ZOPA represents the distance between each party's respective **resistance point,** or the point at which a party is willing to walk away.[2] Consider a very simple example: a negotiation between two parties on one issue, the price for a specific product. Assume that two parties meet through an online selling website such as Craigslist. One party is trying to sell a motorcycle, and the other party is trying to buy the same motorcycle. Each party has their own resistance point, and it is the overlap in the resistance points that determines the ZOPA. If the buyer is willing to pay up to and including $3,000 to buy the motorcycle, and the seller is willing to take any amount at or above $2,750 to sell the motorcycle, they have a positive ZOPA of $250. This is shown in the first part of Figure 2.2.

It is possible, however, that the seller is only willing to go down to $3,000 to sell the motorcycle and the buyer is only willing to pay $2,750. In this case they have a negative ZOPA; –$250 (as shown in the second part of Figure 2.2). That is, there is no dollar amount that will, on the surface, satisfy both parties. At this point negotiators should realize that in order to solve this negotiation they have to *change something*. The two obvious resolutions to this problem are (1) one or both sides could influence the other side to change their resistance point and (2) one or both sides could walk away from the negotiation. Final settlements of negotiations almost always fall between the resistance points unless some other strategy is used.[3] There is a third alternative, however, and that is to create value to bridge the gap. If value can be added to the negotiation, it might be a way to change the negative ZOPA to a positive ZOPA.

The idea of the resistance point is not only relevant in one-issue negotiations, however. Even in multiple-issue negotiations resistance points can impact whether or not negotiators are able to reach agreement. This can happen for two reasons. First, in a multiple-issue negotiation a negotiator could have a resistance point on a specific issue that they care about. For instance, a job applicant might be negotiating a signing bonus,

Figure 2.2   Positive and Negative ZOPA

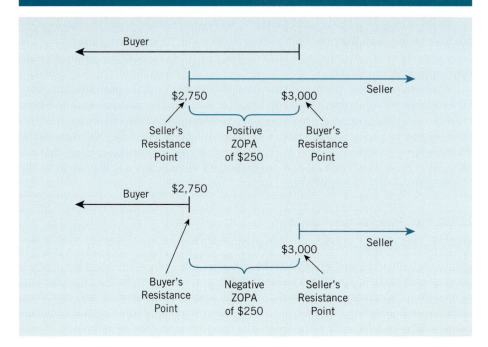

moving expenses, starting date, a new computer, and salary; because salary is the most important issue to the applicant, the applicant will have a resistance point on salary that will impede the ability for the applicant to say yes to a deal with a salary below that point, regardless of what is being offered on the other four issues.

Second, a negotiator could have a resistance point that is formed from the combination of positions on various issues. If the applicant needs $5,000 to relocate, then the applicant's resistance point would be $5,000 for the combination of signing bonus and moving expenses. That is, the applicant doesn't particularly care which "pot" of money it comes from, as long as he or she is getting a total sum of $5,000 before the job starts.

Creating vs. Claiming Value

Some negotiators find it helpful to distinguish between different types of negotiations and the processes within them. One of the most popular distinctions is referred to as creating vs. claiming value. **Creating value** is the process by which negotiators find ways to increase the total value to be gained from the negotiation. If we start from the premise that individuals have a fixed-pie bias (see Chapter 1), we can see how important creating value is to negotiation effectiveness. This creation involves one or more negotiators overcoming this fixed-pie bias and realizing that there might actually be more value that could be added to the negotiation rather than splitting (or compromising on) the obvious issues. While there are multiple ways to create value, this typically happens when negotiators recognize that because they have different interests, they can make trades where the cost to one side does not equal the benefit to the other. When negotiators successfully create value, it is often said that they have reached an **integrative agreement**.

In the motorcycle example, the seller could throw in a helmet ($100 value to buyer) and saddlebags ($150 value to buyer) to close this gap. This tactic is called adding issues (discussed more thoroughly in Chapter 4). This creates value because these items are worth nothing to the seller. The seller is getting rid of the motorcycle, so there is no value in keeping the helmet and saddlebags. If anything, the seller probably wants to be rid of them to free up storage space. By adding these issues, $250 of value has been created in the process of negotiating. Once these issues have been added, the buyer and seller should be able to come to agreement at the price of $3,000.

Claiming value, on the other hand, is the process by which one party attempts to negotiate in such a way as to cause the other party to give up something without getting anything in return. This is related to one of the mistakes discussed in Chapter 1—assuming you know what good negotiation looks like. Many individuals believe that good negotiation is only about claiming value, that is, forcing the other side to capitulate or give in. While such tactics can work and in some cases are needed, negotiation is more than claiming value. When two negotiators only claim value, they are said to have reached a **distributive agreement** because they are merely "distributing" rather than creating value.

Summary. The concepts of interests, positions, issues, and the understanding and convincing approaches will be ones we refer to repeatedly in this book. The reason so much negotiation teaching and research is focused on understanding the other side is because it does not come naturally to negotiators. The basic human instinct is to protect your resource and "fight" with the other side to convince them as much as possible. You should know, however, that there is another way to negotiate, a way that will likely get you even better deals and bring you more value. The path through understanding is difficult because you have to collaborate with the person you initially thought you would be fighting with. This willingness to be vulnerable will open the door to many types of agreements not previously possible.

PREPARING FOR THE ETHICS OF NEGOTIATION

While not all negotiations involve critically important ethical dilemmas or difficult ethical choices for the individual, almost all negotiations, by their very nature, will involve some ethical component because most negotiations involve invoking some manipulation of another party. We will consider the question of ethics from a variety of perspectives, examining not only the question of what exactly ethics, and being ethical, means in negotiations but also various examples of behavior that might be considered unethical, the reasons people engage in unethical behavior, and the many things that may determine whether or not a particular behavior is ethical or unethical in a given situation or context.

What Are Ethics?

Ethics are social standards for what is right or wrong and are rooted in considerations of philosophy and morality. In other words, ethics are generally accepted rules or expectations for what is appropriate and inappropriate behavior. Originating in moral philosophy, ethics are more specific than general social norms or manners. It might be normative in a society to not loudly burp, but deciding whether or not to engage in such behavior in a crowded elevator is not necessarily an ethical question. Ethics are usually more narrowly focused on issues of right and wrong, virtue and justice.

The context of negotiations can be a somewhat tricky and slippery area for ethics. Negotiation inherently involves attempts to influence another party for your own benefit. The practices used to do this and the results of the negotiation are likely to relate to ethics because although people benefit by negotiating, they also may be denied benefit or even harmed. Clearly some ways of trying to manipulate other people, or some agreements where people are worse off afterward, could easily be considered unethical.

Why Are Ethics Important?

People care a great deal about fairness and justice, and behavior that is perceived as being "unfair" and "unjust" is typically considered unethical because "right" and "wrong" are tightly linked to perceptions of justice and fairness. Organizational researchers have spent decades studying and refining concepts of fairness and organizational justice,[4] demonstrating the importance of justice perception in social interactions. The study of fairness and justice has led to the development of research into different types of justice (distributive, retributive, and procedural) and the realization of how crucial employee perception of fairness and justice is to the psychological contract, job satisfaction, and motivation. Evolutionary psychology researchers suggest that humans are particularly sensitive to issues of unfair allocations of resources and are extremely conscious of status, a trait that presumably goes back far beyond the ancestral environment of *Homo sapiens*. We know this because research shows that primates demonstrate similar concern about equitable allocations and status.[5]

It is easy to think of examples of fairness or justice "violations" that cause conflict, anger, and resentment in modern organizations. This includes things like people taking credit for someone else's effort, people being compensated differently for the same work, supervisors abusing their power, or a company not living up to promises about bonuses, promotions, and layoffs. It is important to observe how relatively small things, but things that are perceived as being "unfair," can have a profound impact on conflict and relationships in organizations.[6] Not surprisingly, using tactics that are ethically questionable does not necessarily benefit negotiation performance and can leave negotiators quite unsatisfied.[7]

Research in economics and game theory has also demonstrated how people place considerable value on fairness. The "ultimatum game" (or dictator game) is an experiment in which two people decide on the allocation of a resource.[8] A typical example of an ultimatum game involves two strangers. These two individuals are each told that they will have the chance to share a resource, but the division of that resource will be decided in a specific way. The first person will propose a split (it could be 50:50, or 70:30 in his or her favor, or even 99:1 in his or her favor—he or she can suggest any split). The second person will then decide whether to accept that allocation or reject it. If the second person rejects the split, neither person gets anything and the interaction is over, with no further contact or additional interaction. The key to this type of "game" is that traditional economic theory tells us that the first person *should* suggest a very uneven split (in his or her favor), because the second person *should* accept any allocation that results in a benefit. In other words, since $5 is better than $0, if the first person proposes a $95 to $5 split, the second person should accept that deal, since $5 is better than $0.

From an economic perspective, the choice between accepting the $95 to $5 split and rejecting it is in principle no different than the choice between being offered $5 and $0. However, as many studies have repeatedly demonstrated, people care a great deal about the potential "unfairness" of an uneven allocation. An allocation of $95 to $5 will almost always be rejected, leaving both parties with nothing. Even allocations of $70 to $30 will most often be rejected, even though, in theory, people should pick $30 over $0 all the time. These studies have even been replicated in societies where $30 represents a substantial sum. What this tells us is that people place a substantial value on perceptions of fairness and justice. Interestingly, this not only affects the second party in an ultimatum game but also the first party. What is typically seen in these types of scenarios is that the initial split is usually very close to a 50:50 split, showing that not only is the second party sensitive to the unfair allocation, but so is the first party.[9]

Negotiation is clearly a context in which issues of fairness and justice are going to be particularly salient and visible. Not only are there obvious ways in which the outcome of a negotiation might easily be perceived as unfair or unjust (by one party or both parties), but the process itself can potentially create perceptions of unfair or unjust behavior, all of which can be thought of as unethical. People often look back on negotiations and feel that they were treated unfairly or poorly, especially with the clarity of hindsight.

Having a Personal Standard

With respect to process and practices, much of this book discusses different tactics negotiators can use. Often, these tactics manipulate or manage the perceptions of the other party. Yet even the word *manipulate* has an almost pejorative connotation, implying unclean motives and questionable ethics. But manipulation of perceptions in some form must happen in negotiation; otherwise, people will not change their minds or their positions or their offers. This is why a discussion of ethics in the context of negotiations is so important. What makes it very difficult is that there is much more gray area than black and white.

Consider the fact that most societies agree that lying is generally an inappropriate and unethical act. Although people may acknowledge that there are occasions when "white lies" are not too inappropriate, or when a lie told to help someone (or protect someone from harm) might be acceptable, the general consensus is that lying is wrong. However, the process of negotiation is inherently deceptive, often on multiple levels. For example, if the other party asks what your bottom line is, either you don't answer (i.e., withhold information), or you are vague and obfuscate or imply that your position is a strong one (i.e., deception), or you bluff and actually answer the question but with an inaccurate answer (i.e., outright lying). Now, depending on the particular negotiation context, the specifics of the situation, and even the attitudes and cultures of the people involved, all of those possible behaviors may be entirely appropriate. Thus, throughout this book, we are not prescribing rules; rather, we pose questions to ask so that you can make sense of what you think legitimate behavior would be.

For example, in the United States, giving preferential treatment to social connections (e.g., friends, family) with respect to contracts and employment is frowned upon or illegal. In China, the concept of *guanxi* implies an obligation to give preferential treatment to those in your social network with respect to contracts and employment. Neither is universally "right," but both guide what ethical behavior means in that cultural context.

If you were negotiating for a job at a major firm, say, a large investment bank in New York City, it would almost certainly be considered inappropriate to outright lie about your education (e.g., claim to have degrees or certifications you do not have). However, exaggerating your abilities or skills in certain areas may or may not be considered inappropriate. One interviewer might see an exaggeration of skills as being a sign of the kind of ambition and drive that an investment bank wants, whereas another might perceive the exact same behavior as evidence of weak moral fiber. It is up to you to discern what is expected and appropriate in the context and behave accordingly.

Finally, there might be instances where lying would not be considered inappropriate. Suppose you do not have any other job offers from competing investment banks, but when negotiating salary, you suggest that the employer would have to offer you $10,000 more in order to make you pick them over other offers. Again, some observers might consider such a "bluff" to be entirely acceptable negotiating behavior, whereas others might consider it dishonest and unacceptable. If such a bluff is used, even the manner in which it is done can be the difference between someone perceiving it as dishonest or not. In other words, if a claim is made of a specific competing offer that doesn't exist, it obviously runs a greater risk of being perceived as dishonest than if you make a vague suggestion that you might have other options to consider.

The previous examples highlight two important aspects to ethics. The first is that the perception of something being ethical or unethical can depend on a lot of different factors, both *between* contexts (e.g., buying a rug in a Turkish bazaar vs. negotiating with an investment bank for a job) and *within* contexts (e.g., lying about your degree vs. lying about a competing offer). The second aspect is that the perception itself can depend on a lot of different factors, most based on the individual differences (in beliefs, values, attitudes, etc.) between people observing the same behavior. Since there is no rule, we advocate people have a clear personal standard.

Integrity is one of the most valuable things you can possess—not just in negotiations, but in life. Some people would even argue that it might be one of the few things you can really "own," in that it cannot be taken from you without your permission (unlike material possessions, money, health, etc.). A reputation for integrity can be particularly valuable in a negotiation, because it provides an additional and sometimes powerful source of influence. If the other party is aware that you have a strong reputation for integrity, building trust is going to be much easier than if you have no reputation (or have a negative one). As we will discuss in other chapters, trust can be a critical component in finding solutions that create value for both parties. Integrity essentially means that people believe you behave in an ethically laudable way. Integrity is also something that leads people to respect you. People are much more willing to help and accommodate those whom they respect, as opposed to those whom they do not.

Bad People or Bad Behavior?

The reason that having a personal standard is important is that many examples of unethical behavior and ethical lapses are not necessarily the result of "bad" people or individuals who consciously decided to do "bad" things, but are often the result of people in an unfamiliar context or situation who end up behaving in ways that they would not have done in other situations. The field of social psychology is replete with examples of how the situation can be a much stronger predictor than personality, values, or any individual internal characteristics. Well-known examples are the studies on obedience by Milgram, the studies on conformity by Asch, the Stanford Prison Experiment by Zimbardo, and the studies on bystander apathy by Darley and Latané.[10,11,12,13] In all of these research studies the context leads individuals to behave in ways (often morally reprehensible) that they would not have otherwise.

Our argument is that the more you have carefully thought about ethical issues that may arise—both generally as well as specifically in the negotiation situation you are about to enter—the less likely you are to be swayed into behavior that might be inconsistent with your values or that you might later regret.

As an example, imagine that on behalf of your company you have traveled to another country to negotiate the sale of some raw material to a local manufacturer and one of the officials you are meeting with on your trip is from the customs agency. Suppose that during your discussions with this person, you get the clear impression that you are being asked for a bribe to "facilitate" your product getting through customs and prevent it from being unnecessarily delayed or stuck in bureaucratic limbo for months.

Our purpose in this book is not to tell you, the reader, what you *should* do in that situation. We have no basis for providing the "correct" answer that can supersede your personal views on ethics and morality. Some people reading this book would not hesitate to pay the bribe, whereas others would categorically refuse to do so based on principle; still others would try to find some other way to solve the problem, perhaps by hiring a local, who understands the local norms and expectations, to manage the situation.

What we are telling you, however, is that having a clear insight into your personal standards, and an understanding of what you are willing to do and what you will not do, will help you resist undue influence that the situational context might provide. Following the previous example, if you plan to do business with officials in a foreign country, you must not only have an understanding of how behavior is perceived and interpreted in that culture (in order to avoid misperception and miscommunication that might result in an incorrect judgment of unethical behavior) but also have made decisions ahead of time in terms of what you are willing to do and not willing to do. Agreeing to pay a bribe in order to help your company succeed in the specific situation will not be useful if you are fired by your company the following week for violating their policy.

A rule of thumb that is often useful when faced with a difficult decision or ethical dilemma in a negotiation (or in any situation, for that matter) is to ask yourself if you would mind if your friends or family knew about your behavior in the negotiation. It's essentially the "billboard" test: If you would not mind your behavior described on a giant billboard in your home town, then it almost certainly doesn't violate your personal standard. However, if you would be embarrassed and mortified if such a billboard were put up after the negotiation, then you may have violated your personal standard. When faced with a difficult choice, thinking about such questions might help you figure out what course of action is appropriate for you.

CHAPTER REVIEW

Discussion Questions

Consider the following scenario happening in the Belk family:

The Belk family has four members: parents George and Michelle and their two children, Adam (2 years old) and Katie (6 years old). They live in Fairfax, Virginia. George is a teacher in the public schools and commutes to Arlington, every day, about 30 minutes away. Michelle, his wife, is a marketing executive for a small consulting firm in Herndon, also about 30 minutes away. Michelle works in the office 4 days a week and works at home 1 day a week. Michelle has just recently gone back to work after caring for Adam at home since he was born.

The Belk family have found themselves in some conflict about what to do regarding child care for Adam. Currently Katie, in kindergarten, is dropped off at school at 7:30 am and picked up by George at 4:30 pm. The conflict has arisen over how much to pay for child care and where to send Adam, with Michelle willing to pay more than George.

In anticipation of talking with Michelle, George spoke to his parents in Florida, who told George that couples in their neighborhood pay about $600 a month for child care for a 2-year-old. George also spoke to a coworker who lives close by in Maryland who has a neighbor providing day care for $800 a month. Going to Maryland is too far for them to travel, however. Michelle, on the other hand, has researched one local day care center, KidTime, which charges $1,000 a month. To date they have not found any neighbors who are currently offering day care.

Michelle prefers KidTime because it is close to their house, so either one of them could take Adam in the morning and pick him up in the afternoon. George's target is $600, and he is willing to pay between $500 and $800. Michelle's target is $900, and she is willing to pay $700 to $1,000. She thinks they have to pay a minimum of $700 to get quality care for Adam. Here are the discussions between Michelle and George.

Michelle: We need to solve this child care situation. My mom is leaving next week and we have no child care plan.

George: Yeah, I know. I've seen the KidTime brochures you've been leaving around the house. I just don't know how we can afford that.

Michelle: But it's everything we want! After seeing these awesome brochures, I went to visit the place on my way home from work and found it amazing! They have rubber mats everywhere, slides for the kids, even a pretend farm that the kids can play at! A farm! Just unbelievable!

George: Well, what snacks do they give?

Michelle: Uh, I don't know. I didn't ask.

George: Who works there? Are they college students, or are they more experienced providers?

Michelle: I'm not sure.

George: I'm just not comfortable spending our entire savings on $1,000 a month at KidTime. If we could just limit child care expenses to $800, we'd be able to put more money into Adam's college fund.

Katie: Mommy, Adam put a raisin up his nose! Help!

George: Go help the kids. I'll do some research and let's talk tomorrow, okay?

(The next day)

George: So I've looked around a bit and found another place, ToddlerCare, that is only $900 a month. I know it's more than I want to spend, but it will still save us $1,200 a year versus going to KidTime.

Michelle: Where is it?

George: It's about 20 minutes away, and it's on the way to your office. You could drop off Adam around 8:00 am and one of us could pick him up in the afternoon.

Michelle: What's it like?

George: Well, I went on their website to get all of the relevant information. They have a staff-to-student ratio of 6:1; they only give organic, nonsugary snacks; they have no staff under age 25; and everyone has at least 5 years of experience. They also do not have infants in the facility, which means more attention is paid to the kids. This is really important to me as I want Adam to get a lot of attention.

Michelle: Do they have a pretend farm?

George: Well, no, but they do have plenty of toys and an outside play area for when the weather is nice.

Michelle: I suppose we could go take a look. Thanks for doing that research.

(The next day)

Michelle: So I've been thinking about this, and I have a bigger concern after talking to my friend Janice at work today. She kept talking about how her kid was sick all the time when he was in day care and I'm wondering whether a day care center is a great situation or not.

George: Why didn't you say this *before* I did all this research?

Michelle: I'm just being honest.

George: But Janice is a hypochondriac—since she's always sick maybe her kid is always sick.

Michelle: Yeah, I know, I thought of that too, so I went online and found an article that says kids are twice as likely to get sick in day care centers as they are at home.

George: How could we keep him at home, though? You want to go back to work.

Michelle: Well, what if we get a nanny for 4 days and I keep him the fifth.

George: Can we afford that?

Michelle: Well, I didn't think so, but I looked into it, and nanny prices for 4 days a week seem to range from $600 to $900 per month. With my flexible schedule I should be able to make that work.

George: I don't know if I'm comfortable leaving my kid with a stranger.

Michelle: Well, we can get references and do interviews, and if we don't like the nanny, we can either switch or go to one of the day care centers.

George: How can I help find a good one?

Answer the following questions based on the scenario:

1. Who are the parties at the table?

2. Who are the background participants?

3. Who are the background nonparticipants?

4. How do the background participants and nonparticipants influence the negotiation?

5. What are Michelle's interests?

6. What are George's interests?

7. What are the obvious issues in the negotiation?

8. What are the potential issues in the negotiation?

9. What are the positions brought up in the negotiation?

10. What's the ZOPA?

Concept Application

1. Find a public dispute (one being written about in the media) and infer what the interests and the positions are. Report these to the class, along with the evidence for your inferences. State why it is important in this negotiation to separate out the interests from the positions.

2. Think back to a negotiation you were recently in. Answer the following questions and report your answers to the class.

   a. What were your interests? How were they reflected in your desired positions?

   b. What were the other party's interests? How were those interests reflected in their desired positions?

   c. Why was it helpful in this negotiation to understand the distinction between interests and positions?

   d. What were the issues negotiated in this negotiation? Of those issues, which were obvious issues and which were potential issues?

   e. If you negotiated over money or some other quantifiable item, did you have a positive ZOPA? A negative ZOPA? How do you know? How did this ZOPA impact the negotiation? Did you have to try various tactics in order to reach resolution?

CHAPTER 3

PLANNING TO NEGOTIATE

INTRODUCTION TO NEGOTIATION PLANNING

At this point in the book you should understand what a negotiation entails, the common mistakes negotiators make, basic negotiation terminology, and approaches to negotiation. You should understand the distinction between an understanding approach and a convincing approach to negotiation and what it means to create value in negotiation. In the chapters on the various negotiation levers that follow this one (Chapters 4–10), we will go into the *why* and *how* of negotiation, including understanding individual negotiator behaviors and tactics you can use in negotiation to obtain value in various ways.

But before you learn how to think about negotiations and how negotiations work, you need to understand how to plan for negotiations. Why learn about planning first? To borrow from a famous author, because we want you to "begin with the end in mind."[1] The goal is for you to be able to fill out Table 3.10 (which you will find at the end of this chapter) or at least a shortened version of Table 3.10 in your own mind *before* you start negotiating. This includes the ability to anticipate potential challenges and opportunities in each negotiation, understand your own needs and wants and anticipate others' needs and wants, and craft a cohesive strategy that considers the specifics of your negotiation. So, while you will not understand each and every tactic just yet, this chapter will give you a guidepost for where you want to end up so that you can be prepared for sitting at the table.

Having a plan does several things. First, and most importantly, it makes you a more confident negotiator, which will allow you to feel more comfortable and less anxious in the negotiation. This confidence increases your ability to create value by working with the other party, instead of fearing that the other party is going to take advantage of you.[2] Second, it allows you to have a consistent and

Learning Objectives

1. Articulate the purpose and utility of planning before negotiating.

2. Describe what a negotiation plan contains and how plans may differ depending on the context of the negotiation.

3. Create a preference table based on the issues in the negotiation, and use the preference table in your own negotiation.

4. Create a complete negotiation plan along with appropriate contingencies for use in a negotiation.

5. Argue for both the benefits and the detriments of creating and using a negotiation plan.

6. Describe the ethical questions related to knowing a great deal of information about those with whom you are negotiating.

$SAGE edge™

Master the content at study .sagepub.com/rockmann

focused approach in your negotiation. By planning, you can align your interests with your planned strategy and tactics in order to have the best chance to get what you want. Third, it allows you to *resist* tactics from others, because having a plan will lower your uncertainty. If you are expecting what the other side might do, when they actually do it you will not be anxious or taken off guard—you will be ready.

THINKING ABOUT PLANNING

As discussed in Chapter 1, one of the most common mistakes novice negotiators make is failing to plan for a negotiation. You plan so that you do not have to think through and figure out every aspect of a negotiation as it happens "on the fly." You plan so that you do not have to rely on your instinct. Sometimes following your instincts might be successful and result in excellent outcomes, but that is not a viable long-term strategy, especially when you end up faced with negotiations that may be outside of your experience or familiarity. By planning, you will have anticipated and prepared for a variety of possible situations that might occur. Furthermore, planning helps you to react effectively in situations when people are trying to convince you of something. A good plan helps you look for ways to facilitate an understanding approach rather than a convincing approach to negotiation. It does this by keeping you both focused and adaptable.

Planning is a sophisticated activity that requires you to think critically about yourself, other parties, and the context of the negotiation. The plan puts these together into a usable guide that you can rely on as you try to navigate the negotiation process. A negotiation plan can therefore draw upon any of the material from this book, although you will need to be selective about which material is important or relevant to a given situation.

Most people fail to plan for negotiations because it is not clear to them *why* planning is necessary, or *how* they should be doing it. Since planning is not something people typically do before they negotiate, they do not have a good framework to help them do it. To think about planning, let us use this analogy: You are stranded in the middle of nowhere and a storm is coming. No one can get to you before the storm hits, so you need to figure out how to weather it. What do you do? You cannot really answer that question yet because you first need to know something about the kind of storm that is coming (snow, rain, hurricane, tornado, etc.). You also need to know where you are, what resources you have at hand, and what you are capable of. (Are you in the woods? Is your car nearby? What wilderness skills do you have?) The answers to these questions tell you what you might be able to find, use, or create to help you shelter yourself. Planning requires that you take your general knowledge and think about what you will do in a specific situation.

Continuing with the analogy, let's assume you are in the woods, a rainstorm is coming, you know something about building shelters, and you have no extra clothes. In this case you might make keeping dry a high priority, and so you look around for materials to build a good watertight shelter. If you know what you are going to do, then, even if the storm starts, you can keep focused on executing your task. You don't want to be figuring out what to do while the rain is pouring and you are getting soaked—you won't be able to think clearly. Similarly, you don't want to be figuring out what to do while arguments are flying at you in a negotiation—you won't be thinking straight. A negotiation plan is something you will use during the negotiation to keep you focused on what you want to accomplish. When you are negotiating, you will be simultaneously communicating, influencing and resisting influence attempts, attending to others' moves, and adapting to others' strategies. Planning must therefore provide a clear objective and way to assess progress toward that objective.

You cannot plan for everything, but you can plan for a lot of things.

A good plan makes allowances for managing a situation as it evolves. The path that a negotiation will follow is not fully predictable, much like the weather. Thus, it is probably more important for a plan to be flexible rather than exact. Luckily, even though the course of a negotiation can always deviate from the expected path, negotiations tend to change in fairly predictable ways, some of which can be anticipated. To go back to the rainstorm, some new hazards might turn up (lightning, flooding), but many will not (smoke, blizzard), and if you think about what is likely, you can have contingencies for them (e.g., build the shelter on higher ground in case of flooding).

The best plan is, therefore, one that is adapted to the situation and comprehensive enough to cover the important features. At the same time, the plan must be easy to use. It tells you what you need to keep in mind but no more. It offers guidance that is general enough to apply as the negotiation evolves but is specific enough to guide decisions at any point in time. It provides a way for you to act but is flexible enough to change as new things emerge in the negotiation.

INFORMATION GATHERING

Negotiation plans are situation specific, as nothing in negotiation works the same way all the time. While you may have general knowledge about negotiation, what you need to figure out when planning is how to accomplish your negotiation goals in your specific situation. This is where information comes in. Information helps you apply the concepts and tactics correctly and effectively. Suppose you receive a job offer from Microsoft. Table 3.1 gives examples of the kinds of information you may need.

Table 3.1 shows you how important planning is to the negotiation process. No matter which tactics you wish to use in your negotiation, you need information supporting those choices and information to carry out those choices. Our goal in this chapter is to walk you through this process.

What Is "True"?

The value of information relates to how much the negotiating parties believe the information to be an accurate representation of reality. As first discussed in Chapter 1, a mistake you must avoid is the false-consensus effect, that is, assuming the other side believes what you believe. While some information you have may be fact (e.g., the salary they are offering me is $45,000), far more often you form a biased conclusion based on the information at hand. For instance, you might assume, based on the salary being $45,000, that

Table 3.1 Types of Information

Example of (Hypothetical) Information	Example of How That Information Can Help You Plan
Knowledge about what Microsoft wants from its employees	You can think about what assets or resources you have that you could offer.
Knowledge of the role of the person you are negotiating with	You won't waste time asking for things they can't give (e.g., HR hiring staff may have no authority to discuss promotion schedules).
Knowledge of other potential job offers	You can set more or less aggressive goals for the negotiation.
Knowledge that Microsoft doesn't negotiate salary	You may think about adding other issues to the bargaining mix.
Knowledge of the HR manager's wariness of "losing" the negotiation	You may decide to ask them for their ideas as to how the package can work for both of you.
Knowledge of the standard package that is offered to new hires	You can use this information for deciding how persistent to be.
Knowledge of whether you will ever see this HR manager again	You can think about how aggressive you should be (because there is little possibility of a future relationship).

the company (a) has not offered more than that in the past, (b) has little money to spend, or (c) has other qualified candidates. Are these conclusions true? Perhaps, but perhaps not. The danger is in assuming they are true and therefore negotiating as if they are true.

In our example, if you were to believe "c," that one of the other candidates will take the offer if you do not, you will assume you have low formal power in comparison with the company. This may lower your confidence, lower your persistence, and make you less willing to ask questions in order to create value out of fear that the company will hire someone else. Thus, your belief, which is based on an assumption, NOT fact, is affecting your ability to obtain value from the negotiation. The correction is to practice critical thinking when you gather information. Have you gathered all the relevant information? Have you considered and discounted alternative explanations? Do you know how to figure out if you are wrong in your assumptions when you get to the negotiating table?

Relevance

Relevance is how important a particular piece of information is in a particular negotiation. The fact that you are CEO or a store manager is great, but probably won't matter too much to your children in a negotiation over bedtime. Relevance is a question about whether information that *could* matter *does* matter, and if so, how? This is critical to think about when you are gathering information because you want to seek out information that the other side will perceive as relevant to the negotiation. Take the following example:

> Andrea and Jamison are at odds over where to send their daughter Caroline for day care. Their interests range from money to location to quality of food to atmosphere to the quality of the curriculum to extracurricular activities. They can't seem to reach agreement. Jamison decides to do more information gathering. Specifically, he makes a spreadsheet of all the day cares in their town, what they cost, and what extracurricular activities are offered in the afternoons. He presents this to Andrea thinking this will finally help them make a decision. Andrea says: "So what, this doesn't matter."

Jamison has made the mistake of assuming what is going to be relevant to Andrea. He thinks because cost and type of activities are his two most important interests, Andrea will respond to research based on those criteria. Jamison has fallen victim to the false-consensus effect. To Andrea, however, it is much more about the *feel* of the day care and her interactions with the teachers. She needs to feel comfortable dropping Caroline off there, and that is only going to come from her own interactions with the staff. Jamison's research was useless in meeting her interests.

As you think about what is relevant, realize that you might have to find information that *may* be useful. In most negotiations, the need to simplify and be as conservative as possible in your assumptions about what could happen is paramount. However, creating value in negotiations is in large part about exploring what *could* happen. Discovering and/or creating these possibilities will require the inclusion of information that may be atypical for a negotiation. Put differently, if all you consider are obvious issues, your ability to create value will be severely limited. You have to plan for potential issues. (See Chapter 2 for a discussion of obvious and potential issues.) Both obvious and potential issues are pieces of information that have the potential to create value, and so you may need to be a bit more generative (in the brainstorming sense) when it comes to data gathering about value creation.

Remember that each party has their own filter on what they believe to be true and relevant, and when you think these things are wrong, it will often be quite difficult to get the other side to abandon their beliefs. If you are planning to negotiate with a **free-riding** team member (i.e., one who gets by on less than his fair share of effort), to get him to increase his effort, you should think about whether this team member shares that opinion. He may see himself as an active contributor; he may even feel this way in the face of clear evidence to the contrary. When questioned about his performance, he may offer, "I have A's in all my other classes" as (irrelevant) evidence for his contribution. If you are going to negotiate with this person, you cannot dismiss that information. Thinking you will show him how he is wrong (a convincing approach) is a strategy doomed to fail. Better to accept that perception as information (an understanding approach) and try to find a different tactic or set of tactics to use.

Anticipating Negotiation Tactics

If the fundamental process in a negotiation is obtaining value, then you will need to assess in each negotiation situation what the potential tactics are that you can use. These are the tools that can be used to change others' beliefs and behaviors. You must plan not only for which ones will be useful for you to use, but which ones are likely to be used on you. For both, you can think about how to use them effectively and also how they can be resisted.

As you read through the next section of the book, you can think of these chapters as "levers" in a machine you can pull to influence the other side. You can pull one lever at a time or multiple levers at once. In each negotiation, you want to think through, as you plan, what is likely to work and, more importantly, why.

To assess the likelihood of effectiveness, one of the first steps is to think about relevance: What assets do you have at your disposal (e.g., time, resources, motivation, knowledge, etc.) that will help you obtain value from the other side? Generating this list will help you plan. For instance, if you have a reputation for honesty and integrity, you can leverage this to your advantage. When thinking about how you are likely to be influenced, you must similarly think of the assets that others have at their disposal. Sometimes this is a function of the other party (e.g., what they are expert in) or formal power (e.g., they are your boss's boss). But you should also consider what they probably think will work on you. How are you perceived by others? What does this mean for the kinds of tactics people think will work upon you? If you are generally soft-spoken, then you should consider that others may mistake this for weakness and may try to be aggressive. This is what you need to plan for.

When thinking about what tactics will probably be used, you should also think about how these will be resisted. If you intend to use formal power to obtain value from your subordinates, you should be realistic about what will happen if they want to resist. Will they try to make excuses? Say yes but then not do what you ask? Look to get you to do unpleasant things in return? Each of these would imply different courses of action. It is naïve to think that the other person will just cave to your request, so you should think a few steps ahead in anticipation of this resistance. And if you know the levers that are likely to be used by the other side, you can anticipate possible countermoves or responses. In all cases, the questions to ask when planning are "What tactics do I have at my disposal to obtain value from others in this situation?" and the complementary "What tactics will others use to obtain value from me?"

Planning for Value Creation

Value creation will almost always involve creativity of some sort, or at least deviation from your normal negotiation routine. Why creativity? Because what has value and the ways value can be obtained from negotiations vary depending on the people involved, the context, the time, the issues, and so on. While it is easy to apply a standard, noncreative approach to negotiation, that often leaves a great deal of value unclaimed.[3] This is because value creation typically comes from creatively adding or packaging issues. To uncover such issues requires gathering information on what people have that is tradable and connecting it to their interests. This information may not be readily known and thus might take some creativity to uncover.

Creativity is a cognitively demanding activity that requires a level of openness and thinking flexibility. Therefore, the easiest time to do this is not when you are busy trying to figure out how to respond to the other party's attack, or when you are managing the negative emotion that comes from being engaged in conflict, but rather before you sit down at the negotiating table.

Creativity comes from thinking processes that typically happen unconsciously and automatically. While the input to creativity is often an explicit question (e.g., "What could I offer Josefina to work longer hours?") and other information (e.g., "I have time and expertise at my disposal"), how these things combine into novel and useful solutions happens largely in the automatic thought processes that you cannot directly control.[4] What's more, the harder you try to force solutions using your conscious, deliberate thought processes, the more likely you are to fail.[5] So, not only do you have to gather data on what people want and what you have to offer, you also need some time to let these data "percolate." Engaging in activities that put a large load on your conscious thinking processes (such as negotiating) limits the amount of unconscious thinking that can happen. And being in a negative emotional state limits the flexibility of your thinking with respect to seeing novel solutions to a problem. This is, again, why a plan is useful.

This brings us to the last point about planning for value creation. Value creation takes time and effort, and sometimes the situation is simply not worth the bother. If you want our meeting to be at 9 am and I want it at 10 am, it may be most efficient and effective to compromise (9:30 am) or for one side to accommodate the other (9 am or 10 am). One needs to assess the context in order to figure out whether the time and effort required to come up with ideas, pitch those ideas, and implement those ideas are worth it.

BUILDING A NEGOTIATION PLAN

We will now walk you through the main components of planning for negotiation. Are these the only things you will ever need to plan for? No, but thinking through each of these next sections will give you a solid basis from which to work. Do all of these things always matter? No. Every negotiation is unique, so every negotiation will have areas of emphasis that other negotiations will not.

Negotiation Participants

The most obvious participants are the parties at the table. These are the individuals directly responsible for reaching agreement. Every negotiation has parties at the table. For most negotiations, even if just between two people, there are also likely to be background participants and nonparticipants. As discussed in Chapter 1, background participants are the people who may be "pulling the strings" of the participants at the table or who may need to give their blessing to any ultimate agreement. Nonparticipants are those who have an interest in the outcome of the negotiation but do not have direct control over the parties at the table.

In a contract negotiation, the representative for the supplier and the representative for the purchaser are the parties at the table. The supplier's boss and the purchaser's boss are background participants as they have final say over the deal but are not directly negotiating. Nonparticipants could include coworkers, other suppliers or buyers, stakeholders, and the like. These individuals may have an interest in the outcome of the negotiation and may enter the minds of the parties at the table, but they do not have direct influence over the negotiators.

Very quickly the parties at the table, background participants, and background nonparticipants can get complicated (especially if influencing person A will negatively affect person B, or you need to get C's buy-in before recruiting D). Such complexity is hard to manage in the moment, so it is useful to think of the negotiation parties beforehand. In all cases, one must plan for who needs to be influenced, how they (in particular) should be influenced, and possibly in what order this must happen.

Interests

One of the first questions you should ask when planning is "What are my interests?" But in a specific situation, the question is really "What interests can be satisfied in this negotiation?" Once you know what you want, you need to think about the various ways you can meet your interests in your situation. This links your interests to the obvious and potential issues that should be included in the bargaining mix. Situations differ in what issues can be negotiated and hence what interests can be satisfied.

You also need to anticipate what others will want (their interests) and how you might be able to meet those interests. Knowing what issues or positions can be traded, and the benefits and costs associated with such trades, will allow you to determine the range of acceptable deals between what you hope to get (your goal) and what is the least you'll take (your resistance point).

A plan that keeps what you want clearly in mind helps you stay focused in your negotiation. A plan that keeps what others want clearly in mind helps you stay on target with what you offer. Remember that your habit, a very strong habit, will be to start with some kind of position, so it is always worthwhile to compensate by digging for the underlying interests. Do this the usual way: Keep asking yourself why you/they want that position. Watch out for the false-consensus effect (don't assume!), and try to have evidence for your conclusions about what others really want. They *might* have this interest, but you should conclude that only after you have evidence.

> Kiera is negotiating with her mom regarding her curfew time. Her mom says, "Kiera, you know I want you home by 11 pm, no later." Kiera assumes her mom's main interest is to keep her safe, so she replies, "Mom, I'm only going to be at my best friend's house. Why can't I stay there until 12?" Mom says, "No, 11 pm." Kiera has assumed incorrectly. Mom's real interest is in having Kiera get a good night's sleep so that she can finish her homework in the morning. If Kiera had asked about her Mom's interest, she might have discovered this and figured out a creative way to do her homework before she went out for the night.

As you will see in the forthcoming chapters, coming up with creative solutions that satisfy both parties relies on your ability to trade things that are important to the other party for things that are important to you. Discovering what those things are is therefore crucial in order to be effective in a negotiation. Perhaps you might only be able to discover these interests and their relative importance during the negotiation, but the more you can anticipate what these interests are ahead of time and think about issues that the other party may care a lot about, the easier it may be to uncover them during the negotiation.

Issues and Creating a Preference Table

Issues are the things you negotiate (money, time, flexible work, company car, cell phone reimbursement, grade in a class, vacation destination, etc.); they are the building blocks of negotiated agreements. The more kinds of issues you have, the more ways you have to get to agreement. The best issues for you to find are ones that have more value to you than cost to the other side. The more issues you have, the higher the likelihood that some of these will have this quality. Here again, the habit to avoid is to think only about what first comes to mind (e.g., in the job negotiation thinking of only salary, benefits, and time off). Better to answer these questions: "What other resources do these people have that could meet my interests? What do I have that might meet their interests?"

Not all issues may be usable in a negotiation. If you go into a negotiation with your boss with only the issue of telework to negotiate and your boss is prohibited from giving you that, you walk away with nothing. The more issues you've thought about beforehand, the more you have to work with. Having thought of potential issues beforehand can help with further discovery.

In Chapter 2, we distinguished between obvious issues and potential issues. You need to plan for both. The obvious issues are those that both sides know must be negotiated. Brainstorm beforehand what other issues could be on the table. It is much easier to do this brainstorming before the negotiation begins, because during the heat of the negotiation when emotions are high, it will be harder to think of other issues.

PJ has just taken a new job downtown, which is about a 30-minute commute away. A challenge for PJ is that his new company did not offer him a parking spot, which is critical as PJ does not have easy access to public transportation. He sees that a nearby hotel is offering parking spots for $220 a month. This sum is more than he can afford, so he plans for the negotiation by thinking about potential issues that could be added beyond the issue of price. These include room discounts at this hotel, hotel vouchers at other locations, special event preferred pricing, use of the hotel fitness facility, and discounted meals in the hotel restaurant. When negotiating with the hotel manager, PJ asks about all of these potential issues. The hotel manager lights up at the restaurant idea and ends up offering PJ free buffet breakfast every morning. It turns out he wants more people in the restaurant in the morning and offering PJ breakfast costs him virtually nothing as the hotel is already making the food for the buffet. PJ is also able to decrease the price to $200 a month and lock in that price for 2 years. Planning was critical in this instance, as it is unlikely PJ would have thought of this issue during the negotiation.

We can now use our issues to create a preference table. The central task of making a **preference table** is to figure out (roughly) how much you might be willing to give of issue A to get more of issue B, C, and so forth. Essentially, you need to clearly be able to prioritize your issues in terms of which are more important to you and which are less important. The more issues you add, the more likely that the levels of the issues may use different units (money, time, more abstract things such as level of respect), and these are not always easily tied to a common denominator. Intangibles are not so easily converted into tangibles; even when they can be, the result may be less than satisfactory. For example, economists try to use "how much you would pay" as the common denominator to make things simpler. But by that logic, one should trade one less day of vacation for a 0.4% raise, or one less week of vacation for a 2% raise. Why? Because this is what you would get if you convert vacation days into pay. But vacation days mean something beyond money, and most individuals would not take this seemingly "rational" trade.

The pragmatic problem is creating a system that allows you to compare issues that are seemingly quite different. There are a number of ways to do this, but in all cases you are trying to find "good enough" ways to evaluate offer equivalence. Good enough is defined as the right balance of simplicity (for ease of use) and accuracy (so you can make good trade-offs). Not precise enough is easy to use but leads to bad trades. Too complex can lead to precise trades but will be very hard to use in real time. The tool to use is called a preference table.

Let's say you are going to negotiate with your significant other, Pat, about where you want to go for dinner. Here's how you might negotiate without thinking through a preference table:

You: So where you do want to go to dinner tonight?

Pat: I dunno. Where do you want to go?

You: Uh, I dunno. How about that new pizza place—Anthony's?

Pat: Fine, if that's what you want.

You: No, that's not necessarily what I want. I was just throwing it out there.

Pat: No, it's fine, let's go there.

You: I don't even really want pizza, though.

Pat: Then why did you suggest it?

You: Because I thought that's what you might like!

Pat: Let's just go, OK?

You: Fine.

Who "wins" in this negotiation? No one! Who loses? Both you and Pat. Why? Because neither side talked about his or her interests in going out to eat or the important issues tied to those interests.

So, let's try this again. You are going to negotiate with Pat over where to go out to eat. The issues tied to your interests, issues that you care about, are price, atmosphere, type of food, and distance from where you live. Four possible positions for each of these four issues are listed here, ranked in order of most attractive to least attractive to you (Table 3.2). Note that this is YOUR preference sheet; Pat would have his or her own.

Table 3.2	Basic Preference Table			
Attractiveness	**Price**	**Atmosphere**	**Type of Food**	**Distance From Where You Live**
Most attractive position	>$50	Romantic	Mediterranean	Very close (<15 minutes)
	$40–$50	Relaxed	Italian	Close (15–30 minutes)
	$30–$40	Loud	Asian	Not that close (30–45 minutes)
Least attractive position	<$30	Family	Mexican	Far (>45 minutes)

An ideal solution for you would be an expensive, romantic restaurant that serves Mediterranean food close to where you live. Why are these positions more attractive to you? Because of your interests. You just got a promotion at work, so you'd like to celebrate with an expensive meal. You love Pat and would like a romantic setting with Pat. Mediterranean food is something you haven't had in a while but is a cuisine you very much enjoy. Finally, you are hungry, which is why you want to go somewhere close by.

However, that "ideal" restaurant may not exist! That's OK. This preference table is not about getting everything you want; rather, it's about thinking through *what* you want so that you and Pat can create value and come to a better agreement.

This first preference table is very basic, though, and does not let you make distinctions across issues (e.g., is a romantic atmosphere OK if the food is not very expensive?). One improvement to the preference table would be to rank the issues (Table 3.3). For instance, let's say you value price the most (you'd really like to spend money on dinner!), then atmosphere, then distance, then type of food.

The added benefit in this preference table is now you know which issues are most important to you. This helps you decide which trade-offs you might be willing to make. Because type of food is your least important issue, if Pat wants to go to an expensive, romantic Mexican place, this might be fine with you given that type of food is your least important issue.

This preference table is still limited, though, because we don't know the *relative importance* of the positions within the issues. For instance, this table does not reflect your interest of, for example, hating Mexican food. In fact, you are pretty much fine with any type of food as long as it's not Mexican.

Table 3.3   Preference Table With Issue Ranking

Attractiveness	Price	Atmosphere	Type of Food	Distance From Where You Live
Most attractive position	>$50	Romantic	Mediterranean	Very close
	$40–$50	Relaxed	Italian	Close
	$30–$40	Loud	Asian	Not that close
Least attractive position	<$30	Family	Mexican	Far
Issue Rank	1 – Most Important	2	4 – Least Important	3

To improve your preference table to take these relative values into account, you can rank all of the positions within the issues in terms of relative importance to each other. In this example (Table 3.4), since there are 16 choices, a rank of 1 would be the most important outcome to you, and a rank of 16 is the outcome you are least interested in.

You see that this preserves the relative preference order of the issues, while also giving information about preference between positions within those issues.

Table 3.4   Preference Table With Position Ranking *(Position rank in parentheses)*

Attractiveness	Price	Atmosphere	Type of Food	Distance From Where You Live
Most attractive position	>$50 (1)	Romantic (2)	Mediterranean (5)	Very close (6)
	$40–$50 (4)	Relaxed (3)	Italian (9)	Close (7)
	$30–$40 (8)	Loud (13)	Asian (10)	Not that close (11)
Least attractive position	<$30 (15)	Family (14)	Mexican (16)	Far (12)
Average Position Rank	(1+4+8+15) / 4 = 7 – Most Important	(2+3+13+14) / 4 = 8	(5+9+10+16) / 4 = 10 – Least Important	(6+7+11+12) / 4 = 9

Table 3.4 gives us even more clarity about what we want. Now we can see what we truly value, as spending money and having a romantic or relaxed atmosphere comprise our top ranked positions. We can also see what we definitely do not want, namely, a cheap dinner in a Mexican restaurant that is loud and family-friendly.

By assigning ranks to specific positions, we have already refined our interests, but ranks still may not adequately reflect the magnitude of difference between positions within the issues. It is possible for us to clarify our interests even further, in a way that captures more information about what we really value. The best way to add such specificity is to take the rankings and distribute points across possible positions, and then calculate your resistance point and goal in terms of these points. The advantage of points is that they can, for example, better take into account your hatred for Mexican food. A ranking of 16 merely tells you it is your least preferred option. Allocating a point value to each option allows you to better distinguish how least preferred it is. There's no particular scoring system you need to use. The important thing is merely that your scores capture the relative difference in how much you value (or do not value) the options. In this case, the scoring system has the extreme ends of +50 for things you really want and −50 for things you really want to avoid. If two items have the same score, that implies that you have a relatively indifferent attitude toward them. As Table 3.5 shows, you do not care whether a restaurant is Italian or Asian, so both are given the same score.

Table 3.5   Preference Table With Position Scores

Attractiveness	Price	Atmosphere	Type of Food	Distance From Where You Live
Most attractive position	>$50 (30)	Romantic (25)	Mediterranean (10)	Very close (5)
	$40–$50 (20)	Relaxed (20)	Italian (0)	Close (5)
	$30–$40 (0)	Loud (−10)	Asian (0)	Not that close (0)
Least attractive position	<$30 (−15)	Family (−15)	Mexican (−50)	Far (0)

This preserves your issue and position rankings but has the added benefit of allowing you to set a specific and measurable goal as well as a resistance point. You might say your goal is 55 points and your resistance point is 30 points. This means you want to figure out how to get to 55 points, but you'll say yes as long as you get at least 30 points.

Given these point allocations, you can now brainstorm some restaurant possibilities that are acceptable to you; that is, they provide value at or above your resistance point (Table 3.6).

Table 3.6 Preference Table for Each Restaurant

Restaurant #1: Zayteen *(35 total points to you)*

Attractiveness	Price	Atmosphere	Type of Food	Distance From Where You Live
Most attractive position	>$50 (30)	Romantic (25)	Mediterranean (10)	Very close (5)
	$40–$50 (20)	Relaxed (20)	Italian (0)	Close (5)
	$30–$40 (0)	Loud (–10)	Asian (0)	Not that close (0)
Least attractive position	<$30 (–15)	Family (–15)	Mexican (–20)	Far (0)

Restaurant #2: Tabbouleh *(55 total points to you)*

Attractiveness	Price	Atmosphere	Type of Food	Distance From Where You Live
Most attractive position	>$50 (30)	Romantic (25)	Mediterranean (10)	Very close (5)
	$40–$50 (20)	Relaxed (20)	Italian (0)	Close (5)
	$30–$40 (0)	Loud (–10)	Asian (0)	Not that close (0)
Least attractive position	<$30 (–15)	Family (–15)	Mexican (–20)	Far (0)

Restaurant #3: Anthony's *(30 total points to you)*

Attractiveness	Price	Atmosphere	Type of Food	Distance From Where You Live
Most attractive position	>$50 (30)	Romantic (25)	Mediterranean (10)	Very close (5)
	$40–$50 (20)	Relaxed (20)	Italian (0)	Close (5)
	$30–$40 (0)	Loud (–10)	Asian (0)	Not that close (0)
Least attractive position	<$30 (–15)	Family (–15)	Mexican (–20)	Far (0)

Restaurant #4: P.F. Chang's *(45 total points to you)*

Attractiveness	Price	Atmosphere	Type of Food	Distance From Where You Live
Most attractive position	>$50 (30)	Romantic (25)	Mediterranean (10)	Very close (5)
	$40–$50 (20)	Relaxed (20)	Italian (0)	Close (5)
	$30–$40 (0)	Loud (–10)	Asian (0)	Not that close (0)
Least attractive position	<$30 (–15)	Family (–15)	Mexican (–20)	Far (0)

Armed with this information, your task now becomes to use this information in your preference table to negotiate with Pat. If you take an understanding approach to this negotiation, your goal is to try to figure out what Pat's preferences are. Essentially, you want to be able to construct these relative values by asking Pat questions about Pat's interests. You might find out that while Tabbouleh is #1 on your list, Pat had Mediterranean food for lunch and really does *not* want Mediterranean cuisine. Pat's preferences might look like Table 3.7.

Your combined values then look like Table 3.8.

So what's the best solution here? Well, it depends on your stance toward Pat in this negotiation. If you don't care at all about Pat's interests, then Tabbouleh would seemingly be best for you. But we know that's not likely to be the case and that you probably want the best restaurant for both of you. In this case, P.F. Chang's is the best option. This is called **logrolling**—you've traded an issue that is less important to you and more

Table 3.7 Your Negotiation Partner's Preference Table With Scores

Attractiveness	Price	Atmosphere	Type of Food	Distance From Where You Live
Most attractive position	>$50 (0)	Romantic (15)	Mediterranean (–10)	Very close (5)
	$40–$50 (5)	Relaxed (10)	Italian (0)	Close (5)
	$30–$40 (10)	Loud (–10)	Asian (40)	Not that close (0)
Least attractive position	<$30 (10)	Family (–15)	Mexican (20)	Far (0)

Table 3.8   Scoring Values for Each Restaurant Possibility

Restaurant	Points of value to you	Points of value to Pat	*Joint Value*
Zayteen	35	−15	**20**
Tabbouleh	55	10	**65**
Anthony's	30	30	**60**
P.F. Chang's	45	60	**105**

important to Pat (cuisine) for an issue that is more important to you and less important to Pat (price). In discussing interests, you also open the possibility of finding a more romantic Asian restaurant, which would create further value for both of you.

And to think, without the preference table you were going to go to Anthony's![6]

One important note is also the idiosyncratic nature of these interests, rankings, and scores; some of them (if not all of them) are only valid today and for this particular situation. You may generally not want to spend a lot of money when you go to restaurants, but because you wanted tonight's dinner to be a special occasion, you do care a lot about that issue today. By the same token, Pat may normally really like Mediterranean cuisine, but because Pat had it for lunch, it is not something that Pat values very highly for dinner today. Thus, these scores are specific to the situation and time and can be very different if you and Pat have a similar discussion tomorrow. The ideal outcome tomorrow, in the exact same negotiation, might be very different from what you arrived at today. This highlights that you need to approach each negotiation with this type of mind-set and not make assumptions about the other party's interests or preferences.

Let's be realistic. Are you going to create a preference sheet for every negotiation? Of course not. But going through the exercise of making a preference sheet *forces* you to think about your interests in a way that is detailed and specific. This helps you know the issues that are important to you, the relative importance of those issues, the trade-offs you are willing to make, and what goal or resistance point you might set for the negotiation.

Even though this might seem cumbersome and time-consuming, the key to success-ful value creation is to be able to logroll: trading the issues that are less important to one party against issues that are more important to the other party. Thus, it is important for you to know exactly which issues are more important to you and which are less import-ant. To be effective and find the best outcomes, it is equally important to uncover which issues are more important to the other party (or parties) and which are less important. Once you know that, you can identify which of the issues important to the other party but less important to you you would be willing to concede on, in exchange for the other party conceding on an issue that is really important to you but not as important to them. Much of the "discovery" of which issues are more or less important to the other party will occur during the course of the negotiation itself and the communication that occurs. However, as with our discussion of interests earlier, the more you can anticipate and gather information in advance about which issues may be more or less important to the other party, the better prepared you will be to look for this information.

Goals

In Chapter 10 we will talk about the characteristics of good goals and how they can impact motivation during negotiation. Goals serve as a measure (and anchor) of performance. Planning for goals guides against the contamination of emotion. If you can think beforehand (when you are presumably less anxious) about what you really want to walk away with, and the point at which you don't want to continue to negotiate, then you have something to keep you grounded when the emotions start to swirl during negotiation. If you have a clear, specified goal, you will be motivated to persist in the negotiation.

As will be discussed in Chapter 10, with goals there is the danger of **overspecification**, that is, specifying a precise amount for each issue (making a goal of $80K salary, 2 weeks off, and 2 days a week teleworking with a resistance point of $70K salary, 1 week off, and 0 days a week teleworking). An overspecified goal leaves only one way to reach it. This increases the danger that you will miss a creative opportunity (e.g., the other side adds an issue you had never thought of) because you are laser-focused on reaching your goal. Overspecification also can lead you to want to go through issues one at a time, which prevents value creation. Thus, you want to set your goals such that you are motivated to persist without narrowing your focus so much that you lose sight of your broader interests.

Alternatives

You must always identify your alternatives and specifically your **BATNA** (best alternative to a negotiated agreement). Your BATNA represents what you can do if you fail to reach agreement with the other side. It should be clear and explicit in your mind before going into the negotiation; otherwise, you cannot reap its benefits. If your BATNA is weak, you may not want to use it. Or you can take steps to strengthen it as part of your preparation for negotiation. That is, you could develop alternatives to negotiating that would serve whatever purpose you ultimately desire. For example, if you were going to negotiate with a contractor for remodeling your home, rather than seeing your BATNA as limited to the same job done by other contractors, you could consider doing the work yourself, moving to another house, or finding some other way to accomplish whatever you wanted to get out of the remodeling (e.g., if it was building an exercise room, you could think of a gym membership as a BATNA; if it was building a home office, you could think about joining a coworking space). Even if you wind up having a very weak BATNA, knowing what it is prevents you from making threats you cannot deliver upon, or rejecting offers that, while not attractive, do actually improve your situation.

As will be discussed in Chapter 9, BATNA is absolutely central to negotiation. Not only does the relative BATNA of your situation determine how confident you are in a given negotiation context, but it can give you leverage over the other side. BATNAs can also help you determine your goals and resistance points, as you know what you can get elsewhere. The worst deal you are willing to accept is the deal that is slightly better than (or as good as) your BATNA. Obviously you would not easily agree to an agreement that is worse than your BATNA, since you could just walk away and take your BATNA.

Your resistance point is usually determined by your BATNA. A clear, well-defined resistance point gives you information about when to walk away and guards you against influence attempts during the negotiation. If you know what your bottom line is and people are trying to get you to cross it, you can convincingly say, "This won't work for me." Either the other side will capitulate, or you will stop wasting your own time negotiating. It is understandable to want closure. Things like **sunk cost bias** make "completion" an attractive-looking endpoint, as we are driven to engage in future actions to justify past costs. These forces, however, bias judgment in a way that is ultimately mal-adaptive in that value is left on the table. Some deals should not be signed.

Individual and Cultural Differences

Much of what we focus on in this book is about what is possible—what leads to influence, how to align yourself with others, when there might be more possibility to negotiate, and so forth. However, there are often aspects of situations that limit possibilities. These aspects include the individual and cultural differences that impact negotiations (Table 3.9; also see Chapters 11 and 12). You need to understand the relevant characteristics of the situation before you go into the negotiation so that you don't waste time and effort trying to accomplish or change something that you actually can't.

Table 3.9 Individual and Cultural Differences	
Difference	**Example**
Gender	This can impede your ability to influence by changing how you are perceived.
Personality	Some negotiators may be overly conflict avoidant, making some negotiation tactics difficult to use. Others might be overly confident.
Ability	Certain negotiations are complex and may be more difficult for some negotiators to grasp.
Diversity	Diverse negotiators may be assumed to have certain preferences or characteristics, impeding the ability to create value. Diversity among negotiators also increases the potential for misunderstanding and miscommunication.
Emotion	Heightened anxiety creates defensiveness, impeding the ability to take an understanding approach to negotiation.
Culture	Cultural differences can make certain tactics unacceptable, create communication difficulties, and engender a great degree of uncertainty.

You will also need to think about the logistics of the negotiation, such as where to negotiate, when to negotiate, which technology to use (see Supplement B), and so on. Further, many negotiations have barriers such as resource and time constraints (see Supplement F).

Approach and Tactics

As you work through this book you will gain a significant amount of information about the tactics associated with negotiation. As you plan to negotiate, you will have to decide which tactics to use. The first choice, as shown in Figure 2.2 in the previous chapter, is whether you are going to take a convincing or understanding approach during the negotiation.

If you take a convincing approach, are you going to use formal power? Alternatives? Uncertainty? Persistence? If you take an understanding approach, are you going to focus on reciprocity? The relationship? Intangible interests? And then, within each, which tactic or tactics are you going to use? Once you've decided on a set of tactics, you might find it helpful to write down specifically what you will say. Over the years we've seen our students struggle with finding the words to use in opening a negotiation and, more often than not, default to a weak opening defined by conflict avoidance. When you write down how you'd like to open, you have a **planning script** to follow, which reflects what you truly wish to convey.

Negotiations evolve in a way that is not perfectly controllable by any one person; therefore, a good plan should be adaptable to unexpected conditions. Plans can go awry in an infinite number of ways, so there is no way to prepare for all contingencies. However, you can identify the critical pathways or milestones and have backup plans for these. These are the places that would make you vulnerable or weakened if they did not work out. Some unexpected events could include the following:

- What if they open the negotiation first when you planned to open?

- What if you are trying to understand and they insist on convincing?

- What if they do not care about future interaction and you struggle to build trust or liking?

- What if you find out new information that strengthens or weakens your arguments?

Because people tend to be pretty poor at prediction, you should not get carried away trying to presage all the possible ways in which negotiations can get off track. It is much better to have a focused and flexible set of tactics in case you need a "Plan B." For example, when negotiating with a friend, maintaining the relationship should be critical, and you should have a backup plan in case the negotiation starts to devolve into a fight. Or, if you walk into a negotiation thinking that your awesome BATNA gives you the leverage you need, have a contingency for what you will do if the BATNA turns out to not be very strong at all. If you spend the time to at least think of a few things that might go wrong and how you might respond or change your plan, you will have an advantage over people who do not engage in some basic contingency planning. Asking yourself, "What are the three main things that might go wrong in this negotiation?" can be a very useful thought exercise as part of your planning process.

MAKING A PLANNING WORKSHEET

There isn't one fixed way to plan for a negotiation, and obviously lots of negotiations can vary in many different ways—hence the need for flexibility in your planning. However, as a general rule, it's always good to prepare a worksheet (see Tables 3.10 and 3.11) ahead of time and to make sure that all of the "boxes" have been filled out as much as possible with available information. Not only does this get you in the habit of making sure that you are thinking about all of the important aspects of the negotiation ahead of time, but also the empty areas of the worksheet clearly tell you what information you still need to find.

Once you have filled out a worksheet as completely as possible, the missing gaps will tell you what additional information you need to be searching for (before the negotiation) and trying to discover (during the negotiation). You should also use the worksheet to help you figure out *how* you might try to convince or understand the other party. Does the worksheet tell you anything important about what tactics the other party or parties might be susceptible to? Does the worksheet help you understand how you might overcome different barriers that you might be anticipating during the negotiation? What type of tactics and approach are you going to use, now that you have this information? Most importantly, does looking at the worksheet suggest possible avenues for finding creative solutions that might benefit both parties? In other words, can you already start to get an idea for what low-priority things you might be able to trade away to another party that they might really value, and what things they might not value that could be really important to you?

A planning worksheet is not by any means the only preparation or planning you need to do for a negotiation. As outlined in this chapter, there are many factors that you need to plan for and contingencies to consider. However, a planning worksheet (see Tables 3.10 and 3.11) is something that can help you organize information and think about creative solutions that can lead to effective outcomes. Having a worksheet like this can be a "safety blanket" to help the inexperienced negotiator feel more prepared and confident. As you become a more experienced negotiator, you may eventually not need a paper worksheet in front of you to write on—you may keep much of this in your head—but it remains important to organize and categorize the information in a systematic way.

Tables 3.10 and 3.11 are a start, as for most negotiations this worksheet will capture the important features of the negotiation at hand. As you prepare for a particular negotiation, you might decide that other categories need to be represented in your worksheet. Perhaps there is history between the two individuals that should be captured, or you want to note your own proclivities for the common negotiation mistakes. Use the worksheet, then, and supplement based on the particular situation you are facing.

Table 3.10 The Planning Worksheet

1. **Parties**	Who are the parties in the negotiation?	
2. **Interests**	What are your interests in this negotiation?	
	What do you believe are the interests of the other side in this negotiation? Why might your answer to this question about the other side's interests be wrong?	
	How might you be able to create value in this negotiation?	
3. **Issues**	What are the obvious issues to be negotiated?	
	What are the potential issues to be negotiated?	
	What are your preferences/rankings on those issues?	
	Create a preference table for your negotiation, including possible positions (in the left column) on each issue (across the top row). Include either rankings or point values for each possible position on each issue.	
4. **Goals**	What is your goal (or goals) for this negotiation? Is this goal SMART? How is this goal going to motivate you to be persistent in this negotiation?	
5. **Alternatives**	What is your BATNA? What is the strength of your BATNA? What is the other party's BATNA? What is the strength of their BATNA? What is your perception of your/their BATNA? What is their perception of your/their BATNA? What is your resistance point, or the point at which you will walk away?	

(Continued)

Table 3.10 (Continued)

6. **Individual and cultural differences**	What individual and cultural differences are likely to be in this negotiation? How are these likely to impact your negotiation? Personality, ability, gender, etc.	
7. **Approach, levers, and tactics**	Which approach are you going to use in this negotiation—convincing or understanding? Why?	
	What negotiation levers are you going to try to "pull"? What tactics will you try first?	
	What specifically will you say? How will you open the negotiation?	
	What tactic(s) will you use if your first option(s) is not successful, and why?	
8. **Their approach, levers, and tactics**	What approach, levers, and tactics do you anticipate the other party using?	
9. **Logistics**	Where will you negotiate? How will you negotiate? What are the resource and/or time constraints of this negotiation? Will you need to use a mediator or arbitrator?	
10. **Other?**	What else is likely to matter in this negotiation? History between the parties? Proclivities for making negotiation mistakes? Contract details? Other?	

Table 3.11 Sample Negotiation Plan

This negotiation plan is adapted from an MBA student named Sobek. In anticipation of a negotiation with his boss Julie, he put together this negotiation plan. This is written from Sobek's perspective and was used to negotiate a pay raise, additional responsibilities, and security clearance sponsorship from his employer.

1. **Parties**	Who are the parties in the negotiation?	There are two parties at the table in the negotiation: my supervisor Julie and myself. In addition to these two parties, there are three background participants who can affect the progression of the negotiation because of the influence they have on my supervisor. These are the three companies I perform work for, who were assigned to me by Julie. These companies have influence because if they are not satisfied with my work, they can tell Julie that they no longer need me.
2. **Interests**	What are your interests in this negotiation?	<ul><li>I want to be able to pay off my student loans as rapidly as possible. The interest on my student loans begins to accrue once my classes are over, so an increase in my rate would help me to address this.</li><li>I want to take on additional responsibilities with the work I'm performing so that I may become more knowledgeable about the federal contracting space and make myself more attractive to potential employers.</li><li>By increasing the frequency at which I perform work for my supervisor and receive feedback, I can build a stronger relationship with my supervisor and get more exposure to our clients.</li><li>As my future is in the government contracting space, sponsorship toward a security clearance will open career path options for me.</li></ul>
	What do you believe are the interests of the other side in this negotiation? Why might your answer to this question about the other side's interests be wrong?	<ul><li>My supervisor wants to keep the three companies I work with as happy as possible so she does not lose them as clients.</li><li>My supervisor does not want to lose me working for her as a project analyst because I perform competitive research for the clients she works with.</li><li>My supervisor does not want to damage the mentor–mentee relationship she has with me because I am, in part, a reflection of her.</li><li>My supervisor wants me to succeed because she has invested in me and my success will reflect positively on her.</li></ul> I might be wrong because I'm not in Julie's shoes. I don't have her perspective on the broader business, nor have I had a negotiation like this with Julie before.

(Continued)

Table 3.11 (Continued)

		How might you be able to create value in this negotiation?	I can create value by adding issues and hopefully facilitating logrolling. This creates values if these issues are more important to me than to Julie. If Julie is able to give me my preference on issues #2, #3, and #4, then I would be willing to forgo a $5 increase in pay.
3.	**Issues**	What are the obvious issues to be negotiated? What are the potential issues to be negotiated?	Obvious (What's on the table): • My hourly pay rate Potential (What could be on the table): • I would like additional responsibilities from Julie related to working with our technology platform. This platform is used by our government clients to coordinate projects, and it is something that would help me greatly in my career. • Increasing the frequency at which I perform a number of my assigned duties and report them to my supervisor. Currently I only report weekly but would like to report more frequently. • My supervisor sponsoring me for a security clearance.
		What are your preferences/rankings on those issues?	*(In order of importance)* 1. My hourly pay rate 2. Additional responsibilities 3. Frequency at which I report tasks and get new assignments 4. Sponsorship for a security clearance

Create a preference table for your negotiation, including possible positions (in the left column) on each issue (across the top row). Include either rankings or point values for each possible position on each issue.

	Hourly Pay Rate	Additional Responsibilities	Feedback Frequency	Sponsorship
Position 1	+$5/hr (100)	Yes (50)	Daily (40)	Yes (30)
Position 2	+$3/hr (80)	No (0)	3 times/ week (30)	No (0)
Position 3	+$1/hr (20)		2 times/ week (20)	
Position 4	No change (0)		Weekly (0)	

(Overall points of value to me in parentheses)

4.	Goals	What is your goal (or goals) for this negotiation? Is this goal SMART? How is this goal going to motivate you to be persistent in this negotiation?	I will gain 150 points of total value as determined by the preference table. It is specific, time-bound, difficult, relevant to my interests, and I've set it myself. I have not made this public.
5.	Alternatives	What is your BATNA? What is the strength of your BATNA? What is their BATNA? What is the strength of the other party's BATNA? What is your perception of your/their BATNA? What is their perception of your/their BATNA? What is your resistance point, or the point at which you will walk away?	• **What is your BATNA?** My BATNA would be to simply continue working at my current hourly rate. • **What is the strength of your BATNA?** The strength of my BATNA is low. • **What is your perception of your BATNA?** I perceive my BATNA this way because of the low resource power I possess and the belief I hold that, in part due to my close relationship with my supervisor, she is aware of my BATNA. • **What is your perception of their BATNA?** I perceive her BATNA to be strong since she has legitimate and resource power. Also, her BATNA is strong because there are many candidates who can perform the same work that I do. • **What is their perception of your BATNA?** I believe that her perception of my BATNA is that it is weak. I state this because she knows she holds significant resource power but, more importantly, I strongly believe that my supervisor is aware of my BATNA. • **What is their perception of their BATNA?** My supervisor is aware of the job market and the prevalence of individuals with my skills. As such, I feel that she believes she has a strong BATNA.

(Continued)

Table 3.11   (Continued)

6.	**Individual and cultural differences**	What individual and cultural differences are likely to be in this negotiation? How are these likely to impact your negotiation? Personality, ability, gender, etc.	Julie may not want to be seen as "soft" since she is an aspiring woman leader in the organization. She may be sensitive to this. I need to explore her intangible interests for how she would like to be viewed coming out of this negotiation. I'm generally conflict avoidant and need to remember to keep asking questions and pursuing a positive agreement with Julie.
7.	**Approach, levers, and tactics**	Which approach are you going to use in this negotiation— convincing or understanding? Why?	I want to use an understanding approach to this negotiation. I would feel uncomfortable trying to convince Julie of anything, and I want this to feel as much like solving a problem as possible. In other words, I don't want to get into a tug-of-war with Julie. Because she is serving as my agent, I need her to be on my side during this negotiation so that she is able to represent my interests along with hers to the client(s).
		What negotiation levers are you going to try to "pull"? What tactics will you try first?	• *Relationships* (Chapter 6). I will begin by exchanging pleasantries and working to build rapport. The relationship is by far and away the most important thing to me in this negotiation, and I will make sure Julie knows this. • *Intangible interests* (Chapter 5). From this point, I will tell her how grateful I have been and continue to be for the support and guidance she has offered me. Julie, my supervisor, views me as her mentee and, as such, I believe would respond well when I express my sincere gratitude for all that she has done for me and be completely honest with her by clearly communicating both the things that I need and the things that I would love to have. This should promote a problem-solving approach to the issues at hand rather than an adversarial one. • *Reciprocity* (Chapter 4). Sharing information by openly and honestly communicating with her about my "needs" versus my "love-to-haves" will only act to further the trust that we have with one another. As a result of furthering this trust, she will be even more willing to be forthright with me and explain why she could or could not approve of or address the issues I have communicated. • *Reciprocity* (Chapter 4). I will ask her if it is OK to ask about *adding issues.* If she says yes, I will present all four of the issues in my preference table.

		What specifically will you say? How will you open the negotiation?	"Julie, I just want to tell you how much your guidance has meant to me over the past couple years. From hiring me immediately after I left my personal training job, to teaching me the fundamentals about federal government contracting, to writing my recommendation letter when I chose to pursue my MBA, you have believed in me and supported me when others did not. I am forever appreciative of this! Thank you. As I finish up the last classes of my MBA over these next few weeks, I am increasingly looking 'down the road' in terms of my financial situation. Now, I absolutely hate to ask this, but I always want to be completely honest with you. In order to effectively pay down the student loans I have taken out, I'd like to discuss possibilities regarding an increase in my hourly rate as well as other possible job opportunities. Is this OK to discuss?" *(Wait for answer before proceeding.)*
		What tactic(s) will you use if your first option(s) is not successful, and why?	• *Reciprocity.* If my supervisor responds by saying that she does not think she can increase my hourly pay, I can suggest a contingent contract. The contingent contract would state I would get paid $25 for my hourly work rate for 3 months and if, by that time, I do not have a new job, the hourly rate would go back down to $20. • *Alternatives.* I'll try to strengthen my BATNA by obtaining another job offer. If I'm able to do that, I can then use that BATNA to threaten to walk away and take another offer.
8.	**Their approach, levers, and tactics**	What approach, levers, and tactics do you anticipate the other party using?	• *Relationships.* I really like Julie and her husband and this makes it very difficult for me to ask her for value. Even if she doesn't explicitly "use" her relationship power over me, I know this can influence me. • *Background power.* Julie can say that her hands are tied because of the contract that we are working on.
9.	**Logistics**	Where will you negotiate? How will you negotiate? What are the resource and/or time constraints of this negotiation? Will you need to use a mediator or arbitrator?	• I'd like to get out of the office and negotiate with Julie at a local coffee shop. I think this will make for a more relaxing environment. • Julie may not have the resources to increase my pay because she is constrained by the contract we are working on. • I'm unable to directly negotiate with the three companies that I perform work for. In this sense Julie is my agent. I have to speak with Julie, who, in turn, must speak with the three companies about increasing my hourly rate. This will potentially decrease my ability to know the interests of the three companies.

(Continued)

Table 3.11 **(Continued)**

10.	**Other?**	What else is likely to matter in this negotiation? History between the parties? Proclivities for making negotiation mistakes? Contract details? Other?	• Julie and I met when I was a personal trainer at a local gym and Julie and her husband joined as my clients. I am forever grateful to Julie and her husband for being early clients of mine, and I think this is going to impact how willing I am to ask Julie for things now. I need to remember that this is a business deal and Julie is interacting with me as my supervisor, not as my personal training client.

ETHICAL CONSIDERATIONS

Planning is surprisingly important from an ethical perspective. This is surprising because you may not consider the planning stage of a negotiation as one where difficult ethical choices or dilemmas might present themselves. To a certain extent, this is true; the ethical consideration here is more one of trying to proactively avoid getting into those situations in the first place.

Often, when individuals engage in unethical behavior, it is not necessarily because they are bad or evil people or their intent is selfish or unethical. Rather, it can be because they are placed in unfamiliar situations or are exposed to unexpected pressure—either from other people or from a "strong" situation—and they react with behavior that they might not have otherwise engaged in if they had more time to consider their action or been able to step away from the situation. There are volumes of research in social psychology that demonstrate these kinds of effects,[7] and being well prepared and having a specific plan can "inoculate" you against many of them. Instead of being caught off guard and finding yourself in an unfamiliar and confusing situation, you can rely on your preparation and stick to your plan.

There is a saying among SCUBA divers: "Plan your dive, and dive your plan," which is a rule of thumb designed to prevent people from getting into trouble during a dive. Many fatalities in SCUBA diving occur because divers (often relatively inexperienced ones) end up putting themselves in situations they had not planned for and end up in considerable danger. The logic for negotiations should be the same: The more you have a plan for unexpected things that might happen, or things that can go wrong during the negotiations (as mentioned earlier in this chapter), the less likely you are to find yourself in an ethically compromised position.

Another important way that planning is relevant to ethics is in terms of thinking about your personal ethical standards *before* you enter a negotiation. The more you have a clear idea of what you are willing to do and what you are not willing to do, and exactly where your line is, the less likely you are to accidentally cross that line. For instance, if you are negotiating on behalf of your employer and someone offers a bribe during the negotiation to influence you toward a deal more beneficial to them, you should not have to consider whether or not to take it; you should already *know* the answer. Most difficult choices will not be as blatant as this example and might involve considerable nuance and ambiguity. Gathering as much information about the particular context and norms related to the negotiation ahead of time, so that you can determine how your personal standard applies, is an important part of preparation. Even if you have very clear personal ethical standards, you will still need to think about how they apply in a particular context. Will your standards for appropriate behavior be different when negotiating a used car purchase than for a salary negotiation with a prospective employer? Probably.

Ethics Discussion Questions

1. Are there conditions under which offering a bribe, or accepting a bribe, might be acceptable? What would those conditions be?

2. If you are preparing to negotiate with a company for a contract, and an old college friend of yours contacts you to sell you confidential information on the bids of your competitors (which would give you a significant advantage), how would you respond?

3. Would you be prepared to tell an outright lie during a negotiation? If so, under what conditions? Would you ever include lying in your negotiation plan?

4. If you are negotiating on behalf of your employer, and you were explicitly told by the CEO to not reveal particular information, how do you respond if someone asks you about the information during the negotiation? What do you do if the other party offers what appears to be a really good deal for your company if you reveal the information?

CHAPTER REVIEW

Discussion Questions

1. What appropriate information could you gather prior to a job negotiation?

2. What are all the responses you should be prepared for when you ask a car salesman whether he can lower his price?

3. What would be the danger in developing one part of the plan thoroughly without the other parts of the plan?

Concept Application

1. Following Tables 3.10 and 3.11, make a negotiation plan for each of the following situations, and then conduct the negotiation.

   a. A one-issue negotiation

   b. A negotiation with a close friend or family member

   c. A negotiation with multiple parties

2. Report back on how and why the plan was helpful and where it could be improved.

3. Also report back on whether the plan was restrictive, and if so, in what ways.

$SAGE edge™

Visit study.sagepub.com/rockmann **to help you accomplish your coursework goals in an easy-to-use learning environment.**

NEGOTIATION LEVERS

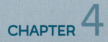
RECIPROCITY

Learning Objectives

1. Describe what can be reciprocated in negotiations.

2. Demonstrate the paradox of reciprocity.

3. Use the paradox of reciprocity to identify why individuals face difficult choices when negotiating.

4. Predict how and why reciprocity works between individuals, and how reciprocity can be used to create value in negotiation.

5. Describe the tactics associated with reciprocity and illustrate how those tactics can be used to obtain value.

6. Understand the ethical questions surrounding the leveraging of reciprocity in negotiations.

Master the content at study .sagepub.com/rockmann

CHAPTER EXAMPLE

Delana is in need of a new garage at her house. She recently had items stolen out of her carport, which means she can't keep any tools, bikes, or other items there without worrying they'll be stolen. She did research on contractors on several home improvement websites and received three different bids. The three bids came in at $48,000, $58,000, and $81,000. Given that the $48,000 bid was from a brand-new contractor that had only done one job and the $81,000 was outside her budget, she decided to negotiate with the company that bid $58,000: ARI Contracting.

Being a savvy negotiator, Delana didn't just want to say okay to the $58,000 price. She wanted to *add value* to the negotiation. She knew that the $58,000 included demolition of the carport, a new concrete pad for the garage, and construction of the new garage (including siding, roofing, electrical, and a new garage door). However, Delana wanted more. Delana presented a counter-offer to Omar, her sales representative at ARI. She agreed to the $58,000, but asked for the following:

- Everything in the original proposal

- Demolition of a 14 × 10 storage shed also on her property

- An additional 14 × 20 concrete pad for a new storage shed

- Two additional exterior lights on the garage

- A new electrical box in the garage for a possible electric car

- A $1,000 discount for every week past 4 weeks that the project was not complete

Omar replied the next day and said that the additional electrical work would cost $2,000, but he could add the additional demolition, concrete pad, and lights at no additional cost. He expressed concern about the final item, the $1,000 discount for every week past 4 weeks the project was not complete. He told Delana that his concern was the weather, that if the temperature drops below freezing he cannot pour concrete and work on the garage. Delana stated that was reasonable. She changed her proposal to $1,000 for every week past 4 weeks of working days during which the average temperature is above freezing. Omar was satisfied with this condition and that day they settled on $60,000 for the entire job.

******

INTRODUCTION TO RECIPROCITY

The next several chapters (through Chapter 10) cover the underlying "levers" of negotiation, or the concept(s) explaining why certain negotiation tactics work. The goal of each chapter is to focus on one major concept underlying negotiation and specifically negotiator behavior. Each chapter is presented in the same way. The first part of the chapter will be on understanding the psychology behind the negotiation lever. The second part of the chapter will be on understanding tactics, or negotiator behaviors, associated with that lever. Each chapter concludes with a discussion of ethics, concept application, discussion questions, and a role-play exercise (full role-play instructions are available to instructors online). The goal in presenting the material this way is so that you understand the underlying concept first and then learn how it applies specifically to negotiations. This will help you see why things happen in negotiations the way that they do and, in turn, make you a better negotiator.

Many people think of negotiations as being about "winning," with the implication that the negotiator who is not winning is probably "losing." We believe, as others do, that these terms of "winning" and "losing" are misleading and not reflective of reality.[1] There is rarely a true "winner" or "loser" in a negotiation as winning and losing are subjective concepts that are open to interpretation. Take a simple example of a husband convincing his wife to go to South Carolina for vacation instead of Aruba. You might say that if they end up going to South Carolina, the husband has "won" the negotiation. But what if the wife resents her husband after the negotiation because she has to go to South Carolina? Further, what if the wife protests engaging in various day trips on vacation because she harbors this resentment. Has the husband truly won? We don't believe so.

We thus take the focus away from winning and losing and place it on value. How much value has each side obtained from the negotiation? At the heart of reciprocity is the idea that we can obtain more value by understanding the interests of the other side and making trades and exchanges that leverage those interests. The use of reciprocity allows you to utilize resources often in nonthreatening ways, which can open up the door for many understanding negotiation tactics and, ultimately, better negotiation outcomes.

Reciprocity Defined

One of the fundamental motivations you can use to your advantage is **reciprocity,** or another's willingness to return equal goods or services to you when goods or services have been given to them.[2] Reciprocity exists because a **feeling of obligation** is created when someone gives something or does something for someone else. Because reciprocity is a powerful social rule or norm, people are generally reluctant to violate it, which is why it can be used to obtain value in negotiation. Further, people have a natural preference for equity or fairness in a relationship, and reciprocating is one way by which people judge whether they are being treated fairly or whether we are treating others fairly. As such, the feeling of obligation that is created when someone gives you something can be a powerful way to obtain value.

Have you felt like you had to give someone a gift after they've given you a gift?

Have you felt like you had to hold the door for someone after they've held it for you?

Have you felt like you had to listen to a story after someone listens to one of yours?

Then you already know what it feels like to engage in reciprocity!

The other reason for reciprocity (as will be discussed further in Chapter 7) is uncertainty. If you meet someone for the first time, for example, on a first date, you may not know what to expect or how to behave. You may have a mental model (see Chapter 1) for how to behave on a first date, but even with a developed mental model, you still have uncertainty for exactly how to engage this new individual. The best piece of information you possess to figure out how to act toward this new person may come from how they act toward you. If they ask you about your job, it's a cue to ask them about their job. If they tell you a story about their family, you tell them a story about your family. This is reciprocal behavior, a remarkably easy decision rule for how to behave in the context of an uncertain social situation.

Reciprocity is based on the fundamental calculation of equity. If X = my contributions to the relationship or situation and Y = your contributions to the relationship or situation, then my goal is for:

$$X - Y = 0 \text{ (formula for reciprocity)}$$

That is, you seek to minimize the difference between what you perceive the other party has put into the deal with what you have put into the deal. The outcome of this is that if you provide something, the other party will reciprocate in order to maintain that perception of equity. Reciprocity is a basic and powerful aspect of human interactions, especially when there is no history between the parties.

Have you ever received a letter in the mail that contained return mailing address labels with your name preprinted on them? Or a request to complete a survey along with a $1 bill? Robert Cialdini notes that receiving those popular address labels around the holidays makes individuals *three times* more likely to contribute to the charity.[3] Why? Because they feel guilty and have an inherent desire to "balance the scales" by reciprocating toward the charity. The same principle of reciprocity occurs with the $1 bill. Individuals don't want to throw the $1 bill away so they keep it and consequently feel compelled to fill out the survey.

What makes reciprocity so valuable is that it can overpower other, more self-interested motives in negotiation.[4] Individuals reciprocate in situations even though it might be in their economic interest to not reciprocate. For example, perhaps a salesperson has given you a small discount on an item. How do you reciprocate? You say yes to the deal, even though economically it is in your interest to keep negotiating. We engage in this behavior because we don't wish to feel uncomfortable in the social setting.

What Is Reciprocated?

In negotiation, reciprocity exists in many forms. Yes, offers can be reciprocated, but so can trade-offs, threats, emotional statements, and even conflict avoiding behaviors.[5,6,7] One of the most important behaviors that can be reciprocated is tactics, the behaviors negotiators engage in to obtain value. Many have suggested that it is in the reciprocity of understanding tactics that better negotiation agreements are reached.[8] Take trust, for instance. An act that is perceived as trusting shows the other side a willingness to cooperate; the other side then is more comfortable cooperating.[9] Similarly, convincing behaviors are reciprocated as well. Once a convincing behavior is reciprocated, it can evolve into a destructive cycle of conflict that is difficult to break.[10,11,12]

The first, more traditional notion of reciprocity is that individuals reciprocate **concessions**. A concession is giving some value to the other side in a negotiation. One side gives a discount on a product they are selling. The other side reciprocates by agreeing to buy more units. Each side has conceded value to the other, facilitated by reciprocity.

While concessions involve positions, reciprocity can also revolve around an exchange of information about interests. If one side provides a piece of information that is personal or sensitive about why they truly believe something or want something, the other side usually will reciprocate and also share information. Further, if one side shows an interest in learning about the *other's* interests, the other side will usually reciprocate and inquire about interests as well.

Laurie Weingart and colleagues conducted a research study on negotiation reciprocity in which they coded strategic behaviors by each party in a negotiation.[13] Each negotiator behavior and the corresponding behavior from the other negotiator were tested to see if one predicted the other. Collaborative behaviors were found to lead to more collaborative behaviors, and competitive behaviors were found to lead to more competitive behaviors. This is reciprocity in action.

Although much of reciprocity is based on the conscious exchange of benefits, the psychology goes deeper than that. Think back to grade school days. Can you remember a time when you felt left out? When you were the only one who didn't know what was going on? Perhaps you were the new kid at school or camp? Did you have that sinking feeling in the bottom of your stomach, thinking that everyone was looking at you?

People generally have a need to be liked and to feel included.[14] People don't want to feel left out or feel stupid because everyone else seems to know what is going on while they don't. Yes, they engage in conscious reciprocity to minimize this, but this feeling is so strong that they also engage in reciprocity at the subconscious level by mimicking others. At this level, individuals mimic facial expressions, emotions, postures, and message content.[15] This means individuals engage in these behaviors without being aware of doing so. The subconscious form of reciprocity demonstrates how deep-seated is the need to follow norms in social settings—by reciprocating, we increase our chance of feeling included. In negotiation settings, mimicry has been found to increase deal-making as it facilitates trust between the negotiating partners.[16,17]

Reciprocity Over Time

Consider the most traditional negotiation, the one-time negotiation of price for an item. I offer you $4,000 dollars (my initial position on the issue of price) for your car, and you return with a counteroffer of $6,000 for the car (your initial position on the issue of price). We already see reciprocity—an initial offer has been reciprocated with a **counteroffer**. If on the next move I counter with an offer of $5,000, a typical response by you is to again reciprocate with a similar concession of $1,000. In this example, both sides have given a similar concession. Neither side feels that they "owe" anything else to the other side at the end of the negotiation because what each gave up was equal. Will this outcome always happen? Of course not. I might know that $4,000 is the correct price for your car based on my research and so I am unwilling to budge off that figure. This echoes the point that reciprocity drives human behavior more so in uncertain, rather than certain, situations.

When there are multiple issues, we have the possibility to create trades where the felt obligation between the parties going forward, after the negotiation, will be positive. For example, say we have a two-issue negotiation where the issues are the price per item and the number of items to be purchased. Now we begin to have the possibility of setting up positive (or negative) cycles of reciprocity. Let's say that the item in question is one that I have a frequent need for (e.g., reams of paper) and one for which you have a decent-sized profit margin. In this situation, price is most important to me, whereas volume is more important to you. If I am about to buy 50 reams of paper and you say, "Buy 75 and I'll give you 15% off the price of each ream," then value has been created on both sides. I feel I have come out ahead because I gained on what was important to me (I reduced my price per ream 15%). You feel you have come out ahead because you gained on what was important to you (you moved from 50 to 75 reams). This is logrolling—trading on issues of unequal value to each side.

The example that opens the chapter is one of logrolling, in that trade-offs are made which are of unequal value to both sides. When she adds the issues, Delana is betting that providing this extra labor and work is easier for Omar to concede than lowering his cost on the overall project. Similarly, she knows that she values getting this extra work done at the same time far more than perhaps saving a couple of thousand dollars in haggling over just the price of the garage. This is why this proposal is so effective. She agrees to pay Omar's price (his #1 issue, lower priority for her), and he agrees to provide quite a bit of extra work for her (her #1 issue, lower priority for him).

Reciprocity impacts negotiator behavior over time as demonstrated in Table 4.1. As a result of my getting my #1 issue, I feel like I've gotten more out of the negotiation than you (X > Y, per the calculation presented earlier). Similarly, as you have also received your #1 issue, you feel like you've gotten more out of the negotiation than I have (Y > X). Given the principle of reciprocity, in the next negotiation we will continue to seek to help the other side in order to "balance the account" in the relationship. This is a very productive place for you to be in with the people with whom you have to negotiate. If you always leave negotiations feeling like you've gotten a lot of value and they think the same thing, the next conflict will be that much easier to solve. This is why taking an understanding approach in continuing relationships is preferable to taking a convincing approach.

While we have provided a positive example here, the reverse is possible, too—that both sides perceive that they got *less* in the negotiation than the other. This would mean, again per reciprocity, that you would want to even the score in future negotiations by harming the other side.[18] Also, emotions arise as a matter of course during this process. These emotions have the capacity to accumulate over time and amplify or complement the feelings of obligation that accompany reciprocity. Although there are many sources of emotions in negotiation, for now let's just consider what arises as a result of exchange distributions. Typically when we perceive we were treated fairly (or better than fairly), we experience positive feelings. When we perceive we were treated unfairly, we experience negative feelings. Those feelings will influence our attitudes toward the other side and how we judge what is fair in future negotiations.

Keep in mind that X's perception of the negotiation need not be the same as Y's. X's and Y's perceptions are just that—perceptions, not facts; thus, they need not be symmetric. You can have situations in which both sides perceived they got "less" than fair and situations in which both sides perceived they got "more" than fair.

Table 4.1   Reciprocity Over Time

Perceived Distribution (from X's perspective)	Obligation to Other Side	Feelings Toward Other Side	Relationship With Y in the Future
Even trade (X = Y)	Small	Neutral	Habit, willingness to work with Y again
X < Y	High (negative)	Negative: X feels as if they "lost"	X seeks retribution in future negotiation(s) with Y
X > Y	High (positive)	Positive: X feels indebted to Y; X perceives relationship with Y like a partnership or a team	Increased trust, liking, and engagement with Y

The Paradox of Reciprocity

In negotiation there is a **paradox of reciprocity**: Although sharing information leads to more information from others (via reciprocity) and the opportunity to create value, negotiators don't share information because they fear they will lose value (see Figure 4.1). Or, to state this another way, fear of being taken advantage of causes you to avoid the thing that will help you (sharing), which ultimately hurts you (by not sharing).

Let's explore this further. Uncertainty makes you wary or suspicious of others and especially of sharing information that could be used against you. Because many people tend to think of negotiations in terms of a fixed-pie (Chapter 1), they fear that revealing information about their motives or underlying interests might allow the other party to take advantage in an opportunistic way. Thus, often, the fear of being vulnerable results in people holding on to information that, if revealed, would make the negotiation much easier and lead to better outcomes. Thus, while you may know you need to share information, you don't want to—hence the paradox.

Think about reciprocity as a siphon, whereby a liquid moves from one container at a higher elevation to another container at a lower elevation through some type of tube or pipe. Siphons work because of gravity: The force of the liquid flowing through the tube continually "pulls" the liquid from the higher container to the lower container. However, you can't just stick a tube or pipe into these two containers to start the siphon; simply connecting them will not make any liquid flow. To start the siphon, you have to pump (or suck) some of the liquid into the siphon. Once you accomplish that, the system will keep going and the liquid will move. Without priming the system in this way, nothing will happen.

Sharing information works in the same way. To prime this "reciprocity pump," one of the negotiating parties has to make themselves vulnerable and share information

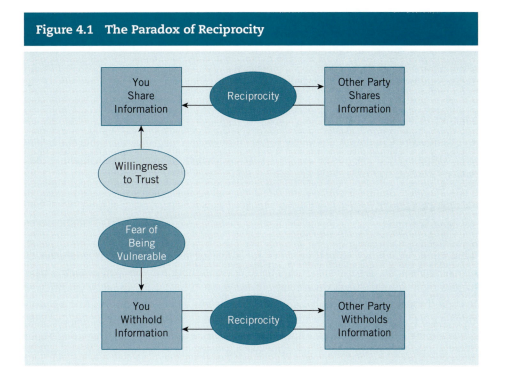

Figure 4.1 The Paradox of Reciprocity

(or show interest in the other side or add issues or some other action that is seen as collaborative).[19] Once this happens, the other side will have the opportunity to reciprocate and the cycle will continue. If no one primes the system, suspicion will remain and very little information will be shared. Thus, it takes a "leap of faith" to overcome the paradox of reciprocity.

Part of what we are talking about here is **trust,** the willingness to be vulnerable to someone else. Trust is the extent to which someone is willing to incur risk in a relationship or interaction with another person. If you trust someone a lot, you will share information without hesitation because you are not worried about them taking advantage of you. If you do not trust someone, you will be very reluctant to share information because of the risk involved. The more a trusting atmosphere can be created in the negotiation context, the easier and more effective the information sharing and reciprocity of information will be.

One advantage to trust that many negotiators don't realize is how *easy* it can be to build.[20] Remember, especially when first meeting someone, you may have very little past information on which to base judgments of the other party—you have no developed mental model. If that second party behaves in what is perceived to be a trustworthy way, voilà!—trust is built, at least temporarily. This is important because this initial trust becomes the basis for the relationship and can foster the use of many of the tactics based on reciprocity that will be described later in this chapter.

To take advantage of reciprocity, you have to be able to give to the other side something that taps into their interests. You must be in possession of something that has value to them, be it goods, flexibility with terms, respect, love, or something else. Don't underestimate the resources you have at your disposal! (See intangible interests in Chapter 5.) You never know what you might have that taps into the interests of the other side.

Interests in Negotiation

As discussed in Chapter 2, a popular belief among many negotiators is that the key to negotiating is about *convincing*. As such, parties often enter negotiations thinking they have to convince the other side to get what they want.

> **MISTAKE: To get what I want I have to *convince* the other side to give it to me.**

This mind-set ignores something very fundamental to negotiation: If you want to invoke reciprocity, or influence someone to do something for you, you generally have to give them something or do something for them. This "something" is usually tied to their interests: those underlying, usually persistent, needs and desires that all individuals have. If you are trying to negotiate, or resolve a disagreement or dispute with someone, it is often going to be impossible to convince them that they are wrong about their position. Arguing and convincing are not typically effective ways to negotiate, and they can sometimes result in conflict or anger, as the other party may end up with the perception that you are not listening to their position or not respecting them. If the other party's position is driven (in part or fully) by underlying beliefs, values, or attitudes, then trying to convince them their position is wrong is implicitly an attack on those underlying factors. You can easily offend or insult the other party and make resolution of the negotiation or conflict far more difficult and perhaps even impossible.

In essence, there are a number of different ways to try to influence someone toward a negotiation outcome that benefits you. Trying to convince them is typically not the most effective way to approach the problem. After all, there's no inherent reason why they should care about what you want. You have to provide that reason, and the best way to find it is by thinking about what they might want, what their interests are.

- Trying to convince an employee that she should work overtime because you think it is important is usually not going to be as effective as offering to pay her overtime or finding some time for her to work when she isn't doing anything else.

- Trying to convince someone that he should help with a cause that is important to you but irrelevant to him is not going to be as effective as asking him to help with a cause that directly impacts his life.

- Trying to convince your single friends to go to a movie may not be as effective as suggesting going to an event where they might meet other single people.

In each of these instances, you are more likely to get what you want by giving the other party something that addresses their interests, as opposed to just trying to convince them that they should care about your interests. As discussed in Chapter 2, what people want can vary widely. Obviously, people want money, promotion, and material things. But many people also want to be important, have high status, and be respected or admired. People also often want to have people care about them and value their contributions and opinions. People care about not feeling embarrassed, ashamed, or guilty. People often care a lot more about many of these intangible and relationship-based factors than we tend to typically think (something so important that we devote an entire chapter, Chapter 5, to this idea).

When you give others what they want in return for their changing their mind or behavior (invoking reciprocity), you are meeting their interests. This can facilitate log-rolling, which involves your giving away something of relatively low value to you but of great value to the other party, and their giving you something that you care about a lot but is of relatively low value to them. In such a scenario, both parties get something of great value but only give up something of relatively low value.

Remember that interests are distinct from positions. Focusing on positions, rather than interests, can lead to a suboptimal solution or an impasse, as in the following scenario between Ben and his boss:

> Ben approached his manager to negotiate for 2 extra weeks of vacation because his job was burning him out. His manager replied, "You're one of my most important employees, and I can't afford to have you gone for that long." Ben argued that because of his high performance, he should get the extra 2 weeks. The manager refused, citing concerns about fairness in the department.

In this scenario Ben is focused on one position, getting 2 extra weeks of vacation, rather than his underlying interest, which is to avoid getting burned out. Unfortunately, when he asked for this position the manager *assumed* that he would lose Ben for large chunks of time on vacation. With Ben focusing on the position (the 2 weeks), it was easy for the manager to end up with this mistaken assumption. It turns out that Ben was not planning on taking one long vacation; he just wanted the flexibility to take a few 3- and 4-day weekends. By thinking ahead of time, and communicating his actual interests (reducing stress and job burnout) to the manager, Ben could have explored several possible solutions that might have satisfied both his and his boss's interests.

Cautions When Using Reciprocity

Does reciprocity always work? No. Not everyone has the same fundamental understanding of what it means to be reciprocal. Research evidence suggests that individuals differ in how important they consider reciprocity in relationships to be and to what extent they engage in reciprocity themselves.[21, 22] Some negotiators may not see reciprocity as applicable to negotiations,[23] which could lead them to be competitive no matter what the behavior is from the other side.

Reciprocity is also impacted by mental models (see Chapter 1). In a study of Palestinian students from the West Bank, researchers found that subjects reacted negatively to unfair offers as compared with fair offers in an ultimatum game.[24] This first demonstrates reciprocity—competitive behavior (an unfair proposal) is reciprocated with competitive behavior (a negative response). However, these students reacted even *more negatively* to the unfair offers when the offers were presented in Hebrew handwriting from Israelis as compared with Arabic handwriting from Palestinians. Israelis had to offer 15% more of a given stake to have the same probability of proposal acceptance. Reciprocity, as any tactic, is not *assured.* In this case these students already had a predetermined belief about what "fair" constitutes and were biased toward members of their in-group (Palestinians) versus members of their out-group (Israelis).

Reciprocity is based on perceiving an equitable, or fair, trade. But fairness can mean many different things to many different people. Take the following scenario:

> Scott and Karen are negotiating over where to go on vacation. Scott wants to invoke reciprocity so he opens the negotiation with this: "Karen, I know you really want to go to Ireland for our next vacation. So let's do that. It actually works out really well because then I can play golf at some of the most amazing courses in the world." Karen is not pleased with this offer as their last vacation was to California, where Scott played golf several days.

The mistake Scott has made here is that he is assuming Karen is seeing his concession the same way he sees it—that because he is "giving" her the location (Ireland), she will concede by letting him play golf during their vacation. But Karen does not see the negotiation in the same way. Karen already feels like she should get to choose the location of the vacation because Scott chose the last vacation. Getting to go to Ireland is not a concession to her; it's her *right.* Thus she feels in no way obliged to Scott for offering something to her that she feels like she has already "earned."

NEGOTIATION TACTICS

Behaviors that *leverage,* or take advantage, of the idea of reciprocity are behaviors you can engage in either before or during your negotiation to obtain value based on reciprocity. But beware! These are also the same tactics that others can use to obtain value from you.

Uncovering Your Own Interests

Before you can make a trade, you have to know what you are willing to trade. One of the first actions to take in preparation for negotiation is to think about what your own interests are. This may seem obvious, but it has been demonstrated that negotiators think primarily about positions, without exploring the underlying interests for those positions. It is important to knowing what your interests are because if you wish to invoke reciprocity, you will have to think about what you actually want and which offers provide enough value for you to say yes. Take the following example from one of our own experiences:

One of our former students called up asking for help negotiating with her company. She said she had a job offer from a different company that provided a good career path, but it would require a longer schedule and commuting to the city 5 days a week. She felt like she was "stuck" at her current company, but she could telework 1 day a week and the commute wasn't too bad. The situation was complicated by the fact that she had a 1-year-old. She asked what she should do.

Our response was to ask her, "What are your interests? What is it that you actually value and care about in your career and job?" She hadn't thought yet about how much the various trade-offs mattered to her and her husband and thus how to evaluate the various opportunities. She was only thinking about the various positions in the negotiations. Once she considered her interests, it revealed that she would be best off trying to be creative about career paths with her current company OR be creative about flexible work options with the new company.

Without knowing your own interests, it is difficult to know what to offer in order to get something from someone else.

Perspective Taking

Just as you need to know about yourself to invoke reciprocity, you also need to understand the other side. We can take one of our most important negotiation lessons from Atticus Finch's lesson to his daughter Scout in *To Kill a Mockingbird*.

If you can learn a simple trick, Scout, you'll get along a lot better with all kinds of folks. You never really understand a person until you consider things from his point of view, until you climb inside of his skin and walk around in it.[25]

Because understanding is central to leveraging the concept of reciprocity, you would do well to heed such advice and try to improve your ability to engage in this behavior. **Perspective taking** is defined as a negotiator's "cognitive capacity to consider the world from another individual's viewpoint."[26] This is critical in negotiation for several reasons. First, it allows you to find resources you have that the other side may value. This helps you avoid mistakes such as the false-consensus effect (Chapter 1). This ability can lead to more creativity in negotiated agreements and to the ability to create value via reciprocity-based tactics.[27, 28] Second, perspective taking helps you avoid being overly self-interested and falling victim to the endowment effect or the confirming evidence bias (Chapter 1). You shift from trying to protect your own value to trying to find ways to create value by partnering with the other person rather than trying to compete with the other person. Third, perspective taking eases your anxiety and emotions. When your resources are threatened, you get defensive. This defensiveness shuts down your ability to think calmly about the various alternatives to present in the negotiation, as you become nervous you are going to *lose*. Perspective taking, by taking the focus off yourself and placing it on others, relaxes this reaction.

Asking Interest-Based Questions

As discussed in Chapter 2, positions are the things that negotiators ask for (e.g., $84,000 salary), while interests are the personal needs that underlie those positions (e.g., *I want to feel valued in my new company*). If you want to give yourself the best chance to invoke reciprocity, you first have to know what the other party wants. That means understanding the interests behind the positions.

Asking questions of the other side is an important way to uncover interests in a negotiation. We often go into negotiations with little if any knowledge of the other side's interests, so why not ask? Besides gaining information, asking questions also communicates to the other party that you care about their interests. The phrase *"This is what I want"* communicates a much different message than *"How can I help you get what you want?"* By asking the other party what he or she wants, you are uncovering potentially important information that you can use to further the negotiation. However, not all questions are created equally. Consider this question from Tarik to his wife Laila:

Tarik: "Honey, where would you like to go out for dinner?"

Laila: "I don't know. Where do you want to go?"

Seemingly innocent, right? Unfortunately, Tarik has started this negotiation with a position-based rather than an interest-based question. Instead of asking about Laila's interests (e.g., type of food, money to spend, location, wait time, dress attire, etc.), he has asked for her position. She has reciprocated his position-based question with another position-based question (*"Where do you want to go?"*). They are now stuck. Perhaps they exchange restaurant names, but even if they decide on a place, they have learned very little about the other person and what the other person's interests really were in picking a place to eat dinner.

Figure 4.2 demonstrates a continuum between interests and positions. On the position side are the restaurant names. To move away from these positions Tarik might ask, "Do you want Mexican food?" While these questions are interest-based, Tarik is still flailing a bit as he goes through each and every cuisine possibility. Better questions take a purely interest approach: "Do you care about the type of food?" "Do you care about money?" These interests are further down the continuum and better represent the core of what Laila is thinking about. From these answers Tarik can then know what Laila is thinking about and ask follow-up questions building on that knowledge, for example, "Ah, so you care about food. Is there a specific type of cuisine that sounds good?"

Even in questions that are designed to acquire information about interests, there can be missteps, such as being demeaning (e.g., "Why are you acting this way?"), threatening (e.g., "Are you *sure* you want to take that position?"), or insulting (e.g., "Would you be willing to share your underlying needs, because right now I can't figure out what the heck you are talking about"). Key to using questions as a tactic is that it has to open up the other side to sharing information. As mentioned earlier, parties can often be reluctant to share information during negotiations, out of fear that they might reveal something that could be used against them by the other party. The more you can create

Figure 4.2 Probing for Interests

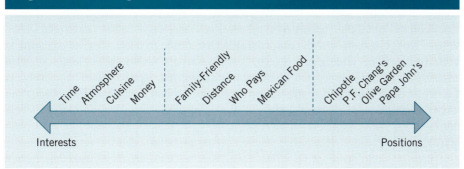

Time · Atmosphere · Cuisine · Money | Family-Friendly · Distance · Who Pays · Mexican Food | Chipotle · P.F. Chang's · Olive Garden · Papa John's

Interests   Positions

a trusting atmosphere and a sense that both parties will share information reciprocally, the more successful you can be in terms of discovering one another's interests.

One of the major hurdles you encounter during the process of negotiation is when you reach an impasse, or a point in the negotiation where you are stuck on your positions and are not making progress. At this point most negotiators do not know what action to take or how best to resolve the situation. You know you are not getting through to the other side, but you are unsure how to proceed. The major mistake negotiators make at this moment is to continually repeat the same arguments, as if the other side has a hearing problem or does not understand. Not only will this action not further the negotiation, it is likely it will harm the negotiation, as the other side is going to get increasingly frustrated and resentful at your attempt to convince them of something you want. Remember, people care first about their own interests. In this moment the good negotiator will ask interest-based questions of the other side in order to understand the nature of the impasse. This is difficult because this behavior is not natural. When you reach an impasse, you usually focus inward to understand what you are doing right or wrong. If you want to leverage reciprocity, you need to focus outward, to understand why the other person is behaving the way that they are and why the proposal on the table does not satisfy their underlying interests. These impasses can often be dissolved by reframing the discussion:

> "It seems we are at an impasse and I know we are not going to get anywhere if I just restate my arguments. Can you tell me more about your positions? How do those best satisfy your needs?"

Compromise

Compromise is a negotiation tactic based on reciprocity whereby the parties agree to "meet in the middle" or "split the difference" on a particular issue in order to reach resolution. Compromise works because of the fundamental notion of reciprocity and fairness—I will give X dollars if you agree to also give X dollars. That, to most people, is perceived as a fair trade-off. This is precisely why compromise is used so frequently as a tactic, because each giving the other side the same amount of dollars (or items being traded) is *measurable and knowable*. We can agree on what is fair when all of the information is on the table. The fundamental motivation to reciprocate allows us to take advantage of that. The danger with compromise is that although both sides are engaging in reciprocity, without adding any issues to the negotiation both sides are at least somewhat unsatisfied. No value is created when compromising. Yes, we've "solved" our problem, but we've done it by each giving up something we wanted and without discussing our underlying interests.

Adding Issues

Adding issues is one of the simplest tactics negotiators have at their disposal and means exactly what it says—adding a potential issue or issues to the list of issues being negotiated. For example, in a job negotiation, if the employee asks about having a new laptop as a part of the job package in addition to salary, he or she is *adding* the issue of having a laptop to the negotiation. When issues are added, it gives both sides the opportunity to state whether that issue is important to them or not, which facilitates logrolling, a tactic described later in this chapter. If both sides want the employee to have a new laptop, then adding the issue of a new laptop to the negotiation involves no conflict and value has been immediately created in the negotiation. This is one way negotiators can create value, by finding issues in the bargaining mix that they have in common or by trading issues in the bargaining mix of unequal value. The best way to get there? Have as many issues in the bargaining mix as possible! While adding issues helps in this regard, adding issues does not guarantee creating value, as some issues may not be able to be put on the table or an issue could be added that is valued equally by both sides.

Think about buying a car. If all you have to negotiate is price, no value will be created and you will have a zero-sum negotiation. Now think about adding other potential issues in, for example, extended warranty, roadside assistance, oil changes, maybe even general maintenance for a set period of time. Each of these can add value because each costs the dealer less than it would cost you to get it on the open market (e.g., an oil change costs the company a fraction of what it costs you at a local garage). Now if you can think about some things the car dealer may want, you will really be in a position to bargain. What might these things be? One is loyalty and future business. This can be harder to guarantee, so this is where you need to be creative. You could guarantee that you will bring the car in to the dealer's service shop and perhaps make the deal "stick" by offering that you can get your free maintenance every other visit (ensuring you still use the dealer's shop). Or maybe you give the dealer the information of your friends and promise to provide a positive referral.

Adding issues is discussed along with reciprocity because by adding issues to the negotiation you are trying to encourage the other side to either (a) add issues of their own or (b) reciprocate with information.

Even in a simple negotiation like where to go on vacation with your significant other, issues can be added. What is the obvious issue in this negotiation? Location, of course. But there are many potential issues that can be added, including budget, activities,

The example that opens this chapter provides a good example of the power of adding issues. Delana knows it might be difficult to haggle over the $58,000 bid, so she creates value in the negotiation by adding issues. She adds the issue of demolition of the storage shed, the new concrete pad, the lights, and the electrical box. Were she to agree to the $58,000 and then try to bring up these things later, she would likely have to pay for each item because the contract would already be signed.

time spent, traveling companions, and so on. Each one of these issues may be of unequal value to the parties, which creates the foundation for logrolling and creating value.

Logrolling

Logrolling, as noted, involves finding issues to trade which parties value unequally.[29] The trade is made such that each party receives a lot on their highly preferred issue and gives a lot on their less preferred issue. For logrolling to occur, there *must* be multiple issues and those issues must have *different* value to each party. For example, let's say we work together and we come to discover that you like to have long weekends off but don't mind working long hours during the week, whereas I can't work long hours during the week but don't mind working the weekend. We therefore make a trade so that I cover your weekends and sometimes Mondays in exchange for your covering me anytime I have to work a double shift. How would this look?

- Issues: Work on weekends, covering double shifts during the week

- My interests: Not feeling overworked during the week

- Your interests: Party time on weekends

- Non-logrolled solution: I ask you to cover my double shift. You respond yes or no.

- Logrolled solution: We trade off the two issues. I cover your weekends and you cover my double shifts.

For another example, think about a job negotiation. If the employee desperately needs moving expenses (highly important) but is willing to be flexible on the retirement plan (less important) while the employer has extra cash and is willing to pay moving expenses (less important) but desperately wants to save money on retirement contributions (highly important), the two parties can logroll these issues, make the trade-off, and have a higher quality agreement.

Packaging Issues

Packaging issues involves making an offer with multiple issues. Although logrolling is always making a packaged offer, a packaged offer does not necessarily involve logrolling. The importance of making a packaged offer, and thus keeping all issues on the table tentative until agreement is made, is that it gives negotiators a chance to see all the possibilities for adding further issues and subsequent logrolling.

The other benefit of packaging issues or making packaged offers is that you get information about what the other side values relative to other issues. Table 4.2 shows packaged offers to the other side in a negotiation for a supply contract.

Table 4.2 Packaging Issues				
	Delivery	**Price**	**Length of Contract**	**Buyer Response?**
Supplier offer 1	1 week	$10/lb	2 years	NO!
Supplier offer 2	1 week	$12/lb	1 year	No
Supplier offer 3	2 weeks	$10/lb	1 year	Yes
Supplier offer 4	1 week	$11/lb	3 years	NO!
Supplier offer 5	2 weeks	$9/lb	3 years	No

For the seller trying to figure out the buyer's needs, packaging issues together in multiple offers allows the seller to discern what the buyer cares about. It turns out that for the buyer a shorter contract and low price are more important than delivery schedule. This is why the buyer prefers Offer 3 presented by the seller. By packaging issues the seller makes sure of only making offers the other side is willing to say yes to, while at the same time increasing the odds of finding a combination of issues to which the buyer will also say yes.

In many negotiations where negotiators find it difficult to talk about interests (perhaps they are too personal or too emotional), packaging issues can provide a great deal of information. A parent can ask his or her teenager if she would rather have 11 pm curfew, homework completed beforehand, and using Uber or Lyft rather than driving to her friend's house OR 12 am curfew, homework completed in morning, staying at home, and having her friend come over. Which offer the teenager prefers will provide some information about her interests. Additional packages of issues provided by the parent will continue to help in this regard.

Contingent Contracts

Negotiators often face difficulty because they have different beliefs about what is going to happen in the future.[30] A baseball player may believe that he is in the prime of his career and is going to remain valuable to the team. The team, on the other hand, believes that the player is at the end of his career and is becoming decreasingly valuable to the team. As such, they cannot agree on salary terms for the player's next contract. It may be hard to see how these two parties would invoke reciprocity in this situation, because there is nothing they can (obviously) trade.

As noted, contingent contracts can be particularly effective for athletes. In the following quote from cornerback Richard Sherman, he is discussing the contingencies that are built into his new contract with the San Francisco 49ers, which he signed in March 2018.

> Once I make a Pro Bowl, $8 million the next year is guaranteed for me. It gives me the ability to control my destiny. The 49ers have skin in the game. I have skin in the game. In my former contract, no matter what I did this year, nothing would be guaranteed to me next year. I couldn't feel secure in my contract. Now, if I play the way I know I'm capable of playing, I know I'm going to get paid.

Notice the language he uses, that both sides have "skin in the game." This is one of the benefits of contingent contracts, that they motivate performance on both sides. In this case the 49ers are motivated because they want to win games and have a productive player. Sherman is motivated because he wants to earn more money in the future. So, despite the risks involved in this type of deal (e.g., if he were to get injured), Sherman clearly appreciates having a degree of control over his destiny.

Source: http://www.espn.com/nfl/story/_/id/22730284/richard-sherman-san-francisco-49ers-says-signing-vengeful-choice-seattle-seahawks

There is a tactic they can use, though—the **contingent contract**—which involves negotiators placing a bet on a future event in order to resolve a potentially difficult issue facing them in the negotiation. That is, what one side gives to the other side is going to be *contingent* on some future outcome. This allows negotiators to focus on their actual interests rather than their disagreements about the future.[31] What the player *truly* wants is to be respected and to be paid fairly. What the team wants is to protect themselves in case the player is no longer able to perform at the same level. To solve this impasse they can set up a contingency, for example, a performance-based bonus based on the player's future statistics. The team agrees to give the player the salary figure he wants if he performs at the level they want. The player agrees to take the salary figure the team wants if he doesn't perform at the level they want. An added benefit of the contingent contract is that it gives the player incentive to continue to work hard because he wants to prove that he is worth every penny.

Another classic example of this is television ad revenue. Let's say a company and a network cannot agree on a price for a set of advertisements for a particular show (e.g., a new sitcom). The network wants $5 million, and the company only wants to pay

$3 million. At the heart of this debate is the number of viewers that are going to watch the network when this new show is on. Of course neither side knows for sure what that number will be, so to solve this conflict they can make payment *contingent* on how many viewers tune in. This is the bet—how many viewers will be attracted to the show. A simple contingent contract could be that if 10 million watch, the company pays $3 million; if 12 million watch, the company pays $4 million; and if 14 million watch, the company $5 million. The reason contingent contracts help negotiators find better solutions is that if 14 million watch, the company is happy to pay $5 million, and if the viewers don't watch, the company doesn't have to pay the full price.

Contingent contracts are a great way to invoke reciprocity because they emphasize that individuals have different expectations or beliefs about the future, and instead of *convincing* each other about what the future is going to be (which is impossible to know), they can simply place a bet. One piece of advice we often give to students negotiating job offers is to make their compensation *contingent* on their performance in the first year. They are motivated to work hard, and the company gets what they want—a hardworking employee. If the employee works hard, the company is happy to give the raise and everyone wins. If the employee doesn't perform, the company does not need to pay extra.

A few words of caution.[32] Contingent contracts require a degree of continued interaction after the negotiation, as the final terms of the deal will not be known until some point in the future. Second, it needs to be clear that the contract can be enforced. In sports, enforceability is easy because contracts are signed and there is a labor union. In other contexts, enforceability may be more difficult. Third, there needs to be a high degree of clarity and measurability. Basing a contingency on "good" performance, for example, is a problem, because what does "good" mean? That term will be open to interpretation and likely cause a conflict in the future.

Case Sidebar

The final component of the negotiation between Delana and Omar is a contingent contract. One of her main interests is getting the project done on time. To satisfy this interest she could argue with Omar about how he can possibly complete the project on time. This argument, though, is not likely to be productive. Instead, she proposes a contingency—she'll pay full price if the work is done on time. Omar believes in his crew and is willing to make this bet, but he is concerned about the weather. He's fine with the time restriction, as long as they exclude days that are below freezing. Thus, his interests are served because he believes his crew will complete the work on time, and her interests are served because she is protected in case the work runs long.

BENEFITS TO LEVERAGING RECIPROCITY

The benefits to using reciprocity can be seen in the range of deals that become possible when negotiating this way. Adding issues, logrolling, and contingent contracts are not only less threatening tactics to use but can lead to more creative agreements that contain more value. When combined with effective communication and information sharing, reciprocity is at the heart of effective negotiations. When implemented well, it will result in the type of value creation described in Chapter 2, which should be the goal of every negotiator. Ideally, every party to the negotiation will get more than they otherwise would have gotten—making the solutions more optimal and all of the parties more satisfied.

An additional advantage of reciprocity is that it will also make future negotiations among the parties easier, because the reciprocity (and hopeful value creation) will likely facilitate trust development, which in turn will make information sharing and more reciprocity more likely in the future. In this way reciprocity forms the basis for the later chapters on intangible interests (Chapter 5) and relationships (Chapter 6).

COSTS TO LEVERAGING RECIPROCITY

The first cost to using reciprocity is the time it takes to discover interests and resources and how to trade them. So, although the outcome in using reciprocity will usually be far superior, there is no doubt that it will usually also be more time-consuming. If negotiating over the price of a pack of gum, the time may not be worth it. If negotiating for the purchase of a house, or a valuable business deal for your company, or vacation with your significant other, it is likely to be worth the time.

Going back to the paradox of reciprocity, it can also make you feel vulnerable to negotiate in this way. You have to be willing to change the negotiation from a convincing to understanding effort, which is not how most people traditionally think about negotiation. So for some, using reciprocity may be a somewhat unfamiliar and uncomfortable feeling when first attempting.

One of the examples used in the preface of this book is a situation where adding an issue *doesn't* invoke reciprocity. Why would this potentially happen? Consider this scenario:

> Barbara is negotiating with Paul, a local contractor, to install a new patio at her house. The contractor is willing to install the patio for $6,500, but this is above Barbara's budget of $5,000. She wants to keep a good relationship with the contractor as she might need work in the future and wants him to do a high-quality job, but she is also struggling with the price. She ponders what issues she might add to the negotiation. While exercising one day, she has a revelation: Perhaps she can leverage the fact that she is on the board of her local community association. She calls Paul and says, "Paul, I have an idea. If

you are looking to grow your business in my neighborhood, which has about 1,000 houses, why don't I host an open house for you and your company after the installation so that neighbors can come and look at the patio, learn about your business, and ask you questions." Paul pauses and says he has to think about it. The next day Barbara gets an e-mail from Paul, stating, "Barbara, I'm really not interested in your idea. I have to cover my costs and I just can't go any lower. Let me know what you'd like to do."

What happened here? Why didn't Barbara's tactic of adding a fairly *creative* issue (hosting an open house) not work? Because it didn't address Paul's interests. Whether smartly or not, Paul is focused on his immediate costs and immediate bills and is in no position to take Barbara up on her offer to hold an open house. If anything, using this tactic *soured* the relationship, given Paul's curt reply. Perhaps he is offended that she wants to be involved in his business. Perhaps he thinks she is trying to take advantage of him. All we know is that trying to leverage reciprocity to gain understanding and create value wasn't effective and likely cost Barbara something in this negotiation.

ETHICAL CONSIDERATIONS

The ethical considerations here are somewhat less important or relevant than the ethical considerations in later chapters, where we will be discussing attempts to manipulate or change the thinking of the other side. Because using reciprocity is generally about *understanding* rather than convincing the other side, when you use these tactics you are likely being open about what is important to you and what you are able to offer the other side. As mentioned at the beginning of this chapter, reciprocity is a very powerful and systemic aspect of human interaction, and we are all susceptible to its influence to some extent. This raises a larger and much more ambiguous question about influencing someone's behavior through reciprocity.

A tactic that shows how reciprocity could potentially be unethical is what Robert Cialdini calls the "door in the face" technique;[33] this involves asking for something significantly greater than what you actually want, and then, when people refuse, asking for what you really want. Research has showed that doing this results in a 50% compliance rate, as compared with only a 17% rate in the case of just asking for what you wanted up front. A real-life example of this tactic is a manager trying to negotiate with an employee regarding how much overtime the employee is going to work next week. If the manager wants the employee to work 2 hours of overtime but knows the employee is reluctant to do so and will likely refuse, the manager will be much more effective if he or she first asks the employee to work 8 hours. When the employee angrily refuses to work 8 hours of overtime, the manager will agree that eight hours is unreasonable and ask if the employee would be willing to do 2 hours. The likelihood of the employee's agreeing to 2 hours is now much higher than if the manager had asked for the 2 hours up front. The effect works precisely because there is a manipulated perception of reciprocity created by the manager that is intended to influence the employee to agree. When the manager suggests 8 hours and is rebuffed, his or her response of lowering the demand to 2 hours appears to be a reasonable concession he or she is "giving" to the employee, which then creates the reciprocity obligation on the part of the employee to "give" something back. The manager's agreeing to "drop" the request down to 2 hours also gives the impression of some kind of "let's meet in the middle" compromise, and the employee will feel pressured to reciprocate.

The ethical question in the previous example is whether or not the manager's behavior is inappropriate or unethical, because he or she is basically manipulating the employee, or if in fact it is entirely acceptable, and knowing how to get people to agree to work overtime is part of the manager's job, and if he or she can do it well, then that's just a sign that he or she is an effective manager. People may disagree on how appropriate such behavior is, and we all may want to pause and consider our personal ethical standards before using such techniques.

Another example of an unethical tactic is the **bogey**, which is a deceptive tactic by which a negotiator pretends to value an issue only to later give a concession on that issue in order to get something that is truly valued.

> Jim doesn't care what day he starts his new job. The organization wants him to start January 1, so he pretends he wants to start March 1. When salary is discussed, Jim "gives in" to starting January 1 in order to get a higher starting salary.

Jim lies in this scenario about his true interests in order to get something else he wants. Because Jim is actively deceiving the company with his request, this would seemingly be unethical. It is also dangerous as the company might really believe Jim and think that giving him March 1 is beneficial to him, when it truly is not.

These ethical questions come back to one's personal standard—whether engaging in deception and manipulation through reciprocity violates what one stands for. In the previous example of Jim, is this how Jim would want others to negotiate with him? Does Jim believe it is okay for individuals to deceive companies in order to obtain additional value? We will keep coming back to these issues as we struggle with what it means to be ethical in negotiation.

Ethics Discussion Questions

If another party is willing to collaborate with you, these behaviors can potentially be used to take advantage of that person:

- Withholding information about your interests
- Mischaracterizing information about your interests (e.g., using a bogey)
- Using information that plays on another's fears or hopes
- Pretending to be emotional or in distress

For each behavior in the previous list, answer the following questions:

1. How might this behavior unethically take advantage of the other party's willingness? Be specific in your examples.

2. Where would you draw the line with respect to what is ethical or unethical when using this behavior?

3. If faced with an opportunity to engage in this behavior, how are you going to decide whether or not it is ethical to do so?

4. Consider the following scenario:

   You are in officer's training in the military, and one of the required tests before graduation is a physical fitness test involving exercises like pullups, pushups, situps, and distance running. All scores are aggregated into an overall score that will be reported at graduation. The running events are timed and supervised by the officers in charge, but because there are a lot of cadets doing the strength tests at the same time, you will be paired up with a partner and you will report each other's performance to the officers on the honor system.

   You are paired with Jaime, who says you should go first. Unfortunately for you, the first test, pullups, is your weakest. The whistle blows and you do as many as you can: FIVE. You finish, jump down, and wait for everyone else. The officer in charge walks over to you and Jaime reports on your performance: "TEN."

   You are shocked and speechless. Before you can do or say anything, the officer walks to the next pair. Now you have a choice: You can let it go, or you can make a big scene by interrupting the entire process, calling the officer back, and publicly stating that Jaime must've been mistaken. Doing so would obviously expose Jaime as a liar, even if the officer accepts the "mistake" story. As you are contemplating this, the whistle blows and Jaime is up on the bar. You now realize why Jaime lied about your score. Jaime can only manage THREE pullups. Jaime winks at you as the officer heads over to get the next round of scores.

   What do you do?

   Do you think you would act differently in the heat of the moment?

CHAPTER REVIEW

Discussion Questions

1. Read the following list of tactics. For each tactic, define it, state how it is linked to reciprocity, and give an example of its use in negotiation.

- Adding issues
- Asking interest-based questions
- Perspective taking
- Packaging issues

- Logrolling
- Contingent contracts

2. Reciprocity often takes place over an extended period of time. If you do something for me and I *immediately* do something for you, we might call it an exchange. With reciprocity, though, I might do something for you in the belief that you will repay that debt in the future. Given this, what are the challenges to balancing the accounts between two people? Can you think of any times when someone tried to create reciprocity with you—meaning that they will owe you a favor—when you were sure this debt could not be collected? Have you ever tried to get a free favor from someone?

3. Your employee comes in and asks for a raise.

   - Think about as many interests as possible that could underlie this request.

   - If you were to negotiate, try to think how you could add an issue for each interest you identified.

   - Which of these issues has logrolling potential for you? Why?

   - How could you design and enforce a contingent contract for this employee?

Concept Application

1. Perform a negotiation where you ask interest-based questions. Report to the class what these questions were, why you chose them, and how they helped influence the other side.

2. Negotiate using one or more of these tactics: logrolling, packaging issues, contingent contract. Report on how you used them and if they worked.

Role-Play Exercise: Expat

This case is adapted from the case *New Recruit* by Margaret A. Neale. To obtain *New Recruit*, please contact the Dispute Resolution Resource Center at Northwestern University (negotiationexercises.com).

This is a two-person negotiation where one side is playing the role of Chris Miller, a new manager at INCM, and the other side is playing the role of Stevie Jones, a human resources director at INCM. Chris has been promoted, and one of the expectations when taking on a managerial role at INCM is that the new manager will spend at least a year overseas. Chris and Stevie must now negotiate the terms for Chris's upcoming expatriate assignment.

This negotiation has seven already defined issues: country, number of trips home, housing allowance, move date, duration of assignment, salary increase, and schooling for employee children. To reach agreement, Chris and Stevie must agree on all seven issues. This is a scored negotiation, meaning that negotiators will be able to see at the end of the negotiation how well they performed.

$SAGE edge™

Visit study.sagepub.com/rockmann to help you accomplish your coursework goals in an easy-to-use learning environment.

THE STAGES OF NEGOTIATION

OPENING

The first thing to think about when opening a negotiation is to determine the location. A location is not just a place to sit and have a conversation; a location connotes *meaning*. Say, for example, that every time you negotiate with your boss you do so with your boss behind his or her desk and you in the seat in front of the desk. What does the choice of this location mean? Power, in that your boss has formal authority over you by his or her place behind the desk. What else? Perhaps psychological distance between the two of you, in that there is a big piece of wood or metal separating you. The location of the office also might convey that the two of you are going to negotiate *as you've always negotiated.* You are in the same seats, having a similar conversation, working toward a similar outcome. The problem occurs when you want to *change* how you negotiate with your boss. If you want to negotiate with your boss in a different way regarding your future at the company, then you should choose a different location. Go for a walk, grab a coffee, use a different office. You might need to set a different routine if you want to leave that negotiation with something you haven't received before.

You also need to think about the proper time to engage in negotiation. Negotiation, unlike conflict avoidance, takes work. If you are taking advantage of reciprocity, whether that is with tangible or intangible (Chapter 5) interests, for example, you will need to be able to engage the other side in a meaningful conversation about what is truly important to that person. This means the other side needs to have the energy and time to engage in such a dialogue. If you are looking to negotiate with your spouse, picking a time when she or he is bathing your three kids and trying to get dinner on the table is probably not a good idea. Stopping your boss in the hallway to negotiate a raise is also not likely to go well.

You may be timid about starting a negotiation. You don't want to bring up the conflict, or perhaps you don't want to be the first to ask for something. Remember that how you behave is likely to be reciprocated by the other side. If you are empathetic, the other party will more likely be empathetic toward you. If you trust the other party, they will likely trust you. If you are open about your interests, they will likely be open as well. As you open the negotiation, then you have an opportunity to set the tone for how the negotiation is going to proceed. Is your negotiation going to be defined by two people trying to convince one another or understand one another?

When you don't open the negotiation, you sacrifice this opportunity. This can put you at a serious disadvantage because it lets someone else set the tone for the negotiation, throwing off your negotiation plan (Chapter 3). Further, you give up the opportunity to anchor the negotiation in a way that allows you to leverage the uncertainty of the other side (Chapter 7).

What you want to do is set the negotiation on a path that makes sense given your relationship with the person. If you are in a simple negotiation where the main thing is to convince on a particular issue, the critical opening is to *make the first offer* with a data-based argument (making it objective rather than subjective). If the negotiation is more complicated, the first thing you should do is communicate that you trust and respect the other person, so as to evoke a productive dialogue. This will allow for the flow of information and joint problem solving.

TAKING BREAKS

Negotiation can be very emotional. When you get emotional, your ability to process information is hindered. Put simply, when you are anxious, defensive, worried, angry, or frustrated, you cannot think. Your brain is occupied with the emotion, and you are simply not able to process all of the information that might be coming at you. So what do you do? Take a break.

Breaks are one of the most important negotiation actions you can take, not because of how it influences the other side but because of what it does for you. Go to the bathroom, go get some water, postpone the meeting until the next day, call someone back in an hour, do whatever you need to do to give your emotions time to calm down so that you can restore your cognitive functioning. If you get a job offer over the phone, thank the caller for the information and ask to call back the next day. This gives you time to process all of the information so that you don't agree to something (or NOT agree to something) you might regret later. This is the same reason it's not good to send e-mails when you are angry—you lack the ability to be objective about the content and the situation. *Just wait.* Give yourself some space to be objective and reset, and then reengage when you are able. For some negotiations a few minutes can do the trick; for others it could be weeks or even months. Negotiating with heightened emotions will rarely get you what you want, as it will prevent the use of almost every tactic presented in this book.

IMPASSE/STALEMATE

Negotiations frequently get to a point where you get stuck. This can be due to heightened emotions that interfere with your judgment, such as when you are frustrated and have devolved into squabbling. At such a point, you might be so focused on fighting and getting back at the person on the other side of the table, you lose sight of the problem at hand. The key at this point is to engage in emotional regulation. Emotional regulation is the ability to control your emotions in the moment or express an emotion helpful to a situation that is not actually felt.[1] As noted in the previous section, taking a break can help in this regard. One must de-escalate the situation so that the negotiators are willing to engage in problem solving again.

Another cause of impasse could be if you cannot seem to figure out what to do next to get to resolution. Maybe you feel that you have run out of options or are still too far apart and cannot bridge the chasm to reach an agreement with the other side. In this case the difficulty comes from a lack of ideas, not emotional interference. The key in this situation is to ask why. For example, if your supplier says, "I just can't give you that many units at that price," do not keep arguing why he should; instead, ask him *why*. This can give you clues for how to get over the impasse. Even if the other side is reticent and says, "I just can't," you can say, "If I know why you can't, perhaps we can figure out a workaround." Note the importance of emotional tone here. That same statement can be understood as a sincere attempt to help or as pushy badgering, depending on the tone you use. Using contingent contracts can be an effective tactic in these situations, especially if the impasse is due to different beliefs about something that is going to happen in the future (see Chapter 4).

CLOSING

"Your job is to get them to sign on the line that is dotted" is what Alec Baldwin's character says in the movie *Glengarry Glen Ross*. You have made all this progress and trades, have gotten people to share, and now it is time to get commitment. When closing, you want to make sure that both sides know exactly what is being agreed to. This results from clear and consistent communication. As seen in the sidebar example from the NBA, even negotiations involving millions of dollars can get fouled up in the closing. *Be clear*. "Just to recap, I'm agreeing to provide X and you are agreeing to provide Y. Is that your understanding as well?" If it's still not enough value for the other side, you can consider adding an issue at the end. This is called a sweetener—an added issue that adds just a bit of value so that the other side will say yes.

If there is a contingent contract as part of the deal, make sure everyone knows exactly how the contingency will play out. For example, "If your performance rating in 6 months is a 4, you will get a 5% raise. If your performance rating in 6 months is a 5, you will get a 7% raise." This contingency and closing leave no ambiguity, especially if they are provided in writing.

One of the most bizarre trade situations in recent memory will likely make things very awkward in three NBA locker rooms. A three-team trade involving the Phoenix Suns, Memphis Grizzlies and Washington Wizards fell through Friday night, according to multiple outlets, over a strange miscommunication about which player named Brooks would be included. The Suns thought they would be acquiring Dillon Brooks from the Grizzlies. However, the Grizzlies were under the impression they'd be trading MarShon Brooks. When the teams began to set up a trade call with the league, the confusion came to light, according to David Aldridge of The Athletic. Once the teams were on the same page, Memphis was unwilling to trade Dillon Brooks, and Phoenix had no interest in MarShon Brooks. According to ESPN's Adrian Wojnarowski, the Suns and Grizzlies did not initially communicate with each other directly, instead using the Wizards as a go-between to facilitate the deal. That is reportedly where the confusion arose between Dillon and MarShon Brooks. Wojnarowski later reported the Wizards believed they were told Dillon Brooks by the Grizzlies, who insisted they said MarShon Brooks.

Source: Eppers, M. (2018, December 15). Suns-Grizzlies-Wizards trade falls through over bizarre miscommunication about player involved. *USA Today*. Retrieved from https://www.usatoday.com/story/sports/nba/2018/12/15/suns-grizzlies-wizards-trade-falls-through-miscommunication-dillon-marshon-brooks/2320324002/

CHAPTER 5

INTANGIBLE INTERESTS

Learning Objectives

1. Articulate intangible interests and provide examples.

2. Define the four main sources of identity, and delineate between identities resulting from each of these sources.

3. Anticipate how identity threat impedes negotiations.

4. Provide examples of when cognitive dissonance and consistency would impact behavior in negotiation.

5. Develop a list of interests in principle that may be relevant in your negotiations.

6. Help others "save face" in negotiations.

7. Understand the calculation of tangible and intangible interests. Devise creative strategies in order to provide intangible resources to others.

8. Distinguish between the various benefits from leveraging intangible

CHAPTER EXAMPLE

Solomon is a School of Health administrator tasked with developing a new master's program in health administration. This is a year-long multiparty negotiation that is complex because Solomon wants to design the program so that courses are offered over 10 weeks instead of the traditional 14 weeks. The shortened time period allows the program to be more competitive because students would earn a master's degree sooner than they would otherwise. Solomon and his staff have already done the market analysis and know that this 10-week structure is the only way to make the program thrive. The task now is to get the rest of the university on board. Solomon and his team have engaged the following university departments in order to negotiate: provost's office, registrar's office, billing, veterans administration, institutional reporting and compliance, and financial aid.

There are a few factors that make this negotiation particularly challenging. First is that each of the parties at the table in this negotiation has different interests. The registrar's office, for example, wants the new master's program to fit within the university master schedule so that classrooms can be assigned efficiently and effectively. The billing office would like the tuition schedule set to the same rates as other master's programs to ease the logistics surrounding student payments. Veterans administration would like to see the program not have significant gaps in course scheduling so that students can maximize VA benefits while in the program. Institutional reporting and compliance would like the terms to be structured in such a way to make compliance documentation more straightforward. The provost's office wants to see the new program launched as quickly as possible.

Over the course of a year Solomon and his staff have many conversations with each of the departments and are able to design a program satisfying every party at the table except one. The department head of financial aid, Elizabeth, has not yet agreed to support this new program. Here is a typical exchange between Solomon and Elizabeth:

Solomon: I think we are all on board with a 10-week program schedule beginning in August.

Elizabeth: I can't support that schedule.

Solomon: Why not?

Elizabeth: The federal rules for funding.

Solomon: Can you help us understand the rules?

Elizabeth: It's way too complicated. There is just no way for students to get federal assistance in a program with this type of schedule.

Every time Solomon asks about a unique solution or a different possibility, the answer from Elizabeth is no. Every time Solomon inquires about the specific rules prohibiting program offerings, Elizabeth answers in vague terms and repeats how difficult and complicated the rules are to understand. At one point Solomon asks Elizabeth what it would take to get her to say yes. She responds that the program needs to be structured like existing programs on a 14-week schedule, a solution that Solomon cannot support given that it would make the new master's program non-competitive in the market.

Finally after a year of disagreement, Solomon is at a loss. He has tried every negotiation tactic he can think of and nothing has worked. Without an agreement from financial aid, his new program will be dead. In a last gasp effort, he decides to download and read the *Federal Student Aid Handbook*, a 1,321-page downloadable PDF from the Department of Education website. By searching through relevant sections, Solomon learns that 10-week programs can be funded in certain circumstances. He discerns from this research that it isn't that Elizabeth can't fund the new program; for some reason she doesn't *want* to. He sends the following e-mail to Elizabeth:

Elizabeth,

I'm trying to help you all find an answer to the problem we've given you. I've been reading the federal guidelines and have a naïve question for you.

What type of funding model does our university use? It looks like there is some discussion in the federal guidelines about students attending

interests. Articulate how each benefit is more or less relevant to your own negotiations.

9. Develop an ethical understanding of leveraging intangible interests.

Master the content at study .sagepub.com/rockmann

shorter-term classes in abbreviated semesters, which seems to be what we are talking about with our new master's program. It seems as if there are funding possibilities here.

Thanks, as always, for your help on this.

Best,

Solomon

Elizabeth responds early the next morning.

Solomon,

I am really sorry that you felt the need to take your personal time researching the federal guidelines as we are actually very familiar with these regulations. The answer to your question is that our university is on a Type III funding model and we are unable to support anything else due to the staff size and time and the lack of necessary resources. Please call me so that we can discuss.

Elizabeth

At this point Solomon finally knows what the problem has been all along. Elizabeth believes that she is facing a staff shortage. Instead of being open about this shortage, Elizabeth has used the federal guidelines to deflect the inquiry. Had she been open about the staff time allocation from the beginning of the negotiation, her skills as a manager might've been called into question. Solomon knows she is a relatively new manager, and this might be an uncomfortable topic for Elizabeth. He also now can guess why she is so defensive, as any discussion of how her department is run might be seen as threatening.

Solomon calls Elizabeth and begins the conversation with the following question: "*I had no idea you were facing a staff shortage. How are you able to manage over there?*" Elizabeth tells how she is trying to support new programs and initiatives but has been stonewalled by the administration from hiring more staff. Solomon just listens and gives her the occasional "*Sure*" or "*That has to be hard*." He can tell during her story that she is near tears, that this managerial role is really taking its toll on her.

When she has finished telling her story and Solomon has asked a few follow-up questions, he finally offers her staff time from his department. He tells her that she can use the staff however she would like. Elizabeth reciprocates by telling Solomon that with this extra support she will find a way to support the new program. The program begins the following fall and is a huge success.

******

INTRODUCTION TO INTANGIBLE INTERESTS

One of the mistakes we reviewed in Chapter 1 is that negotiators can become overly self-interested. Underlying this mistake is the incorrect belief that all negotiators care about are outcomes. In one fascinating research study, Curhan, Elfenbein, and Xu categorized everything that negotiators *value* when they negotiate.[1] Yes, negotiators value outcomes, but negotiators also value feelings about the self, feelings about the negotiation process, and feelings about the relationship. This is supported by research showing that making more money does not necessarily make you feel more accomplished or satisfied.[2] The reality is that negotiators care just as much if not more about intangible interests such as one's ego and relationships than they do about tangible outcomes such as money or goods.

In this chapter we will demonstrate that there are tactics that affect individuals based not on tangible interests (e.g., jobs, positions, money) but on intangible interests. Intangible interests are interests, in that they represent what people want. But they are intangible in the sense that they cannot be held or touched or traded as easily. Respect, saving face, feeling valued, being listened to, having a say in the final decision: These all represent possible intangible interests (see Table 5.1). We use the concept of identity to help you think about intangible interests because identity guides you to understand what, of all of the possible intangibles, actually might be at play. This will help you as a negotiator understand the intangible interests of the other side so that you may be able to give intangible value in order to get what you want.

Table 5.1 Tangible and Intangible Interests	
Examples of Tangible Interests	**Examples of Intangible Interests**
Money	Respect
Resources	Recognition
Jobs	Feeling of being involved
Working conditions	Fairness and justice
Length of contracts	Reputation
Time to oneself	Self-image/ego
Decision-making authority	Relationships

The "Self" and Identity

We have talked at length in this textbook about the interests of the parties in a negotiation, and we mentioned in Chapter 2 that interests can be both tangible and intangible. Tangible interests, such as financial security, manifest themselves in positions that can easily be traded in negotiation, such as money. Intangible interests, such as recognition, loyalty, and respect, cannot as easily be traded. This is because intangible interests are often fulfilled through the discourse of the negotiation itself and not necessarily in the outcome of the negotiation. Consider a wife who is in a negotiation with her husband over what size television to buy for the family room. Whereas the husband's interest might be hosting great football parties for his friends, the wife's interest might be that she is simply included in the decision-making process. If the husband assumes that his wife wants to spend less and wants a smaller TV, then he will try to satisfy the wrong interests and may end up with a smaller TV than he wants! He has ignored her intangible interests.

Underlying intangible interests can come from how one defines oneself; this is one's **identity**. Identities help provide a sense of self-worth.[3] People have an underlying need to feel that they belong in the world, and identity is one way in which those feelings are built and maintained.[4] It feels better to be a part of a group, a club, a family, a profession, a demographic, because belonging helps you to know your place. When you have a developed identity, it allows you to be happier, to try out new things, and to feel comfortable in the world.

Sources of identity provide us with meaning for who we are. This meaning serves as a guide for how to behave in many situations, including situations involving conflict such as negotiation. When individuals believe that the outcome of a negotiation could strengthen or, more importantly, weaken part of their identity, they frame the negotiation around that identity.[5] That means in their mind the negotiation has become about not just the outcomes but about who they are as a person. Is identity at stake in every negotiation? Of course not. But your task as a negotiator is to understand when it might be at stake and to offer intangible interests that support identity.

The skill you need to develop is to understand when someone else's identity may be enhanced by providing, usually intangible, value. This could be either because an identity is important to someone and you can provide value to validate that identity or because an identity is threatened and you can provide value to address that identity threat. Identity threat causes a range of negative outcomes, including depression, poor health, and conflict.[6] Thus, when individuals are threatened, moving toward understanding and reciprocity can be a challenge. Your task in a negotiation is to figure out which identities are *activated*, that is, which identity or identities for the person you are negotiating with are particularly meaningful or salient in the context of that particular negotiation.

Where Does Identity Come From?

Identities can originate from multiple sources, including group, roles, relationships, and symbols.

Group-based identity originates as you see yourself as a member of a social group. Groups can be almost anything, including clubs, schools, organizations, companies, teams, family, religion, and even demographic-based groups (e.g., gender, sexual orientation, ethnicity). When you identify with a social group, you are biased in favor of that in-group and biased against relevant comparison or out-groups.[7] To maintain and increase your self-esteem, you tend to see actions and characteristics of your in-group more positively than you do out-groups.

Consider a simple negotiation over a new bicycle. The salesperson is not only trying to sell a bike and settle the issues; in addition, she *sees* her bike shop in a favorable light and the bike shop across town (the competitor) in a negative light. This might imply a bias toward her own bike shop ("Our service plan is so much better!"). To help the salesperson say yes, the customer might need to be sensitive to that sense of identity the salesperson holds. The customer might compliment the shop or say something negative about the shop across town. Each of these statements would likely resonate with the salesperson because of her intangible interests to see her own bike shop positively. This is a simple example of one person (customer) supporting the identity of another (salesperson).

Role-based identity results from the roles that you hold. As seen in Figure 5.1, these can be work-related roles such as supervisor or coworker or non-work-related roles such as spouse, parent, or friend. Individuals who negotiate a great deal might also see themselves in the role of *negotiator*, which could be quite meaningful to them. This role-based identity is especially critical as they may be *more* threatened by the possibility of "losing" a negotiation than someone who does not have this role-based identity.

Figure 5.1   Sources of Identity

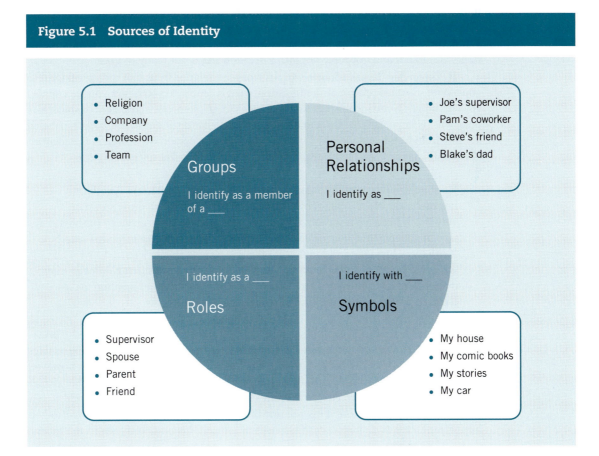

Consider Diane, a new manager in a health insurance organization.

> Bill, one of Diane's new direct reports, has been lobbying for a year to investigate a new information technology (IT) system for the unit. His argument is that greater efficiency can be achieved if medical records can be updated from phones, tablets, laptops, and desktops. Upper management has been ignoring this request because the dominant thinking for a long time has been to "stay away" from handheld technologies. Bill now brings this request to Diane.

In addition to her tangible interests of profit, Diane has an intangible interest that is wrapped up in her role-based identity as a new manager. She perceives her role as a manager as one of importance and expertise and that she should be "the boss." Thus, it is hard for her to champion Bill's request because she would feel as if she is "giving in" to Bill and not acting like a manager. In her mind she convinces herself that Bill's request is not really appropriate for the organization. So even though Bill might make the company money, Diane is predisposed against his suggestion because her role as a manager is making it difficult for her to see Bill's proposal in an objective way. Giving in to Bill seems to her as if it violates her belief as to what she should be doing as a manager (i.e., making decisions), and as such she is predisposed to be skeptical toward him. For Bill to get what he wants he will need to understand that this part of Diane's identity is important to her and not force her into a decision she is not ready to make.

Relationship-based identity results from the relationships that are meaningful to you.[8] With so-called relational identification, what is central to you is how you see yourself vis-à-vis others. If you identify as being someone's friend, someone's coworker, or someone's boss, what is important to you is that relationship. What distinguishes relationship-based identity from role-based identity is that another, specific person is involved in this identity. You identify because you are Joe's supervisor or Pam's coworker or Steve's friend.

> Keith reluctantly agreed to take a vice president job when his predecessor unexpectedly left the company. Although he is not averse to more work, he very much liked his prior job. One of the first tasks Keith is given by his boss is to hire a new executive director in his department. After an extended search, Keith hires Judy. He and Judy hit it off right away as she is eager to learn about the business and take on many of the innovative tasks that Keith and his department have been charged with. Seeing Judy grow in her position makes Keith happy and motivates him to continue as a manager.

In this scenario Keith does not identify as being a manager as Diane does in the previous scenario. Power and authority are not important to him, and while he appreciates the added salary, he liked his old job just fine. What is meaningful to Keith, however, is the relationship with Judy as Judy's mentor. He finds himself invested in her career development and wants to ensure that she continually gets opportunities to add to her skillset at the organization. This relationship gives meaning to Keith and will be an important factor as he negotiates on behalf of himself, his unit, and Judy in the future.

Symbol-based identity is based on the things, not people, that help you define yourself. There are two main types of symbol-based identity. The first is possessions. Consider the following scenario of Diego, who is selling his house:

> Diego has spent the past 15 years restoring a house built in the 1890s. He loves this house "more than life itself" and credits the restoration project for getting him through a tumultuous divorce, the death of his mother, and numerous job changes. He always knew that on the weekend he could work on the house as an "escape" from reality. Unfortunately for Diego, he is now out of work and is simply unable to find a job. Desperate to stay off welfare, Diego decides to sell the house. The first agent who comes to the house takes a look and tells Diego, "This would probably be a teardown." Diego is crushed.

Diego's identity is wrapped up tightly in this house. In a sense, Diego *is* this house. When Diego thinks about who he is, he thinks about the house. Any buyer negotiating with Diego has to *know* that they are not just negotiating with someone who is selling a house, they are negotiating with someone who *is* the house. Insulting the house or pointing out flaws in the work that Diego has done will feel like a personal insult to Diego, making it much less likely that Diego will say yes to the buyer.

Symbol-based identity can originate from other inanimate things such as one's stories. When someone tells and retells a story of oneself as a fair and kind person, the story becomes the source of identity rather than the original event. In this case individuals are motivated to support that identity to be consistent with how they see themselves. If you are interested in the power of symbol-based identity, watch the movie *Big Fish* by director Tim Burton (2003). In this movie a dying father's entire identity is defined by the stories he has told about his life. His son, who is not interested in those stories, is trying to negotiate with the father while negating or diminishing those stories. Not surprisingly, the son does not get very far in the negotiations because he violates the dad's symbol-based identity.

Multiple Sources of Identity

The concept of identity is not straightforward. It is not as if any one individual has one role or one social identity; rather, individuals have multiple identities.[9] A woman who is an executive in an engineering company negotiating a supplier contract may have the following identities: woman, engineer, manager, executive, successful contract negotiator, mother, spouse, and possibly others. Individuals differ in terms of the importance they place on any one identity; identities also differ in terms of relevance to any one negotiation.

In negotiations, her identity as a successful contract negotiator or engineering professional or manager will likely be most relevant to her.[10] But it does not mean that the other parts of her identity are *not* relevant. If you, as a potential supplier, make a joke disparaging kids, and this activates her identity as a mother, you may find yourself with less ability to collaborate with her.

Identities can also be multifaceted or layered, in that what is seemingly an easy identity to understand is much more complicated from the perspective of the identity holder. You might assume, for example, that a chef has a professional identity that is centered on knowing how to work with multiple types of food. In this case the chef's identity would be closely related to the technical skills he has developed. But it is equally likely that the chef might see himself as an "artist" by virtue of his profession.[11] Why is this relevant? Because when you are negotiating a catering contract with that chef, validating his identity as an artist might go a long way toward getting you what you want.

Thus, to understand the identity-based interests of an individual, you need to understand that individuals hold multiple identities, these identities become relevant depending on the situation and conversation in the negotiation, and these identities can be threatened, leading to negative reactions.

Identity Threat

Identities are relevant because, if threatened, they can inhibit your ability to obtain value from negotiation. This can happen if you threaten someone else's identity or if they threaten yours. **Identity threats** are experiences in which an individual perceives "harm to the value, meanings, or enactment of an identity."[12] To perceive a threat, the individual needs to see harm to the identity in the present or, for a more intense threat, in the future. Consider the following example adapted from Petriglieri's article (see note 12) on identity threat:

> A middle manager who aspires to a senior executive position is standing in line to buy a coffee shortly after her return to work from maternity leave. While waiting, she overhears two strangers denigrating working mothers and questioning their career commitment. On a different occasion the woman overhears her boss and a close colleague having a similar conversation. Whereas in both situations the woman may feel that her professional identity is devalued in the moment, in the second situation she is more likely to project future negative consequences, such as being passed over for promotion and being less able to claim a potential senior executive identity, her current manager identity, or her mother identity at work. While she may appraise both experiences as harmful to her identity, the threat is likely to be more intense in the second situation.

What we can see from this example is that not all identity threats are created equally, just as not all identities are equally important. It is your task as a negotiator to understand which identity (or identities) are activated and the severity of associated threat. What do individuals do in response to identity threat? They can give up their identity, but identities may be quite difficult to discard, especially to the degree they are more central to one's self-definition, such as a gender or racial or even religious identity.[13] This is one reason particular intractable identity conflicts, such as the one between the Israelis and Palestinians, last for many generations.[14] Others have argued that the intensity of such disputes is based on the need to protect and preserve held national and religious identities.[15]

Case Sidebar

The problem Solomon faces in getting Elizabeth to agree to this new program structure is that Elizabeth's identity is threatened throughout this negotiation. Elizabeth's identity is as a manager, and she desperately wants to be seen by her peers across the university as someone who is competent at running a unit effectively yet with limited resources. Elizabeth perceives the questions that Solomon keeps asking as threatening this identity, because she would have to get into a discussion of how she is allocating resources and managing her unit. She thus begins to distance herself from Solomon and avoid conversation so as to protect that manager identity.

Rather than discard a held identity, what is more likely in negotiations is that when one side is threatened, that side makes a negative judgment of the person who caused the harm, which could cause one to simply not negotiate.[16,17] This means that if you threaten someone else's identity in a negotiation, one of the ways they can manage that feeling of harm is to think negatively about you. This becomes a problem if you are seeking to take an understanding approach to negotiation as understanding is based on open exchange of information; once you are seen as nontrustworthy, that open flow of information is likely to stop.

> Olivia walks into the car dealership. Aman, the new salesperson, greets her and asks what he can do for her. She replies that she is interested in a small SUV for her family. Aman replies by asking what her husband thinks.

Oops! Within 30 seconds of meeting a potential client, Aman has threatened Olivia's identity as a self-independent woman and mother capable of making her own purchase decisions. No matter what happens after this, Olivia is going to see Aman differently and is much less likely to trust him, let alone buy a car from him. Aman has not understood the lesson of identity threat.

Cognitive Dissonance and Consistency

Have you ever been in a negotiation with someone where they "dig in" to their position? Or they refuse to talk about something they consider already decided? Or they won't even put an issue on the table because they already said that issue is nonnegotiable? Individuals do this because they want **consistency** between their current and prior actions.[18] In this case their prior action is stating a preference for a position or a decision on an issue or saying an issue is nonnegotiable. If they were to waver off of that position, they would be inconsistent and potentially **lose face**. This is threatening to one's identity, which is one of the intangible interests. It's not just that someone *wants* something, it's that they have become psychologically attached to that prior position by publicly stating its importance. This is the opposite of having someone **save face**, which occurs when someone is put in a position where a past position is supported or a valued identity is upheld.

Cialdini, in writing about consistency, gives the example of a subtle change in the reservation policy of a restaurant, which was struggling because people who made reservations failed to show. Instead of saying to the caller "Please call if you have to change your plans," the receptionist started asking, "Will you please call if you have to change your plans?" The caller would then have to give a verbal response acknowledging that she would, in fact, call back if she needed to cancel. By making this verbal commitment to call and cancel, the caller would now have to put in the time to call back and cancel in order to be consistent in her past actions (saying that she would). This simple intervention dropped the no-show rate immediately, from 30% to 10%.

Underlying consistency is the concept of **cognitive dissonance**, developed by psychologist Leon Festinger in the 1950s and 1960s. Cognitive dissonance describes the process by which you seek to align your actions with your thoughts or cognitions.[19] In one classic experiment subjects engaged in a boring task of filling in spaces with letters on a grid. After completing this task they were paid either $1 or $20 and were told to describe the task to a waiting subject in the next room. Surprisingly, those that were paid $1 were more likely to give a positive impression of the task than those who had been paid $20. Why? Because those who had been paid $20 now had a *reason*—a big payout of $20—that helped them justify why they had to complete such a boring task. Those that had only been paid $1 had no such justification, so they (unconsciously) convinced themselves that the task wasn't so boring. This cognitive shift allowed them to resolve the dissonance between doing a boring task and being paid poorly.

Cognitive dissonance can occur in all types of situations. A classic example of this idea (and the origin of the expression "sour grapes") is expressed in the fable *The Fox and the Grapes* by Aesop (ca. 620–564 BCE). In the story, a fox sees some high-hanging grapes and wishes to eat them. When the fox is unable to think of a way to reach them, he surmises that the grapes are probably not worth eating, that they must not be ripe or that they are sour. This example follows a pattern: One desires something, finds it unattainable, and reduces one's dissonance by criticizing it.[20]

Dissonance can take other forms as well. You could imagine a child wanting $20 from a parent. Upon asking, the child gets $10, which if they had been asked beforehand, would be seen as not sufficient. However, after the negotiation the child thinks, "Well, I'm sure that's all my dad could give" or "That's how much I *really* wanted anyway." Again, one desires something, finds it partially attainable, then justifies it in order to feel better.

In one study researchers found that negotiators compare themselves with others so as to make their own demands seem fair and reasonable.[21] Why do they do this? Because they want to feel good about the demands they are making; they want to believe that the offers they make are fair and appropriate. After all, no one wants to believe that they are unfair and untrustworthy. The dissonance in this case makes negotiators biased and potentially blind to the truth. After all, just because you believe your offer is fair and reasonable does not mean it *actually* is.

Consistency can work in other ways as well. Consider a negotiation in which you have already decided beforehand specifically what you want. For example, you know you are going to buy a new MacBook. In this case your belief is that the MacBook is a great laptop and well worth the money. Dissonance means you want your negotiation behavior to be consistent with your beliefs. You will pay attention to information supporting that belief in order to stay cognitively consistent. This means that when the salesperson tells you great things about the MacBook, you will be nodding along thinking, "Yes, yes, I knew this was a good idea!" Unfortunately, this also means you will be more likely to ignore information that may suggest an alternative course of action, for instance, if the MacBook was not reviewed as highly as other laptops. Why do you do this? Because if you were to accept the bad information about the MacBook, you would be admitting to yourself you were WRONG to love this particular computer. That is threatening to your ego. So you ignore this information in order to protect yourself. These cognitive gymnastics are associated with a classic bias known as the confirming evidence bias (Chapter 1). The negotiator (you, in this case) will only pay attention to information that confirms existing beliefs or supports your own identity. This protects (and reaffirms) the self and makes you feel better about who you are (and what you want).

Case Sidebar

Part of the added challenge for Solomon in negotiating with Elizabeth is that she is victim to cognitive dissonance. That is, she has likely convinced herself (or wants to convince herself) that she is a good manager, meaning she is unwilling to engage in solutions that put that belief into question. She is paying attention to information (the federal funding restrictions) that is consistent with her belief that the problem is at the federal level, not with her department. This is frustrating for Solomon as he doesn't know the federal funding guidelines, until he decides to read them and force Elizabeth into facing the realities of the situation.

Interests in Principle

Beyond one's identity, there can be intangible interests concerning what is fair or what is right. Lax and Sebenius call these intangible interests **interests in principle**.[22] These interests can originate from how individuals have negotiated or been treated in the past or from what they see as appropriate or ethical in a situation. Interests in principle can apply to both the way issues are traded as well as the process of the negotiation. Some negotiators will care a great deal about how the negotiation proceeds, whereas others will not. These interests could include desires over who speaks when, how the discussion flows, who is at the table, and so on.

In February 2018 the teachers in West Virginia went on a 5-day strike. The news coverage surrounded the fact that West Virginia ranked 48 out of 50 states in terms of teacher compensation. Many *wrongly* assumed this strike was only about salary and benefits, that is, *tangible interests*. As noted by Christine Campbell, president of the American Federation of Teachers West Virginia, teachers cared about more than tangible interests. In addition to tangible benefits, they were concerned about "attacks on their voice." Teachers did not feel as if they were valued or treated with respect, that is, *interests in principle*. Most teachers don't believe they will get rich by teaching, but they do expect to be treated with respect, valued in the community, and listened to. It was these fundamental rights that, in part, led to this strike. Once the governor realized this, getting the teachers back to work by providing a small wage increase and a good faith effort for future negotiations was relatively straightforward.

Source: Larimar, S. (2018, February 27). West Virginia teachers expected to return to classrooms Thursday as Gov. Jim Justice announces deal. *Washington Post.*

While interests in principle can originate from one's held identity (or identities), they also can originate from one's underlying values.[23] Negotiators have diverse backgrounds, which lead to diverse values and diverse intangible interests. The mistake here, as discussed in Chapter 1, is falling victim to the false-consensus effect, whereby you assume that what *you* see as fair is what others will see as fair; what *you* see as how a negotiation should proceed is what others see as how a negotiation should proceed. Negotiating with false consensus violates these intangible interests of others, causing you an opportunity for reciprocity by providing intangible value to others at a relatively low cost.

Respect

While trust is a willingness to rely upon another person that is based in the idea that the other person will not harm you, respect is the worth that is owed to everyone simply based on the fact that they are a person.[24] It is entirely possible to show someone respect but not necessarily feel a lot of trust toward that person. For instance, you might respect an enemy, but you probably would not trust him or her.

Respect is a good example of an interest in principle. Seeing value in other people makes one want to know and consider their thoughts and feelings. It also makes people behave in a particular way toward them. When people feel respected, it improves both their mental state and ability to perform.[25] In a negotiation context showing someone else respect (as seen in the sidebar about Bill) makes it more likely that they will engage in cooperative behavior.[26] People's compliance with behavioral expectations, and their ability to willingly and gracefully accept losses, often hinges on the treatment they perceive themselves getting. If you do not show respect for the other party in negotiation, you are cuing to them that they have no value, decreasing the likelihood that they will reciprocate any offer in the future.

Bill Mansfield, a former private investigator, was interviewed on the Planet Money podcast regarding his work to prevent international companies from counterfeiting American manufactured goods and selling them around the world. This is an excerpt from the podcast:

Host: Bill has found that in China local authorities have a ton of power. So what he does now is set up lots of meetings, meetings with the people who can launch investigations, conduct raids, seize counterfeit products, and arrest counterfeiters.

Bill: I always prefer criminal action, an arrest is always what I'm looking for. Some time in jail is never worth selling counterfeit glue.

Host: If you ask Bill, this is how to stop counterfeiters in China and elsewhere. Lots and lots of meetings. . . . He's traveled to 55 countries, gotten at least a dozen people convicted, and millions of dollars of counterfeit goods destroyed.

Host: How do you reward these local authorities after a raid goes down? Do you take them out to dinner?

Bill: I reward them with the key currency all bureaucrats love, which is a "thank you." And, often, a small plaque they can put in their office . . . that says you helped us. . . . *People want to be appreciated for their work*.

Host: Are you sure you never bribe people Bill?

Bill: No. Never.

Source: From Fountain, N., & Chang, A. (Producers) (2019, March 15). The stolen company. *Planet Money* [Audio podcast], No. 900, NPR. Retrieved from https://www.npr.org/sections/money/2019/03/15/702643451/episode-900-the-stolen-company

When one party is dismissive or derogatory of another's interests, it can be seen as disrespectful because interests are based in values. Imagine your friend invites you to take a month-long trip around the country with her. How do you respond in a respectful way? If you say the idea is ridiculous, you are questioning her values regarding vacation. If you say driving around the country for a month instead of working is lazy, you are questioning her values regarding work. Even if you say nothing, you might be seen as disrespectful because she is looking for validation of her choice. If you say you are not interested, you might be threatening her role-based identity as your friend. Any of these outcomes could be detrimental to her perception of you and, in turn, your ability to create value in future negotiations with her. One idea, rather than saying yes (which you don't want) or no (which would harm her), would be to ask about her interests, so that you can craft a plan that works for both of you. This is both satisfying her interest of being respected and helping her save face.

NEGOTIATION TACTICS

Helping Others Save Face

You need to remember that for you to get what you want, the other side has to say yes. However, saying yes to an agreement can be very difficult for the person you're negotiating with if he has already made statements suggesting he would not reach agreement on a particular issue or if he is otherwise particularly sensitive to the threat of losing face.[27] This is because of consistency. Consider the following example:

> A teenager is trying to get her parents to let her use the car on the weekend. But her parents have already told her that she can use the car only when she has no homework. This creates a problem because she is planning on using the car on Saturday and not finishing her homework until Sunday. Allowing her to use the car on Saturday would thus cause the parents to lose face, meaning they would have to agree to something that directly contradicts what they have already publicly said. So what should the teenager do?

She needs to help her parents save face by suggesting an alternative that would not go against their previous statement. She must remember that her parents want to be consistent in their words and actions. Here are a few possibilities:

- She could forgo her plans on Friday night and finish her homework then.

- She could ask for a contingent contract (Chapter 4), such that she only gets to use the car on Saturday contingent on her completing her homework on Sunday. If she is unable to produce said homework, this deal will not be possible in the future.

- She could lay out her situation, explaining that the plans cannot be moved to Sunday and that the group she is doing homework with can only work on Sunday. Then ask her parents for advice on what she might do in this unusual situation that is not likely to happen again.

The key is for her to give her parents a reason to let her out of the original deal, but without making them think what they've said is not important or relevant. This is a challenge because when negotiators are threatened in this way, they naturally become more competitive.[28]

Framing Positions to Match Intangible Interests

Because saving face is a critical component to agreement in negotiation, it may be necessary to frame certain issues or positions on issues in a way to help the other party save face. It might just be a superficial change, but it may be enough to get the other side to say yes and stay consistent between their cognitions and behaviors. One key example of this was the budget negotiation between the Republicans and Democrats in April 2011. The Republicans, fresh off a victory in the 2010 elections, were under pressure to cut the budget to support the various Tea Party supporters in the party. This made their stance on budget cuts seemingly intractable. To get them to say yes, the Democrats had to give them a number they could take back to their constituencies. They ended up agreeing on $38 billion in spending cuts. When the details of the final agreement were released, however, it was discovered that most of these cuts weren't cuts at all but programs that were not renewed and/or savings that would only be realized several years into the future. According to an analysis of the budget by the nonpartisan Congressional Budget Office, actual cuts to spending amounted to only $325 million. Nevertheless, the presence of the $38 billion figure allowed the politicians a talking point to save face to constituents.

Take another example of an employee who wants a new task assignment at work. He wants to take on budgetary responsibilities in addition to technology work, but his boss is worried he is going to slack on his current job. Instead of calling it a "new job" with a "title change," which is unpalatable to his boss, the employee proposes that he serve as the "backup budgetary" person. He can still work with the budget folks and learn about the job but at the same time satisfy his boss. This solution allows his boss to save face and gets the employee what he wants.

Utilizing Intangible Resources

Every negotiation represents an exchange of resources between two parties. As you first learned in Chapter 2 (and in Table 5.1), resources, as with interests, can be both tangible (e.g., money, cars, boats, etc.) and intangible (e.g., empathy, trust, respect, etc.).[29] In this way negotiation is no different than any time you purchase something at a store. You say yes to buying a box of cereal because you think the value of the cereal (e.g., $4.19) is as great as or greater than the value of $4.19 to you.

Thus, as a decision rule, individuals need to cognitively balance the exchange in order to say yes to a negotiated deal. They need to believe that what they are receiving in the offer equals or exceeds what they are putting in. You can think of this in terms of the following equation:

For Party A to say yes:

$$A_{(received)} >= A_{(given)}$$

For Party B to say yes:

$$B_{(received)} >= B_{(given)}$$

That is, what A receives must be greater than or equal to what A gives for A to say yes. Similarly, what B receives must be greater than or equal to what B gives for B to say yes. You can see from these equations that A is particularly concerned about what A receives versus gives and B is particularly concerned about what B receives versus gives.

Let's assume Party A is selling a saxophone for $500 and Party B is willing to buy it for $400. As denoted by the arrows in the figure, what B is giving A ($400) is equal to what B receives from A (a saxophone worth $400). However, the value given by A (a saxophone worth $500) is not equal to what A receives from B ($400). Using the same two equations above, the negotiation at this stage looks like this:

For Party A:

$400 >= $500 → *"NO"*

For Party B:

$400 >= $400 → *"YES"*

These equations demonstrate that when only tangible resources are being exchanged, there is NO DEAL. B is offering $400 to A for a saxophone worth $400 to B and $500 to A. This represents a –$100 zone of potential agreement (ZOPA; see Chapter 2). So what is the outcome? With only these resources on the table, A is going to say no to this deal and B will say yes, meaning there is no deal.

What can B do? B needs to influence one of the components of the equation so that A's equation balances. Here are some of B's options:

1. Convince A the saxophone is only worth $400. (Present A with data-based arguments; see Chapter 7.)

2. Allow himself or herself to be convinced the saxophone is worth $500, thereby increasing the offer to A. (Allow A to present data-based arguments; Chapter 7.)

3. Add another issue (instrument, case, lessons, etc.) and logroll the issues. (Adding issues and logrolling; see Chapter 4.)

4. Provide A with intangible resources to help A say yes in the negotiation.

Options 1, 2, and 3 have been or will be covered at length in other chapters, so we will not rehash them here. Option 4, however, is a different way to manage this equation as it leverages B's intangible resources, which are valuable because of A's intangible interests. Many things that people want are intangible and are related to how they are treated by the other party in the negotiation. If you are able to tap into an intangible interest of the other side (respect), the other side will be more likely to say yes to your deal. Instead of just thinking about what is received and what is given, we can think about both the tangible and intangible resources that are received and given.

For Party A to say yes:

$$A_{(intangible\ received)} + A_{(tangible\ received)} >= A_{(tangible\ given)} + A_{(intangible\ given)}$$

For Party B to say yes:

$$B_{(intangible\ received)} + B_{(tangible\ received)} >= B_{(tangible\ given)} + B_{(intangible\ given)}$$

If B realizes that A would value some intangible good (to validate A's identity), B can provide that for very little (if any) cost to B.

Going back to the saxophone example, say A has symbol-based identity to the instrument which is partly driving A's assessed value. B can say something like "So, tell me how you got into playing the saxophone?" or "I'm fascinated with this instrument. What all can you tell me about it?" B could also flatter A by genuinely stating how impressed B is with the instrument and how A must have taken great care of it. If A is worried about who is acquiring this instrument, A may be quite pleased to sell to a buyer who actually shows genuine interest in the instrument. B might follow with additional questions in order to show A that B really cares about taking good care of the instrument. This empathy (which costs B $0) toward A might provide enough value ($100) for A to say yes to the deal. A now feels more comfortable selling at a slightly lower price to B because of B's providing of intangible value in the negotiation. In this case both parties will say yes.

For Party A:

$100 + $400 >= $500 + $0 → "*YES*"

For Party B:

$0 + $400 >= $400 + $0 → "*YES*"

However, perhaps A doesn't feel $100 worth of "warm fuzzies" over B's interest in the instrument and instead says something like "B, I appreciate your interest and because of that I'll be perfectly honest with you. I'll come down to $425 but that's as low as I can go." B, whether because of reciprocity (see Chapter 4), because of the magnitude of the concession, because B likes A (Chapter 6), or because B feels that A is treating B more than fairly, agrees to the deal. A has given B intangible resources (respect, fairness, trust, honesty) in addition to the tangible concession of $75. In this case while B still values the saxophone at $400, B says yes because of the intangible resources received from A. In this case the equations look like this:

For Party A:

$75 + $425 >= $500 + $0 → "*YES*"

For Party B:

$25 + $400 >= $425 + $0 → "*YES*"

The importance of understanding intangible interests and trading intangible resources can be seen in the show *American Pickers*, an example we come back to here because of the show hosts' ability to manage tangible and intangible interests. The premise of the show is that two business owners (Mike and Frank) from Iowa drive around the country and "pick" antiques and collectibles from individuals who typically have large collections on their property. They then sell the items in their shop for (hopefully) a profit. Because Mike and Frank are almost always buying from original owners (who are deeply invested in their own possessions), the owners tend to overvalue what their items are worth, because they have an (irrational) emotional attachment to the items. Their identity, and the identity of their family in many circumstances, is wrapped up in these possessions. Mike and Frank typically utilize the following strategies:

1. Convince the owners the item is not as valuable as the owners think.

2. Reassess what they think the item is worth (often by calling experts).

3. Add other items and logroll.

4. Provide the owners with intangible resources.

While Mike and Frank rarely use #2, they often employ #1 and #3 when trying to make deals. They also realize the importance of #4 by asking questions such as "How did your dad get into collecting?" and "What do you love about these items?" They try to validate the sellers' identity; in doing so, they provide intangible resources to the owners, resources that cost them nothing but time. The owners, because they typically have an intangible interest of feeling good about the buyer, find it easier to say yes to Mike and Frank than they might to a stranger who is *only* interested in price.

Note that intangible interests are not just whether someone *likes* someone else. Liking is another way that negotiators can get what they want from others (discussed in Chapter 6).

The Emotional Appeal

An **emotional appeal** is essentially the equivalent of saying "Please help me" to the other party. With the emotional appeal, you are tapping into the intangible interests of the other side.

Manager:	I need you to cc me on all of your e-mails to customer X.
Sales Employee:	Why?
Manager:	Because I am under a ton of stress and upper management is breathing down my neck, and it would really help me out if you did this favor for me.

In this case the manager is trying to get value from the negotiation simply by asking for sympathy. The emotional appeal can work for a number of reasons. One reason is that people sometimes respond favorably to an expression of vulnerability—they feel bad for the asker. Second is that the issue is meaningful to them and they are motivated to help. Perhaps you are asking for money for a cause that is personal to the potential donor. Another reason is that, even though you are not offering anything in exchange, the principle of reciprocity may still motivate the other party. After all, even though you have no power *now*, you possibly will have resources, knowledge, or authority in the future which might be valuable. So by helping you now, the other party may expect some future benefit from you, as a form of logrolling or delayed reciprocity. Finally, it could be that they help you because of the relationship you have with them (see further discussion of relationships in Chapter 6).

Another factor in whether or not an emotional appeal might work is essentially "the luck of the draw" in terms of individual differences (discussed more in Chapter 11). Some individuals may have more of a helping disposition or may be more generous and charitable than others.[30] Whereas one person might easily be able to ignore an emotional appeal, another may feel obliged to help. The better you know the people who surround you, the more accurate you will be in predicting who you might be able to influence with an emotional appeal.

Using Standards

As you are negotiating with someone else, you can use cognitive dissonance and the idea of consistency to your advantage by invoking what is termed *standards*. A **standard** is a "practice, policy, or reference point that gives a decision legitimacy."[31] Company policies can be standards, fairness can be a standard, even the process of negotiating can be a standard. To use a standard means that the negotiation party has adopted some belief that you can use in order to frame the negotiation as a matter of consistency.

Imagine you are negotiating with a company about a return that is slightly past the return date. Perhaps the company has a policy that "The customer is always right." In this case you can ask the company representative whether that standard applies in this situation. The policy of the customer is always right might trump the return policy. That is, the manager might bend the rules on the return policy in order to be consistent with the policy that the customer is always right.

Many standards are based on the idea of fairness. If your daughter is arguing that *she* should pick the movie for movie night rather than her sister, you could reply with formal power: "No, I decide whose turn it is," which may result in tears, or you could reply with standards: "Do you think that everyone in the house should have a chance to pick the family movie for movie night?" If she says yes to this question, then, to be consistent, she is more likely to relent and let her sister choose.

BENEFITS TO LEVERAGING INTANGIBLE INTERESTS

When you seek out intangible interests you are engaging in an exploratory exercise to diagnose not only what someone wants and why, but how that ties to who the other person is—their identity, their values, their beliefs, and so on. Their intangible interests describe how they see the world and how they believe they (and everyone else) should be treated in negotiation. This viewpoint gives you the opportunity to understand not just the tangible resources they desire but the intangible resources that will help them say yes. So, why does this help you?

- *Reciprocity*. You learned in Chapter 4 the various tactics that are opened up to you via the path of reciprocity. Leveraging intangible interests, as discussed here in the tactics, just gives you more opportunity to do so.

- *Shadow of the future*. You don't know what is going to happen in the future, such as whether or when you are going to be negotiating with this person again. It is of course then in your best interest to satisfy the other side's intangible interests so that they form a positive impression of you. Due to cognitive dissonance, if they have a positive impression of you, it will make it much more likely for them to say yes to not only your current but also your future requests.

- *Relationship Management*. Do you want to try to figure out someone's identity and underlying beliefs every time you negotiate? Of course not! This is a giant waste of time. Better to try to truly dig in and understand their underlying intangible interests so that negotiating becomes more efficient in the future. If you have ever been in a bad relationship, you know that position-based bargaining over every single thing is draining, both for the individuals and for the relationship. Avoid this by learning intangible interests early.

- *Ethics*. Responding to others' intangible interests is the right thing to do. It shows empathy for them and it communicates that you want a negotiating environment where each side's values and beliefs are not violated.

COSTS TO LEVERAGING INTANGIBLE INTERESTS

There are also several potential costs to using intangible interests. First, remember that intangible interests can be quite unpredictable. You could spend entire negotiations (or lifetimes) trying to discern which intangible interests truly matter to the person on the other side of the table. Part of this reason is that even the person may not truly know what their intangible interests are, or even if they do, they may not be able to articulate those interests and/or why those interests are important. One way that you can learn about intangible interests is to not talk about interests at all but rather ask many, many questions about possible offers so as to detect what the tangible and intangible interests truly are. This is costly, though, in terms of time and effort.

Another potential downside of focusing so heavily on intangible interests is that if the other party realizes they are being influenced using intangible interests, it can backfire if you are not genuine in your attempts. If you are only trying to seek their identity in order to obtain more value, it could be perceived as a negative negotiation tactic. This is why it is important to be genuine. Intangible interests are helpful to learn because it strengthens the relationship and because you believe it the right thing to do, not just because you want to obtain value.

Finally, if you focus on intangible interests, you might learn something you did not want to know. Perhaps you find out that someone's conservative identity is very important to them, and you are a liberal. Or you find out that someone's religious identity is very important to them, and you are an atheist. In this circumstance the knowledge of the identity could impede your ability to take an understanding approach to negotiation, because certain stereotypes may be invoked that make it more difficult for you to engage the other side.

ETHICAL CONSIDERATIONS

If you are genuine about finding out about others' intangible interests, it is unlikely that you would be engaging in unethical behavior. You are seeking to understand by trying to step inside the shoes of someone else. As with perspective taking, you are trying to provide them with the valued resources they seek in order to make it easier for them to say yes to what you want. The ethical quandary you may be in is why you are choosing this set of tactics.

Take, for example, helping someone else save face. If you are truly helping someone else save face, you are taking the management of their ego as your own personal task, which shows that you can see the negotiation through their eyes. In essence you are helping them feel better about themselves so that they can say yes to what you want. Would you like others to treat you this way? Being sensitive to your needs and your ego? If so, then this tactic will be something that would likely uphold your own personal standard. If not, then you should question whether helping them save face is ethical in your situation.

An ironic side effect to genuine attempts to understand other people's intangible interests and trying to step inside their shoes is that you may inadvertently discover information about them that you can take advantage of during a negotiation, as opposed to just understanding their interests. Suppose, for example, that you discover that a coworker you are negotiating with (and that you need some resource or information from) is very insecure about his job and is constantly worried about upper management getting a negative impression of him. If you have influence or relationship ties with anyone in upper management, it would be relatively easy to influence this person with subtle hints that you might mention his "lack of cooperation" to your friend in upper management. If a genuine desire to understand the other party's interest ended up giving you a potential advantage and additional lever to use to influence him, is that just a lucky break for you to help you achieve your goals in the negotiation, or is it ethically problematic?

Case Sidebar

Do you think that Solomon's behavior in this negotiation is ethically questionable? He went behind Elizabeth's back and read up on federal funding guidelines that are clearly *in her domain*. What if Solomon had taken that research to Elizabeth's boss? After this negotiation Solomon asked himself whether what he did was the right thing to do, whether he would have been comfortable with someone else doing this to him. If he had to do this over again, Solomon would have kept trying other tactics and questions with Elizabeth before invading her "turf." For example, he could have asked her permission to look at some of the federal guidelines or talked to other people at the university to uncover some of the problems she might be having.

Ethics Discussion Questions

1. Imagine that you are in a negotiation with a coworker over whether to continue to update a document before sending it to the boss. You want to send it to the boss and your coworker wants to keep editing. You know that if you say that you are the "content expert" and you should have final say, it will threaten the identity of your coworker, who just wants to be seen as an equal. However, you also know that if you say this, you will likely immediately get what you want, which is for your coworker to give up and let you send the document in. What do you do? How would you feel if someone did this to you?

2. You make more than your significant other and this is causing tension in your relationship when you have to decide how to spend money. You feel more comfortable going out to eat, buying nice clothes, than does your significant other. What might the intangible interests be in this situation? You basically just want to tell him or her to "get over it" so that you can have normal conversations about buying furniture, taking vacations, and spending money on other things. Is this an ethical thing to do? If not, how might you approach the intangible interests better in this situation?

3. Many states have passed so-called apology laws, whereby individuals or companies can apologize to a victim or victim's family *without* putting them at risk of being sued. For example, if a hospital makes a mistake and a patient dies, a representative of the hospital can apologize to the family of the patient. This sounds good, right? One perhaps unintended consequence of the apology is that the victim's family is much less likely to sue if they've received the apology (an intangible resource). This raises the question: Is the apology given because one is truly sorry? Or is the apology given because one doesn't want to be sued? What do you think about the nature of apologies in these types of situations?[32]

CHAPTER REVIEW

Discussion Questions

Consider the following scenario:

Two months ago Brock was placed on an inter-departmental team with four other individuals. One of Brock's fellow team members, Erin, is the only member of the team with an information technology (IT) background. The rest of the team is from finance or management. Erin's preferred style is to immediately identify a problem and set out to fix it, much as you would a piece of software code. Brock's problem is that the team is tasked with setting a strategic vision for change for the organization, which is complex, multilayered, and long term. Given the divergence between the team's task and Erin's preferred problem-solving approach, the team members often discount Erin's ideas, which usually consist of immediate action.

One day during a team meeting, this issue came to the fore as Brock was leading the team through the 4-month rollout of a new strategic initiative. Erin wanted to e-mail the company that day telling them the change, which Brock and his fellow team members knew was not going to work. They had to get buy-in for the idea first. Erin finally had enough and told the team, "You clearly all don't value my ideas, so just decide what you want to do and I'll support the team."

Whereas some of the team members were fine with this solution, Brock was not. He knew that without Erin's full buy-in, she would not be as motivated, she would not provide valuable input, and she would not sell the strategic changes to her home department.

He could sense that Erin was defensive in team meetings and was starting to "check out."

1. What should Brock say to Erin?

2. When should he approach Erin?

3. What do you think Erin's intangible interests are in this situation?

4. What are the benefits of probing into Erin's identity?

5. What are the costs to probing into Erin's identity?

6. What if Erin tells Brock that she is not going to fall for any "gooey-feely" stuff?

Concept Application

1. Imagine you are not pleased with a test grade and you want to send your professor an e-mail.

   a. What are your tangible and intangible interests in this type of negotiation?

   b. What are the tangible and intangible interests of the professor in this type of negotiation?

   c. What identities might be activated by this negotiation for the professor and the student?

   d. How do you address both your interests and your professor's interests?

   e. Now write the e-mail and share it with your classmates.

2. Find a close friend, family member, or colleague who is willing to open up to you about their intangible interests. Ask them about a negotiation they were involved in that did not involve you. Ask them the following questions to understand whether intangible interests played a role in determining the outcome of the negotiation:

   a. Were you treated fairly? How do you know?

   b. Do you share the same beliefs and values as the other person? What information did they give you that leads you to believe this?

   c. Did you feel threatened in the negotiation? Or defensive? What happened that led to those feelings?

d. Would you negotiate with that person (those people) again? Why or why not?

3. After performing an in-class negotiation, ask the person you just negotiated with how well you did at managing their intangible interests. You may ask them the following questions as a starting point:

   a. Did I treat you fairly?

   b. Would you want to negotiate with me again? Why or why not?

   c. Did you feel threatened or defensive? What did I say that caused that reaction?

   d. Would you have appreciated different behavior from me during the negotiation? How so?

4. Use standards. This could be in a negotiation with a company, a negotiation at work, or even a negotiation at home. The key is to try to get the other side to agree on a *principle* and then influence them based on that principle. This is often possible if a company has a mission statement or policy of standards (e.g., "the customer is always right") that is public. Come to class with your example(s).

Role-Play Exercise:
The Science Department

ACME Publishing produces textbooks for various high school subjects, including English, history, science, and math. Each subject area has a department head, who is in charge of all editing and sales. Each department has approximately 30 employees, who are split equally between editing/author support and sales. The editing/author support teams are located on-site and work on updating already existing editions of textbooks as well as working with new authors to produce new textbooks. The sales employees are distributed across the country and each is responsible for a particular region.

Due to scandal involving sexual harassment as well as poor leadership of the divisions, the chief executive officer (CEO) of ACME Publishing was removed by the board of directors 3 months ago. While a nationwide search proceeds, an interim CEO was put into place by the board. The interim CEO, Doug Williams, has been charged with getting a handle on the performance of all of the departments (see Figure 5.2).

After 2 months in his job, Doug sent this message to the entire ACME staff:

> After listening to many of you at ACME during the past 2 months, I have decided that the best course of action is to open up all four of the department head positions in english, history, science, and math. I know this may come as a shock to many of you. The department heads have been doing what had been asked of them, but the environment of textbook publishing has changed, and it has come time to reevaluate where everyone is in relation to those goals. The current department heads are welcome to apply for the positions as well. This action is meant to "restart" our strategic efforts at ACME and make sure that the best people are leading us into the future. Regardless of the outcome of each of the positions, it is my intent that every current employee of ACME will have a position at ACME going forward.

Sam Jakist is the current department head of science and has been for the past 15 years. Sam has decided to reapply for the department head position in science.

Blake Rogers has been in sales in science for the past 12 years, working under Sam the entire time. Blake, too, has decided to apply for the department head position in science.

After a series of interviews, Blake Rogers is hired by Doug Williams, the interim CEO, to be the next science department head. Doug offers Sam a choice of staying within the science department or moving to one of the other departments.

The negotiation takes place between Blake Rogers and Sam Jakist after Blake takes over as department head.

Figure 5.2 ACME Publishing Organizational Structure

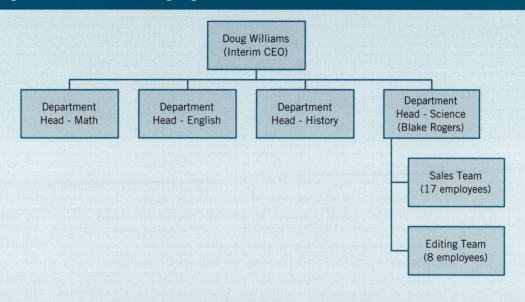

NEGOTIATION AND TECHNOLOGY

A textbook on negotiations written a generation ago might not even have mentioned technology, but in today's world it is a constant and pervasive presence in our lives. As modern generations are growing up surrounded by technology and communication devices, the standards for how and when people communicate are changing.[1] A member of one generation might initiate a phone call for something that a member of a different generation would have texted or sent an e-mail about. One person might be offended at having received an "impersonal" text or e-mail instead of a phone call, whereas another person might be annoyed at having been interrupted by a non-urgent phone call when a text could have sufficed. Both examples could result in annoyance or conflict, even if the offending party was trying to be courteous. From how we communicate, to the various methods and media we use, to the availability of information and analytical tools, modern technology has affected negotiation in many substantial and significant ways.

TECHNOLOGY VS. FACE-TO-FACE

The use of technology in communication has fundamentally changed negotiation. With the use of simultaneous video and audio through smartphones, tablets, computers, or dedicated video-conferencing meeting rooms or facilities, the idea that negotiators need to physically be present is a thing of the past. This allows for incredible flexibility, making negotiation much easier and more available. Whereas in the past, negotiations would require physically meeting, now people can negotiate in any place and at any time.

There are potential advantages and disadvantages to the increased flexibility and convenience that technology provides in communication. Although people may like the convenience of instantaneous communication via texting, for example, overreliance on it may undermine benefits that might exist in richer communication media. The benefits of in-person presence, which allows for the full "range" of communication (including body language, eye movements, and other subtle signals), will be increasingly lost as the bandwidth of communication is reduced. Whereas little information might be lost in high-resolution video-conferencing meeting facilities, video on a small mobile phone screen clearly is more limited. As we move down the spectrum to voice or asynchronous text, clearly we are potentially giving up on a lot of data, something that researchers in media richness theory noted even before the advent of the Internet.[2] The ability to develop more nuanced communication and to build relationships and trust—which can be crucial to effective negotiation—is clearly constrained when using electronic media.[3,4]

There are a few things that happen when you are not face-to-face during a negotiation. First, it makes it much more likely that someone will lie to you. Research has shown that lying increases when individuals are not face-to-face, possibly because of the anonymity that communicating via text may provide.[5] This anonymity also can provoke individuals to take extreme stances or be overly aggressive, as communicating through e-mail or other non- face-to-face platforms makes it easier to avoid social norms of constraint.[6] On the positive side, though, negotiating through technology provides a *record* that might be useful, especially in complex negotiations. If you are attempting to buy a car and you are trying to understand monthly payment, annual percentage rate (APR), oil change charges, fees, trade-in value, and accessory pricing, negotiating through e-mail might help you keep many of those facts straight in a way that negotiating face-to-face does not. Negotiating via technology might help you avoid being taken advantage of due to your uncertainty (see Chapter 7).

What you want to think about is whether the choice of communication mode *matches* your intended tactic. If you are trying to build a relationship or uncover intangible interests, being face-to-face can help, as it will allow for more and deeper information to be transferred between individuals. If, however, you are using formal power, or alternatives, you might benefit from a more straightforward approach over e-mail.

Ultimately this is but one of the many choices you have to make when you negotiate. You might prefer a multipronged approach, where you *start* a negotiation face-to-face but continue the negotiation virtually once you've built trust with the other side. You will have to balance the likelihood of being lied to or otherwise treated negatively with the benefits of having a clear record of what is being negotiated.

INFORMATION AND ALTERNATIVES

An entirely different way that technology has changed—and continues to change—negotiations, is not just as a medium of negotiation but via the increased availability of information. The vast amount of information available via the Internet and other electronic resources has clearly made it much easier to find relevant information in negotiations. For example, the Internet helps negotiators (whether buyers, sellers, or other roles) to more accurately estimate the other side's BATNA (bottom line) and to understand the availability of alternatives.

A simple example is the purchase of a used car. Twenty years ago there would be relatively little information available for the buyer, and any estimate of the seller's bottom line would be largely guesswork. Developing a good BATNA would be very difficult and time-consuming and would involve limited sources of information like classified ads in local newspapers. Today, on the other hand, there is a wide variety of information available that is largely without cost and relatively easy to access. Various websites will provide estimates on the value of a used car, including specifics like options and mileage, and will typically provide estimates of both how much a private buyer is likely to pay and what a dealership is likely to pay.[7] In addition, various auction sites typically provide data on past sales. Combining multiple such sources can give the buyer a relatively detailed impression of what the actual value of a particular used car is and what others in the local area would typically be willing to pay for such a car—giving a good estimate of the seller's BATNA. Furthermore, the buyer would also be able to much more easily locate similar used cars for sale, both locally and farther away, to develop a superior BATNA themselves. In this example, the availability of technology to provide this information has completely changed the dynamic of the negotiation, substantially shifting the power from seller to buyer.

Obviously, most negotiations are more complicated than buying a used car and involve more issues and/or parties, but the underlying benefit of increased access to information remains. If a company is negotiating with a potential new vendor, for example, electronic searching can likely provide a lot of information about the vendor, their past activities, any federal contracts they might have, complaints lodged against them, and other information. If a company is publicly traded, it is likely possible to find annual reports and financial statements, all of which can provide useful information about possible reliability, stability, interests, BATNA, and other data that could be useful for planning a negotiation.

CHAPTER 6

RELATIONSHIPS

CHAPTER EXAMPLE

Ann and Deb have been married for 25 years and have two daughters, Sarah and Julie. Julie, the younger of the daughters, has just finished high school and is heading off to university next month. For several years Ann and Deb have discussed how they can't wait to downsize and move into a smaller house or condominium once both Sarah and Julie are in college. This discussion typically has come up in the past when complaining about the yardwork they have to do at their current house, as well as the work involved in keeping such a large house clean. Now the time has come to negotiate over the "terms" of this potential move.

Ann and Deb were both living on the north side of Chicago when they met. Ann had just finished law school and secured a job clerking for a prestigious judge. She was just beginning her professional career and was learning about what it meant to be a lawyer, a clerk, a judge, and how she was going to fit in the legal profession. Deb, on the other hand, was doing accounting work for a small startup. The company was doing fine until the founder was thrown in jail for buying illegal drugs and the company folded. When Deb met Ann, she had no job, had little savings, and was thinking about moving back home to Detroit where a family friend had guaranteed her a job. Ann was her lifeline to staying in Chicago. They met, started dating, fell in love, and the rest, as they say, is history.

In the past several years the discussion about downsizing has come up several times.

Typically, Ann brings up the idea that the yardwork or the housework is too much for the two of them to handle on their own,

Learning Objectives

1. Distinguish between a relationship and relationship power.

2. Illustrate how a relationship can change the perceptions of others' negotiation tactics.

3. Describe the process of social exchange and articulate how positive exchange is built in the context of relationships.

4. Distinguish between trust and liking, and think about the implications of each in the context of negotiation.

5. Provide examples of how trust is built, violated, and repaired.

6. Strengthen relationships within the context of negotiation using various relationship-based tactics.

7. Be sensitive to the ethical implications of leveraging relationship power.

$SAGE edge™

Master the content at study .sagepub.com/rockmann

and Deb agrees. This is because they have a half-acre lot with several garden beds. Also, their house is approximately 3,000 square feet, with five bedrooms and four bathrooms. Ann likes to say, "It's a ridiculous house for just two people to live in." Because Deb has never said otherwise, Ann believes that Deb agrees with her on this 100%.

Deb doesn't wish to upset Ann, so she hasn't shared her true feelings on the house and downsizing. Deb is emotional about the house, partially because it is the house where Sarah and Julie spent their entire childhood. After thinking more and more about downsizing, Deb realizes she would like to stay for several more years, mainly so that Sarah and Julie are coming "home" when they return from college to visit. She thinks they have many more memories to create together in that house and doesn't want to move right away to what she believes will be a "soulless" condo. She has been reticent to mention this to Ann.

Without telling Deb, Ann has made an appointment with their longtime friend and realtor, Kate. Deb sees the appointment on their shared calendar and feels a pit in her stomach. Deb feels devoted to Ann. Ann is the person with whom she has crafted a wonderful life with two great kids. However, Deb has this strong emotional attachment to the house and this overwhelming sense of sadness about leaving. She doesn't know what to do.

******

The importance of relationships and the influence you have as a result of them cannot be overstated. One of the primary ways you obtain value in your daily interactions is as a result of the power inherent in relationships that have developed over time. If your significant other cooks a terrible meal, aspects of your relationship might influence you to still eat it and pretend to like it. If your significant other wants to go to a Monster Truck show but you would rather go to the opera, aspects of your relationship might lead you to end up going to see Big Foot and Gravedigger, instead of getting to enjoy the *Magic Flute* or *Tosca*. While you might be perfectly willing to pay for a colleague's lunch, you are not as likely to pay for the stranger who claims to have forgotten his wallet. As relationships develop over time, things like trust, respect, and liking can be created, all of which have power in negotiations.

Many of our negotiations are going to take place with people that we already know. Some of these relationships may be relatively "weak" such as with colleagues that we rarely interact with or neighbors that we wave at but never speak to, and some of them may be very "strong," such as those with spouses, parents, children, some coworkers, or lifelong friends. While we often take these effects for granted, and may have an intuitive working understanding of the power of relationships, it is important to augment that with an analytical approach and an understanding of some of the specifics involved. Understanding the research on relationships—in particular, how you are affected by relationship power and how you affect others with relationship power—is the goal of this chapter.

Negotiating in the context of an existing relationship has benefits and risks. On the one hand, an existing relationship, compared with a new relationship, may allow for much more trust, respect, liking, and understanding. All of these things can improve communication, which will help resolve a dispute or reach an agreement. On the other hand, an existing relationship may complicate what might otherwise be a fairly simple problem and turn it into something involving considerable emotion, suspicion, concerns about equity and justice, future obligation, or other factors that might make the resolution or agreement far more difficult. Thus, although the existence of a relationship may lead to more options being available in terms of how to approach the negotiation, it can also make resolution more difficult.

INTRODUCTION TO RELATIONSHIPS

Relationship Power

Relationship power is the potential influence an individual has as a result of relationships or personal ties with other people.[1] A person is said to have relationship power (or what French and Raven refer to as referent power) over you to the extent that you identify with that person or want to be closely associated with that person. Such relationships can be mutual and reciprocal, or they can be more one-way in that only one person out of the two wants to be closely associated with the other. If a negotiator comes across as friendly, reasonable, and generally nice, you may be more likely to listen to an argument or to agree to a certain concession.

However, most of the time, relationship power is the value you obtain from others as a result of the strength and type of the relationship you have with them. A family member or a long-time close friend can influence you to do many different things that you would never do if a casual acquaintance or colleague asked you. Coworkers who have worked together for many years on the same team, can develop a lot of relationship power toward each other. A new member of the team may come into the situation with a lot of expert power (say, as a recent engineering graduate, with the latest knowledge and techniques) but may have no relationship power at all.

Relationship power does not arise from simply being interdependent—or in a relationship—with someone. Being in a relationship with someone (e.g., a family member) may give them relationship power over you, but it is not necessarily the case. Being in a relationship simply means that you are interacting with someone with whom you are interdependent—you are reliant on that person to reach some goal together. The source of power that person has over you is based on how you view that person. If you are willing to be influenced because that person controls resources that you want or is able to force you or coerce you in some way, that person has formal power over you (see Chapter 8). If, however, you are willing to be influenced simply because of the nature of the person, it is relationship power. What, though, is the source of relationship power? We review a few of the individual factors that lead one to have relationship power over someone else: positive social exchange, liking, and trust.

Social Exchange

A relationship can be thought of as a series of transactions between two individuals, where tangible and intangible goods between two interdependent individuals are traded, or exchanged.[2] But while relationships involve giving and receiving between individuals, relationships are not built solely based on whether what has been given is equal to what has been received. Relationships are built to the degree that what is given is judged favorably. The standards by which one judges another's actions in a relationship are called the **rules of exchange**. Over time, if the rules of exchange are met or exceeded, the relationship evolves into one marked by trust, loyalty, and commitment.[3] On the contrary, if the rules of exchange are not met, the relationship devolves into one marked by distrust, antipathy, and revenge.

The complication of negotiation is that different individuals may have different rules of exchange—what they expect to get from a relationship and how they evaluate what is returned to them. As a negotiator you want to understand the rules of exchange that the other party is playing by. You also want to understand the rules of exchange you expect so that you know how likely it is that you are susceptible to relationship power. Here are a few possibilities:[4]

- *Generalized exchange:* You are willing to provide to someone else without knowing if or when you might be "paid back." You can also think of this as **altruism**, or costly acts that benefit others.[5] When in generalized exchange, your goal is to keep the other person happy without regard to your own expense.

  EXAMPLE: Your best friend Jie and you have known each other since you were kids. You have tickets tonight but Jie calls and asks you to drive 3 hours to pick her up because her car died. You quickly forget about the concert tickets and go pick up Jie. You don't care if or when you get "paid back" for this favor, and you don't consider what is coming to you in return in this "negotiation," which lasts all of a minute. You have willingly changed your plans simply because Jie asked. Jie has a great deal of relationship power over you. Your rule for your relationship with Jie is generalized exchange.

- *Reciprocal exchange:* You want to be paid back for what you provide, but you don't necessarily care when. You have trust in the other person that you will be treated fairly and "compensated" for what you are agreeing to give the other person. You value an equal footing over the long term within the relationship.

  EXAMPLE: Your coworker Keith asks you to help him with a new customer service interface your company just rolled out. You know that while Keith struggles a bit with the technical aspects of customer service, he has great contacts which will likely help you in the future. You agree to help him because you know that if you cement a positive relationship with him, Keith will likely help you in the future. Keith has some relationship power over you. Your rule for your relationship with Keith is reciprocal exchange.

- *Negotiated exchange:* You need to know right now what you are getting back if you are going to give up anything. This is termed *negotiated exchange* because it is how we traditionally think of negotiations—you decide in the moment what you give and what you receive.

  EXAMPLE: Your boss Tamika wants you to work an extra 10 hours this weekend. You state you are willing to do this only if Tamika pays you overtime. Based on your relationship, you are only willing to do things for Tamika if you get "paid" immediately. Tamika has no relationship power over you. Your rule for your relationship with Tamika is negotiated exchange.

As you can see in these examples, where relationship power clearly has a role in negotiations is when one or both sides sees the relationships as being in generalized exchange. One possibility for why you might have generalized rules for exchange is because you've experienced an anchoring event with someone—perhaps you served in the military together, or you dealt with an abusive supervisor together, or that person was simply there for you during a personal crisis.[6] Just know that if this is the case for you and your negotiation partner, you likely are in generalized exchange and are susceptible to significant relationship power. This can lead to ironic situations where close friends, who we would think would collaborate well together, create less value because each is so eager to give in to the other.

Case Sidebar

One of the reasons the dynamic is so interesting between Ann and Deb is because Deb clearly views the relationship with Ann as being in generalized exchange. This is because they have been through so much together in 25 years, including having two kids. This makes it *very* difficult for Deb to say no to Ann because she truly wants Ann to be happy. Ann clearly has significant relationship power over Deb.

Table 6.1 outlines a negotiation between two friends—Gbemi and Meggan—over where to go on their next vacation together. Within each example are some of the problems that could occur if two parties do not have similar rules for exchange.

The rules of exchange thus are a tool we can use to diagnose advantages in some relationships as well as difficulties in other relationships. It's a good place to start if you are (a) trying to increase your relationship power and/or (b) trying to understand why you are failing to increase your relationship power. It's also a helpful place to start if you are struggling to understand why the other side is responding in the way that they are. Perhaps they are thinking about your relationship differently than you are.

Table 6.1   Gbemi (Pronounced "bee-me") and Meggan

Example	Gbemi's Rules for Exchange in Her Friendship With Meggan	Meggan's Rules for Exchange in Her Friendship With Gbemi	Potential Negotiation Problem
A	Generalized	Reciprocal	Meggan allows Gbemi to pick the location and will be waiting for Gbemi to reciprocate during the vacation by, for instance, letting Meggan pick a restaurant or day trip. Gbemi may have no idea Meggan is thinking this and may upset Meggan if she does not offer.
B	Generalized	Negotiated	Meggan is willing to allow Gbemi to pick the location only if Gbemi immediately agrees that Meggan will be in control of all day-to-day activities. Gbemi struggles to understand why Meggan is so insistent on firming up day-to-day activities. After all, Gbemi knows she would gladly let Meggan choose whatever she wants whenever she wants. Gbemi wonders whether she should go on this vacation with Meggan if every activity/meal is going to feel like a "negotiation."
C	Reciprocal	Negotiated	Meggan is willing to allow Gbemi to pick the location only if Gbemi immediately agrees that Meggan will be in control of the day-to-day activities. Gbemi is happy to let Meggan choose the day activities as that would be a fair trade, but she struggles to understand why it needs to be done immediately.

Liking and Similarity

Liking is perhaps not as intense or deep a feeling as being in generalized exchange, yet it still conveys some relationship power. Liking involves a general assessment of whether or not you want to be affiliated with another. When you like someone, it makes you less likely to adopt counternormative arguments.[7] What this means is that if someone you like says something you agree with, you are happy because their likability aligns with what you already know. Further, if someone you like states something you do not agree with ("counternormative"), you will be less critical of that argument than were you to hear it from a stranger. It's simply harder for you to be critical because your liking of the person gets in the way. In negotiations this can end up being a major source of influence as many of the arguments given in negotiation are arguments you may not agree with. If you are negotiating with someone you like, you might choose to believe their data-based argument (see Chapter 7), rather than evaluating that argument critically, in order to preserve your feeling of liking of that person.

There are many reasons we like others, many of which we may not be consciously aware of. We may like people because they have some characteristic or trait we find appealing, or because they engage in activities that we admire, or simply because we enjoy their company for reasons that we cannot articulate. We may also like people because we find them attractive, an effect that can lead to attractive people getting more value from counterparts in negotiations.[8,9]

Another source of liking is the perception of similarity.[10] The research on in-group and out-group effects, for example, suggests that we often end up liking people in our in-group better, because of perceptions of similarity and shared group membership.[11] These effects include not only the allocation of resources and willingness to do things for those we consider our in-group but also the beliefs and assumptions we have about in-group members versus out-group members.[12] Research has found that we share more knowledge with people we see as members of our in-group which can facilitate creating value in negotiations.[13] As a result, if you are negotiating with someone that you consider to be similar to yourself, you are going to be much more likely to make concessions, give them a better deal, and trust them, than if you were negotiating with someone that you consider to be quite different from yourself. This helps you avoid the paradox of reciprocity as illustrated in Chapter 4. As noted in the discussion of intangible interests in Chapter 5, when you give a concession to someone from your in-group, you get *intangible value* because you are helping someone from your in-group, which makes you feel better.

Consider a situation in which Tina is negotiating at a street fair over a wooden-framed mirror that she admires. She sees the price tag of $250, which to her seems very expensive. She is preparing her arguments: The size of the mirror is modest, the mirror seemingly costs more than other similarly sized mirrors at the fair, and so she decides her opening offer will be $150. However, when Tina sees the seller is wearing a college sweatshirt from the same small liberal arts college that Tina went to (which is surprising because the school is located on the other side of the country), Tina's arguments immediately go to the back of her mind. Instead of opening with discussion of the mirror, she opens with a question about the school. This changes the discussion from a potentially contentious negotiation to a conversation between old (although previously unknown) friends. The liking that she immediately has for this other person makes Tina feel more at ease with paying full price. Further, even if Tina does pay full price for the mirror, from Tina's perspective this may not be a bad outcome. Tina was afforded the opportunity to support someone from her alma mater, and this feels quite good to Tina (provides her intangible value; see Chapter 5). Without even knowing it, the seller has used relationship power on Tina.

As such, we need to be constantly aware that we may be more favorably inclined to do something for one person as opposed to another, based not on reasons related to the negotiation but rather on unrelated perceptions of liking, whether that be from in-group or out-group membership, physical attractiveness, or other characteristics. Note that these effects are neither fair nor just, nor are they particularly rational or logical. Nonetheless, they are real and powerful sources of influence, and as a result we need to be aware of them and understand them.

Trust

Trust is the willingness to be vulnerable to the actions of another party.[14] Another way of thinking about trust is as the willingness to act on the words, actions, and decisions of another party. Both of these definitions describe vulnerability and risk in a relationship. Trust is essentially the belief that another person is not going to take advantage of, or otherwise harm, you. The more trust there is in a relationship, the easier it is to negotiate.[15] Trust enhances cooperation and information sharing, which in turn enhance trust.

Trust is therefore an important component in being able to obtain value from others. The more someone trusts you, the easier it will be to reach an agreement with that person. If you are negotiating with someone who trusts you (as a result of a long relationship, for instance), a statement such as "I cannot possibly pay more than $10,000 for your used car" will likely be believed, whereas if that statement were made by a stranger, it would be less likely to be believed, and if it were made by an employee at a used car dealership, it almost certainly would not be believed. Trust also allows for delayed reciprocity in relationships. If one party trusts another and expects future negotiations, it is possible to accept a worse agreement on one negotiation in exchange for the expectation of a better agreement in another, future, negotiation. Such an example illustrates how trust is a willingness to incur risk. If you have complete trust in someone (say, a family member you have a very close relationship with), you would not hesitate to expose yourself to such a risk. If, on the other hand, you have only just recently met someone and do not know much about them or their past behavior, it is highly unlikely that you would agree to such an arrangement.

Trust between two parties typically results from a variety of factors but primarily from the history of the relationship between the parties. Every interaction you have with someone in a relationship provides you with additional information about that person's actions and decisions. It allows you not only to evaluate their consistency over time but also to make inferences about their values, attitudes, and beliefs—all of which can contribute to your assessment of how much risk you are willing to expose yourself to in dealings with that person. However, in addition to these factors, there can also be individual and situational factors that can contribute to the trust in a particular negotiation. For instance, there may be particular situational factors in a given negotiation—including rules, contracts, or other forms of enforcement, as well as cultural or normative factors—that might increase or decrease the trust between the parties. Individuals can vary in terms of their predisposition toward trust. Some people tend to be more suspicious and wary, whereas others tend to be more open and trusting in relationships.

Lewicki and Bunker proposed three "stages" to trust development, in which trust is based on calculus, knowledge, and identification.[16] Their first stage, calculus, is a very cognitive/informational and quantitative approach to trust, in which individuals decide how much risk they are willing to expose themselves to, based on an assessment of benefits versus costs, and the probability of opportunism by the other party. The second stage, knowledge, results from the accumulation of information about the other party, as a result of the relationship over time. The more a person learns about the other party and can observe their actions and decisions, and the consistency over time, the more accurate predictions about the probability of opportunism can be estimated. Thus, the more interaction and communication there is in a relationship, the more accurate this knowledge can be. The third stage of trust is based on a shared history and perceptions that interests (and often beliefs, values, and attitudes) are aligned or complementary between the two parties.

As a result, it is always in your interest to have the other party trust you as much as possible, since it will make them more likely to share information, agree to requests, and generally agree to give you value. As mentioned earlier, while much of the trust that develops in a relationship results from the observations of behavior, it can also be affected by perceptions of similarity and familiarity, as well as situational factors. The more you can manage these factors, the more trust can be created in a relationship, and the more value you can obtain.

Trust Repair

A very important issue to consider in negotiations is the possibility of the perception that trust has been violated or broken. Because people care a lot about being treated fairly, the perception that trust has been violated can be very damaging to a relationship (see Figure 6.1). Given that trust has a wide range of benefits for negotiations, undermining or losing it can create a serious problem in a negotiation, making it much more difficult to reach agreement. Obviously, the simple rule for a negotiator is to not only build trust but also be sensitive to the possibility of accidentally violating trust or even creating the perception that trust was violated. The concern about the perception of a violation becomes particularly important when you negotiate with people from different cultures, because the norms and values can obviously differ from yours, and a behavior that is innocuous in one culture can be inappropriate or deeply offensive in another. The better informed you are and the more you understand such things, the better you can protect yourself against the perception of a trust violation.

Case Sidebar

One of the dangers in the negotiation between Deb and Ann is that, if Deb were to bring up the possibility of remaining in the house after Ann has already scheduled a meeting with the realtor, Deb would be harming trust. Ann might trust Deb to tell her when she disagrees—Deb would potentially be violating this trust by not saying anything. Deb needs to think carefully about her relationship with Ann and how to communicate her concerns without breaching trust. She also might consider employing the following strategies: Apologize, let Ann vent her frustration, and work immediately on communicating her concerns in a timely way going forward.

Apologize. If the other party perceives that a violation of trust has occurred, the critical question for the negotiator is how to best repair it. One of the best ways to repair trust is via a sincere apology.[17] However, research has found that many negotiators are reluctant to apologize unless they believe that they will be forgiven.[18] Apologizing carries risk, and as was discussed in Chapter 5, negotiators want to protect their identity—apologizing without belief that a forgiving response is forthcoming is threatening to one's identity.

Let Others Vent. If you are trying to repair trust in a relationship, you first have to realize that the other person has been harmed by your actions. Rather than talking through the problem or the details of what happened, it may be helpful to listen to the other side vent about their frustration and disappointment. This helps to restore a sense of fairness, in that you are showing an interest in understanding their concerns and how they feel they were mistreated.[19] But you might also find that letting people vent and being supportive causes people to feel more justified in their decisions and thus less willing to change their mind about concessions.

Figure 6.1   Trust Issues

Engage in Trustworthy Actions. Another way to repair trust is to consistently engage in a series of trustworthy actions after trust has been broken.[20] Research shows, however, that this method of repairing trust works only if the initial untrustworthy actions were not accompanied by deception. Others might forgive you for making what they deem to be an "untrustworthy" decision, but if you *lied* about that decision, you might never regain trust.

Obviously, never having the trust violation in the first place is the best way to not have to worry about whether or not the violation will be forgiven by the other party. As a general rule, the more trust has built up over time, the more resilient a relationship will be to a one-time violation. As you think about how much relationship power you have in negotiations and whether you want to increase that power, you need to think about how much you are trusted and, if you are not, what steps you need to take to restore that trust.

The political environment in 2018 in the United States was fraught with partisanship. Any Republican or Democrat seen to give *anything* to the other side in a negotiation was labeled a defector, putting his or her seat at risk in the next election. Thus, it was surprising to see a spirit of collaboration between Republicans and Democrats in the state of Virginia.

An article in the *Washington Post* describes the months-long process to secure additional Medicaid funding in the Virginia state budget, an issue that state Republicans had long been against and state Democrats had long been in favor of. At the heart of the deal is the friendship, built over many years, between the Republican house speaker, M. Kirkland Cox, and the newly elected governor, Democrat Ralph Northam.

"Taciturn and deeply conservative, Cox is not a politician who seems open to hobnobbing with Democrats. But Northam has always been friendly with Republicans; they tried to recruit him to change parties earlier in his career. Shortly after he was elected, Northam began meeting with Cox. . . . They talked baseball. Northam played in high school. Cox was a coach. . . . The two formed such a bond that Northam joked about it at a recent event. 'Kirk actually picked out my tie for me this morning. He said it really brings out my eyes.'

"With Cox and Northam on such good footing, the way was clear for another powerful Republican—House Appropriations Committee Chairman S. Chris Jones—to [take on] the nitty-gritty work of building a state budget that included Medicaid expansion. Jones, a pharmacist, had an even deeper relationship with Northam, having teamed with him in 2009 in the bipartisan push to ban smoking in Virginia restaurants.

"After additional lobbying in both the State House and Senate, the measure passed 23-17 in the Senate and 67-31 in the House, providing a key victory for the governor, who mentioned that these negotiations 'set the stage for us to be able to do some really good things working together.'"

Source: Schneider, G. S., & Vozzella, L. (2018, June 5). How VA lawmakers expanded Medicaid. *Washington Post*, pp. B1, B4.

Summary. To return to the beginning of the chapter, the idea here is that relationship power is going to impact negotiators in very specific ways. How they view the other person (or people) will change their behavior, either relaxing them and making them open to collaboration and understanding or restricting them and making them anxious and defensive. The three rules of exchange, liking, and trust are all indicators of how any specific negotiator might behave in a negotiation. As your task is to understand and hopefully predict negotiator behavior, each of these is a tool you can use to determine whether the relationship will be a significant source of power.

NEGOTIATING TACTICS

Because relationships can be a powerful way to obtain value, negotiators should always try to do what they can to build and strengthen them. If engaging in a one-time interaction, there is obviously going to be much less that can be done than if engaging in a series of repeated negotiations over an extended period of time. That said, because some of these effects on relationships—such as liking, perceived similarity, attractiveness—are very subtle, there are a number of actions that can be taken to build the relationship, even if the negotiation is a one-time interaction.

Appear Friendly and Open

While this may seem to be one of the more obvious pieces of advice, it may not be intuitive for everyone. People differ in their general affect; some just tend to come across as more open and friendly, whereas others may give an impression of being more standoffish, or even negative. However, because liking can be a source of relationship power, the more likable the other party perceives you to be, the better you can accomplish this. This involves a conscious management of appearances—**impression management**, if you will. Rather than simply "being yourself" in a negotiation setting, particularly in the early stages of a relationship or the first time you are interacting with the other party, it is very important to be sure that you are giving the impression of being friendly, open, trustworthy, and likable. This is called **self-monitoring**, the ability to know how you are being perceived by others. This might include, for instance, actively listening to the concerns and questions of the other side intently rather than internally thinking about your arguments and responses. It also might include asking questions that communicate empathy—that you care about the interests of the other side. Even in a seemingly contentious negotiation, engaging in small talk or other nonthreatening discussion can help the other side see you as likeable.

Have a Professional Appearance

People tend to like attractive people more than unattractive people. Of course, it is not easy or feasible for you to change your physical features, but it is possible to present that appearance in as positive a light as possible. Suppose you are trying to gain admission into a graduate program. You know that your undergraduate grade point average is not the best, and you very much want to influence the admissions officer. If you walk into the meeting wearing a freshly cleaned suit and nice shoes, with well-manicured hands and neat hair, you are probably more likely to influence the admissions officer than if you walk in wearing a dirty T-shirt and shorts, with unkempt hair. The admissions officer is not just looking at your application materials but also making an assessment of whether you will succeed and fit into the program. Dressing appropriately communicates that you take the opportunity seriously and that you are willing to do your best to succeed.

Be Consistent

Another obvious method for building relationships and trust is to be as consistent and transparent in your actions as possible. The more you behave in a consistent way—in the actions, decisions, and attitudes you communicate—the easier it will be for the other party to develop a clear perception of you and a belief that they can predict your actions. Since trust is essentially a willingness to expose yourself to risk, the more confident the other party feels in their ability to predict your actions, the more they will be willing to place trust into the relationship. As with trying to appear likable, a large part of this is a matter of impression management and self-monitoring. The more you are aware of— and thinking about— all of your actions and statements, the more you can manage them to be consistent.

Be Dependable

To build relationship power, you need to be a good friend. Being a good friend often means that you are dependable—that you are going to respond when others ask for your assistance. This has several positive effects on your future negotiations. First, it will build the perception of trust, as part of trust is assessing whether someone else is dependable. Second, it makes you more likable, as individuals who are there for others when they need them will be judged more positively. Third, over time, it changes others' rules for exchange with you, moving them toward generalized exchange. That is, they are willing to help you simply because of the relationship you have with them. When you make it a habit to be dependable, you obtain value from your relationships in the future.

> Trey has worked for the same company for 15 years. Over that span of time he has demonstrated his dependability as a coworker, as a boss, and as a friend. When Trey's son recently had to go to the hospital for an extended stay, Trey needed to negotiate with a friend to take his other two children for several days. Trey worried needlessly about which coworker might help him out. Once they learned Trey had this problem, four different people came to Trey offering help. Trey's relationship power at work was truly unbelievable to him and gave him so much value in this "negotiation," which never really happened.

Always Reciprocate

Because of the crucial importance of reciprocity (see Chapter 4), it is always important to be able to send the signal that "yes, I follow that rule" as clearly as possible. This can sometimes be accomplished by simply drawing attention to actions that you might have taken anyway. Instead of just paying for the cab because the other party paid for lunch, explicitly say, "Since you paid for lunch, I will pay for the cab." This removes any ambiguity and signals to the other party that you value and adhere to the norm of reciprocity. Similarly, it can be used in a normative way to make requests. For instance, if you share a piece of information about your interests or priorities on particular issues in the negotiation, you can explicitly invoke reciprocity by saying something akin to "I just told you about my interests on this matter. Would you be willing to tell me about your interests?" This implies the tit-for-tat reciprocity of information sharing. Such influence attempts can be very successful, especially if you have reinforced that you adhere to norms of reciprocity. The reason we mention this here, in addition to Chapter 4, is that following the norm of reciprocity can change the form of exchange and trust within the relationship. You are now seen as someone who is trustworthy and willing to pay back debts; this gives you relationship power in the future.

Share Experiences

Social exchange is built over time as a result of positive interactions. If you know that you are going to be negotiating with someone in the future, share experiences with that person *now*. You do this with friends, right? You spend time with them, and you likely solve conflicts with them as well. Part of the problem we have negotiating with others is that we lack the relational history. The more frequently we can interact with the other party, the more we can build the relationship. So, at a very basic level, to build relationships, we need to spend time interacting. In addition, the more experiences you share—particularly outside the negotiation context itself—the more the in-group perception can be activated, and the more you can benefit from all the positive benefit created by the identification and perceived similarity.

Find Similarities/Common Ground

In addition to creating new shared experiences that can increase identification and strengthen in-group perceptions, try to identify experiences in the past that may do so. An example of this is if two people who have just recently met discover that they were both in the army around the same time or realize they grew up in the same town, or share a friend, or went to the same high school. Any number of experiences two people have in common can increase the perception of in-group membership. By the same token, discovering shared beliefs, values, or attitudes can accomplish this as well.

> When Walker goes into a meeting with a new potential client, he always looks around the office for something he can use to establish similarity. While this can be something obvious like pictures of the family or diplomas, the absence of those things can also convey information. For example, when Walker met Naomi, he noticed no pictures of her family, and nothing really of substance to personalize her office. This made Walker think that Naomi was potentially a teleworker or otherwise wanted to communicate an identity of strict professionalism. He worked telework into the conversation and it turned out she had been teleworking for several years. He shared his experience with teleworking and this helped establish similarity between the two of them.

BENEFITS TO LEVERAGING RELATIONSHIPS

Perhaps the most compelling benefit to using relationship power is the fact that there is no direct cost; that is, no concession on any particular issue needs to be made in exchange for the value received. In one sense, using relationship power is a very "cheap" way of obtaining value in negotiation. It is important to remember that because relationships are based on the pervasive norm of reciprocity, there will still likely be a cost; the cost is just likely to be delayed. However, the intelligent negotiator will think about this future reciprocity as another opportunity for a mutually beneficial exchange.

Perhaps most important in terms of benefits, using relationship power may allow you to obtain value from negotiation that might not otherwise have been possible. Depending on the strength of the relationship, it might be possible to get another person to do something that they would simply not do using other (more convincing) tactics.

Take Erik, for example. Nobody would be able to convince Erik to do yardwork (e.g., digging, weeding, removing trees, etc.) for anything even remotely resembling a reasonable wage for such work. Even offering Erik far more than a normal prevailing wage for such work would not induce him to use his valuable free time on such unpleasant work. However, if a good friend asked for help with their yardwork, Erik would likely do so without complaint or any thought of compensation. That's the benefit of relationship power.

Someone might be willing to move to a town that they really do not want to live in if it would substantially help their spouse's career, or might agree to go to a Monster Truck show instead of the opera, even if they would never go to such an event on their own. It is easy to think of examples like these, that those with whom we have the strongest relationships (such as spouses and family) can influence us to do, that nobody else could make us do, no matter how much money or incentive were offered in a negotiation. This, of course, is the greatest benefit to using relationship power—the potential power that can reside in relationships. The stronger the relationship is, the more value can be obtained.

COSTS TO LEVERAGING RELATIONSHIPS

Earlier in the chapter we discussed the difference between generalized exchange and reciprocal exchange. In generalized exchange you don't need to be paid back—you are giving to the other without knowing if or when you'd be paid back. In reciprocal exchange you *do* want to be paid back, eventually. If one or both parties in a negotiation sees the relationship in terms of reciprocal exchange, it leads to a significant cost: reciprocity. If you take from someone and you see the relationship in terms of reciprocal exchange, you may feel an obligation toward them that extends into future interactions. If you give to someone and you see the relationship in terms of reciprocal exchange, you want *them* to feel an obligation to pay you back in the future. This creates messiness, as individuals are essentially "keeping score" regarding who owes what to whom and who needs to be paid back. Any misalignment in belief about the score or miscommunication could result in feelings of unfairness and a breach of trust. We saw the potential for this in the example of Gbemi and Meggan in Table 6.1.

One of the costs (or risks) of using relationship power is that it can eventually weaken or damage the relationship if not reciprocated. As discussed, positive social exchange is built upon successful reciprocity and exchange over time.[21,] If one party uses relationship tactics without future reciprocity, it will eventually strain and possibly undermine the relationship. Nobody minds helping out a friend once in a while, which is part of the accepted relationship that one has with a friend. But once the perception develops that one friend is constantly asking for help but is never available to help when asked, the relationship will be damaged and the potential to wield this power will be weakened or completely eliminated. ***Thus, relationships are a resource that can be used, but they also need to be replenished***.

Another downside is that this type of power—by virtue of its indirect and subtle nature—can be difficult to assess or manage. In other words, you may try to negotiate through the various mechanisms or tactics described in this chapter, but it will be difficult to predict the effectiveness of such attempts, and it may often be difficult to accurately assess the effectiveness of a particular tactic. As a result, in terms of planning to negotiate, relationship power can be unreliable. Clearly, the stronger a relationship is, the easier it should be to predict whether or not the other party will be susceptible to relationship power. This is in part because strong relationships are almost always based on a long history of interaction that not only creates a long sequence of reciprocity and obligation but also provides each party with a lot of information about the other party. But if we are faced with a negotiation in which there is no existing relationship, predicting relationship power as a function of perceived similarity, in-group membership, and liking is difficult.

Ironically, using relationship power to negotiate may affect the amount of relationship power you have. This is in contrast to expert power, which is not affected by whether or not you use it. If you influence someone in a negotiation as a result of your expertise, you still have all of your expertise. However, if you use relationship power to induce your parents to loan you money at a very low rate, or you sell your friend a car that had some undisclosed problems, using that relationship power to your advantage will likely reduce how much relationship power you have in the future. While not everyone keeps track like a bank account, individuals are perceptive to how often you use relationship power versus how often they use relationship power over you.

You can also imagine how this happens in the workplace. Consider the popular supervisor at work, who has a very good relationship with the workers on the shift she supervises. If she uses some of that relationship power to get the workers to work unpaid overtime, it certainly can affect the strength of that power in the future.

Cautions such as "Never lend money to family" or "Never sell a car to a friend" are often considered truisms precisely because you put yourself in a significantly disadvantageous position if you are trying to negotiate with someone who has significant relationship power. Because they can obtain a lot of value from you (unrelated to the issues being negotiated), you are far more likely to agree to outcomes that are far worse for you than if you were negotiating with a stranger.

Another problem when negotiating with relationship power is that it can shut down the ability to create value in negotiation. This is because those in existing relationships might be uncomfortable with the conflict inherent in negotiation and may resort to more compromise.[22,23] To create value, you have to accept the conflict and be willing to persist and ask questions about what issues are possible, what trades can be made, how individuals think about different valuations, and so on. Creating value takes work, and those with strong relationships might too often resort to the comfort of compromise, as discussed in Chapter 1.

ETHICAL CONSIDERATIONS

The optimistic view of managing relationships over a long period of time is that you are trying to improve how others see you. This attempt to improve others' perceptions of you brings happiness to everyone involved. When individuals have more positive relationships, whether in a professional or a nonprofessional setting, they have greater enrichment in their lives and find themselves to be happier in general. If you are playing a part in this, it means you are adding good to them personally, to organizations in which you share membership, and to society.

The pessimistic view is that you are manipulating others over a long period of time in order to get what you want in future conflict situations. You gain liking and trust through behaviors toward the other person, and at some point in the future they give you more than you deserve in a negotiation because of how you have come to get them to see you.

Which is correct? It goes back to your personal standard. Do you actually *want* to have positive relationships with others? Or are you just trying to manipulate them? If it's the latter, then there are clear ethical implications. Consider Henry Fonda's character (Juror 8) in *12 Angry Men* (1957). Is there any question that he is genuine? Not usually, as most viewers see him as genuine. The other side of this argument, though, is that (spoiler alert!) he ends up influencing (manipulating?) almost every other person in that room. Now, what if you knew that Juror 8 knew that boy and had a vested interest in getting a not guilty verdict? Would your feelings change? Probably, because now you may not believe that he is genuine. You may now believe that his motives are suspect. This is what you need to ask yourself, whether your motives support your personal standard and whether that is something you can comfortably live with.

Ethics Discussion Questions

1. How would you feel if you knew that someone at work was being nice to you because they wanted you to put in a good word for them for a promotion?

2. Unlike others who just ignore them, you say hi to the information technology (IT) staff every day on your way into your office. You always address them by their first names, because you know how important IT is to your job. One day the IT director comes to your office, closes the door, and asks if you'd like a $3,000 upgraded computer because the IT department got a demo version and no one is tracking where it goes. He specifically mentions how much nicer you are to the IT staff than others. Do you take it?

3. State whether you agree or disagree with the following statement: The key to a successful friendship (or marriage) is manipulation.

CHAPTER REVIEW

Discussion Questions

Read the scenario and answer the following discussion questions.

Meredith is deeply worried about her father's health, as she has witnessed him gain 30 to 40 pounds in the past couple of years. She would now like to negotiate with her father to change some of his eating and exercise habits in order to restore his previous good health.

Her father, Stephen, has been living alone since Meredith's mother passed away from cancer 3 years ago. Stephen had retired from a successful career in finance 2 years prior to that. Thus, for his first 2 years of retirement he largely nursed his wife and took care of the house.

Meredith is worried that her father is depressed, and as such her first goal is to get him to talk honestly with his doctor about what he is experiencing and feeling. She knows this is not going to be an easy conversation, but she is motivated to see this through and to help him, no matter what it takes.

1. How might Meredith approach her father in this negotiation? What can she do *prior* to the negotiation to ascertain her relationship power? What can she do *during* the negotiation to use her relationship power?

2. How would Meredith's stance toward her father be different if her father sees their relationship in generalized exchange versus reciprocal exchange?

3. Should Meredith be thinking about this negotiation as a "short" or a "long" game? Defend your answer.

4. If Meredith is seen as dependable, what are three relationship advantages she gains?

Concept Application

1. Think about how you are perceived by others. Do others trust you? Do others keep you informed of critical information? Do others seek your advice or counsel? Answering these questions will help you understand your ability to obtain value this way.

2. Notice how another person dresses, how they sit or stand, and whether they make eye contact in interpersonal situations. Understand how *others* are viewing this person and forming an impression of them. Report back to class what you notice.

3. Realize that using a relationship power is often a "long game" in that for it to truly take effect it may take a long period of time. That is, you cannot develop meaningful levels of trust immediately, nor are you going to invoke a strong sense of liking just by saying hi and appearing pleasant. These things help form initial impressions of trust, but the other party will be looking to your behavior in every situation (not just in negotiations) to confirm whether those initial impressions are correct or whether they need to be updated. Knowing this, how can you develop a long-term plan toward someone you know you are going to have to negotiate with in the future (e.g., a supervisor, an important coworker, or a parent)?

Role-Play Exercise: The Raw Form

Anthony Martonali is on the verge of securing funding for his newest restaurant venture, The Raw Form. He just won the pop-up restaurant challenge on the reality TV show *Pop Up Start Up*. With this exposure, Martonali could make the comeback he has so desperately wanted since he was forced to close his last restaurant to fight a battle for custody of his son. The negotiation, however, seems to be at a stalemate.

On one side of the negotiation are Anthony and his partner and best friend, Chris Gascol. On the other side of the negotiation are the two stars of the TV show, the people who judge and then potentially bankroll the restaurant: Jose Abbondanza and Jim Felicity. The way it usually works is that if the pop-up does well, one or both of the investors will offer a deal to the restaurateur. In this case, Anthony's restaurant did spectacularly well—100% of the people said they liked the food and would come to the restaurant regularly; this had never been achieved in the show's history. As such, both investors made an offer:

Jim offered $225K for 85% ownership of the business and would give Anthony a salary of $40,000 a year. After Jim makes his investment money back, Anthony would be able to buy back ownership percentage points (up to 50% total) at a cost of $6,500 per point.

Jose offered $235K for 85% ownership of the business and would give Anthony a salary of $55,000 a year. After Jose makes his investment money back, Anthony would be able to buy back ownership percentage points (up to 50% total) at a cost of $9,750 per point. Jose also offered Anthony 40% profits interest (i.e., Anthony is entitled to 40% of the growth in the valuation of the company should it be sold).

Both deals were compelling, although Anthony had originally wanted to retain 70% ownership (60% for him and 10% for Chris). Anthony also had to consider that Jim had less of a reputation and empire in the restaurant world than Jose. But the real problem, what caused the stalemate, was what to do about Chris.

About a minute after these deals were proffered, Jim said, "But let's get to the elephant in the room. Chris, we asked you to prove that you were worth 10% of this business, and from what I could tell, you are nowhere near worth anything close to that." Jose

then cut in. "We didn't see *anything* from you. So if you want to make a deal with me, you gotta get rid of *him*," Jose said to Anthony as he looked across the table at Chris.

They were putting Anthony in a tough spot, basically asking the man to cut his best friend out of a potentially lucrative restaurant deal. But this was business. And as both Jim and Jose told Anthony at the outset, Chris needed to prove himself. Chris was a high school history teacher with no restaurant experience.

"Can I say something?" Chris asked.

"No," Jose said.

"Let the man have his word," Jim interjected.

Jose cut him off, saying, "You had your chance. Restaurants are serious business, and I don't waste time with people who show up from the schoolyard wanting to bus tables."

"Please, with all due respect, I—" Chris tried to continue, but Jose just kept talking.

"Let's review, shall we? Anthony shows me his menu and it's fabulous. We agree to let him try his food in a pop-up restaurant. He agrees to manage the kitchen, and you say you will take care of the finances and the front of the house. But it turns out you can do neither.

"It takes you forever to do the food cost averages, and when we came to look at the food costs, you had numbers that *cannot* be right.

"Then we saw how you were a hindrance in the kitchen as Anthony was trying to prepare the food. We knew it meant you would be a hindrance when it comes to actually managing the wait staff. So Jim brought some of his people in to help.

"Then when you opened the pop-up, it became clear you know absolutely nothing about management. You had no plan for table service, table sharing, or plate sharing. In fact, you can't even clear a table properly. This whole operation would have been a disaster had Anthony been forced to rely on you for *anything*.

"About the only good decision I have seen you make is to shave that stupid braided goatee off your chin." Jose picked up his appointment book and spat, "If I bought the book of Anthony, this is the page of

Chris" as he tore out a page, crumpled it, and threw it onto the floor.

The four men sat in stony silence.

All of what Jose had said was true, and they all knew it. Chris had messed up pretty much everything he was asked to do. Chris had burned mushrooms, he almost ruined an expensive piece of fish by storing it improperly, and he cut tomatoes at a glacial pace. When Chris first met Jose and Jim, he had a braided goatee that was about three inches long. Jose had commented on it at that first meeting. Chris had gotten the hint and shaved it off.

"So Anthony, are you putting your friend before a business deal?" Jim finally asked.

"We need a minute," Anthony said to Jim after receiving the ultimatum. Anthony and Chris got up from the table and walked into the next room.

NEGOTIATING WITH MORE THAN ONE PERSON

While we often think of negotiation in terms of two people sitting across from each other, negotiations can take many forms. You might have negotiations in which there are multiple parties negotiating simultaneously, and you might have negotiations in which there are multiple parties negotiating but not necessarily at the same time or in the same room. You also might have a negotiation where you are one person in a team negotiating with another team. Alternatively, you can have negotiations where you are not negotiating but are represented by an agent who negotiates on your behalf. All of these examples introduce new dynamics and complexities that may change various aspects of the negotiation, which can have substantial effects on outcomes.

NEGOTIATING IN TEAMS

A common scenario is that there are multiple people representing each side in the negotiation, even though there may still be only two sides (i.e., two parties). This type of scenario essentially maintains the "classic" two-party negotiation but adds people to each side. The presence of multiple people on each side of the table introduces potential complexities of group psychology to the mix. Instead of an individual negotiator making decisions, processing information, communicating, and so on, we now have to worry about all of the effects of the group context on each side of the table. This in effect becomes two negotiations—one negotiation *within* the team on one side of the table[1] and one negotiation with the team on the other side of the table. There has been an enormous amount of relevant research on groups and teams over the past hundred years; to cover such information you need an entirely different textbook.[2] However, we can highlight a few of the most important effects that the addition of multiple people to a negotiation team might have.

- *Information sharing and communication.* Having a team at the table seems to have a positive effect on both negotiation process and outcomes, in part because more information is shared and more perspectives and potential solutions can be proposed by the additional individuals involved in the negotiation. The literature on teams has shown that multiple people can generate richer and more complex solutions than individuals.

- *Decision making.* There are many studies showing effects of team membership on decision making, including such effects as group polarization and "risky shift," conformity and normative pressures ("groupthink"), as well as internal information sharing and communication constraints. As a result, the effect of teams representing sides in a negotiation can be varied—it can range from very helpful effects that will facilitate creative thinking, richer problem solving, and consequently more integrative solutions, to negative effects that can result in suboptimal solutions as a result of biased in-group/out-group perceptions, conformity and defensiveness, and inaccurate and skewed decisions.

- *Conflict.* Introducing additional individuals into a negotiation scenario will by necessity increase the potential for conflict, as additional people may have different goals, interests, and positions on issues, as well as differences in personality, values, attitudes, preferences, communication styles, and many other issues that can cause conflict either within teams or between teams in the negotiation.

As illustrated, the addition of teams to a two-party negotiation can very much be a double-edged sword. Additional people can contribute to better information sharing, increased creativity and decision making, and superior outcomes.[3] However, being in teams can also result in increased conflict, biased perceptions and decision making, and inferior outcomes.[4] While teams being productive and collaborative is contingent on many factors, one key factor central to negotiations is that the team members have a *shared understanding* of what the team is, what the team's goals are, and what role each member is playing in the team.[5] As such, this can be an extremely important contextual feature that influences negotiations in substantial ways. The better negotiators understand teams, the more they can avoid pitfalls and harness the positive effects that teams can have on negotiations.

One simple piece of advice for those negotiating in teams is to take such negotiations *one at a time.* Negotiators who ignore the first negotiation, or who fail to treat the intrateam discussion as a negotiation, might find it more difficult to create and obtain value in the second negotiation. Of course, because each of these is a separate negotiation, all of the tactics, concepts, and lessons that you have learned about in this book can apply to both negotiations. Also, just because the team is involved in both negotiations does not mean you will necessarily use the same tactics in each. In the first negotiation, with your team members, you might use interest-based questions (Chapter 4) and intangible interests (Chapter 5). In the second negotiation, with the other team, you might use contingent contracts (Chapter 4) and a strong BATNA (Chapter 8).

MULTIPARTY NEGOTIATIONS

The overall dynamic of a negotiation can change completely not only with the addition of more people to the traditional two-party negotiation but also with the addition of more parties to the negotiation. Having four or five different, possibly independent, parties in a negotiation, for example, creates an entirely different context than the traditional two-party negotiation. A simple example would be a group of managers needing to negotiate a new staffing schedule. Each manager is a unique person representing their own interests.

In addition to various social effects (including those mentioned previously), there are also several unique effects that can occur when multiple parties sit at the same negotiating table. One of these is the increased amount of information to process; any one party may be concerned that their interests may get "lost in the crowd," so parties generally seem more eager to share their interests early, to make sure that everyone else at the table is aware of them. This can of course greatly help the negotiation, since a common problem is that negotiators do not sufficiently communicate interests and instead focus on positions (see Chapter 1). However, it can be overwhelming if everyone is trying to communicate at the same time! This invites other procedural problems such as how to structure the conversation, who talks when, who leads the negotiation, and so on.

Another unique dynamic that is introduced when a negotiation involves more than two parties is the potential for coalition formation. In the traditional two-party negotiation, power is distributed between the two parties. With the addition of more parties, the distribution of power can become much more dynamic and fluid, as parties can form coalitions in order to be more powerful and influential at the negotiating table.[6] Coalitions should always form around shared interests, and thus parties who share interests can gravitate toward such alliances. The tricky part is that parties may share interests on some of the issues being negotiated but not others, and resolving those differences can become a separate negotiation nested within the larger negotiation. Once we have multiple parties and multiple issues in play, it is clear how there may be overlap on some issues between some parties. This can create a complex situation for parties to manage, which once again illustrates the importance of understanding the interests and priorities of other parties. If not managed well, coalition building can be unstable and ineffective; for instance, if two or more parties try to develop a joint strategy around shared interests on two issues but fail to realize that they have divergent interests on a third issue. In such a situation, the eventual realization of their unresolved differences on the third issue could break their coalition and undermine their attempts to give themselves more power and influence in the negotiation.

It's also important to note that the issues involved in teams and in multiparty negotiations can "stack" in the sense that you can be dealing with a context in which both occur: You can have negotiations in which there are four or five parties, and all of them are represented by teams of negotiators rather than individuals. Predicting exactly how the negotiation process and dynamics—not to mention outcomes—will be affected in such a scenario is practically impossible. In such a complex context for the negotiation, your challenge is to have a sophisticated understanding of how this added complexity might affect the negotiation and of the potential pitfalls to be avoided. As with so many of the sections and chapters in this book, the inescapable conclusion always remains that the better-informed and better-prepared negotiator is always likely to do better in the negotiation. Start with identifying each party, the interests of each party, and how each party views the others at the table.

NEGOTIATING THROUGH AGENTS

Agency in negotiations—that is, having someone else represent you and negotiate on your behalf—can introduce a whole new series of dynamics, constraints, and possible conflicts. One of the most important questions is how closely aligned the interests of the principal and the agent are; this is a classic potential problem in agency theory.[7]

For example, questions arising from the relationship between real estate agents and their home-buying clients have been studied extensively. One potential agency problem is the matter of how the agent is compensated. A real estate agent typically receives a percentage of the agreed-upon sale price as a fee. This means that the buyer's agent, who is supposed to be representing the interests of the buyer, will actually make more money if the sale price is higher. As a result, there is a lack of interest alignment between the principal and agent, as the buyer's interest is in a lower price, but the agent's interest is (at least partly) in a higher price. This is an illustration of one of the most crucial issues that arise when using an agent in negotiations, and it raises obvious ethical questions.

As such, if you are planning on using an agent in a negotiation—or are required or pressured to do so—it is important to think very carefully about all of your various interests across all issues in the negotiation and consider if there might be potential conflicts between you and the agent. The more we can recognize potential conflicts ahead of time and attempt to resolve them (or clarify them in contracts), the fewer problems we may run into.[8] When using an agent, the onus is on you to actively manage the relationship—not only to plan ahead to try to anticipate potential conflict or ethical dilemmas but also to clarify how the relationship will function during the negotiation, in terms of factors such as communication, compensation, and decision-making authority.[9] The less clarity and specificity there is in the arrangement, the more potential there is for unanticipated conflict.

CHAPTER 7

UNCERTAINTY

CHAPTER EXAMPLE

Xue (pronounced "shweh") is an accounting major in the College of Business at California Central State University (CCSU). She came to the United States from China before she enrolled as a first-year student. Now in her senior year at CCSU, Xue has earned the dean's list six straight semesters and completed an unpaid internship in San Francisco at a "big four" accounting firm between her junior and senior years.

As graduation approaches, Xue starts looking at the job market. During her time in the internship she realized that, although she performed excellently, she was uncomfortable with the high-pressured environment of a large accounting firm. She is therefore looking for a position at a smaller, boutique accounting firm in Los Angeles or San Francisco, both because she has made many friends who are from those cities and so that she can easily travel back to China.

Complicating Xue's hiring process is that she has been in the United States on a student visa; thus, she will need any employer willing to hire her to also sponsor her on a work visa. She knows that her Chinese background could be advantageous to firms doing business with China. Finding a firm interested in her because of her background could help her travel to China occasionally and help the firm make a case for her to get a work visa.

After a couple of months of looking, Xue finally has secured a job offer with Buckner Davis Consulting, a firm of 400 employees doing work on the Pacific Rim in addition to California. This seems to Xue like an excellent fit. The home office is in San Francisco, and they have satellite offices is Beijing, Seoul, Tokyo, Hong Kong,

Learning Objectives

1. Identify the different types of uncertainty that might be present in a negotiation.

2. State in your own words how uncertainty affects individual judgment via sensemaking.

3. Articulate how and why differences in information impact negotiators, specifically via anxiety.

4. Predict how uncertainty will impact negotiations through estimates of expert power and tolerance for ambiguity.

5. Compare the relative benefits of data-based (objective) arguments versus non-data-based (subjective) arguments.

6. Demonstrate how to use the anchoring and planning concessions tactics in a job negotiation.

7. Critique the use of leveraging uncertainty in the context of the ethical implications of such tactics.

Master the content at study .sagepub.com/rockmann

and Singapore. The firm has committed to helping her get a work visa, and if they are unable to get the visa immediately, they've agreed to let her start work in Beijing and come back to San Francisco when the visa is acquired.

Here is an excerpt of the offer letter from Buckner Davis:

> Buckner Davis Consulting will pay a starting salary at the rate of $52,000 per year, which is appropriate based on the applicant's expertise and market conditions. This is payable in accordance with the standard payroll schedule, beginning June 1. This salary will be subject to adjustment pursuant to the company's employee compensation policies.
>
> The employee will be eligible for 5 days of paid vacation leave per year. Paid time off is additional to sick days, bank holidays, and days that the company does not operate.

Xue is confused and filled with uncertainty. She does not know what she should be getting and has no idea whether or not $52,000 is a good offer. She does not know whether the company is taking advantage of the fact that she does not have a visa. Perhaps they are discounting her salary because they have to do extra work to secure her visa? She does not know whether they are taking advantage of her ability to communicate in both English and Chinese. She does not know what offers other new hires are receiving and doesn't know who to ask to find out this information. She is worried about having only 5 days of paid vacation, as she would like to take time to visit her family in China. But perhaps this is company policy?

Most of all, Xue is scared to ask *any* questions for fear of ruining what might be an excellent job opportunity.

With the deadline to return the offer letter fast approaching, Xue signs it without negotiating further and sends it back to Buckner Davis. She begins her job as noted in the offer letter on June 1.

******

INTRODUCTION TO UNCERTAINTY

Negotiators never have complete information about a situation. Rarely is someone 100% sure about what their *own* interests and goals are, not to mention the interests and goals of the other side. This creates both a challenge and an opportunity. The uncertainty surrounding a negotiation means that information is critical, and negotiators who have more information increase their ability to get value from others, as well as to analyze how well or poorly a negotiation is proceeding. It also means that negotiators can benefit from another party's need to seek information, by trying to bias their perceptions and thought processes.

Obviously, if you are selling something, you want the buyer to believe that it is more valuable than it costs, and if you are buying something, you want the seller to believe that it is less valuable than it is. Similarly, if you are interviewing for a job, you want the interviewer to think you are even more impressive than he or she might think based solely on your résumé. Managing these impressions, or beliefs, is central to how to leverage uncertainty in negotiation, as the perceptions of the other parties at the table are crucial to getting what you want.

Uncertainty in Negotiation

There are some things that you know to be true, and others that you know to be false; yet, despite this extensive knowledge that you have, there remain many things whose truth or falsity is not known to you. We say that you are uncertain about them. You are uncertain, to varying degrees, about everything in the future; much of the past is hidden from you; and there is a lot of the present about which you do not have full information. Uncertainty is everywhere and you cannot escape from it.1

Have you ever felt a sales pitch working on you? Perhaps it's because there is a special coupon or offer? Or because the salesperson has told you something about the product you didn't know beforehand? Do you want to know why these tactics work? Because that salesperson is leveraging your uncertainty. There is something you do not know about the product or situation, and you sacrifice value due as a result of a piece of information given by the other side.

Ann's diamond engagement ring is slightly broken, as one of the prongs that holds the diamond secure has fallen off. She takes it into the jewelry shop where it was purchased. After looking at it, they describe the problem to her and tell her the price to replace it is $395.

What is going on in Ann's mind? When she walks into that store she has no idea how much it costs to repair a ring. They could've told her $50 or $500 and she wouldn't have known whether it was a good deal or not. What do naïve negotiators in Ann's situation do? They pay. They allow the salesperson to take advantage of the uncertainty they have when they walk through the door. Our goal in this chapter is to help you understand when you are susceptible to uncertainty as well as how you can leverage the uncertainty of others so you do not find yourself in this unenviable situation.

Uncertainty is one reason that so many people dislike negotiating and why they often feel anxiety and unease in negotiations. Whether you like it or not, uncertainty affects your behavior and perceptions in significant ways, so in a manner of speaking you are often at the mercy of uncertainty unless you learn how to understand it, manage it, and use it to your advantage.

Uncertainty is everywhere in negotiations. There is uncertainty with regard to the parties, the issues, the interests, the possible positions, the BATNAs, the resistance points, the power, and so on. Most of what matters in negotiations is unknown to the parties before they begin or even during the discussion, and so parties are left to guess about what others may be thinking. This is critical because in negotiations what other parties think and feel determines which of your tactics are going to be effective and which are not. If you don't know what others are thinking and feeling, you have a degree of uncertainty entering the negotiation and may be less effective as a result.

Perhaps you are uncertain about your *own* interests. Have you ever gotten into a conflict where you realized afterward you didn't know why you were arguing? One of the reasons that planning (Chapter 3) is such a critical tool in negotiation is because it helps you to think through why you want what you want. Planning reduces uncertainty. When we counsel students on their personal negotiations, they often make statements or claims like "I really want this car" or "I want a starting salary of $75K." But remember from Chapter 2, these are statements of positions, not interests. When asking probing questions such as "Why do you think that?" or "Why do you want that?" students often shrug and struggle to clearly articulate why it is they want (their interests) what they want (their desired position[s]). This line of questioning can lead them to realize that they don't really know why they want what they want. Knowing your interests helps reduce uncertainty, which helps you gain control in the negotiation. This uncertainty, as will be discussed in this chapter, leaves negotiators vulnerable to tactics from other parties in the negotiation.

In Figure 1 ("Negotiation Levers") in the Preface of this textbook, the bubble for Uncertainty is placed between a more understanding approach to negotiation and a more convincing approach to negotiation. This is because when you leverage uncertainty, you are opening the door to *both* understanding and convincing. It opens the door to understanding because reducing uncertainty gives you a great deal of information about the other side. Information about the other side opens up the many tactics that you learned about already in Chapters 4, 5, and 6. Leveraging the other side's uncertainty, however, can also help you convince them to change their mind about an issue, a position, or even you. Many of the tactics discussed in this chapter are described in this way. We start with a discussion of what uncertainty does to people, how you might recognize uncertainty, and then, of course, how to use it to your advantage to get more in your negotiations.

Knowledge and Uncertainty

This will be helpful to remember as you go through this chapter: ***Knowledge reduces, but does not eliminate, uncertainty.***

Doing research, anticipating problems, and planning help generate knowledge for the negotiation, and knowledge can definitely reduce how much uncertainty someone perceives. For instance, Ann could've called a couple of jewelry repair shops for quotes or searched online to get an estimate for what jewelry repair might cost. This knowledge helps Ann to know whether she is being fairly treated or not. But does this eliminate uncertainty for Ann? No. Ann is never going to know as much about diamond ring repair as the jeweler, and so she is vulnerable to statements such as "*Unlike other shops who use low-temp heat to repair the gold band, we use high-temp heat and the best rhodium to not only permanently bond the gold but make it look as if it were brand-new.*" How can Ann possibly know if this is true or not beforehand? Asking the salesperson to hold on a minute while she Googles "rhodium" on her phone might be impractical or embarrassing.

Take another example of a negotiation to purchase a new roof:

Trevor is buying his first roof. He is anxious about the situation and therefore has spent a couple of weeks doing research in preparation for the negotiation. He knows the type of shingles he wants and has talked with his parents about how much they spent on their roof. He has even gotten offers from some roofing companies through e-mail. Stephen, the roofing salesperson with 20 years of experience, has not met Trevor and doesn't really know anything about Trevor, yet he is ready when he shows up at Trevor's house.

What distinguishes Trevor from Stephen in this negotiation? While Trevor has prepared at length for this negotiation, Stephen has been conducting this negotiation in various forms every day for 20 years. No matter how much Trevor knows or thinks he knows, it is Stephen who has the upper hand in this negotiation and is the one who can leverage uncertainty.

Stephen is unlikely to perceive uncertainty in this negotiation because he "knows" that the actual roofing prices and alternatives are less important details than how he manages Trevor once he gets here. He is likely to be able to guess Trevor's interests and positions before he even meets Trevor. He will also know what to do with whatever information Trevor throws at him. His familiarity with the situation in general, despite not having any specific knowledge about Trevor, will make him better able to handle any uncertainty that Trevor throws at him. Trevor, on the other hand, is susceptible. Yes, he has research, but because he is anxious, he might forget to use it or forget the numbers in the moment. Or perhaps Stephen presents him with a "limited-time offer" and Trevor is unable to process quickly whether that is a good deal or not.

We describe Stephen in this case as someone with a more developed mental model of how this negotiation is going to go. As discussed in Chapter 1, a mental model is a cognitive representation about how something works in the real world.[2] In this example, Stephen's mental model regarding what happens in a roofing company–homeowner negotiation is based on 20 years of negotiating with every different type of buyer. We can think of Stephen's mental model as a professional-level playbook. Stephen is an expert; Trevor is not. Stephen has a prepared response to every type of action or tactic from any potential buyer, including Trevor. Although Trevor has spent a couple of weeks preparing, his preparation has resulted in a novice (only a page or two) playbook. Trevor has a set of tactics he is prepared to try, but if things do not go exactly as planned, Trevor will be faced with significantly more uncertainty than Stephen.

Uncertainty, Anxiety, Sensemaking

Uncertainty. Understanding how uncertainty can affect perception and behavior process ensures you can use it to your advantage and not have it exploited against you.

Figure 7.1 provides a very general model, outlining the somewhat predicable process by which uncertainty can affect a negotiator. Uncertainty creates anxiety in the negotiator, and that anxiety and uncertainty create the need for sensemaking, or the search to understand the situation. As people engage in sensemaking they will pay attention to certain pieces of information and ignore others. Using those perceptions, they will then make judgments about what is happening in the situation and use those judgments to guide their action and behavior.

Anxiety. One of the side effects of uncertainty, or not having information, is the tendency to experience anxiety or nervousness about the situation at hand. Negotiators worry when they don't know what is going on or what to expect. As a consequence, they feel threatened and anxious, which, unfortunately, creates a serious problem in negotiations. The research on anxiety suggests that cognitive problem solving and creativity are hindered when individuals feel threatened.[3] The brain essentially goes into protection mode, thus making it difficult to evaluate information, think in creative ways, and process large amounts of information. The problem is that negotiation is characterized by the need to make evaluations about information, think in creative ways, and process large amounts of information. Anxiety also causes us to become more egocentric and makes it more difficult to take others' perspectives, largely because of the uncertainty we perceive in the situation.[4] This egocentrism is crippling in negotiations, as we know that more options for successful resolution are possible when we can realize others' (rather than just our own) motives and interests. This is central to the understanding approach discussed in Chapter 2.

Because of this effect, the anxiety present as individuals engage in the perceptual processes limits the ability to accurately perceive information. As noted, this may be a problem for the party experiencing the uncertainty because the other party can take advantage of the uncertainty and anxiety to convince you to take less, especially if they

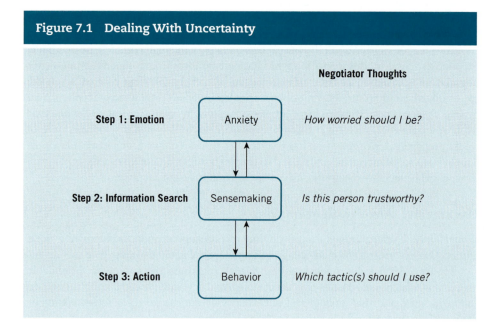

Figure 7.1   Dealing With Uncertainty

Negotiator Thoughts

Step 1: Emotion — Anxiety — *How worried should I be?*

Step 2: Information Search — Sensemaking — *Is this person trustworthy?*

Step 3: Action — Behavior — *Which tactic(s) should I use?*

are not experiencing the same level of uncertainty or lack of information. Take the following example:

> Lakshmi just got a job offer from CompuTech. When negotiating for salary, the vice president of human resources (HR) presented Lakshmi with a lowball (significantly below market) offer. Lakshmi was ready to add issues to the negotiation, including a new computer, training classes, and more vacation time, but when she heard the lowball offer, she suddenly got quite anxious. She scrambled to come up with an argument to counter such a low offer. She began to question not just whether she should take this job but also whether the issues she was planning to add were even possible.

In this example, not only was Lakshmi's outcome harmed by the surprise of the lowball salary offer, but the overall negotiation outcome was harmed as well. Had Lakshmi been able to pursue her strategy of introducing multiple issues with integrative potential (the ability to create value), both parties would likely have ended up better off. Instead, as a result of the anxiety she experienced, she reevaluated what was possible and decided not to ask.

Case Sidebar

Anxiety over negotiating is a major impediment to Xue in this case. Her anxiety stems from her belief that if she does not just accept what Buckner Davis is offering, she might lose not just this offer but also an opportunity to make a life in the United States. Her anxiety also stems from her uncertainty around anything having to do with the job market. She simply does not know what she is worth, and this keeps her from negotiating with Buckner Davis and seeking to gain a better deal.

Sensemaking. Negotiators, like all individuals in uncertain situations, have a fundamental need to make sense of their surroundings, a process some researchers refer to appropriately as **sensemaking**. The idea behind sensemaking is that individuals seek information in the context in order to figure out why things are happening. Sensemaking is marked by several features that are relevant to negotiation:[5]

- Sensemaking is inherently social.
- Sensemaking is ongoing.
- Sensemaking involves information search.
- When sensemaking, seekers prefer plausibility over accuracy.

The first of these characteristics has to do with the fact that individuals draw knowledge about their environment and contexts from others around them. In negotiation this process is going to occur primarily between the parties at the table. Second, sensemaking is ongoing, in that it is never a completed process. As we interact with other parties, we are continually learning new information that we then need to make sense of, form judgments about, and use to update our mental model of what is happening in the negotiation. This is why you see arrows going in both directions in Figure 7.1. Individuals are always trying to figure out what is going on around them so that they can feel more comfortable. It is that sense of discomfort, especially among those who don't like to negotiate, which causes individuals to resolve the situation. The problem is that the urge to make sense of the situation causes some people to agree too quickly on simple but ineffective solutions.

Third and fourth, sensemaking is about information search, and such information does not need to be accurate. Although not a negotiation, there is a classic story that illustrates the process of sensemaking nicely.[6]

> Susan arrives at the train station 30 minutes early. She buys a newspaper and a packet of cookies so that she can sit and do the crossword puzzle and have a snack while waiting. Because the station cafe is crowded, she ends up having to sit at a table with another person. This man looks like he is on break from his job cleaning the train station, as he is wearing overalls. As she sits down, she puts her packet of cookies and newspaper down on the table and picks up the section with the crossword. She realizes she forgot a napkin, goes to grab one, and then comes back to the table.
>
> Much to her surprise, when she gets back she sees the man eating from the packet of cookies. She is now faced with uncertainty and an extremely unfamiliar situation, and the following thoughts rush to her mind:
>
> - Did this man really just steal a cookie from me?
>
> - Why is this man eating my cookies?
>
> - Is he hungry?
>
> - What am I going to do now?
>
> - Do I confront him? What would I say?
>
> - Should I take my cookies and go?
>
> Not knowing how to respond or what to say, she confronts him by reaching for the packet, taking out a cookie, and very deliberately eating it, staring angrily at him. He does not react to her anger at all, and instead responds by reaching in and eating another cookie. Stunned, she can think of no other response than to eat another cookie herself. This continues, and the two of them alternate eating cookies, one after the other, until the packet is empty. Then, the man politely gets up and departs, leaving her sitting there trying to understand what just happened. At this moment, her train is announced, and she gets up to leave and picks up her newspaper and sees HER packet of cookies, which were lying underneath her newspaper the entire time.

In her haste to make sense of the situation, Susan valued plausibility ("He stole MY cookies") over accuracy ("I stole HIS cookies"). She is trying to make sense of the situation, and these types of immediate judgments are typical of what we do when faced with uncertain and unfamiliar situations. This is precisely why **stereotypes**[7] are so powerful: Stereotypes help individuals make sense of situations by placing images, people, and situations into familiar categories. **Stereotyping** is the attribution of traits, values, and motives to individual members of a group, based on generalizations about the group. Stereotypes are essentially cognitive shortcuts that our brains take, often without our being consciously aware of it. As Nobel Laureate Daniel Kahneman points out in his seminal book *Thinking, Fast and Slow*,[8] we often fall back on shortcuts such as stereotyping or in-group/out-group perceptual effects when we are faced with unfamiliar situations or are asked to make unexpected decisions. A salient negotiation example would be the assumption that all used car salesmen are shameless liars and only trying to take advantage of you. Entering a negotiation to buy a car at a used car dealership with such an assumption about a salesperson you have never met before (and know nothing about) might make your negotiation tactics and behavior more inflexible and less open to possible integrative solutions, resulting in nonoptimal or dysfunctional outcomes.

Now, imagine a similar sensemaking scenario in negotiation. A prospective client walks into a shop to inquire about buying blinds for her new house. There could be a great deal of uncertainty here, potentially having to do with how much blinds cost, who she will be negotiating with, whether the salesperson will actually negotiate, what the issues of the negotiation are, what store policies might be, and so on. She will be attempting to make sense of the situation, so she will seek information as soon as she walks in.

- How does the "look" of the store feel?

- What do the signs in the store say?

- Does someone come and meet me?

- What do they say?

- What do they look like?

- What does the handshake feel like?

- Do we sit or stand?

And so on. She is going to want to feel like she has the "lay of the land." Thus, she will form a mental model based on the information she perceives and then will update (sensemaking is ongoing) that picture based on additional information she receives later. Every interaction with a salesperson will potentially provide new information to help update her picture.

Information Asymmetry

The reason uncertainty and sensemaking provide a fertile ground for obtaining value in negotiation is because uncertainty can create a state of vulnerability for the people who are exposed to it. They need a framework within which to operate. If you provide them that framework, you can obtain more value. They are in effect searching for information, and to the degree that you have information and are willing to share it or use it in a strategic way, you can "shape" the perceptions and judgments of the other party, influencing them and the negotiation. This is an example of **information asymmetry**, where one side has more information than the other.

Think about someone who is impressionable, such as a child. Why are children seen as impressionable? A big part of the explanation is that they lack information about the world, and they are constantly striving to make sense of it. As an example, they may not yet know fully what a "stranger" may be, what normative or appropriate behavior may be, or even what opportunities exist for them. This is because their world is so, comparatively, small. When they experience something new, they are on the lookout for information to help them make sense of that situation. Should I feel safe? Can I explore? How should I behave? Adults who leverage information asymmetry to provide such information can relatively easily make an impression on children and change their behavior.

The same principle applies in negotiation. Being able and willing to provide information, or to use the information you have that they don't have, is to provide context for someone who might be in an unfamiliar context. This is the basis for signaling theory, the study of behavior when information asymmetry exists. Many of the tactics described later in this chapter center around how one side communicates, or *signals*, to the other side a piece of information they have (or do not have).[9] How the communication is received determines whether that signal is effective in getting the provider additional value.

Research in psychology over the past half-century has demonstrated that your behavior is particularly vulnerable to influence when you are in unfamiliar and uncertain situations, that is, when others are perceived to have an information advantage over you. As we have already noted in this chapter, most people engage in a negotiation to buy a car once or twice every decade, whereas the car salesperson does so as often as multiple times a day. To the car salesperson, the negotiation is a very familiar, controlled, and comfortable situation, whereas to the car buyer it is a very unfamiliar situation, filled with uncertainty and discomfort. This makes the buyer vulnerable. Uncertainty, therefore, is a big problem for negotiators. The more you can reduce your own uncertainty, the more effective you can be during negotiation, and the more likely you are to achieve your goals.

Tolerance for Ambiguity

There is an important individual difference which can change how susceptible individuals are to uncertainty. This **tolerance for ambiguity** represents how comfortable or uncomfortable an individual will be in uncertain situations.[10] Individuals who are more tolerant of ambiguity are more comfortable and calm in situations characterized by uncertainty and thus are more resistant to some of the tactics described here. The reason for this comfort is because individuals high on tolerance for ambiguity see such situations as challenging and interesting. On the other hand, the person low on tolerance for ambiguity will experience anxiety and stress and may seek to avoid such situations altogether.

This implies that the effect of uncertainty in negotiation will depend in part on one's tolerance for ambiguity. It is the anxiety inherent in uncertain situations which drives the search for information. If someone doesn't feel that anxiety, they will not feel the similar need of sensemaking and may not be paralyzed or indecisive in uncertain situations.

Tolerance for ambiguity varies across cultures.[11] In low-ambiguity cultures members prefer rigid rules and procedures to guard against future uncertainty or risk. In high-ambiguity cultures members are more comfortable with broader, less defined agreements and arrangements. When individuals are less tolerant for ambiguity, they compromise more;[12] this is not surprising given compromise is one way to *avoid* dealing directly with conflict. In general, Western cultures are less tolerant and Eastern cultures more tolerant of ambiguity. It may help you to think about where you are from and how comfortable you are with uncertainty compared with the person or people with whom you are negotiating.

Expert Power

Remember from sensemaking that negotiators are always on the hunt for information. To the degree that you have knowledge, or *expertise*, that the other party sees as valid, it will increase your ability to obtain value in that negotiation. ***As the old saying goes, knowledge is power***. **Expert power** is the extent to which individuals have knowledge or expertise that allows them to influence people.[13] This type of power is both variable and malleable and, as with all power, is given. Someone who has considerable expert power on one topic or in one situation will not necessarily have expert power on a different topic or in another situation. Just because you might listen to your college professor in terms of advice on conflict resolution and negotiation, you may not be particularly convinced by his opinions on bear hunting in Alaska. By the same token, the grizzled float-plane pilot from Alaska is probably not going to have a lot of influence over you when it comes to your salary negotiation with an investment bank. Your ability to obtain value based on your expertise is thus based on their willingness to believe in your expertise in a given situation.

Expert power can be changed. If one employee attends a particular type of training, she may become more influential at work as a result. Alternatively, a situation can change, suddenly making the information or expertise that a particular person has more (or less) valuable. For example, an HR specialist in a company may have little power despite being an expert on HR law and discrimination lawsuits, but that employee may suddenly become very important after the company is faced with multiple, very expensive lawsuits. On the other hand, an air force engineer who may have enjoyed considerable power as a result of expertise on the B-52 long-range bomber might have far less power in the organization once the B-52 fleet is retired and the air force moves on to newer and different technologies in which his expertise is no longer relevant or accurate. Both examples involve some outside event changing the value of a person's expertise;

in these cases the individual would do well to change their own expertise by pursuing additional training or education.

Having lots of expertise in itself does not guarantee negotiation success. It has to be expertise that (a) other people value and (b) is scarce or difficult to acquire. The more those two conditions hold, the more power is created by having that expertise. In terms of negotiation, you are more likely to believe claims made by someone who appears to have a lot of expertise. The perception of someone else's expert power (especially if combined with relative ignorance on your part) can make you particularly vulnerable in a negotiation setting. By the same token, the more expertise and knowledge you have, the more likely you will be to be able to get value from another party who does not have such knowledge. Again, as with everything else in the negotiation context, this all depends on perception. If another party *believes* that you have relevant knowledge and expertise, then you will have expert power over that party. If they do not believe that you have relevant expertise, then you will have no accompanying power, even if in reality you actually do have the expertise.

NEGOTIATION TACTICS

Doing Research

Because you need information to avoid being susceptible to low levels of uncertainty regarding the pending negotiation, the first tactic is one that occurs before the negotiation begins and continues to take place throughout the negotiation process; this tactic is doing research. Doing research means you are on a hunt for *unbiased* information, which is information based on data or other objective sources, not information that you choose simply because it confirms your prior beliefs. This could be information relevant to the issues at hand, the parties at the table, the background participants, the likely tactics to be used, and so on. Anything relevant to the negotiation could be a potentially important piece of information used to negotiate with the other side.

One important reason to do research is that having information will lessen your anxiety because it reduces the amount of uncertainty present for you in the negotiation. Doing research relaxes you rather than leaving you susceptible to uncertainty-fueled anxiety, so you hear the content of the message being communicated to you instead of being emotional, confused, and uncertain. This also reduces the possibility of buyer's remorse, in which you agree to something and then realize it was not a good deal.

So where should you go to get information? With ubiquitous technology, the problem is really more about getting unfiltered or unbiased information. Information that is unbiased is typically closer to "truth," and it allows you to decide for yourself what that information means (rather than having its meaning decided for you). This is not to say that you should avoid experts, who by definition will be telling you what they think information means; it is just to say that you need to be aware of their biases. Surgeons often advocate operations as means to solve health problems. They are not being self-serving; that is just the way they have been trained to solve problems. Table 7.1 provides some general tips on sources and their pros and cons.

Table 7.1 Gathering Information

Information Source	Pros	Cons	Suggestions for Use
Internet	Large amount of information; skill at surfing can unearth an amazing number of things.	Can be very time-consuming, and for certain types of research there is no verifiability.	Good place to get an initial idea of what is out there. Can tell you what questions you should delve deeper into.
Your network of associates (i.e., the people you know)	Provides detailed information that is probably easiest to understand and synthesize. You can also make good judgments as to the quality of the information.	People who know you tend to know what you do. Unfortunately the further out you go, the less well you know the person and the harder it is to assess information quality.	Best to talk to "weak ties" (i.e., friends of friends). This balances your ability to get understandable information with getting new information. Friends often just tell you what you want to hear.
The other party(ies)	They know best what their own interests are and where they are coming from in the negotiation.	Some other parties will try to deceive you regarding their interests. Some won't share information about their interests at all.	This should be your goal when you want to move to a more collaborative atmosphere in the negotiation. Also, it never hurts to ask someone what they want or why they want it—the worst that can happen is that they say "no."

Data-Based Arguments

Using arguments that are based on data (evidence) rather than opinion is more influential (see Figure 7.2). Actual data could be facts, figures, and statistics, anything that is defendable with nonbiased information. Data-based arguments differ from opinion-based arguments, which reside only within one person's mind and are based on one's perceptions. Data-based arguments are effective because they are rooted in logic, not perception, and are therefore more difficult to refute. Here are some examples:

- *Opinion: I don't think this offer is fair.*

- *Opinion: This car doesn't seem very high-tech.*

- *Opinion: But I'm worth more than that.*

- *Data-based: This day care center has the lowest sickness rate of any in our city.*

- *Data-based: According to our alumni survey, the average salary for students with my degree is $54,000.*

- *Data-based: Per square foot, this house is listed for $1,400 more than the comparable sales in the neighborhood over the past 6 months.*

Arguments based on data work under three conditions:

1. The other party has uncertainty about something in the negotiation and is looking for information.

2. The data used are seen as believable and credible.

3. The data are seen as relevant to the negotiation.

Take the following example of someone looking at taking a government job:

> Jessica leaves her job at Hi, Price, and Lawyers, LLC to go work for the Department of Justice. The fact that she used to get paid a lot more should help her argue for more money. Her previous salary represents a piece of objective criteria that is irrefutable. However, the government may respond by saying that everyone makes the same amount coming in. Again, this piece of data cannot be easily refuted by Jessica. Jessica is thus convinced by this objective piece of evidence to take a lower salary than she had before.

Figure 7.2   Evidence-Based Argument

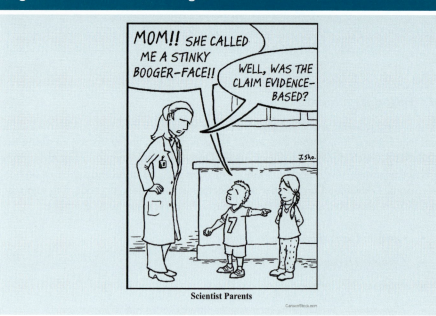

If we look at the three conditions with regard to the government, in order to assess whether Jessica can use data-based arguments, we see that perhaps the conditions are not all met. Although the government negotiator would believe Jessica's previous salary (#2), the government probably does not have a lot of uncertainty (#1) and probably does not believe that particular piece of data is relevant to the negotiation (#3). On the other hand, Jessica probably *does* have uncertainty, is likely to believe the government negotiator when he says everyone makes the same amount, and is also likely to think that piece of information is relevant. Because of this, the government likely is better positioned to use data-based arguments, and Jessica will probably lower her salary position.

Planning Concessions

One of the many things you can signal in a negotiation is how far you are willing (or not) to go to reach a deal. As such, when negotiating you want to think through your concessions carefully. You want to strive for mutual (both parties) rather than unilateral (one party) concessions so that you don't concede too much value. Negotiators who make smaller and fewer concessions tend to get more, as compared with those who make larger concessions and who make concessions more frequently.[14] Offering concessions is a way to reduce tension in negotiation, which can help the parties work together toward agreement.[15]

Besides signaling a willingness to work together, concessions in a negotiation also communicate information to the other party and thus can be leveraged to obtain value, especially when the negotiation is focused on one or two issues. When you give a concession of $100 off a desk you are selling at $200, it tells the other party you don't think much of the desk, at least at the $200 price. If you give a concession of $5, it communicates that you think the price should be very close to $200 and that you value the desk at around $200.

Similarly, when you give a concession of $100 off a $20,000 car that you are selling, it suggests you are *not* willing to move very much off the current price. One tactic that can communicate clearly to the other side how far you are willing to go is to decrease the amount of sequential concessions you make. For example, in a car negotiation, by giving a $500, then $300, then $100 concession, you communicate to the other side that you are approaching your resistance point. Table 7.2 shows how that might look for a potential buyer.

Notice that the amount of each concession for the buyer decreases from $500 to $300 to $100. This tells the seller that the buyer cannot go much higher, if anything, than $18,400. The seller, on the other hand, makes each concession $500. The buyer, by strategically reducing concessions, has conceded in total far less ($900) than the seller ($1,500).

Planning concessions like this is a nonthreatening way to communicate to the other side you are losing your willingness (or ability) to negotiate. Examples of poorly planned concessions are when a negotiator makes all concessions the same value (e.g., you continually give $500 with every concession as the seller does in the example in Table 7.2) or makes **unilateral concessions**, multiple concessions in a row without a concession from the other side.

Table 7.2 Planning Concessions

Opening offer:	**$17,500 (buyer)**
Counteroffer:	$20,000 (seller)
Second offer:	$18,000 (buyer, a $500 concession)
Counteroffer:	$19,500 (seller, a $500 concession)
Third offer:	$18,300 (buyer, a $300 concession)
Counteroffer:	$19,000 (seller, a $500 concession)
Fourth offer:	$18,400 (buyer, a $100 concession, accepted offer)

Opening Offers/Setting an Anchor

People are often timid about starting negotiations. They don't want to bring up the conflict, or if they do, they don't want to be the first to ask for something. Being timid puts you at a serious disadvantage because it lets others frame the negotiation in a way that advantages them. Alternately, a good negotiator makes the opening offer to **anchor** the negotiation because then the other party has to deal with that offer (even if they don't want to). The research is consistent in showing that, if you have information, you are better served making an opening offer, with an objective (data-based) justification.[16] If you can make an opening offer, you take advantage of the other party's uncertainty by placing the negotiation in your target range. This raises the question, what should the opening offer be? Ideally, the opening offer will be something that you can (objectively) justify that would (a) exceed your goals in the negotiation and (b) not anger the other side. Take the following example:

> Sarah is buying her first new car and has decided to be as prepared as possible. Once she knew which particular model and configuration car she wanted, she spent a lot of time and effort researching prices and finding information on the dealer cost. She found information telling her the invoice price of the car (what the dealer pays), as well as additional charges like the destination fee, dealer holdbacks, and other costs. She also found some information on what a reasonable profit margin for dealerships usually is. Armed with this information, Sarah concluded that a reasonable price to expect to pay for this particular car would be $20,000. Preparing herself for the negotiation, she planned to open the negotiation at $18,000 and expected that the dealer would probably ask for $22,000. Then, they could negotiate back and forth, making concessions and eventually end up agreeing somewhere around $20,000.
>
> When Sarah arrived at the dealership, she found the precise model car she was looking for. Much to her surprise, the salesperson mentioned that the price for the car would be $25,000, and it would be difficult for

him to come down much from that price. When Sarah expressed surprise, the salesperson told her that lots of people do research on the Internet and think they understand the cost structure of the dealership, but they do not take various additional costs into account. The salesperson explained that the dealership had to spend a lot of money on advertising, mortgage and utilities, the "appearance package" of the car, and labor costs to inspect the car to make sure everything was perfect. Sarah started to wonder if her estimate of $20,000 had been overly optimistic and that perhaps there were costs that she hadn't taken into account. Maybe, she thought to herself, $21,000 or $22,000 is a more reasonable price after all.

In this example, the salesperson was able to use a strong anchor to his advantage to make the customer doubt (and reevaluate) the information she had previously gathered. Because Sarah knows little about how a car dealership operates, it is difficult for her to refute the arguments that the salesperson is making, arguments that cause her to doubt the accuracy of her initial judgment.

Case Sidebar

Buckner Davis effectively uses the offer letter as an anchor in this negotiation. They not only give out the salary number ($52,000) but they include a statement referring to this as "appropriate based on the applicant's expertise and market conditions." Xue believes this is a strong justification. She has a great deal of uncertainty, thus causing her to believe the $52,000 offer is fair and reasonable. Buckner Davis has leveraged her uncertainty. She chooses to accept the offer rather than negotiate.

Another way to think about opening offers is to equate them with price tags. How do price tags work? By reducing uncertainty for the consumer and by giving the consumer time to decide whether he or she will pay that price. The price tag is thus the opening and final offer in millions of negotiations every day! You can use an anchor as a price tag. In a negotiation where the other side is not sure what to "pay" or what the issues may be in the negotiation, the opening offer fills in those gaps and, as with most price tags, goes a long way to determining the form of the final deal.

Using Expertise

Uncertainty exists not just about the issues in the negotiation but also with regard to the people involved in the negotiation, as we've discussed in Chapter 2 with BATNAs (best alternatives to a negotiated agreement). When individuals perceive that others are experts in a certain area, they convey to them a sense of power. This expert power works more effectively when there is uncertainty. Also, it works in the eye of the person without the expertise. They see someone who seemingly has a great deal of knowledge, which makes the person more believable.

Titles are one way that society often signals expertise. A researcher with a PhD or the title of "professor" is often assumed to be indicative of expertise. One illustration of this is a study that found that an overwhelming number of nurses (95%) were willing to give a dangerous and unauthorized level of medication to a patient, based on nothing more than a phone call to the hospital from a stranger claiming to be a medical doctor.[17]

Another way expertise can be signaled is with intricate knowledge of a situation. Take the following example of two car salespersons:

Salesperson 1: In order to finish the deal, I'd like to offer you a special deal on undercoating. We're running a special today, only $400!

Salesperson 2: Have you thought about how oxidation is going to affect your under-carriage? The reason I bring it up is because around here the county uses magnesium chloride on the streets when the temperature drops below 25 degrees. That chemical can get into the exhaust system and, within about 2 years, it can rot away. The cost to replace it is typically about $1,000. If you are interested in protecting your car, we sell an undercoating product at a fraction of the cost of replacing the system. Is this something you'd be interested in?

So not only is the salesperson framing the cost of the product as a gain (+$600), the expertise can be very convincing to a naïve customer who might concede to paying for the $400 cost. If the customer *knows* what undercoating is and that it's not worth $400, this lowers the customer's uncertainty and the tactic is not successful.

Framing as Gains

Individuals are more sensitive to potential losses versus potential gains,[18] a bias you can use to your advantage when discussing various offers. Individuals tend to respond in a *risk-seeking* manner when a problem is framed in terms of a possible gain and a *risk-averse* manner when a problem is framed in terms of a possible loss.[19] This builds from prospect theory, which has shown that individuals are more sensitive to losses rather than equivalent gains.[20]

When using the tactic referred to as **framing as gains**, you state your offer in a way so that it is framed as a gain instead of a loss.

> *Gain: My offer of $60,000 is a $10,000 increase over your last job and $5,000 more than we typically pay. We're so pleased to be able to give this to you.*

> *Loss: I'm sorry we can't give you $70,000. The best we can do is $60,000.*

Functionally this is exactly the same offer, but it will be much easier for the potential employee to accept the salary when framed as a gain versus framed as a loss. The "gain" makes the potential employee feel better about the offer and about what he or she is getting out of the negotiation.

As with the other tactics in this chapter, this only works when the other side has uncertainty about what is fair in the negotiation and what to expect on a certain issue. By framing the offer this way, you are helping the other party make sense of the concession you are giving, and you are doing it in such a way that it benefits you!

Cialdini mentions a study that demonstrated how a bias against loss resulted in different responses from people when given the same option but framed in a different way.[21] In the study, homeowners were told about insulating their houses. Half of them were told that they would save a certain amount by insulating and the other half that they would lose the same amount if they did not insulate. This first group framed the problem as a gain (saving money) and thus engaged in risk-seeking behavior (not insulating their homes). The second group framed the problem as a loss (losing money) and engaged in risk-averse behavior (insulating their homes). Service providers use framing to their advantage. Think about this the next time someone offers to do work on your house or a mechanic offers to do work on your car. If they frame the service as a potential loss for you, you might be induced to purchase the service, even if you don't need it.

BENEFITS TO LEVERAGING UNCERTAINTY

Since individuals are extremely susceptible to these negotiation tactics when they lack information, have uncertainty, or are in unfamiliar situations, there is clearly a huge potential benefit to being able to leverage uncertainty and use information to your benefit. The tactics described in this chapter (e.g., anchoring, planning concession, or framing as gains) can work extremely well to convince and better understand someone else, especially if that person does not have accurate information about you. The larger the "information gap" is, the more you can use it to your advantage. For instance, the effects of anchoring can be substantial, and there's little cost to an individual using such a tactic, since it requires little effort. By the same token, a tactic such as telling a potential job applicant "We provide a standard package of benefits to new employees" or "Salaries for your job category are not negotiable" can be incredibly effective; if the other party believes it, it can basically shut down their ability to negotiate.

In trying to defend (or "inoculate") yourself against these tactics when used by others, what really matters is to be able to discriminate good or relevant information from bad or irrelevant information. Having an accurate assessment of the other party's costs, for example, and a strong level of confidence in that assessment (as a result of an extensive search for information), will make it much harder for another party to influence you with tactics such as anchoring or framing as gains.

It has also been found that arguments are most effective when there is logic behind them.[22] In this chapter we have discussed the importance of having data-based, objective evidence to drive this logic. When you are able to obtain and use objective data, whether based on research or expertise, you force the other side to refute those data. And while subjective arguments are quite easy to refute, objective arguments are not. This is why, when you go to the boss to negotiate working fewer hours, you may want to show your boss a spreadsheet documenting all your tasks and hours spent on each task (more objective) instead of just saying, "I've been working a lot" (more subjective).

COSTS TO LEVERAGING UNCERTAINTY

One of the obvious costs to leveraging uncertainty is effort. The other costs revolve around the issues of consequences and ethics. The search for information can involve considerable effort. Although much information is readily available today—especially with the widespread use of the Internet, electronic databases, instant communication, and other technologies—there will still be instances when finding specific and relevant objective information may be quite time-consuming or difficult or may involve having to negotiate for that information (creating separate negotiations "outside" of another negotiation). So, as with any other behavior, you need to determine if the expected benefit of having additional information outweighs the cost involved in acquiring it. Of course, given uncertainty and a lack of information as a starting point, such a trade-off can be difficult to calculate until you actually have the information, creating a bit of a catch-22 situation.

The consequences of leveraging uncertainty and information can also be negative, particularly if we are talking about possible repeated interactions. Several tactics described in this chapter can be perceived as manipulative or dishonest. If one side is benefitting from the lack of knowledge or information of another party, or deliberately using the other party's unfamiliarity with the situation for benefit, this can be perceived as taking advantage. While this is just the reality of negotiations (that the people with better information can be more effective), remember that perception is everything. If the other party believes that you unfairly took advantage of them, that belief will obviously impact your next interaction, may even prompt retaliation, and will undermine trust, respect, and other factors that might be important for reaching future agreements.

ETHICAL CONSIDERATIONS

This chapter is centered on how to leverage uncertainty, but to some readers it might feel more like the art of manipulation. While the former seems mild and strategic, the latter seems unethical and very tactical. What is the truth here? There are two statements that we will look at in turn:

1. Leveraging uncertainty works because it can help you obtain value from others.

2. Leveraging uncertainty may not always be the *right* thing to do.

We discuss the power of uncertainty and information because it can help you get what you want in negotiation. When you have more information than the other side or are simply more comfortable with uncertainty, you will be able to use the tactics described in this chapter to get more negotiated value for yourself. The psychological basis for biases and heuristics is some of the most storied research that exists. There was even a Nobel Prize awarded to Daniel Kahneman for his work in this area with Amos Tversky in the 1960s and 1970s. Their intentions were to show how the mind works: how we take information from our environment, filter it, process it, and make decisions. It was a side effect that this same research can be used to one's advantage. This is where the ethical part comes in.

What is difficult about leveraging uncertainty is that some of the tactics are normative in negotiation; that is, some are acceptable for use in all negotiations. For instance, take the tactic of the anchoring, opening offer. Negotiations always have opening offers at one time or another, and it is well accepted that one or both parties will attempt to anchor the negotiation in their favor. Is this expected? Yes. Is this accepted? Yes. Is this unethical, to simply make an opening offer? Probably not. In this case both parties *know* that this tactic will occur, even if they don't know the advantage it will convey.

Where the ethics can get fuzzy is when there is information asymmetry between the parties, such that one party has more information than the other and that information asymmetry cannot be resolved by the party with the information disadvantage. Take, for instance, the following situation:

> Howard loved scrounging around yard sales and estate sales looking not only for fun and quirky items but also for the occasional deal on old collectibles. Saturday morning he arrived at an estate sale and briefly spoke to the middle-aged couple putting items for sale on tables set up on the lawn. He learned that the lady's father had recently died, and their mother was going into a planned community, so they were selling lots of things from her parents' house. Howard's eye was drawn to an old suitcase by the garage that had an old sword in a worn and damaged scabbard. He asked the couple if the items in the suitcase were for sale and if he could look at them. They replied that the items were definitely for sale, and it was just "old junk" that her father had held onto from when he served in the Pacific during World War II.

> As it turns out, Howard was a collector of old Japanese swords and knew that a polisher could repolish such a sword and it could be almost perfectly restored. When Howard removed the handle, he recognized the signature as that of a famous smith named Inoue Shinkai, who lived in the mid-1600s. A Shinkai blade, properly restored, would easily be worth $100,000 and likely far more. Howard remembered seeing a blade like this sell for $340,000 at Christie's auction house a few years earlier. The restoration would cost several thousand dollars, but Howard was certain that the sword was authentic, making it a minor investment for a gigantic return. Clearly this was a huge opportunity for a spectacular deal at an otherwise pretty boring estate sale.

> Other shoppers had arrived at the estate sale now, and the owners were busy answering questions and occasionally haggling over prices. Howard managed to catch the attention of the wife and asked her how much they wanted for the Japanese sword. "That old rusty, ugly thing?" she replied. "You can have it for $25 if you want it."

The ethical question here is painfully obvious. There is a huge information asymmetry, and it allows Howard to potentially purchase something that is likely worth hundreds of thousands of dollars for practically nothing. Is taking advantage of this huge information advantage unethical?

Some people might feel that the context (i.e., the matter of looking for a deal at an estate or garage sale) is all about finding a "hidden treasure" and so there should be nothing wrong with Howard's paying $25 and chortling all the way to his car. Others might similarly argue that, regardless of the context, it is always the seller's responsibility to engage in the relevant information search before selling something of unknown value, and if the seller chooses not to do so, then the opposite of *caveat emptor* applies, and the buyer has no responsibility.

That said, in this example, many people would probably acknowledge that leveraging the uncertainty in this case is undoubtedly a case of Howard's taking advantage of the middle-aged couple. If Howard is concerned that this is unethical behavior, there are obviously a number of choices available to him.

- He could tell the sellers that he believes the sword may be more valuable and thus would feel bad buying it for $25. Instead, he could offer them more, perhaps somewhere between $250 and $500.

- He could tell them that he is pretty sure that the sword is far more valuable than $25 and offer them considerably more, perhaps somewhere between $3,000 and $5,000.

- He could tell them that he is an expert on Japanese swords and is certain that the sword is worth a huge amount of money. He could then recommend that they spend a couple thousand dollars on professional restoration and subsequently have an auction house like Christie's sell it for them.

Whereas almost everyone reading the example would agree that Howard would be taking advantage of the sellers by buying the sword for $25, not everyone will agree what the "right" thing to do is in such a situation. Some may think that paying the sellers $250 for something they would gladly have sold for $25 is all that is required for being ethical in this situation, since they are now much better off than they would have been. Others may believe that full disclosure, and giving up *all* advantage that his superior information granted him, is the only course of action that would be truly ethical.

As mentioned earlier, it is definitely a difficult and fuzzy issue, precisely because much of business and trade is predicated upon someone being able to leverage better information into a profit. It could be argued that the entire principle of arbitrage and profit that underlies our market economies is based on information differences. As a result, the suggestion that people should voluntarily give up all or some of those differences in the interests of ethics becomes an almost unresolvable conundrum. On the one hand, part of the reason we negotiate is to get a positive and favorable outcome for ourselves, and "doing our homework" (planning and gathering information) is done precisely for this reason. On the other hand, as we pointed out in Chapter 2, both buyers and sellers value fairness, and as such there should perhaps be limits on how much we are willing to take advantage of information asymmetries and uncertainty.

While we can all agree that stealing candy from children is "wrong" (and most of us probably agree that Howard's buying the sword for $25 is not entirely "right"), it is far more difficult to agree on what is "the right thing to do" in a negotiation context that involves one party's having a clear advantage over the other in terms of information.

Although we argued in Chapter 2 that it is not our place to explicitly state what is "right" and what is "wrong" but rather provide a framework for the individual reader to determine what your own personal standards are and to act consistently in accordance with your standards, we do consider the situation of extreme information asymmetry (combined with the inability of one party to learn the information) to be a scenario that is almost certain to include the potential for unethical advantage. In such situations, it is important that the negotiator, who is able to reap positive outcomes as a result of a huge information advantage, be very sensitive to the ethical issues involved and make every effort to consider the ethical implications of taking advantage and consider perhaps instead how much advantage to take of their insurmountable information asymmetry.

One possible compromise in the sword scenario would be for Howard to fully disclose to the couple that he believes the sword may be extremely valuable and that it would be a good idea to have it restored and sell it. Then he could propose that he act as their agent, handling the restoration and sale of the sword in exchange for a percentage of the gain. Considering that the couple would have been willing to sell him the sword for $25 (something he might remind them of), it's very possible that they'd be willing to split the profit with him evenly. In such a compromise solution, Howard could still walk away with a huge eventual gain, but he could do so with an entirely clean conscience and not having taken advantage of anyone.

Ethics Discussion Questions

1. What do you think about the phrase "leveraging uncertainty" versus the term "manipulation"? When do you think it is okay to leverage uncertainty? What are the types of contexts in which it is definitely not okay to leverage uncertainty and why?

2. Have you ever been treated unethically in a negotiation because of information asymmetry? Do you think the other side knew that they had more information than you? If you end up in a situation like this again, what would you do?

3. How can you know before a negotiation is complete whether you have been ethical in terms of leveraging the uncertainty of the other side? Is this even important to think about before the negotiation is concluded? What if you find out after the negotiation that you had a clear advantage over the other party? Even if your intentions in the negotiation were good, should you go back and reopen discussions?

CHAPTER REVIEW

Discussion Questions

1. How will the uncertainty in each of these situations impact your likelihood of obtaining value? For instance, having a first interview for a new job versus solving a family conflict? How will the uncertainty in each of these situations affect the perceptual process and your likelihood of influencing and being influenced?

2. Why does making a strong opening offer help you in negotiation? If you are going into a job negotiation, how might you make an opening offer in a way that is open and friendly?

3. Does leveraging uncertainty necessitate being aggressive? Thinking about reciprocity and collaboration from Chapter 4, how might you use these concepts in tandem? That is, can you leverage uncertainty to collaborate rather than manipulate?

4. How should Sarah respond in the scenario with the car dealer presented earlier in the chapter?

5. How might you think about planning concessions if you are entering a job negotiation?

Consider this follow-up to the negotiation at the beginning of Chapter 4 regarding Omar and Delana.

Three weeks later, once construction had begun, Omar sent the following e-mail to Delana:

> I hope all is well. In talking to my team today about the progress, they mentioned there were a lot of additional personal trash items left in the garage and also that the shed is cinder block construction and not plywood like the garage. I wasn't aware that the shed was cinder block and instead assumed it was similar to the garage material.

I was hoping to dispose of all of this extra trash in our dumpster, but it's requiring another dumpster. I won't charge for any labor to cover this, but I was hoping you could pay for the dumpster fee of $700 due to the much heavier weight than I was anticipating. Please let me know if this is okay.

Delana, instead of getting upset at Omar for asking for $700, sees an opportunity to negotiate. She calls Omar and says the following:

> Omar, I'm going to be perfectly honest that I was surprised at your note. Not necessarily that something came up that was unexpected—after all, that always happens with construction—but because this issue was entirely avoidable. First, you mentioned the weight of the shed. I was a bit surprised at this because your foreman knew the shed was cinder block—we looked at it together. Second, I was surprised at the concern over the personal items. If you or the foreman had called me at work suggesting this would be an additional cost, I would've been happy to tell them to leave the personal items to the side.
>
> This request also concerns me because of the lack of communication. Is this something that is going to keep happening during the rest of this project? My neighbors have already seen the ARI sign in my front yard and are asking how things are going. I guess I'm trying to figure out what to tell them, and to do that I'm wondering if these sorts of "surprises" are going to be the norm.

Omar responded by telling Delana to forget about the $700, that it was his fault and that he should've brought up the issue of the weight much earlier.

6. What tactic(s) is Omar using here?

7. How does Delana counteract that tactic(s)?

8. Why is Delana able to counteract that tactic(s) so well?

Concept Application

1. Negotiate for something using only subjective (opinion) arguments as your main negotiation tactic. Now negotiate for something similar using only objective (data-based) arguments as your main negotiation tactic. Report to the class on the differences in ease and effectiveness between the two.

2. Go find advertisements that try to influence you using the tactics referenced in this chapter. Would you normally be influenced by such advertisements? Why or why not? Does knowing about the various biases change your susceptibility to these advertisements?

Role-Play Exercise: A Question of Value

This exercise is based on a real negotiation (names changed) between Chris Angelis and Charlie Peters. Chris is the founder and CEO of two companies dealing with respiratory health, and Charlie is an entrepreneur who has developed a homeopathic product. They are meeting to discuss a possible business partnership.

In Part A of the case you will serve as an advisor to Chris on the kind of deal he should make with Charlie.

In Part B you will learn the deal they *actually* made and advise Chris again on how to deal with emerging issues with Charlie.

In Part C you will learn how Chris responded to the challenges in Part B and advise him a final time on what to do now.

Finally, you will learn the ultimate outcome.

MEDIATION AND ARBITRATION

There can be numerous reasons for why it might be helpful, or even necessary, for you to have a third party become involved in a negotiation. Often the reason that a third party becomes involved is if the negotiation has reached a stalemate and you do not believe that progress is possible between yourself and the other party. Another reason may be due to a contractual or legal requirement. Labor contracts, for example, often have third-party facilitation written into them, in order to better resolve grievances or disputes. The legal system, by definition, involves a third party (the judge) if a dispute ends up in a courtroom. Sometimes, if there is very little trust (or a high level of suspicion) between two parties, a third party may be necessary to even get a negotiation started. Many famous diplomatic agreements between nations (e.g., the Camp David Accords between Egypt and Israel in 1978) are achieved with the aid of a third-party facilitator (the United States in the Camp David Accords).

The two most common types of third parties are mediators and arbitrators. Whereas both work to help manage the process and reduce conflict and disputes, they differ in terms of their effects on the negotiation process and outcomes. In simplest terms, mediators affect the *process* of the negotiation or dispute resolution directly and the outcome indirectly, whereas arbitrators directly affect both the process and the outcome. Thus, there is a significant distinction in terms of how much control you are willing to give up when using a third party. A mediator will help and assist the negotiating parties toward reaching a deal and might exert quite a bit of control over the process, but a mediator does not have any authority or control over the outcome. In contrast, an arbitrator is granted complete control over the outcome (in many ways like a judge in a courtroom), and both parties agree to give up control. The table on the following page provides an illustration of some of the differences between mediation and arbitration.

As you can see, arbitration involves giving up a lot of control, but it also provides a lot of certainty and structure, which can be attractive to some or might be appropriate for particular contexts. Mediation, on the other hand, can provide a lot more flexibility and many different paths to an agreement. Some mediators may provide a relatively rigid and formalized process, whereas others may primarily help with communication and facilitation but let the parties determine the process themselves. If you choose mediation, you will obviously be able to hire whatever mediator you like, depending on how much process you'd like him or her to control. Many people prefer the flexibility of

Table D.1 Mediation and Arbitration

	Mediation	Arbitration
Your control over outcomes	Full	None
Your control over process	Varies	Low
Formality	Varies	High
Cost	Varies	Moderate
Time	Varies	Shorter
Guarantee of resolution	0%	100%

mediation over arbitration, but it comes at the price of a loss of certainty and structure. If you choose arbitration, then you *will* have a solution, and it will be within a certain time frame. With a mediator, you *might* end up with an agreement, but there is no guarantee. The mediator can help but is powerless to force the parties to agree to anything.

MEDIATION

Mediation can range from the very formal to the very informal. In large-scale and complex negotiations, the mediator often needs to provide structure and exert some control over the process. For example, a mediator from the Federal Mediation and Conciliation Service (FMCS) assisted Major League Soccer and the Player's Union in their labor–management negotiations in 2015 (see box). In this collective bargaining agreement, there were more than 125 issues to be settled.

Major League Soccer . . . spent a couple of weeks locked up with this federal mediator the NFL and the players are using—and both sides left the building swearing by [the mediator] George Cohen. "I don't know that we would have gotten a deal done without his help and his very calming demeanor," MLS commissioner Don Garber told me Sunday night. "A mediator can't do the deal, but judging by our experience, he can get people to move off very solid ideological points to the center.". . .

It was interesting talking to Garber and two MLS stars Sunday night, Landon Donovan of the Los Angeles franchise and Seattle goalkeeper Kasey Keller. They're two of the most respected players in the league, and they, along with Garber, thought Cohen was invaluable in the process. "In most labor fights," said Garber, "both sides tend not to accept what the other side says at face value. I found George to be rational, calm and focused, with no vested interest except in trying to find a resolution. He ensured that all

(Continued)

(Continued)

voices were heard, and I think led us to an agreement that could help us grow the sport."

"Sometimes," said Keller, "it takes a third party to hear an argument for the first time and say, 'Look gentlemen, this is what I think is fair.' In our case, neither of us was flinching first. He gave both parties the sense that it was the other side giving in, and he was suggesting what was fairest to all. I can tell you that we all thought he was phenomenal."

In particular, one of the final sticking points for Cohen was to bridge the gap on minimum salaries—both for rostered players and for the MLS's version of practice-squad players, the developmental players. Minimum salary for active players rose from $34,000 to $40,000; developmental salaries went from $20,100 to $31,250. Cohen looked at ownership and said, in effect, You can't expect players to join a professional team for $20,000 a year. "That was a big deal," said Donovan, "because so many guys in the league either make near the minimum or have made the minimum."

Source: King, P. (2011, March 7). Financial transparency may be next step to the NFL finding labor peace. *Sports Illustrated.* Retrieved from https://www.si.com/more-sports/2011/03/07/mmqb

However, there can also be far less complicated negotiations or disputes in which a mediator might be asked to assist, in which the mediation might be far less structured and formal. For example, mediation could be something as simple as a coworker assisting two colleagues who are trying to resolve the question of who should get the newly vacated office with the large windows and the good view. The mediation might consist of little more than helping each party listen to the other, and suggesting possible solutions they might not have thought of, for example, one of them giving up their good parking space in exchange for getting the office. Consider the following example:

> Jack and his friend Hiram are working on a team project for their biology class. One day in class Hiram sees a text chain between Jack and his friend Emily on Jack's phone, in which Jack texts Emily, "Hiram is kind of stupid." Hiram is incredibly hurt by this but says nothing to Jack because he is angry. Jack is now wondering why Hiram doesn't want to work on the project. Jack has the idea to ask Emily to ask Hiram what the problem is. Hiram doesn't want to tell Emily but finally confides what he saw on Jack's phone. Emily agrees to tell Jack how hurt Hiram is and that Hiram is sorry for looking at Jack's phone. Upon hearing this news, Jack apologizes profusely to Hiram and shows him the entire text chain, in which he said, "Hiram is usually super smart, but on this Bio project Hiram is kind of stupid." He tells Hiram he never should've used those words to Emily and that he is really thankful that Hiram is his partner.

Because of the emotions involved in this situation, it would've been very difficult for Hiram to address Jack directly. Emily becomes an effective third-party mediator in this scenario, as she is able to transmit information between Jack and Hiram without the emotion were they to communicate themselves.

The benefit of mediation is that not only does it tend to be less costly than arbitration, but it also tends to result in greater satisfaction for the parties involved.[1] However, mediation is not always successful since no resolution is guaranteed. Several factors can affect how successful mediation is likely to be, the most important of which is the level of frustration that parties are experiencing. If negotiators have tried to negotiate on their own and have been unsuccessful, then they are much more likely to be open to mediation than if it is suggested earlier in the negotiation. However, timing is important. If too much time passes, animosity and frustration can result, and the parties may end up too angry or emotionally involved to reach a settlement, even with the help of a mediator. Especially when looking at diplomatic and political negotiations, researchers have used the term *ripeness* to describe the point at which the parties are sufficiently (but not too) frustrated for mediation to be most effective.[2] Another factor important to the success of mediation is that all parties have to accept the mediator. Some mediators have personal styles or process preferences that are not acceptable to all parties. It is also possible that one party might perceive a mediator to be unfairly biased, in which case mediation is unlikely to be successful. From that perspective, the choice to pursue mediation might result in a separate negotiation about whom to use as a mediator, because the person needs to be acceptable to both parties. As mentioned earlier, this is where the FMCS or other formal mediation service can be very helpful, especially for complicated negotiations with high stakes.

ARBITRATION

Arbitration tends to be more formal than mediation, in the sense that both parties have to adhere to rules and procedures, particular timing, and other factors, all culminating in a formal ruling by the arbitrator. Arbitration is common in labor–management negotiations, in contractual disputes between organizations, and in international commercial disputes. In many ways, arbitration is similar to the legal process but typically faster and less costly. In a typical arbitration, both parties have an opportunity to explain their side to the arbitrator and to provide supporting materials and evidence. Once the arbitrator has heard both sides and has had an opportunity to question the parties, as well as review any supporting materials and documentation, she or he will issue a ruling. Most arbitration (and what we have been describing so far in this supplement) is what is called binding arbitration in which both parties have legally agreed to follow the rulings of the arbitrator. It is possible for parties to use a third party in nonbinding, or voluntary, arbitration, which essentially follows the same process as binding arbitration, but the parties are not required to agree to the arbitrator's final ruling. This can be useful for the parties to get an idea of how an objective third party would view their dispute and could help to provide ideas for a settlement.

Arbitration can be very attractive precisely because of the certainty it provides. If you submit a dispute for binding arbitration, you *know* that a resolution will be found, and the timing will be predictable. The downside is the risk and uncertainty you incur when you give up all control over the outcome. The concern about a biased third party is going to be much more serious for arbitration than it is for mediation. If you do not like what a mediator who might be biased against you suggests, you can ignore the mediator. But if an arbitrator is biased against you, that may be a serious problem and could result in a bad outcome. As a result, the choice of arbitrator can become a very important, and possibly contentious, negotiation in its own right. Licensed or certified arbitrators will have a public track record, so the parties will be able to get some idea of a particular arbitrator's reputation. As arbitration is particularly common in labor–management negotiations and in labor disputes, it can be important to determine if an arbitrator is more pro-union or pro-management based on their past rulings. One solution to the concern about bias can be to include a list or pool of arbitrators in a contract, with both parties getting to choose half and then alternating between them as disputes occur.

A potential downside to arbitration as a specified method for dispute resolution is that the parties may not try as hard to reach agreement, because they both know that the potential arbitrator can just "solve" their problem for them. This might limit the motivation to explore time-consuming negotiation in order to generate creative and integrative outcomes. This phenomenon has been labeled the "chilling effect."[3] Another downside that can occur is that parties may feel less satisfied with the outcome and be less committed to implementing it. As a general rule, both in negotiations and in management, the more people involved and participating in a solution, the more committed they tend to be to that solution.[4] Sitting back and letting a third party impose a solution upon you can definitely make you less invested in it, since it is not a solution that you helped craft, nor one that you agreed to.

SUMMARY

For most negotiations you are not going to need a third party. But if you do encounter a difficult situation, or you perceive that you are simply not making progress and are headed for an impasse, then it is important to be aware of the different types of third parties and be able to figure out which is going to be most helpful for your situation. For some situations, one may be far more useful than the other, and choosing incorrectly could result in more harm than good.

It is also important to remember that third parties can be useful in all types of negotiation, whether it be high-stakes and complex negotiation (e.g., international relations and treaty negotiations or complex labor–management contract negotiations) or negotiation with far lower stakes and complexity. To illustrate the point, a parent might be the mediator or arbitrator for a dispute between two of their children. The issue of who gets to "ride shotgun" in the family car might be a trivial issue to the parent but could potentially be a time-consuming and acrimonious dispute to the parties (the two children) involved. In this case, mediation or arbitration on the part of the parent will likely provide a much quicker and better solution than leaving the two parties to fend for themselves.

CHAPTER 8

FORMAL POWER

CHAPTER EXAMPLE

Kyler and Steven work for a military contractor. Steven's job involves writing contract proposals to the Department of Defense. He also interacts and networks with decision makers in the federal government as well as other firms and subcontractors. Kyler is Steven's supervisor. Both of them served in the military before joining this company. Kyler was an officer, and Steven was an enlisted soldier.

Steven knocked on the door to Kyler's office, wondering why Kyler scheduled a formal meeting and why it was in his office. Normally, if he wanted to talk, Kyler would just drop into Steven's office, or they'd talk when they happened to run into each other in the course of a day. After getting no response to his knock, Steven waited for a moment and knocked again.

"I'll be right there. Give me a minute," he heard Kyler yelling from inside the office. Steven nodded to a couple of colleagues as they walked past him. "This almost feels like waiting outside the principal's office when I got in trouble as a kid," he thought to himself. After about a minute, he heard Kyler yell "Come in" from inside, so he opened the door.

As Steven walked to the small chair in front of Kyler's large wooden office desk, he was once again reminded of how nice Kyler's office was. "Maybe one day, I'll have an office this nice," he mused to himself. Glancing around as he sat down, he also noticed the number of diplomas and photos that Kyler had on his walls. Two photos in particular caught his eye—one was of Kyler in Afghanistan, posing for a photo with the general who was later to become secretary of defense, and another was of Kyler at the

Learning Objectives

1. Describe personal examples of when formal sources of power have been used in negotiations as well as the reason(s) why formal sources of power were or were not influential.

2. Distinguish between types of formal and informal power.

3. Clearly articulate the distinction between using resource power to understand others versus convince others.

4. Be able to give examples of actual power and perceived power and describe situations under which one or both can be used to obtain value.

5. Use tactics that leverage formal sources of power.

6. Calculate the costs and benefits of using formal sources of power.

7. Describe the ethical implications of using formal power.

Master the content at study .sagepub.com/rockmann

Pentagon with the vice president of the United States. Steven already knew that Kyler had been pretty important when he was in the army, but this was an impressive reminder. Speaking of impressive, the large framed graduate degree from Princeton on the opposite wall also really stood out.

"Hey. Steven," Kyler said, straightening up in the large high-backed leather office chair he was sitting in. "I asked you to stop by so we could talk a little about the MTG radar system that we're going to be bidding on."

"Sure," Steven replied. "I've been doing a ton of work getting that proposal ready. What in particular did you want to talk about?"

"As you probably know, getting that contract is a big deal to the company," Kyler said, and Steven nodded. "In fact," Kyler continued, "I was just talking to Pat the other day at the golf course, and she was saying that if we don't get that contract, we might have to consider some layoffs." It took Steven a moment to realize that when Kyler mentioned "Pat," he was talking about their CEO Patrice Morrison.

"I hope it doesn't come to that," Steven said. "My team is putting together a really solid proposal, and we think it will have a very good chance. We are doing everything we can."

"I appreciate that," Kyler said, "but let me ask you, are you really doing *everything* you can?"

"I'm not sure I understand," Steven replied, genuinely confused. "My team has been going all out on this project, and we all know it's a very important contract."

"That's not what I mean," Kyler said. "Didn't you tell me once that Chris Bushnell was a really close buddy of yours? I'm pretty sure I remember you saying that you saved his life in Afghanistan."

Now Steven was really confused. "Sure, I know Chris," he replied, "and yeah, we all covered each other's back in Helmand Province when things got ugly. He certainly thinks I saved his life, but nobody was keeping score. Why are you bringing up Chris?"

Kyler smiled. "You know he works at the federal office that reviews these contract bids, right?"

"Yeah, I know that, but he's not a decision maker or anything. He doesn't have any influence on who gets awarded the contract. He just reviews them to make sure everything is compliant and then passes them on to the decision makers."

"I'm aware of that," Kyler replied. "But most of our competitors have already submitted their bids, and there's still a week before the deadline. If he could give us an idea of their bids, just the bottom line, that would give us a huge advantage in adjusting our bid so we can win the contract. He certainly thinks he owes you a favor, right?"

Steven was quiet for a moment, multiple thoughts whirling in his mind.

"But that's totally inappropriate, Kyler," he exclaimed. "There's no way Chris could reveal that kind of information. He'd be fired for sure if anyone ever found out."

"How would anyone find out?" Kyler countered. "We would be the only ones who ever knew. Not even Pat would know. But if your team were instrumental in getting our company this bid, I am sure Pat would be very pleased, and it would be reflected in your bonus and would be remembered when promotion decisions need to be made."

"Come on, Kyler. I can't ask Chris to risk his job," Steven protested.

Kyler looked at him. "So, when you say you're doing everything you can to get this contract, that's not really true, is it? If we don't get this bid, and there was something more that you could have done, that probably would be something that Pat would hear about, and it might be remembered when we need to decide on layoffs. And if we don't get this contract, there will be layoffs."

******

INTRODUCTION TO FORMAL POWER

What is your first impression after reading this story of Kyler and Steven? Perhaps you are thinking that this is a *not* a negotiation. After all, they are not discussing salary or benefits or any of the typical issues you might think need to be involved in a negotiation between supervisor and subordinate. That is a misconception. This is a one-issue negotiation, as they are in conflict about how to proceed in the bidding process and they are dependent on each other. Kyler is trying to convince Steven to approach his friend Chris for inside information on the bidding process, and Steven is reluctant to do so. To convince Steven, Kyler has issued a threat to Steven's future employment at the company.

By now you know that in negotiations one of the approaches you can take is to convince others to do something or to believe something (see Figure 1 in the Preface of this book). This ability to convince others can be the direct result of power. The more power you have, the more potential you will have to convince others. This is why we spend an entire chapter on the concept of power. You need to be able to understand what power is, how it impacts negotiations, when it should be used, and perhaps (as shown in the opening example) how it shouldn't be used in negotiations. Power can take on many forms and can come from many different sources. In this chapter we will talk about the sources of power, why sources of power can be used to obtain value in negotiation, and what it means to use formal sources of power in negotiation.

What Is Power?

A very basic definition of **power** is the capacity to produce effects on others,[1] or the potential to influence others. Although power and influence are clearly related, in that one results from the other, it is important to distinguish between them. Power is the potential, or capacity, to cause change in someone's behavior, attitudes, or even values and beliefs. You can have power but choose to not use it. **Influence**, on the other hand, is the degree of actual change in someone's behavior, attitudes, or values and beliefs.[2] Of course, the extent of influence on others can vary quite a bit. You might change another person's behavior in order for that person to work an extra 10 minutes, give a dollar to a charity, or agree to walk the dog in the rain. These examples may seem relatively minor or inconsequential. On the other hand, you might change another person's attitude toward work, increase their motivation, or encourage them to pursue a promotion they otherwise might not have. It is even possible to convince people to change their values and beliefs. For instance, you might convince someone to vote for a different political party or believe in a new religion. At the extreme end, we can think of examples like the Nazi party before and during World War II, when leaders such as Adolf Hitler managed to convince an extraordinary number of followers to commit atrocious crimes against millions. These leaders held extreme power over their followers.

As the goal in this book is to understand what makes negotiators more effective—whether trying to convince your spouse to take the garbage out or convince hundreds of employees to become excited about a new corporate vision for the company—we cannot ignore the importance of power and how such power can be wielded.

Power Is Given by Others

The power you can use in negotiation is based on what other people believe about you. That is, power is *given*. A supervisor only has legitimate power to the degree that others see that power as legitimate. A parent only has resource power to the degree that the child sees that parent as controlling a valued resource. A salesperson has expert power to the degree that the buyer sees that salesperson as an expert. Power, thus, should be thought of as something that is perceived versus inherent to an individual. Consider the following example:

> You are just about done with your purchase. The salesperson comes back and tells you the following: "While many people think that the frame of the mattress has little to do with its longevity, our in-house research has shown that mattresses with the special inverted bow wood frame last 3 years longer, on average. We are running a special and can add this frame to your order today for just $399. Can I add this to your order?"

In this case, what is going to cause you to say yes to the salesperson? Whether the salesperson thinks he or she is an expert? No. You are going to say yes to this based on whether *you* think the salesperson is an expert. It is on you to decide whether to give the salesperson power in this interaction and consequently whether to believe what he or she is telling you. If you give him or her that power, you are more likely to be convinced and say yes to this service.

Similarly, just because you have power, it does not mean you can always use it to get more in negotiations. Power is just the potential to be influential.[3] **Potential**

power may be based on one's position or knowledge or other source of power, as will be defined later in this chapter. **Actual power**, though, is based on the other party *acknowledging* that source of power and their willingness to give you value as a result.

The more power others give you, the more options you will have in terms of what negotiation tactics you might use. If others give you no power, or only power from just one source, it will limit those options. The more options you have available to you, the more flexible you can be in your use of negotiation tactics and the easier it will be to adopt and tailor your tactics to the circumstances and the people you are negotiating with. As a result, you should always be aware of and understand where power can come from and what tactics different sources of power allow you to utilize. The better you understand your power and the power you convey to others, the more effective you will be at maximizing and utilizing it in order to get more.

Types of Power

French and Raven developed a taxonomy of power that provides a good starting point for thinking about power.[4] In Table 8.1, we illustrate their five sources of power and the extent to which we consider them formal versus informal. Some of this is review from previous chapters. Formality in this sense means how well defined, understood, and commonly known is the source of power by all parties involved.

As shown in Table 8.1, these categories are not always black and white in terms of formality. Legitimate power is almost entirely formal, and relationship power is almost entirely informal, but coercive power, resource power, and even expert power can be a mix of formal and informal sources. In this chapter we will focus on legitimate, coercive, and resource power. Chapter 7 covered expert power in more depth, and Chapter 6 focused on relationship power.

Table 8.1 French and Raven's Taxonomy of Power	
Type of Power	**Level of Formality**
Legitimate power	Formal
Coercive power	Mostly formal but can be informal
Resource power	Mostly formal but can be informal
Expert power *(discussed further in Chapter 7)*	Mostly informal but can be formal
Relationship power *(discussed further in Chapter 6)*	Informal

Legitimate Power. An individual's organizational role and status (and resulting authority) determines their **legitimate power**. The professor has the authority to assign students to teams and determine the class schedule, readings, assignments, and grades. The supervisor on the manufacturing line has the authority to hand out job assignments, determine who gets overtime, and report workers for disciplinary actions. The more the organizational members respect the organizational structure and identify with the organization, the more impactful such legitimate power can be.

Manager:	I need you to cc me on all of your e-mails to customer X.
Sales Employee:	Why?
Manager:	Because I am the boss.

The use of legitimate power in this simple negotiation between a manager and an employee acts as a real deterrent to any attempt by the employee to explore alternative solutions. By emphasizing rank and position, the party with the legitimate power in this negotiation is signaling that compliance is what is important, not creative thinking or alternative ways of approaching the issue. Notice that in this example, there is no threat of resource or punishment mentioned—the argument is based purely on the organizational role or status of the manager.

Legitimate power can operate via several mechanisms. Some might be convinced directly by respect for the position or the status of the person who is claiming legitimate power. However, it is also likely that when occupying the position, some resource or coercive power might be implied. So, although legitimate power in itself does not necessarily relate to resource or coercive power, some of the influence may be a result of the other party's inferences about such implied power.

Authority and Conformity. Another underlying reason that legitimate power works is because of the appearance of authority. A classic example of this is the Milgram studies of obedience. The study design involved an actor pretending to be the "learner" of a list of words, who would receive an electric shock at each mistake. The research subject was put in the role of "teacher," in charge of delivering a series of increasingly severe shocks to the "learner" at each mistake. As the shocks were administered, the subject ("teacher") would hear screams, yells, and pleas from the "learner" until finally there were no responses. Thus the subject believed he was in fact tormenting, injuring, and possibly killing another human being. The surprising finding from this initial study of male participants was that over two thirds of the subjects shocked all the way to the most severe setting, based on nothing more than a researcher telling them to do so.[5,6]

So why did they do this? After all, the subjects in the study were *volunteers*, meaning that there was nothing preventing them from either refusing to continue or just getting up and walking away. There was nothing compelling their behavior other than a researcher in a lab coat, instructing them to carry out the task of giving the electric shocks to the other subject. Particularly interesting is that Milgram asked colleagues, graduate students, and psychology majors, after reading a description of the experimental design, to estimate how many subjects would go "all the way" in terms of the severity of the electric shocks. The estimates, by what can be considered experts in the field, were that only 1% to 2% of subjects would give the most powerful shocks, and most would refuse once the actor started demanding to be released or started screaming. When Milgram described the experiment to 39 psychiatrists, their estimates were even lower, predicting that only 1 in 1,000 people (0.1%) would go all the way.

Milgram described the chief finding of his study to be "the extreme willingness of adults to go to almost any lengths on the command of an authority [figure]." This is a powerful illustration of how people with the appearance of authority can exert an enormous amount of influence on people around them. From a negotiation perspective, the perception that you have authority is one of the most valuable characteristics you can have.

Several researchers have sought to better understand *why* the subjects in the Milgram experiment complied with the authority figure. One study, for instance, found that individuals sought to *resist* the authority during the experiment.[7] That is, they were not passive bystanders willing to mindlessly shock the subjects; rather, they were actively troubled by the circumstances yet still found themselves conforming in the end. Although this gives hope that the soldiers at Abu Ghraib, for example, possibly tried to resist, in the end they still committed horrible atrocities.[8] Legitimate authority is more powerful than you think.

We can further see the power of conformity with the numerous tales of sexual harassment, inappropriate sexual behavior, and the culture of misogyny coming to light in the fields of entertainment, sports, business, and politics in 2017 and 2018. So many of the women tell tales of being "obedient," not wanting to question "authority," and "conforming" to the norms in the context in which they were placed. Did they *want* to engage in these actions? No. Did they feel the tension in the moment? Yes. Unfortunately, neither of these forces prevented the horrible behavior from occurring and in many cases reoccurring.[9]

If you are negotiating with someone you see as an authority (e.g., parent, boss, professor, etc.), you may be troubled by what you are being asked to do and may even protest, but in the end the power of conformity may be too powerful to overcome, unless you are prepared for this.

Coercive Power. **Coercive power** results from being able to inflict punishment on another. The playground bully, for instance, is able to convince other schoolchildren to part with their lunch money based purely on coercive power. Consider the same negotiation from earlier in the chapter. In this case the manager is using coercive power:

Manager: I need you to cc me on all of your e-mails to customer X.

Sales Employee: Why?

Manager: Because if you don't, I'll fire you.

This is the most straightforward example of coercion. The employee is convinced to cc the manager because of *fear* of punishment. The employee likely wants to retain his or her job, so he or she gives the manager what the manager wants. The manager can punish in a variety of ways, though.

Manager:	I need you to cc me on all of your e-mails to customer X.
Sales Employee:	Why?
Manager:	Because if you don't, I'll give you a bad performance review, which will prevent you from getting a raise this year.

In this situation, the manager is threatening a punishment along with withholding a future reward. We can see here that coercive power has overlap with the next source of power, resource power, in that the manager controls access to a valued resource: the raise. What separates coercive power is that it is tied to *fear* and *threat*. You are convinced to act because you fear some degree of punishment from someone else. In the same way, a parent might take his or her child to a fast food restaurant as a result of a threat of a tantrum. In this case the parent has *given* power to the child, to avoid the child's future tantrum. This is not wrong or right; this is just what happens as we negotiate power every day in our various relationships.

Resource Power. The ability to obtain value from others as a result of control over a desired resource is called **resource power**. Resources can take many forms in job negotiations, from the tangible resources such as raises, promotions, and bonuses, to the less obvious such as work assignments, schedules, administrative support, technology, to intangible resources such as praise or recognition. While resources are usually available to those higher in the organization, this is not always the case. It is possible for employees to control resources that higher-ups in an organization might value. A common joke in the military is that supply sergeants (those soldiers that supply the units with all of the things they need) have an enormous amount of power—despite their formal rank not being very high—precisely because they can exert a lot of control over valuable resources. So, although an organizational chart might not illustrate one's position as being particularly high or powerful, in practice, such a position can entail a large amount of potential influence.

The organization of labor into unions, for instance, is a way for lower level organizational members to gain power (see the **coalition** tactic later in this chapter). Employee motivation and morale are valuable resources to management, resources that the union can leverage in a variety of ways that management cannot. As a result, a relatively low-level employee in an organization may have quite a bit of power as a result of a higher level position in the union.

Control over resources is one of the most basic features of negotiation. Almost every negotiation is guided in part by giving and receiving resources. To the degree that the possession of those resources is valued describes how much power the party holding that resource has. In a job negotiation, the fact that the company controls the resource of the job often will cause potential employees to perceive they have relatively little power. This may or may not be the case depending on how desirable that applicant is to the company.

An exercise we often use in class is "New Recruit." In this exercise one student plays the role of a recruiter, while another student plays the role of the applicant. Each party has a set of priorities on eight issues and must agree on all eight issues for a negotiated agreement to be reached. One of the questions we always ask after the negotiation is complete is "Who had more power?" Applicants, particularly those who have not performed well in the negotiation, invariably say that the recruiter had more power because they had control over the valued resource: the job. What is often surprising and revealing to the students is there is nothing inherent in the case that gives the recruiter more resource power. This power is given by the applicant to the recruiter because the applicant is worried about not getting the job. Consequently, students who are working in human resource jobs often say the opposite—that it is the *applicant* who has more power. This perception comes from the day-to-day challenge of trying to find good people to fill organizational positions. Power is based on perception.

Note: Visit negotiationexercises.com to obtain "New Recruit."

Resources, as noted, like interests, can be tangible or intangible. A job is a very tangible resource. However, consider a negotiation between a husband and a wife regarding a vacation location for the family. The husband could have significant resource power because he controls his willing participation. Only he can provide that, and to the extent that it is important and valuable to the wife, he has some resource power in the negotiation. This illustrates not only the perceptual nature of power but the inherently interdependent nature of it. If the wife doesn't care at all whether the husband is happy or a willing participant, then his power to withhold that particular resource becomes irrelevant. If, on the other hand, the wife considers it of prime importance that he has to be absolutely thrilled with the location, then his power is obviously very high. Notice that his power in both cases is not only about his ability to control the resource but also about how much value the other party places on the resource. In some ways, simply economic supply/demand logic applies here—your control of the supply of a scarce resource is only valuable to the extent that there is demand for it.

It is important to remember that resource power is not just about frequently negotiated resources like promotions, bonuses, or desirable work assignments—negotiator power can originate from *any* resource that the other party wants or needs. An office assistant's control over scheduling of business travel, for example, might give him substantial power with respect to sales representatives in the organization who want to arrange their schedules in certain ways. Controlling a resource that nobody cares about gives you no power.

Reciprocity Versus Resource Power. Whereas resources are clearly used to leverage reciprocity (see Chapter 4), resource power describes the *overt* action to force others into a position by using resources or rewards. This is a very important distinction between Chapter 4, which focuses on understanding between the parties, and this chapter, which focuses on convincing between the parties. For instance, a manager who chooses to offer set rewards to an employee will develop a much different relationship than a manager who works with the employee on a mutual agreement of rewards based on mutual needs.

As discussed in Chapter 4, the relationship goal when using reciprocity is one of *equality*, based on the idea of exchange between parties. When we use our resources at hand and seek to understand the other side, we are trying to craft an agreement by which not only is each side getting something that they want, but each side is working together to achieve that aim. Here, however, using resource power implies there is really no goal of equality. As with the manager looking to be cc'd on the e-mails, he or she is not interested in understanding the employee; rather, he or she needs compliance and is using the resource to achieve that end.

Case Sidebar

One of the sources of power exhibited in the opening example of this chapter with Kyler and Steven is resource power. Kyler specifically implies that a bonus and/or a promotion could be in Steven's future if Steven is willing to break the rules and contact Chris, his contact in the government contracting office. This negotiation tactic could work if Steven wants those resources. Note the distinction between Kyler's actions and what we might expect of a boss using the tactics as described in Chapter 4. Kyler is clearly trying to use the resources at his disposal to *coerce* Steven to giving him what he wants. There is no spirit of collaboration, problem solving, or involvement of Steven as an equal partner to "solve this puzzle." Further, if Steven is planning to leave the company anyway, then Kyler's offer of a bonus or promotion would do little to change Steven's mind.

Expert Power. Expert power works in a variety of ways. First, if you have expertise or knowledge that others need, this is by definition a valuable resource. In this case, expert power overlaps with resource power. Second, expertise can come in the form of explicit certifications, degrees, or other formal professional affiliations that you may have. In this case expert power overlaps with legitimate power as expertise conveys the appearance of authority. Third, expertise gives you knowledge you can use to convince others. Using knowledge that others do not have is central to the idea of leveraging uncertainty (discussed further in Chapter 7).

Relationship Power. Relationship power, or what French and Raven term *referent power*, refers to the power inherent in the interpersonal relationship between the negotiators. As seen in Table 8.1, this is an informal source of power. With relationship power, you give power to someone else because you want to maintain or improve your relationship with that person. What underlies relationship power are relational features such as trust, respect, and liking. When you like someone, you are willing to give them value to uphold or support the relationship. When you trust someone, you are willing to believe what they say. Given the importance of relationships to negotiations, we devoted all of Chapter 6 to this idea.

Power Imbalance

Having more power certainly does not guarantee that you will be successful in a negotiation. In fact, if there is a large discrepancy between the power of two parties in a dispute or negotiation, it is possible that the more powerful party will force a solution on the less powerful party, and that solution may not be the most optimal for either party. Even though you may sometimes be able to impose a solution that you believe is beneficial to you, you may have inadvertently created a distributive agreement, whereby one issue is "distributed" among the parties (recall the zero-sum bias from Chapter 1). Unfortunately, the overreliance on formal power can cause you to miss an opportunity to create value and craft an integrative agreement, whereby multiple issues are combined in such a way that the solution not only benefits you, it benefits the other party as well.

Why does this happen? Having power makes you less likely to want to listen to others, and can make it more difficult to reach integrative agreements.[10,11] Having power also causes you to focus more intently on your own positions and makes you less likely to talk about, or even listen to, the underlying interests of others in the negotiation. Similarly, if you perceive the other side to have more power, you may acquiesce too easily on a particular position out of fear that the other side will use their power. Or perhaps you walk away from a negotiation that might yield a positive outcome, as a result of perceiving the other party as being "too powerful."

Case Sidebar

Part of the problem we see between Steven and Kyler in the opening example to the chapter is the imbalance of power between these two individuals. Kyler, with more power in this example, is neither listening to Steven nor understanding Steven's interests. Steven is quite worried about his relationship with Chris and about the ethics of what Kyler is asking him to do. Kyler does not seem to care as he is focused on winning the contract. At the end of this negotiation, instead of trying to use a tactic from Chapter 4 such as adding an issue, Steven is likely to walk away because he believes Kyler has significantly more power than he has.

This perceived power imbalance is one reason we often hear from our students that they are "afraid to ask" their supervisor a question about their job. In this common scenario, the supervisor has not necessarily done anything besides having the title of supervisor. The employee, perceiving a power imbalance, believes the supervisor might take actions against the employee if the employee were to bring up an issue. The mistake here is that in many cases these concerns about retaliation are completely unfounded. Rather, the supervisor (in the high power position) is simply not attuned to or aware of the employee's needs; thus the employee assumes incorrectly that the supervisor does not care about his or her needs. This causes the employee not to ask. When students ask us whether they should ask their supervisor for a raise, for example, our response is always "*I can guarantee one thing. If you don't ask for the raise, you won't get it.*"

Summary. One important observation about the different types of power is that any given situation will not necessarily involve just one. For instance, if a supervisor wants an employee to work overtime, there are a variety of options available in terms of how to convince the employee. The supervisor can tell the employee to work overtime (legitimate power), promise a future promotion for the employee (resource power), or indicate that working overtime might make the employee less vulnerable to layoffs (coercive power).

Power is not something that is vested in you (or something that you "own") but rather something that exists only in the interaction with other individuals. In other words, power is always relative and specific to relationships. You do not have resource power in general—you have resource power in interactions with those specific individuals that value resources that you control. Thus, when faculty are in a classroom with students, they have legitimate power in interactions only with students who respect their organizational position and the title as "professor." They have resource power in interactions only with students who care about their grades (or possible recommendations the professor may write or introductions the professor may make), and they have coercive power in interactions only with students who believe the faculty member can put them on a team they don't want to be on or can punish them for plagiarism and so on. It is equally important to realize that a professor has no resource power over a student that doesn't care about his or her grade or whether he or she passes the course.

Table 8.2 summarizes these underlying reasons why power works as a negotiation lever. Depending on the type of effect you want to create in the person with whom you are negotiating, it may help you decide which type of power to attempt to use.

Table 8.2 Why Do We Give Value to Others?	
Type of Power	**Reason**
Legitimate power	Desire to be obedient and conform to normative behavior
Coercive power	Fear of punishment
Resource power	Desire for rewards
Expert power *(discussed in Chapter 7)*	Uncertainty about situation
Relationship power *(discussed in Chapter 6)*	Value in the relationship

NEGOTIATION TACTICS

As Table 8.2 illustrates, there are a variety of ways that one party to a negotiation might try to use power to negotiate with another party or parties. What is important to note in all of the examples is that the use of formal power, such as resource, coercion, or legitimacy, tends to focus on acquiring the desired position(s) of the powerful party. This makes it far less likely that either party will make the effort to try to explore the interests that might be "under the surface" of the negotiation and more likely to lead to dysfunctional or inefficient outcomes.

Using Resources as Leverage

A common use of resource and coercive power is to use resources to get what you want—or to use the threat of the removal of resources as the punishment to get what you want. Particularly in organizational settings, employees, teams, and departments all need resources from other parts of the organization to be able to accomplish tasks effectively. Obviously, such resources can range from financial resources and budgets, to raw materials, to office supplies, to administrative or technical support and anything in between. For any resources that someone might need, there can be someone else that controls them, and this resource dependence creates the potential for power. As a result, individuals with control over desired resources can have considerable power.

Those resources can be used either as carrots (rewards) or as sticks (punishments), depending on whether or not the person in control is offering more resources as a potential reward for compliance or threatening to remove existing resources as a punishment for noncompliance. Both tactics can be effective paths to obtaining more value in negotiation.

The key with using resource and coercive power is that it is aggressive. To use this type of power is to imply, "If you want the resource, you will do X (resource), and if you don't, Y will result (coercion)." These types of power often coincide and can be the sole determinant of negotiated outcomes. One party knows they are more dependent on the other, and so they are willing to make a concession to placate the party with the power.

Consider Wal-Mart. Wal-Mart Stores (including Sam's Club) is one of the largest companies in the world. The sheer size of the company gives it an incredible amount of resource power. In negotiations with potential suppliers, Wal-Mart can be quite persuasive because the supplier needs Wal-Mart much more than Wal-Mart needs any one supplier. This is why Wal-Mart can buy at such low prices and offer the same goods as other retailers at severely discounted prices. Wal-Mart can simply say, "Unless you lower the price we will go with a different supplier." Is Wal-Mart using resource power? Yes. Is Wal-Mart using coercive power? Yes. Does Wal-Mart likely have a good alternative to any one supplier? Yes, although a good alternative is not required to be coercive (see BATNA in Chapter 9). Does Wal-Mart even need to make this statement to get more value in the negotiation? Probably not. The supplier already knows the power dynamic of the negotiation and has prepared to concede.

Sam's Club's buyers summoned major vendors (suppliers) to meetings and told them a "cost gap analysis" showed they should be delivering at a lower price and demanded millions of dollars in discounts on future purchases, according to e-mails reviewed by Reuters and interviews with suppliers and consultants involved in the talks. Unlike in prior talks, which featured give and take, vendors were told they could not ask questions at the meetings, with queries to be handled later via e-mail, according to suppliers and consultants involved in or briefed on the meetings.[12]

We can see in this story from Reuters the threat to Wal-Mart in using this tactic. Were another company to arise (e.g., Amazon?) and offer the supplier a better deal or choose to negotiate based on collaboration rather than coercion, the supplier would likely leave Wal-Mart immediately.

As in the Wal-Mart situation, dealing with formal power tactics based on someone's control of resources can be very difficult, precisely because of the dependence. If you need a particular resource, and the person negotiating with you controls it, then they do have considerable power over you. Exploring alternate sources of the same resource is one of the most important ways to reduce that power, but if there are no good alternatives, then every attempt should be made to turn the negotiation to the question of interests, as opposed to the other party focusing purely on trying to force you to comply with their position.

Using Legitimacy

Another tactic that can be used in the negotiation to take advantage of formal power is to use one's legitimacy. This can be accomplished, as described in the previous example, by simply saying:

I'm the boss/wife/mother-in-law/doctor/teacher, etc.

If the person on the other side of the table sees you as having that legitimate power and authority and values that legitimacy, then this tactic can be particularly effective. This suggests a boundary for this tactic—when the legitimate authority is perceived and valued. If you have a new employee in a retail store or restaurant and you need them to fold clothes or flip burgers, just tell them to do it. If they see you as a legitimate authority, they will comply.

You might be thinking that this is *always* an excellent way to get what you want if you are in that position of power, especially with children. That is a mistake. Young kids especially do not necessarily have a well-defined mental model of parent as legitimate authority, so when you say "I'm the dad" or "I'm the mom," they might just keep screaming. What kids *do* have a developed mental model for is resources—the things they want or like. If you threaten to take a valued item away, the child immediately knows the consequence and can be influenced accordingly.

Building Coalitions

Another use of formal power is the introduction of other people, or the threat of additional people, to the negotiation setting. One traditional way for a person of low power to increase their power in a negotiation is to ally themselves with someone else, forming a **coalition**. In this way the resources of the individuals are pooled together to better leverage power.

Manager:	I need you to cc me on all of your e-mails to customer X.
Sales Employee:	Why?
Manager:	Because I talked to all of the other people on your team, and they agree that this is important and you need to be doing it.

By bringing other people into the equation, the manager adds power to his or her position, because it is likely that the employee cares about what the other people on the team think. The employee is likely to be convinced by the knowledge that the members of the team agree with the manager, not only since it is necessary to work with them on a daily basis and a good working relationship is required but also because individual members of the team may have various types of power (not limited to formal power) over the employee. Thus, when the manager communicates that his or her position is shared by other parties, it strengthens the position.

The power of coalitions in a negotiation setting is a function of strength in numbers. If five parties are attempting to resolve a dispute, and three of the parties join forces behind one position, then clearly that position is much more likely to be the final outcome than if the five parties all supported different individual positions. When a coalition is formed, all of the various types of individual power that members of the coalition may have, in terms of resource, coercive, or legitimate (as well as all the other possible sources of power), get "pooled" to form the power of the coalition.

The key to building coalitions is to identify parties in the negotiation that have shared interests.[13] If two parties have the same interests on all the issues involved in the negotiation, then clearly a natural coalition exists, and those two parties can join forces without any cost to either of them and hopefully exert more power as a result of the joint strategy. More realistically, however, some parties to a negotiation may have some shared interests. They may partly agree on most of the issues, or they might completely agree on some of the issues but disagree on others. The key to building a strong coalition is to identify the issues on which the parties have aligned interests and then try to resolve or minimize the differences on the remaining issues. If substantial differences exist on some issues, then the coalition will break when those issues come up, so parties trying to build a coalition around one negotiation will often have to engage in separate side negotiations ahead of time (or during a break in the main negotiation) in order to resolve the differences on the issues that divide them. If they can do this, then they can (re)enter the main negotiation as a unified front and gain strength through numbers.

Invoking Background Power

Another common tactic in negotiation, using **background power**, takes advantage of formal power by one party mentioning that you are constrained by another party who has legitimate power. This is seen in the following example of a salesperson who is attempting to close the deal:

> If it were up to me, I would say yes to giving you a 20% discount, but I have to answer to my boss and I know she will say no.

In this case the salesperson is attempting to use the legitimacy of a background participant (the boss) to convince the other party to take a smaller discount. This tactic works when the buyer sees the background participant (the boss) as a source of legitimate power. This tactic also works because it shifts the blame for the offer to the background participant rather than the salesperson. This makes it easier to say yes to the salesperson because the salesperson is not the one saying no. Finally, this tactic works because the negotiator using background power is creating the perception of a coalition. If a parent is trying to convince a child that he is not allowed to watch a movie, that attempt is more powerful if the parent invokes the power of the other parent as well. This could be accomplished by saying, *"Both mommy and daddy say no."* This cuts off a potential recourse for the child: asking the other parent.

Managing the Impression of Formal Power

If you want to negotiate via formal power, it is in your interest to be perceived as having as much formal power as possible. Sometimes, the mere act of behaving as if you have power may successfully give people you are negotiating with the impression that you have power. Some of the ways to manage this impression of formal power include the fairly obvious, such as the placement of titles, diplomas, awards, and other recognitions. Power can also be assumed from other features such as office location, size, and the furniture arrangement within the office. Power can be assumed from behavior as well, such as being made to wait outside someone's office or standing while they sit.

Attempts to manage impressions of formal power can even involve material factors such as clothes, cars, watches, and so on, with the attempted implication that if someone drives an expensive car and wears expensive clothes, they must be an important person, which implies they are a powerful person. Obviously, some such attempts can be transparent, but on the other hand, if successful, such attempts can result in significant value, often unperceived by the other person.

Another way to manage impressions can be via subtle behaviors that people are conditioned to associate with high-status and more powerful people. Examples of such behaviors are interrupting during conversations, pointing at and touching other people, or staring and maintaining eye contact. In general, more powerful and high-status people are "allowed" to engage in such behaviors toward lower status individuals. As such, people who want to give the impression of power may deliberately engage in such behaviors to give the impression that they are more powerful than they really

In the case at the beginning of this chapter, you may have noticed that Kyler used a number of subtle tactics intended to convince Steven. He not only insisted on a meeting in his office, which forces Steven to have to spend time coming to him, but he also deliberately made Steven wait in the hallway for a few minutes, emphasizing that he is the superior and Steven is the subordinate, with the implication that his time is more important than Steven's. Furthermore, the office itself sends signals of power and status, not only with its size but also with a prestigious view. Furthermore, the large (leather) chair and large desk can be intimidating, sending the signal of power. Finally, diplomas and certifications on the walls help to bolster the perception of expert power, and photos of Kyler with very important and powerful people also suggest that he is a person of importance and, by inference, power.

All of these small actions and signals can have a cumulative effect and send the subtle message to Steven that Kyler is a powerful and important person. This will aid in Kyler's attempts to convince Steven to do what he wants him to do.

are. If they manage to create the perception that they are more powerful, then they will have gained some ability to obtain value, because power is very much a perceptual phenomenon.

BENEFITS TO LEVERAGING FORMAL POWER

One of the obvious benefits to using formal power is that it is very easy for people to understand. It is what most people expect in a negotiation, and so they are sensitive to it (as opposed to using interests or indirect means, which people may not "get" or may be suspicious of). A related benefit of using formal power is that it can be fast.[14] In some situations, time may be of the essence. There may be a window of opportunity that is closing, or there may be a deadline that cannot be missed, or other urgency. The use of formal power to force other parties to a resolution means that the situation can be resolved quickly.

Power also provides confidence to negotiate. Negotiators who have power have been shown to be more likely to make strong opening offers in negotiations, which results in more claimed value.[15] If you have power, you will be less worried you are going to lose and are thus less fearful about being taken advantage of by the other side. Power can also provide confidence to deal with difficult negotiators.[16]

Generally speaking, having considerable amounts of formal power provides a substantial advantage, but you must know how to use that power for maximum advantage. It is usually a bad idea to start by using power to focus on your positions—as opposed to interests—or force situations. However, power typically works (although sometimes with unintended consequences), so it is good to have as a last resort or as a way to break logjams or force people to come to the table and talk about their interests.

An example here is using formal power to reduce ambiguity that may have existed in terms of who actually has power. Sometimes, negotiations can be difficult—and can even result in impasse—because some parties believe they have more power than they actually do. If the use of formal power breaks those misconceptions, and by doing so, allows a resolution instead of an impasse, then it clearly has served a beneficial purpose.

COSTS TO LEVERAGING FORMAL POWER

One of the primary downsides to using formal power is that it is often based on positions rather than interests. By using formal power to convince the other party (or parties) in the negotiation to accept your position, or to accept a solution that is closer to your position than to theirs, it is very likely that the discussion of interests was limited. After all, if you have the power to force people to accept your position, why even bother talking about interests? Thus, having formal power can be a trap that actually prevents you from spending the time and effort to explore interests and alternative solutions because it is so easy to use that power to negotiate. In other words, if you rely solely on power, you are missing the opportunity to use the tactics from Chapters 4 through 6. This lack of exploring the interests of the other side could be one reason why groups with significant power dispersion struggle to reach agreement.[17,18] Negotiators who have power are also sensitive to retaining that power and may negotiate in such a way so as to protect their own power rather than work on a collaborative solution with the other party. In one study, negotiators with power preferred to delay discussion of consequential issues so as to protect any possible threat to their own power.[19]

On the flip side, however, *not* having power can also lead to more aggressive tactics in negotiation, as a low-power party seeks to use aggressive tactics to balance out the power in the negotiation.[20] This strategy is also not effective.[21] This is why we see the most successful outcomes with balanced power negotiations.

The use of formal power often "leaves money on the table" in negotiation settings, because more optimal solutions that might have benefitted both parties are never explored or discovered. One (or more) party has enough power to dictate the terms of the agreement—terms that the other side either accepts or counters. With either response, no interests are discussed and no value is created.

Another cost of using formal power is that it can substantially harm relationships and future interactions. Think about this. If you force someone to do something via threat, resource, or legitimate power, they are not likely to be happy about it. It should come as no surprise then that most people do not enjoy being told what to do or being forced into a particular behavior. For example, in one study of police officers, it was found that leaders who engaged in more *forcing* behaviors (using formal sources of power) elicited more negative and less positive gossip from followers.[22]

If the negotiation or dispute is a one-time interaction, with no likelihood of future interactions or negotiations between the parties, then perhaps you would be willing to have others think quite negatively about you in the end. However, if future interactions are possible, then the use of formal power becomes particularly problematic, because it is likely to harm your relationship with the person with whom you are negotiating. Some people are likely to resent it, whereas others may not even be bothered by it at all, depending on the situation and the context, as well as their personality, values, attitudes, and beliefs.

Case Sidebar

Although there is plenty of formal power illustrated in the example at the beginning of this chapter, there is also a lot of gray area. While Kyler is definitely Steven's superior, he does not overtly threaten (using coercive power) or offer specific rewards or resources. Rather, he *implies* that there may be rewards if Steven complies with his suggestions and similarly implies punishment if Steven does not. But the coercion is not overt, and although the entire conversation is clearly in the context of his superior role in the organizational hierarchy, Kyler never explicitly orders Steven to take action.

An interaction might involve just one type of power, but often a negotiation will involve multiple sources of power. The example of the supervisor telling the employee to work overtime "because I'm your boss" could just be an attempt to invoke legitimate power (on the part of the supervisor), but the employee might perceive a subtle threat of coercive power or an implied promise of resource power, and each of those types of power may help convince the employee to work overtime. If you are attempting to convince someone with resource power, but that person perceives your attempt to be entirely coercive, then it does not really matter what you intended—the negative consequences of a coercive power attempt are now going to color the rest of your interaction.

ETHICAL CONSIDERATIONS

Among the many ethical considerations to be conscious of when using formal sources of power, most relate to your own personal standard and whether your behavior toward another party (or parties) is in line with what you believe to be that party's "rights." As discussed throughout this book (e.g., Chapter 1), negotiators tend to be very self-focused in negotiations—very sensitive to their own actions and outcomes but not particularly sensitive to others' actions and outcomes. Thus what may seem a perfectly reasonable use of formal power (e.g., invoking formal position power) from your side of the negotiation may in fact be perceived as quite negative from the other party. The ethical question is whether you, if sitting on the other side of the negotiation, would perceive this to be acceptable behavior in negotiation. That is, when does it violate someone's rights to force them into a decision versus using another negotiation tactic? Consider the following examples:

Example 1: Debbie would like to take 2 weeks off over the holidays to visit family. She goes to her manager John to negotiate. John explains that it is very difficult to grant this request as there are many orders that come in over the holidays. Debbie says she understands but that her extended family has not been able to get together for 10 years and this is an opportunity that would be difficult to miss. John states firmly that she cannot take more than 4 days of vacation if she would like a job in the new year.

Example 2: Same scenario, but this time John states that if Debbie wants a favorable year-end review, she'd better be at work during her planned vacation.

Example 3: Same scenario, but this time Debbie states that she and the rest of the office staff know that John has been hiding losses in the office from upper management.

Do the actors in these scenarios violate the "rights" of the other? Do you think it is fair to Debbie for John to invoke his position in Example 1? Do you think it is okay to use resources as leverage as John does in Example 2 and as Debbie does in Example 3? When does use of formal power turn into blackmail?

Is using power to change the behavior of other people inherently manipulative? If it is, is that a problem? In our society, words like *manipulative* and *Machiavellian* have a negative connotation. However, if a manager's understanding of power allows her to be better at convincing employees to work harder, being more committed to the organization, and even being happier, is she not a better manager than the one who doesn't understand these things? The science on persuasion has taught us that if you want employees to work 2 hours of unpaid overtime, they will be much more likely to agree if you first ask them to work 10 hours and, after they refuse, ask them for 2 hours, instead of immediately asking them to work the 2 hours.[23] If a manager has taken the time to understand something like this and uses it to be a more effective manager, is that manipulative and bad? Or does that make them a better and more effective manager? Ultimately, negotiation is about getting people to do things they otherwise might not do or even want to do. So, there is really no way around the reality that negotiation is inherently manipulative.

Being ethically considerate means being able to view situations through various lenses, namely, from your own perspective and from the perspective of others. Being able to engage in this perspective taking will help you see the ethical consequences of your own actions.

Ethics Discussion Questions

1. Do you believe Kyler acted ethically in the example that opens this chapter? If you believe Kyler behaved unethically, at what point in the example does he go from being ethical to being unethical?

2. What negotiation tactics related to using power have the most potential to be unethical? Why?

3. What does your own personal standard say about using the formal power negotiation tactics?

4. We learn in kindergarten the golden rule: to treat others like we would like to be treated. Does that saying impact the tactics you would choose to use in different power-based negotiations?

CHAPTER REVIEW

Discussion Questions

1. Can you leverage power even if people do not like you and do not respect you? How? What are the consequences of using your power?

2. Are there any downsides to having a lot of power compared to the other party (i.e., having a power imbalance)? If you are the powerful party in a negotiation, what are ways that you might be able to minimize or mitigate such downsides?

3. List some ways that you might be able to increase your power to get more value in negotiations you typically face.

4. What would you suggest Steven should do, following his meeting with Kyler? What could Steven have done differently during the meeting?

Concept Application

1. Negotiate at a retail store using formal power. You can negotiate for different things, and you can use more than one kind of power with the same person, but you *must* only use one kind of power for each issue you negotiate. Report to the class on what was effective or not effective about using the different kinds of formal power.

2. Negotiate with two different people, but use the same leverage as a carrot in one instance and a stick in the other. That is, in the first situation offer a reward that you control (the carrot). In the second situation offer a punishment that you control (the stick). Report to the class how these compared in terms of obtaining value in the negotiation and relationship more generally.

Role-Play Exercise: Nuclear

Nuclear power is not the preferred method of energy production in the United States. Due to a relative abundance of fossil fuels, as well as considerable public apprehension about potential dangers and risks, nuclear power accounts for less than 20% of total energy production in the United States. Nuclear disasters at Chernobyl in 1986 and Fukushima in 2011, and to a lesser extent Three Mile Island in 1979, have resulted in increased regulation of nuclear power plants, which has inflated operational costs and led to hard economic times for companies involved in nuclear energy production. In addition, there have been severe cutbacks in funding for nuclear energy research since the mid-1980s. All of these factors have led to a general disillusionment, both on the part of investors and of the public, with nuclear power as a viable energy source.

NuclearTech, a division of a large multinational corporation involved in energy production as well as high technology manufacturing, design and research, hopes that its new type of reactor design will revitalize the nuclear power industry. Central to their design is a new type of fuel rod which they believe will alleviate many of the concerns and potential problems associated with nuclear energy. Early last year, NuclearTech secured a large contact to construct a power plant using their new technology, as well as a new breeder reactor and a fuel storage site. The planned breeder reactor and storage facility would allow for production of the new fuel rods, giving NuclearTech a significant advantage if and when such fuel rods become the new standard for nuclear power generation (which they firmly believe will happen).

NuclearTech has already hired two main subcontractors to do the bulk of the work on this project; BR Solutions, and SL Inc. Both are highly reputable companies in the nuclear construction business, and NuclearTech has used them as contractors in the past. Work on this project has already begun, with preliminary sub-contracts issued last year to BR Solutions and SL Inc., who both very much would like to be the primary sub-contractor on this project. Both firms are also very interested in securing additional specialized sub-contracts that NuclearTech has not awarded yet.

Another company in the nuclear business is NucRes, who has claimed that NuclearTech (and indirectly their sub-contractors) are using designs and technology that infringe on patents and intellectual property belonging to them. They have threatened lawsuits as well as complaints to the Nuclear Regulatory Commission (NRC), but are willing to sit down and talk about alternative solutions before taking those steps.

The Nuclear Regulatory Commission (NRC) is very interested in the construction of new nuclear facilities, and want to be absolutely sure that everything is done according to existing rules and regulations. Given the safety potential of NuclearTech's new design, the NRC is open to the possibility of relaxing some regulatory constraints, which is ultimately what would allow this technology to make nuclear energy much more profitable. At the same time, however, they are also quite concerned that BR Solutions and SL Inc. apparently did not fully comply with existing regulations in the work they have already done for NuclearTech, which will result in fines against either them or NuclearTech, or both.

Out of a desire to resolve these issues, including the questions of who will be the main subcontractor, what can be done to resolve the dispute with NucRes, how to reassure the NRC and determine possible fines – as well as other issues – NuclearTech has requested a meeting of all the involved parties. This meeting will be between representatives from NuclearTech, BR Solutions, SL Inc., and NucRes as well as the NRC. Hopefully, by having all five parties meet together, a comprehensive agreement can be found that will allow the project to move forward quickly and smoothly.

"HARDBALL" TACTICS OF NEGOTIATION

In this section we discuss some of the most common hardball tactics, or "dirty tricks," that you may encounter in a negotiation situation. They are briefly described and are followed by some suggestions on how to respond to them, as well as the strengths and weaknesses of each.

"Beware of the dark side." Always good advice when faced with such tactics even if you're not a Jedi. Do not give in to anger, and do not immediately respond or react unless you can do so with a cool head. Taking a break and asking for a brief recess to give yourself time to think instead of immediately reacting can be very useful. Silence can also be very helpful—giving yourself time to calm down and think about a response, as well as confusing the other party who may have expected a particular response.

Choosing the best way to respond to a hardball tactic will depend on your specific goals as well as the broader context of the negotiation. For example, very different behaviors and tactics may be appropriate (and even expected) in negotiating the price of a used car as compared to negotiating a salary and benefits package with a prospective employer or negotiating with a supplier on behalf of your company. Whom you are negotiating with, what type of relationship you have with them, and your own BATNA will influence how you choose to respond. If your BATNA is terrible, for example, you may respond very differently to a particular tactic than if you have very good alternatives.

GOOD COP/BAD COP

Situation: In this classic situation you are negotiating with two people on the other side. One of them (often a superior, or someone who appears to have authority over the outcome) takes a hard line (the "bad cop"), and the other then appears conciliatory (the "good cop") in order to gain concessions by appearing reasonable in comparison. This happens frequently in car negotiations where the salesperson would like to be seen as the "good cop" while the manager or finance person is the "bad cop." The tactic is designed to lower your aspiration level and to have you reciprocate the reasonableness of the "good cop."

Why this works: This tactic works because of the contrast effect. You are so happy not to be dealing with the "bad cop" that you readily agree to work with the "good cop," who doesn't really have your interests at heart.[1]

Suggestions for dealing with the tactic:

- Once a "bad cop" enters the picture, assume that everyone you're dealing with (no matter how seemingly benign) is a "bad cop".

- Remember your prenegotiation plan.

- Suggest a recess to consider the new demands, but offer no concessions on your return.

- Bring in your own "bad cop".

- Ask for data-based justification or an other objective standard.

- Ask for the "good cop" (e.g., salesperson) and "bad cop" (e.g., manager) to resolve differences between themselves.

- Call the tactic. Explain that you see what is happening and suggest an alternative bargaining strategy.

LIMITED AUTHORITY

Situation: The other side offers a deal but then claims to lack authority to go beyond certain levels or limits. The claim is made that additional approval would be needed to go beyond such limits. This is an extreme version of the invoking background power tactic from Chapter 8. Sometimes, the other side will agree to a tentative deal that is then rejected by a (sometimes illusory) superior and replaced by a less attractive alternative. The superior may be portrayed as difficult and obstinate to preserve the credibility of the negotiator using this ploy (in essence a good cop/bad cop tactic).

Why this tactic works: Both variations are intended to put pressure on you to accept less than favorable conditions rather than have to go through the entire process again and risk losing the deal altogether. Especially if combined with the good cop/bad cop tactic, it is also intended to make you lower your aspiration level.

Some suggestions for dealing with the tactic:

- The best defense is to ask about the qualifications of the other negotiator first. Is he or she the decision maker? If this is addressed early in the negotiation, it may make this tactic nonviable later.

- Ask to negotiate directly with the decision maker.

- (If applicable) Suggest that you have the same problem and that perhaps a meeting could be arranged between your decision maker and their decision maker.

- Ask for specific information about the other party's position.

- Do not allow yourself to be rushed into an agreement.

EXTREME DEMANDS
(HIGHBALL OFFER/LOWBALL OFFER)

Situation: The other party takes an extreme position or opening offer in an attempt to force you to lower your expectations by making you reevaluate your own opening and aspiration and move closer to your resistance point. You know that you should be making between $60K and $80K as a new graduate, and the firm offers you a salary of $25K. This would be an extreme lowball offer causing you to second-guess everything about the negotiation.

Why this tactic works: The tactic works for the same reason a strong opening offer works: It leverages your uncertainty (see Chapter 7). The only difference here is that the demands are considerably different from what you might have expected, causing you to potentially panic because you fear you may not know what the correct terms of the deal should be.

Some suggestions for dealing with the tactic:

- Get commitment around the terms of an interest-based negotiation: "If we are going to do business together we need to craft a fair and reasonable agreement that meets the interests of each other. Would you agree?"

- Ask for a data-based justification for the extreme offer.

- Counter with opposite anchor with your own objective justification.

- Discount the offer; for example, say, "Listen, that is not a serious offer, so let's pretend you did not make it. You know that I can't even consider it."

- Be careful if the other negotiator backs off a little on the extreme offer. The temptation will be for you to concede the remaining points because now the deal looks better than the original extreme offer. This is another example of the contrast effect.

BOGEY (PHONY ISSUE)

Situation: The other party lies about their interest in a relatively worthless (to them) issue to gain reciprocal concessions on a more important issue when they "reluctantly" finally compromise on the phony issue. The objective of this tactic is to make you focus attention on one issue to divert attention from another that holds more importance to the other side. An example would be Caroline (a job applicant) giving in on the issue of vacation time (which she falsely pretends to care about) in order to get a concession on salary (which she actually cares about).

Why this tactic works: It works because you believe you are getting concessions from them so you feel better about the deal. Because of this you are (a) more likely to reciprocate by giving them concessions on other issues and (b) more likely to judge them positively because they are "working with you." Of course, this is a ruse because they are not *actually* working with you; rather, they are lying about what is of value to them.

Some suggestions for dealing with this tactic:

- Listen carefully to understand what is really important to the other side.

- Stick to your guidelines and your prenegotiation plan.

- Make proposals that are of equivalent value to you but have different combinations of issues. The other side's preferences will soon reveal what is important to them.

- Ask for information on why each issue is important as this can expose any bogey issues.

THE NIBBLE

Situation: A deal will supposedly have been agreed to, but at the last minute a minor item (often not raised during the negotiation) will have been added or changed. Often, you are presented with a deal that supposedly has already received the approval of superiors (with the small change or addition) and would be difficult or impossible to change. Sometimes you might be faced with a signed deal, with small alterations. The intent is to pressure you to accept the alteration instead of reopening the negotiation.

Why this tactic works: This works because the concession presented at the end of the negotiation will often be perceived to be too small to lose the deal over it. This also works because of sunk costs; too much work has gone into the deal to risk losing it at the end.

Some suggestions for dealing with this tactic:

- Perceive it as part of the negotiation process rather than as a substitute for negotiation.

- Treat it as a counterproposal, nothing more, and respond as if you were in an earlier stage of the negotiation.

- Tell them that a deal signed by the other side that isn't satisfactory to you is meaningless.

- Ask for a reciprocal small concession on their part.

PLAYING CHICKEN

Situation: This tactic involves one party taking a strong position, or making a commitment that hurts them if they do not get what they want on an issue, in order to force you to concede ("chicken out"). Essentially, they change the negotiation so that they have a strong (often public) reason that they "must" have a certain concession. This makes not getting their position so painful that it's worth fighting hard to get it. Inherently, this tactic focuses entirely on position, because the outcome is already decided and "locked in" for the other party. (For this reason, this tactic is sometimes also referred to as a "lock in" tactic.)

The classic example of this tactic is in the movie *Rebel Without a Cause*, in the scene where Jim (James Dean) and Buzz (Corey Allen) challenge each other to a car race toward a cliff. The first one to jump out of the speeding car is dubbed the "chicken" and loses. While Jim jumps out safely, Buzz's jacket gets caught on the door handle and he is unable to get out in time. This is why "chicken" is such a dangerous game. You are putting yourself out there publicly and betting that the other side will back down and that you will win. A version of this tactic is called the exploding offer, where a deadline is given that determines when the offer will expire, or "explode." This is playing chicken because the party giving the exploding offer is betting that the other side will accept before the expiration date.

Why this tactic works: This tactic works because of fear and power. Whoever chickens out first loses. If no one chickens out, both sides lose as there is no deal.

Some suggestions for dealing with this tactic:

- Resist on principle. (e.g., "My practice is never to yield to pressure, only reason. Let's talk about the merits of the problem.")

- If possible, remove or diffuse the commitment.

- Back off (chicken out) but in doing so say, "I'll give you what you want this time, but I want your agreement to give me what I want next time."

- Be preemptive in negotiating with the other party so that they do not feel like they have to make a public commitment.

- If faced with an exploding offer, try the Farpoint gambit, a strategy popularized by Captain Jean Luc Picard on *Star Trek: The Next Generation*. When faced with an untenable offer from a alien species regarding charges of "crimes of humanity," Captain Picard calmly stated that he agreed, but only under certain conditions. You can do the same with an exploding offer. Agree, but conditional based on terms favorable to you.[2]

ARTIFICIAL FOCAL POINTS

Situation: The other side offers to "split the difference" or split it down the middle based on some artificial position designed to yield a middle point favorable to them. This simple tactic tries to manipulate norms of fairness by catching you off guard with what sounds like a reasonable offer. For example, say you are negotiating rent. You wish to pay $1,400/month and your landlord offers $1,700. You concede $100. The landlord then says, "Okay, you are at $1,500 and I am at $1,700, so let's split the difference at $1,600." This sounds reasonable, but you have conceded twice as much as the landlord.

Why this tactic works: It works if you are not paying attention to what has been conceded in the negotiation. This might sound reasonable, but in reality you may be ceding too much value.

Some suggestions for dealing with this tactic:

- Reject the artificial focal points ("those are not the appropriate focal points in this negotiation").

- Ask for a data-based, objective justification for the focal points.

- Pause or take a break before you say yes.

USING EMOTIONS OR PLAY ACTING

Situation: The other party uses emotional responses like getting angry, raising their voice, or indicating they think you are trying to take advantage of them. The emotional and language intensity is intended to make you lower your expectations, put you on the defensive, and cause you to make concessions to prove you aren't as bad as they seem to think. It is often used in situations of unequal power. Depending on the quality of the play acting, it may be difficult to determine if you are being subjected to a tactic or if the other side is genuinely upset.

Why this tactic works: It leverages your uncertainty about the situation (see Chapter 7), and changes how you are thinking about the other side and about any offer that might be on the table. Once they get angry, for example, you might reevaluate your main argument, which you originally felt was based on data and fairly objective. (For a longer discussion of why emotions work to get value in negotiations, see Chapter 11.)

Some suggestions for dealing with this tactic:

- Don't be thrown off guard and begin to experience guilt. Be aware that guilt may very well be the exact response the other side is looking for.

- Wait for the moment to pass, then calmly restate or paraphrase your last point and ask the other side to explain any concerns.

- Do not respond, and instead pause to allow them to continue.

- If emotion won't abate, request a recess until a later time when everyone may be calmer. You can say, "My intent was not to make anyone upset. Let's take a short break."

- State openly that you perceive the emotion as a tactic and that it will not work. (This is riskier and may cause more offense if they are truly upset.)

- Don't make concessions to appease the emotional party. This is a unilateral concession and will only encourage the other side to use the tactic more frequently.

BOULWARISM

Situation: The other party determines a "fair deal" based on their best knowledge and presents it in a "take it or leave it" manner. This is the final offer, not to be perceived as an opening offer. It may in fact be a reasonable offer. Of course, the other party may just claim this, and in reality be willing to negotiate, and this is just a firmly anchored opening proposal. Many things that people claim are nonnegotiable are often in fact very negotiable. However, if it turns out that the other party is completely unwilling to negotiate at all, then it is a case of boulwarism.

Why this tactic works: You don't like conflict, and this seems like a reasonable proposal, so you accept it, thinking, "That was easy!"

Some suggestions for dealing with this tactic:

- Emphasize the importance of involvement in *process*. Point out that it doesn't matter how good the deal is or isn't, but you want to be involved in the process of deciding what the deal should be.

- If they really won't negotiate, don't waste your time. Either (a) offer a choice between negotiating or immediate impasse or (b) take the deal if it's better than your BATNA.

- Take your BATNA (see Chapter 9).

SLICING

Situation: The other party takes each separate issue and negotiates it at the best possible level, often in a series of separate meetings. Continually, small requests are made, giving you the feeling that it is not worth risking the entire deal over seemingly small issues. Once the other negotiator has gone as far as possible on individual items, you might be asked to make additional concessions if the entire package is to be accepted. Using a series of small requests detracts from how they will add up to a total package, and this tactic (like a nibble) takes advantage of you often not being willing to risk a deal over one small thing. Slicing is a common practice in buyer/seller negotiations. For an overall negotiating perspective, it is a very dysfunctional tactic, since many of the tactics to create value (see, e.g., Chapter 4) may be overlooked by such a one-issue-by-one-issue approach.

Why this tactic works: If you are worried about the complexity of the negotiation, you might be attracted to this tactic because it simplifies the negotiation into separate issues.

Some suggestions for dealing with this tactic:

- Keep all of the issues in the bargaining mix in front of you. Use your negotiation plan (see Chapter 3).

- Negotiate multiple issues at a time. Discuss changes in one issue in terms of consequences for other issues.

- Do not make unilateral concessions (concessions without anything in return).

SNOW JOB

Situation: This is a tactic whereby a negotiator tries to overwhelm the other party with information, in order to take advantage of the other's uncertainty and anxiety. This tactic is intended to distract and confuse the other party. Consider this scenario:

As soon as Bill got out of the car, the salesman started spouting off all the features and additions that are standard on the model he just looked at. Bill could not get a word in edgewise and did not know where to begin.

Why this tactic works: The flood of information creates *more* uncertainty and clogs the sensemaking process. This could make you reconsider your resistance point, rethink your goals, or even make you ignore your interests. The defense to this tactic is knowing what to ignore, as most snow job information is irrelevant.

Some suggestions for dealing with this tactic:

- You can directly confront the other side. Ask, "Why are you throwing so much information at me? Are you hoping it will overwhelm me?" By taking this approach you not only communicate that you know what is going on, but in most cases you imply that the other party's behavior is unprofessional.

- You can be aggressive back. This can send a clear signal that they cannot intimidate you. But beware, this can also escalate the situation.

- Take a break. Pause, evaluate the information you've been given, do the additional research you need to do, then begin negotiating again.

Of course, there are times when (although you may want to) you should not say, "Hey, boss, why are you acting like such a spoiled child?" In this case you need to use more indirect methods. These would be ways to imply your awareness of what people are doing without calling them on it (helping them save face). Lying is a particularly effective place to use this. Calling people out on their lies typically leads to more covering up. It is better if you can help them be honest by asking about their underlying interests. Again, you keep the moral high ground and at the same time may even earn some reciprocity for your forbearance.

The ultimate indirect way to deal with hardball tactics is to ignore them, but in many negotiations you can't ignore them completely. If a person threatens you and you do not react, you want to add something to ensure that you are not communicating that that was not enough and that you need a bigger threat. At the same time, ignoring bad behavior is part of what perpetuates it. Someone who is an aggressive jerk and only has times where his aggressiveness is rewarded or has no effect will never abandon that behavior. Thus, even when you ignore a hardball tactic, you need to make it clear that you are ignoring it and why.

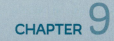

ALTERNATIVES

CHAPTER EXAMPLE

Julise is a study-abroad student, spending the semester in Lima, Peru. She is studying Spanish and has enjoyed her time studying at one of the universities in Peru and meeting several new friends from Peru. During the time of her study abroad, Julise has traveled to Cusco and Machu Picchu, visited Arequipa, and explored the various *barrios* of Lima. There is one thing that Julise has been putting off for weeks now, and her time is running out. She has to negotiate to buy some souvenirs for her parents. After all, they paid for her to come and study abroad and they asked if she would bring home some authentic alpaca goods. Julise has gotten information from her friends on which market has high-quality yet affordable alpaca garments. So, with a heavy sigh and nervousness in her step, she sets out one afternoon for the market.

Part of what is overwhelming for Julise in this scenario is that the market is huge. By her estimate, there are 30 to 40 different vendors selling what look to be the same alpaca garments. Many of these vendors are eager to talk with her. This does not seem to be a low-stress "browse as long as you would like" environment. She is very nervous even making eye contact with the vendors, as she knows if she makes eye contact they will come over and start talking to her.

Julise is not completely unprepared in this situation though, as she has asked her friends what a nice scarf (for her mom) and a sweater (for her dad) *should* cost. Although her friends do not exactly know, they have given her prices ranging from 200 to 300 sol for each item (about $60 to $90 USD). So while she is not exactly sure how much she should pay, Julise knows that she can package both items together (see Chapter 4) to hopefully get a better deal.

Learning Objectives

1. Be able to describe what opportunity costs are and how the evaluation of such costs impacts negotiation.

2. Articulate the definition of BATNA, including what BATNAs are and what BATNAs are not.

3. Analyze negotiations in terms of the two reasons BATNAs can be impactful in negotiation—through negotiator confidence and through resource-based power.

4. Distinguish BATNAs from offers and compromises.

5. Provide examples of how BATNAs can be improved.

6. Recognize and utilize negotiation tactics based on alternatives.

7. Debate the ethical implications of leveraging BATNA, or using knowledge of another's BATNA to take advantage of them.

Master the content at study .sagepub.com/rockmann

After walking around the market for about 30 minutes, Julise decides on three vendor stalls that have nice displays, offer plenty of selection, and do not seem as intimidating as the others. She takes a deep breath and goes into the first stall, ready to use her now excellent Spanish to negotiate with the young gentleman standing there.

Vendor 1: Hello, what are you looking for today?

Julise: An alpaca scarf. Can you show me what you have?

Vendor 1: Ah, we have the best alpaca in the market. Look at this table right here. These are 100% alpaca. My family raise the alpaca high in the mountains and they make all of these scarves.

Julise: How much are each of these?

Vendor 1: Well, these are no ordinary scarves. These are the best we have. 400 sol for each.

Julise: Okay, that seems like a lot.

Vendor 1: I can see that you are a nice *chica*. So for you, I will go to 380 sol.

Julise: I'll think about it.

Vendor 1: Be careful if you look other places. Many scarves are not 100% alpaca. They mix the alpaca with wool, which is much cheaper. We have those types of scarves as well for 270 sol. (He leads Julise over to a different table.)

Julise: Thank you.

Julise, feeling her heart pounding in her chest and starting to sweat, leaves the stall and walks around the corner to rest for a minute. She was not expecting the information about the 100% alpaca versus the alpaca/wool blend. Is this young man lying to her? She has no way to know. She tries a quick search on her phone, but her battery is almost dead. No help there. She heads to the next vendor.

Julise: Do you have 100% alpaca scarves?

Vendor 2: We have the best alpaca. These scarves at this table are 300 sol.

Julise: Are they 100% alpaca?

Vendor 2: 100% alpaca is not ideal in terms of softness. You want some other fibers mixed in to make the alpaca feel nicer on the skin. Look at these colors, aren't they wonderful?

Julise: [Vendor 1] has these same scarves for 270 sol.

Vendor 2: But not in these colors. I can see, though, that you know what you are talking about. I will make my price 270 sol.

Julise: What about sweaters?

Vendor 2: We have wonderful sweaters—each is 400 sol. If you buy both, though [types in calculator], the price for you is 650 sol.

Julise: Okay, I will think about it.

Vendor 2: Wait, wait, don't leave. Let me ask my brother if I can make an even better price. [He disappears for a minute to another stall and returns.] He says we can do 630 sol for both.

Julise thanks Vendor 2 and walks down the main alley of the market. She is feeling more and more comfortable. She now knows she can get both for 630 sol, which seems a bit high but not terrible. She also knows she can go back to Vendor 1 and continue negotiating, although she preferred the colors at Vendor 2. Knowing this, she heads to Vendor 3.

Vendor 3: Ah, welcome, are you looking for alpaca?

Julise: Yes, please show me scarves and sweaters.

Vendor 3: We have 100% alpaca scarves for 360 sol. We have 100% alpaca sweaters for 450 sol.

Julise: [Vendor 2] offered alpaca sweaters for 400 sol.

Vendor 3: We do have some alpaca-blend sweaters over here [takes her over]. These are very nice—340 sol. Much better price than [Vendor 2].

Julise: What about scarves?

Vendor 3: All we have are these scarves for 360 sol. But you seem very nice, so I will make you a price of 650 for both.

Julise: Thank you, I will think about it.

Julise now has more information than she did before and uses that information to go back to Vendor 2, where she liked the colors of the sweaters the best.

Vendor 2: Ah, I see you are back. You clearly know good quality.

Julise: Here's my problem. Your price on sweaters is 400 sol. [Vendor 3] gave me a price of 340 sol.

Vendor 2: Yes, but I also gave you a price of 630 for both.

Julise:	But if I go to [Vendor 3] for the sweater and [Vendor 1] for a scarf, I can get a price of (340 + 270) = 610 sol.
Vendor 2:	You are making this very difficult for me.
Julise:	I just want a good deal.
Vendor 2:	Okay, I can give you both for 600 sol. Do we have a deal?
Julise:	Not yet. Throw in that nice Peru key chain for me that is marked for 20 sol and we have a deal.
Vendor 2:	Fine!

With her goods in hand, Julise left the market.

******

INTRODUCTION TO ALTERNATIVES

Alternatives are a feature of any conflict situation. As a party in a conflict you must always decide whether it is better to keep negotiating with the other party or walk away. Having a good alternative helps you convince others because of resource power: They know they need you more than you need them. And alternatives help you persist because of confidence: You know you have a good option and are resistant to being convinced. In this chapter, you will understand the underlying concept of opportunity costs, the nature of the best alternative to a negotiated agreement (BATNA), and associated tactics based on alternatives.

Opportunity Costs

Opportunity costs are the benefits available from an alternative that must be forgone in order to pursue a certain action.[1] In negotiations the opportunity cost represents the alternative (other agreement, or no agreement) that you must give up in order to pursue a certain action (the current agreement). With every agreement we give up something, and that something represents the opportunity cost. Here is a more complete notion of what opportunity costs entail:

> Opportunity cost is the evaluation placed on the most highly valued of the rejected alternatives or opportunities. It is that value that is given up or sacrificed in order to secure the higher value that selection of the chosen object embodies. . . . The value placed on the option that is not chosen, the opportunity cost, must be that value that exists in the mind of the individual who chooses.[2]

Here are some examples of possible opportunity costs in negotiations, or what benefits the parties are forgoing by coming to agreement:

- A customer at a car dealership could buy the car in front of him, but this may mean potentially forgoing a better deal at another dealership. *The opportunity cost of signing a deal with dealership A is the inability to sign a deal with dealership B.*

- The car salesperson has a choice for how long to continue to negotiate with a customer. *The opportunity costs include the time that could be spent with other customers.*

- You and your significant other are negotiating with an agent to buy a new house. *Your opportunity costs include the other houses that you could also potentially buy.*

- A politician agrees to vote for a piece of legislation. *The opportunity cost is the ability to vote against that piece of legislation.*

- You are about to accept a job offer at a new company. *Your opportunity cost is staying in your current job.*

In looking at these opportunity costs, several things become apparent:

- Opportunity need not be clearly defined.

- Opportunity costs can be similar for both (all) parties.

- Opportunity costs do not have to be related to the specific issues being negotiated.

First, although opportunity costs can be clearly defined, that is not necessary. Take, for example, a car negotiation. The opportunity cost to the buyer is the possibility of buying the same car somewhere else—that opportunity to buy the car elsewhere is often well defined (as prices on cars are widely published). On the other side, though, for the seller, the possibility of another customer paying more for the car is less defined. The salesperson may not know when the next customer is going to walk through the door. When you take an action, you give up the *opportunity* to do something else.

Second, opportunity costs can closely mirror each other. Take the example of politicians negotiating over some policy agreement. The opportunity cost to agreeing to vote on a bill is virtually the same for both sides. For a politician, part of the political calculus is determining the opportunity costs of voting for a piece of legislation. If the cost to voting for the legislation is lower than the cost of not voting for the legislation, technically the politician should vote for it. Much of politics is trying to estimate what the opportunity costs are of taking certain stances in negotiations. How much will the politician's constituents like or hate a bill? Which donors will be pleased or upset? What doors will be opened or closed if the politician votes positively on this bill? All of those questions speak to the nature of opportunity costs. And all of those discussions between politicians? Yes, they are negotiations.

An example of such a negotiation was the health care legislation passed in March 2010, eventually known as the Patient Protection and Affordable Care Act, or

"Obamacare." Many Democrats in the House of Representatives were faced with a difficult choice regarding this law. There was a negotiation between the Democratic leadership and the house members regarding this vote. The leadership wanted each and every Democratic representative to vote for the bill, but this vote came with significant opportunity costs. The choice at hand was whether to vote for it or not. (This choice was not as salient for House Republicans, who almost unanimously opposed the bill.) Each member had to decide whether the benefits of voting for the bill outweighed the costs of not voting for the bill. The opportunity costs of voting for the bill had nothing to do with the legislation itself; rather, they were the benefits of not voting for the bill. That is, what opportunity is lost if they cast a yes vote? Similarly, what opportunity is lost if they cast a no vote? If they cast a yes vote, they would lose the opportunity to claim that they are "fiscally responsible" and "antigovernment," traits that their constituents might value. If they cast a no vote, they would potentially lose future leadership possibilities by not supporting the Democratic leadership and the president. The initial vote in the House of Representatives showed 219 Democrats vote for the bill and 39 Democrats vote against the bill.[3]

While we like to think that politicians are dutifully judging the merits of legislation when they negotiate with one another, we cannot ignore the importance of opportunity costs. Depending on which action is taken, what opportunities are being forgone? This is at the forefront of every negotiator's mind.

Case Sidebar

In Julise's mind, she is worried about losing this negotiation by agreeing too quickly to a deal with any one vendor without knowing what she could get at another vendor. The possible better offers she is missing out on from other vendors are her opportunity costs. We see in this example that Julise is doing a decent job trying to estimate those opportunity costs by investigating prices at multiple vendors. Could she investigate further? Of course! There are 30 to 40 vendors of similar alpaca goods at the market. But she does not have the time or patience to do this. She gathers enough information to generally know what she can get if she walks away from any one specific vendor.

BATNA

You now know what opportunity costs are and how they play a role in negotiations. Opportunity costs in general represent the range of alternatives that are forgone if you agree to a specific outcome. Those alternatives have varying levels of desirability to you.

The best of all of your available alternatives is known as your BATNA best alternative to a negotiated agreement. The BATNA represents your best alternative (among all of your alternatives) were you to walk away or otherwise not be able to reach agreement in the negotiation. BATNA, as Fisher, Ury, and Patton state in *Getting to Yes*, is "the standard against which any negotiated agreement should be measured."[4]

A few important characteristics of BATNAs:

- A BATNA exists outside the current negotiation; it is *not* the best offer in a negotiation or a compromise in a negotiation.

- If you are attempting to negotiate to get someone to do something different, the BATNA is often the status quo.

- Each party at the table has a BATNA.

- BATNA is singular—there is only one "best."

- A BATNA can be bad—you can still have the best of a poor set of alternatives.

Are BATNAs just other offers? No. You might be thinking, given some of the examples used here, that BATNAs are always your next best offer. If you are buying a car, your BATNA is an offer from another dealer. If you are negotiating for a job, your BATNA is an offer from another company. Although these can be BATNAs, they are by no means representative of what BATNAs can be in the minds of individual negotiators. Your BATNA to buying a car might instead be keeping your current car. Your BATNA to negotiating for a job might be keeping your current job. Both of these BATNAs represent the status quo.

Imagine you are negotiating where to go on vacation with your significant other. You are in conflict about which destination to pick. What is your BATNA in this situation? No, it is not that you should go get another significant other (at least let's *hope* that's not your BATNA!). Your BATNA, if you are unable to reach agreement, is to wait and negotiate again or perhaps not to go on vacation (status quo). This is what will happen if you and your significant other are unable to come to terms. So, although BATNAs can be other offers, a BATNA can really be anything that you believe is your best option for what to do to address the conflict if you cannot reach a deal.

I have no good alternatives. Does this mean I have no BATNA? No. You always have a BATNA. Each party always has a BATNA. You may be thinking of a BATNA as another offer, which it is not (see the previous question), rather than as an alternative. Because you have the ability to leave the table or to say no to a negotiation, you always have an alternative. Does this mean your alternative is good? No. Your alternative could be terrible, yet it still exists.

In the movie *Sophie's Choice* (1982), Sophie (portrayed by Meryl Streep), a Jewish woman from Poland, faces an impossible choice upon arriving at Auschwitz. She is told by an SS officer that she can save only one of her two children. She must choose which of her children to save, knowing the other would be put to death in the gas chamber. Sophie's BATNA is not to choose, in which case both children would be put to death. This truly horrible BATNA leads her to comply with the request from the SS officer, saving both herself and her son while dooming her daughter.

Are BATNAs just compromises? No. This is one of most common mistakes we hear from our students in trying to understand BATNA. The thinking here is that if you cannot reach agreement, you and the other side will "settle" on some value in the middle and that this value is the BATNA. For example, let's say you are negotiating with your phone company on the monthly payment. They want you to pay $20/month more for faster Internet, and you are only willing to pay $10/month more for faster Internet. Your BATNA is not $15/month. Your BATNA is taking your business elsewhere or keeping your current contract for Internet service (status quo). Remember, BATNAs are *alternatives* to negotiated agreements. In this case, if you were to settle on $15/month, that would be a negotiated agreement.

Let's say you move into a new house and your significant other has already agreed to spend money for a 40-inch TV. That negotiation is complete. But perhaps you change your mind and want to convince your significant other to purchase a 50-inch TV. In this case you have decided to engage in a second negotiation. Now the 40-inch TV becomes the BATNA in the second negotiation, because you have already agreed to this deal.

Case Sidebar

Julise's BATNA is different in each negotiation, as each negotiation will involve different dynamics. So what are Julise's BATNAs in each of the three negotiations with the three different vendors?

- Negotiation with Vendor 1: Julise's BATNA is to leave and try to get a better deal from other vendors.

- Negotiation with Vendor 2 first time: Julise's BATNA is to go back to Vendor 1 as he had seemingly good-quality products.

- Negotiation with Vendor 3: Julise's BATNA is to go to Vendor 2, as Vendor 2 had better prices and colors than Vendor 1.

- Negotiation with Vendor 2 second time: Julise's BATNA is to get the sweater from Vendor 3 and the scarf from Vendor 1.

Julise's BATNA changes as she gets more and more information about the alternatives available to her.

Are BATNAs always specific? No. You may know, for example, that your car has a book value of $12,000 when you walk into the dealership to trade it in. However, unless someone else has already offered you $12,000 for it, "getting $12,000" is not your BATNA. Without the offer of $12,000 from someone else, your BATNA with the dealer is try to find another offer. Even if someone had offered you $12,000, until you have the money in your bank account there is going to be uncertainty as to your BATNA. In this case the BATNA would be to hope that the person who promised you $12,000 will continue with the deal.

There are two reasons why alternatives and BATNAs impact negotiation: (1) because they affect how the party with the alternative sees the negotiation and (2) because they affect how the other party sees the negotiation.

BATNA and Confidence

As noted in Chapter 7, negotiations are plagued by uncertainty. This uncertainty can center on parties, issues, interests, positions, tactics, mental models, basically anything involved in the process of negotiation. One of the side effects of this uncertainty is inhibited confidence, or a sense of doubt about how beneficial the negotiated agreement will be. Verbal and nonverbal behavior is affected when confidence is low.[5] Verbal communication is affected because you may not be sure what to say or when to say it. Nonconfident individuals won't speak as loudly or as clearly, for example. On the nonverbal side, a lack of confidence might be indicated by lack of eye contact or shifting in your seat. These communication behaviors are picked up by other parties in the negotiation, which reinforce the lack of confidence.

Confidence is not just important in terms of the nonverbal signals you might be inadvertently sending to other parties in the negotiation, but it is very important because it can affect your motivation and subsequent performance. The link between confidence and performance has been studied extensively, and research has found a strong relationship: In general, the more confident you are, the better you tend to perform.[6] Confidence is related partly to self-esteem and partly to self-efficacy. Self-esteem can vary a lot between people, and some people may just have higher "natural" levels of self-esteem, but self-esteem is also improved via experience and skill, which will in turn increase confidence. This is one of the reasons that this book emphasizes the importance of actually practicing the negotiation skills. The more experience you have negotiating, the more familiar and comfortable it will feel (and the less anxiety it can evoke) and the more confident you can become. **Self-efficacy** is another very important characteristic that contributes to your confidence and ultimately performance. Self-efficacy is the extent to which you believe you are able to successfully perform a task. The more efficacy you have, the more confident and motivated you are, and ultimately the better you will tend to perform.[7] Again, the more experience you have and the better prepared you are for a negotiation, the higher your self-efficacy and resultant self-confidence will be.

Having a good alternative can increase your confidence by giving you an "ace in the hole," to use a card-playing analogy. When you know that you have another good option if you don't come to agreement, you are more comfortable in exerting certain tactics. For instance, negotiators with a good BATNA are more likely to make the first offer, which can convey a negotiating advantage.[8] You can almost think of a BATNA as analogous to a safety net under a high-wire or trapeze act. If you KNOW that there is a net that will catch you, then you will be far more likely to jump from one trapeze to the other, because the risk has been mitigated by the safety net underneath you. If there is no safety net, and you could fall and be seriously injured, you probably won't take the risk. In that sense, a good BATNA can be like a safety net giving you the confidence that allows you to take the chance, because even if you fall, you have the BATNA there to catch you.

Take, for example, a simple negotiation between a job candidate and a potential future employer. The issue of salary has come up, and these are the offers on the table:

(Offer) Job Candidate:　$75,000 (goal: $72,000)

(Counteroffer) Employer:　$65,000

There are a range of tactics the job candidate could use to increase the price, but even before she can get to those tactics, she first has to make the simple decision of whether to keep negotiating. Whether the job candidate tries to increase the salary is based, in part, on the alternatives she believes she has. Having a good (or even decent) alternative frees the job candidate to explore the issue of salary with the employer, because the fear of losing the offer is lessened. The simple fact that the job candidate has or doesn't have the offer changes her mind-set, and it is that confidence that affects the ultimate agreement. In other words, a potential job candidate without a good alternative may not even ask about salary, even though negotiating above $65,000 is exactly what the employer expects the candidate to do.

To illustrate this point in a simple way, imagine yourself in two different scenarios. In the first scenario, you are currently working at a job that you like, and your pay is $67,000. You have been looking around at other options, have already interviewed with several other employers, and currently have a job offer that pays $70,000 (with comparable benefits). In the second scenario, you are unemployed, living in your parents' basement, and occasionally delivering pizzas to make some money. You really need a job, and you really want to move out of your parents' basement! In both scenarios, you are scheduled to interview for a job today. Clearly, there is a huge difference in your BATNA in these two scenarios. The strong BATNA in the first scenario will allow you to engage in all sorts of negotiation tactics that you would probably be unlikely to try in the second scenario. In the second scenario, you would probably be very tempted to just accept the opening offer for $65,000, whereas in the first scenario, there is no way you could accept that, since both your current job and your other job offer are better than the current offer on the table. In a sense, the stronger your BATNA is, your confidence makes it easier to use a wider set of negotiation tactics.

Case Sidebar

Julise clearly improves her BATNA throughout this scenario by gaining more information. Part of what this does for Julise is give her confidence. She feels more comfortable dealing with these vendors and asking questions about their products and prices because she knows she can go somewhere else and buy the products she is looking for. This is confidence she does not have when she first approaches Vendor 1 and ultimately helps her obtain value from the negotiation with Vendor 2.

For another example, take the tactic of building a coalition, which was discussed in Chapter 8. When using this tactic, individuals carefully parties together in order to convince the other side to give them what they want. It is possible, though, that, when deciding to use this tactic, how *confident* the negotiator is will impact the success of the tactic. For instance, some negotiators might be thinking:

- How many coalition partners do I need?

- How do I present the coalition to the other side?

- What if they have their own coalition?

- What if my coalition partners defect?

Each of these concerns is valid and can disrupt the effectiveness of the building coalition tactic. These concerns may discourage the negotiator from using this tactic, even though it may be appropriate for the negotiation. This implies that using such tactics necessitate a level of confidence and comfort in order to "pull it off." Having a good alternative helps the negotiator engage with such a tactic because he or she will be less concerned about losing out on the negotiated agreement.

In the same vein, knowing that there are no alternatives has the opposite effect. When you know you have no option but to reach agreement with the party at the table, it may make you less likely and less willing to engage in tactics you think may be risky. Your own perceived resource power is reduced, making it more likely you will judge the other's power to be greater.

Consider the logrolling tactic from Chapter 4. The same principle applies as with the coalition tactic. When trying to logroll, you must be able to discover which issues in the bargaining mix are valued differently by each side. This typically involves asking questions seeking to understand the other party. But as discussed in Chapter 4 (see the Paradox of Reciprocity), you might be scared of asking such questions, fearful that the other side will take advantage of you. Confidence lowers this fear. Having a good BATNA will set your mind at ease, lowering any anxiety you might have and making you feel more comfortable asking the "tough" questions, which ultimately may add value to the negotiation.

BATNA and Power

The better your BATNA is in a negotiation, the more resource power you may be able to bring to a negotiation. Resource power in a negotiation can come from two sources:

- How much the other parties in the negotiation value the resources you hold

- How much you value the resources that others hold

BATNAs work by affecting both of these sources. As your BATNA becomes more favorable, you don't need the resources as much from those other parties at the

Figure 9.1   A Great BATNA

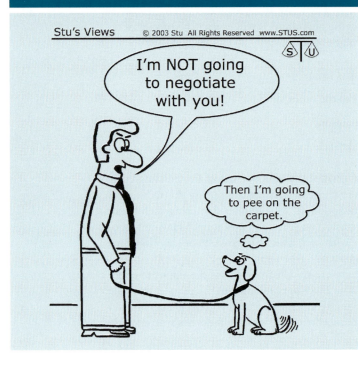

table (see Figure 9.1). As others' alternatives become more favorable, they don't need your resources. The relative strength and weakness of the alternatives available to the different parties determines how much resource power exists in a negotiation, because it determines how dependent each party is on the other.

As shown in Table 9.1, consider a job candidate and a recruiter negotiating the terms of a job offer.

In the first case the candidate has many other job offers and the recruiter has no other qualified applicants. This gives the candidate resource power, which makes the candidate more likely to negotiate a higher salary, better benefits, and so on. In the second case the alternatives for both sides are plentiful, but

Table 9.1   Resource Power Distribution

Candidate Alternatives	Recruiter Alternatives	Resource Power Distribution
Already has several other job offers that he would be happy to take	Has no other qualified applicants for the job	**Advantage candidate**
Already has several other job offers that he would be happy to take	Already has many other qualified applicants for the job who really want the job	**No clear advantage**
Has no other job offers and no other interviews scheduled	Has no other qualified applicants for the job	**No clear advantage**
Has no other job offers and no other interviews scheduled	Already has many other qualified applicants for the job who really want the job	**Advantage recruiter**

because these options are available to both the candidate and the recruiter, resource power is balanced. In the third case resource power is also balanced, but this time it is because neither side has other good alternatives. In the fourth case the recruiter has more and better alternatives than the candidate and thus has a resource power advantage.

In each of these cases the presence of one's alternatives, if known, can change how the other party perceives the negotiation. Perceiving that another has a good alternative (or not) increases the resource power of that individual vis-à-vis the other party at the table.[9]

To further understand resource power in this negotiation consider Table 9.2, which shows, we have to understand the BATNAs in comparison to each other. The job candidate's BATNA seems to be better than the employer's BATNA as the job candidate has an offer already in hand while the employer has much more uncertainty. In this case the employer seemingly needs the job candidate's resource (the job candidate) more than the job candidate needs the employer's resource (the job). This allows for a set of tactics to be used to leverage that resource power.

As with confidence, though, power is based on perception. That is, the job candidate is only going to have additional resource power to the degree that she believes her BATNA is strong relative to the employer. Similarly, the employer is only going to be susceptible to this resource power to the degree that she believes her BATNA is week relative to the job candidate. This becomes a hurdle when individuals have a stereotypical mental model of the power dynamic in the negotiation. If a job candidate believes that job candidates never have resource power in job negotiations, then the ability of the BATNA to increase resource power will be diminished. Similarly, if the employer believes that job candidates always have resource power in job negotiations because it's hard to find good employees, then the employer will give resource power to the job candidate whether she believes the candidate has a good BATNA or not.

Also remember that the BATNA for either side need not be based in reality for it to have an effect. When a BATNA *could* exist but doesn't, it is referred to as a

Table 9.2   Offers and BATNAs

Offers and BATNAs	Description
Offer from the employer	$65,000
Counteroffer from the job candidate	$75,000
Employer's BATNA	Go back to the job pool and try to find someone of similar quality at $65,000
Job candidate's BATNA	$78,000 from another employer (but with a longer commute)

phantom BATNA. Phantom BATNAs are potential, rather than actual, BATNAs. For instance, the likelihood of the job candidate getting a higher offer from the employer does not have to be based on whether that specific offer of $78,000 actually exists (or is presented to the employer). If the employer *thinks* the job candidate has another offer or could get another offer at a good salary, the employer might be willing to acknowledge the resource power of the job candidate and raise the offer accordingly. In this latter case, the potential other job offer, the phantom BATNA, has increased the power of the job candidate.[10]

NEGOTIATION TACTICS

Improving Your BATNA

Often before you can use a BATNA you have to improve it, and to improve it, you have to gather information. As such, this tactic is often used before the negotiation officially starts. Table 9.3 shows examples of generated alternatives that might be used in negotiations.

To the degree that you can do this research and information gathering before you enter the negotiation, the greater the likelihood you will be able to use the tactics discussed next.

Table 9.3   Possible Alternatives

Negotiation	Party	Possible Alternative(s)	Needed Research
Job	Potential employee	Finding another job offer or keeping current job with better benefits	Need to search job market, talk with boss about possibilities for staying
Car	Customer	Another car at a different location	Need to research online and other sources to see what the other offer is likely to be
Vacation rental in Hawaii	Renter	Go to Bahamas instead or stay in a hotel or other rental property	Need to do research on hotel costs, travel costs, benefits of various locations, etc.

In many situations, what you do to improve your BATNA before you negotiate is more important than the actual negotiation. Take, for example, an employee with an abusive supervisor and a terrible job. Any negotiation with the abusive supervisor is likely to be horrible. One of the only things the employee can do in this situation is work to improve his or her BATNA by finding another supervisor or another job before facing the supervisor.

Disclosing BATNA

As noted, your BATNA represents the best option you are left with if the current negotiations fail and an agreement cannot be reached. When disclosing your BATNA, you are communicating to the other side that you have a better offer. This involves saying to the other side, "I have another offer and I'm going to use it." Consider the following example.

> Byron is negotiating the sale of his car with Tarik. Right now, Byron has three other offers from other people: $4,000 from Joe Cheapo, $7,800 from Kelly Bluebook, and $9,000 from Jim Sucker. Byron's BATNA is Jim's offer. Byron tells Tarik that he has an offer for $9,000 from Jim and unless he exceeds it he is going to sell it to that buyer.

This example shows Byron disclosing his BATNA. When disclosing a BATNA at the beginning of a negotiation, opponents make less demanding offers, are more truthful, and settle for less.[11] In this case, disclosing a BATNA will make Tarik less likely to make a demanding offer and more likely to settle for less than he otherwise might were Byron not to disclose his BATNA.

When disclosing your BATNA, it is important to remember that BATNAs work because of perception, not necessarily reality. You may have a great BATNA, but if you can't convince the other side you have a great BATNA, then the

BATNA is not going to increase your resource power in the negotiation. Similarly, if the other party believes you have a great BATNA, even if you don't, (the phantom BATNA) your resource power will be increased. This has implications for how much you disclose. If you disclose a lot of detail about your BATNA, it might be more convincing to the other party, which could advantage you. However, disclosing could lead to a situation where the other party sees what your BATNA is and does not value it as much as you do. Similarly, nondisclosure could help you because the other party will "fill in the gaps" and, out of fear, believe the BATNA to be better than you believe it to be. Or nondisclosure could mean that the BATNA is discounted.

In the example of Byron and Tarik's negotiation, let's assume Tarik offers $8,000 and Byron discloses his BATNA of Jim and the $9,000. Tarik walks away because he doesn't think Jim exists. Byron then goes to Jim. What if Tarik is correct, and Jim backs out of the deal? Now Byron may have to go back to Tarik with "hat in hand" and very little resource power. Tarik now has the upper hand in the negotiation and may be able to demand further concessions from Byron. Without disclosing his BATNA, he would have at least gotten the $8,000 offer.

For an example of the danger in not understanding another party's BATNA, we can again look at the National Hockey League (NHL) labor negotiation and lockout in 2004–2005.[12]

In 2004 the NHL Players Association and owners had to negotiate for a new labor agreement. The old collective bargaining agreement expired on September 15, 2004, and before play could commence for the 2004–2005 season a new agreement had to be in place. Unfortunately, the two sides could not reach agreement before the old agreement expired and on September 16, 2004, the owners locked the players out. The negotiation between the two sides was contentious, mainly because there was a significant difference over the value of the new salary cap. There were other issues on the table, but the two sides focused on this one as it directly affected the owners' bottom line and the players' salaries. The players had already conceded to having a salary cap under the new agreement, but they wanted the cap to be as high as possible. The owners, on the other hand, wanted the cap as low as possible to maximize profit.

After months of negotiations and a series of concessions, on February 15, 2005, the owners offered a salary cap of $42.5 million plus $2.2 million in benefits. They had increased this number several times but communicated that that this was their final offer. Accepting the deal at this date would mean the league could still have a shortened season, with playoffs and a championship. The players association countered at $49 million, which the owners rejected. The 2004–2005 season was then officially canceled.

By offering $49 million, the players were betting that the owners' BATNA was worse than accepting the $49 million offer. They were also betting that offering $49 million was a better alternative than their own BATNA, which was a canceled season. The players association was wrong on both accounts. The owners felt that canceling the season—their BATNA—was preferable to any price above $42.5 million, and consequently the players suffered from lost wages.

(Most NHL players make considerably less than NFL, MLB, or NBA players.) It was the players who lost the most money, and it was the players who had to come back to the bargaining table. When they finally came back, it was clear the owners had more power in the negotiation. The final agreed upon value for the salary cap was $39 million.

In some instances, you may want to expose your *bad* BATNA in order to convince the other side. If your BATNA, let's say, is bankruptcy, which would harm the other party, sharing that information may help the other side move on a particular issue. The classic quote here is "If we walk away, I go out of business and neither of us gets what we want. Is that what you want?"

Exposing Another's BATNA

The flipside of disclosing a BATNA is trying to assess others' BATNAs and exposing them. This is helpful especially when you suspect their BATNA is not as strong as yours—it can increase your perceived power in the negotiation by suggesting you are willing to compare BATNAs. If the BATNA is strong, though, knowing it could lead you to make a more conservative opening offer.[13]

This can be accomplished through information gathering both before and during negotiations. You need to try to figure out what their resource power is by exploring what alternatives they might have. You can also ask them, "What is your alternative if we can't reach agreement here?" One danger is that they may realize their BATNA is weak and could potentially work to improve it. They could also be reluctant to share information, which suggests that (a) their BATNA is weak, (b) they want to wait to use the BATNA, or (c) they prefer to negotiate without using BATNAs.

Walking Away

Walking away is a related tactic that literally means to get up and walk away from the table. When using the power of walking away, you have decided that your BATNA is preferable to the deal on the table and you wish the other side to know that. By getting up and walking away, you are communicating to the other side that you are willing to leave, which may cause them to reassess their resistance point and the offer currently on the table. This works by increasing your perceived resource power in the negotiation.

It is important to note, however, that the power of walking away only works when you actually walk away! If you threaten to walk away or start walking away but come back, it does not have the same effect as actually walking out the door. Walking away forces the other side to make a decision about how they'd like to proceed with the negotiation. It is also important to note the danger in using the power of walking away: The other party might actually let you go. As with the NHL negotiation, if this happens perhaps you misjudged the strength of the other side's BATNA.

BENEFITS TO LEVERAGING ALTERNATIVES

Negotiation is about the exchange of resources, and if you can tip the scale of resource power in your favor, you can obtain more value from the negotiation. Further, because many people who negotiate are relative novices, alternatives are something they understand. When you go to buy a TV, the salesperson may respond to a BATNA but not to a variety of other tactics because the salesperson expects you to walk in with a good alternative. He "speaks" the language of alternatives. Thus, if you have improved your BATNA before going in and are willing to expose your BATNA, you can get a better offer. Car dealerships now expect this, given the relative ease of getting information about car prices. If you do not do the work to improve your BATNA before going in, then the resource power and confidence will clearly be in favor of the salesperson, and it will be harder for you to save money on the deal.

Many companies and organizations have developing BATNAs as part of their company policy or culture. Managers resist increasing your salary unless you prove you can go out on the open market and get a better offer. Why? Because management has decided they are only going to pay for resource power, and they are only going to believe in your resource power if you can demonstrate it. It is in your best interest to know whether any company or organization you belong to or work for has this value so you understand what you are expected to do to increase your salary down the road.

COSTS TO LEVERAGING ALTERNATIVES

Is using your BATNA always good negotiation? Probably not, in that using alternatives to convince can be seen as aggressive toward the other party and is likely to come with social costs. There is no value being created, and there are no creative solutions being generated; it is simply negotiating based on what else could be achieved. Because of this, one of the costs can be hurt feelings. Using your BATNA could be seen as evidence of a lack of trust, which suggests these tactics may be best used when trust does not exist. But when trust does exist? They can be harmful and detrimental, not only to the implementation of the agreement but also to future agreements with the same party.

Remember that parties with unequal power engage in more contentious behavior and use threats and punishments.[14] If you believe that the key to a successful negotiation is to develop a strong BATNA, you might unknowingly be so confident you end up using threats in a such a way that harms the relationship between yourself and the other party. In this case your developing and thinking about resource power leads you down a convincing path even though an understanding path would lead to more value for you and the person you are negotiating with.

ETHICAL CONSIDERATIONS

The same ethical considerations are relevant when using alternatives and one's BATNA that exist when leveraging formal power. First is whether this is the type of person you want to present to others. In the case of Julise, she is seemingly only gaining information that sellers are willing to share and using that in the context of a simple business transaction. Although she is in fact "pitting" the vendors against each other, in the culture of the market the vendors likely expect this and it is not likely to be seen as unethical behavior. But what if Julise left out certain information about what the other vendors were offering? Perhaps she revealed a BATNA that did not include information on whether the item was 100% alpaca or a blend. Now the ethical line gets a bit blurry. Is it okay to use an "incomplete" BATNA in the hopes of making the other side believe your BATNA is stronger than it actually is? This is where BATNA behavior becomes more questionable.

We can imagine other situations where exposing one's BATNA makes people in low power positions feel horrible about themselves.

Boss: I don't care if your kid is sick, I need you to work the night shift.

Employee: But I have no one to watch him, and I told the sitter I'd be home by 8.

Boss: If you can't work this shift, then apparently it means you don't want a job.

Employee: Fine, I'll stay.

The employee has a terrible BATNA—stay home with his or her child and risk losing his or her job. The boss exposes the terrible BATNA of the employee in this situation in order to force the employee to stay late at work. Does this work? Yes, in the sense that the employee complies. But is this ethical? Many would say no.

You could be privy to another's BATNA without them knowing. Going back to the earlier case of the job candidate and the employer, if the employer knows from a friend at the other company that the $78,000 offer is to join a unit that might be merged in the next year or two, the employer could leverage that information to obtain more value from the job candidate. Is this just good business? Or is this borderline unethical? Something to think about as you do research for your own negotiations.

Ethics Discussion Questions

Christine was moving from California to North Carolina for her job. She had found a house she liked and was in the middle of negotiating its price. She had put in a tentative bid and was waiting to hear what the sellers thought of it. Out of curiosity, she decided to Google the owners and found that the seller had a blog. On the blog the seller had written, "We got a potential buyer for the house today. I really hope she agrees to buy. We are in so much debt after my husband lost his job that we need to take practically any offer for this house just so we can get out of here. Soon we are going to need to sell our furniture to stay out of bankruptcy." After reading this, Christine called her broker and changed the amount that she had bid to one much lower.

1. Was Christine's behavior ethical? Why or why not?

2. If not, what should she have done with this information? Why?

3. How much does the seller's personal situation matter in the determination of what is ethical? Would it be different if the seller was in debt due to poor financial decisions or irresponsibility?

4. What if the seller had been a real jerk to Christine? Does that change anything with respect to what is ethically allowable?

5. What if the seller had written, "We got a potential buyer for the house today. I like her and hope she agrees to buy it, but I am not sure if I can ignore the two other better offers. No matter how much I like the buyer from today, I can't refuse that much more money," and it made Christine increase her bid. Is that ethical on the part of the seller?

6. What if this hypothetical blog posting was a lie? How does this compare (ethically) to the original situation?

CHAPTER REVIEW

Consider the following scenario:

Peter is a vice president of marketing and communication for a startup food delivery company called FoodFAST. Part of Peter's job in this role is to find a customer relationship management (CRM) technology solution that fits within FoodFAST's budget and vision. This is critical for FoodFAST for a variety of reasons. First, the company needs to know as much about their customer's preferences as possible so that it can suggest food items customers are likely to be interested in. Second, the company needs to be able to access customer data quickly so that it can troubleshoot any likely problems. Third, it needs a secure solution so that there is never any threat to their customers' data. Finally, because the company might need to sell parts of customer data in the future, it needs a technology that would allow this possibility.

Peter is negotiating with Ben at CRM_One, one of the possible suppliers of a CRM product. Ben has offered him the following terms on the CRM_One Platinum Solution:

- Two-year contract

- Site license for the entire company at $25,000/year

- Free 24/7 tech support

- Web-based CRM access (no need to install software on desktops)

- Mailing program extension included at no extra charge (so that FoodFAST can create custom mailings for different segments of the database)

- Highest level of security along with insurance guarantee if data are hacked

Peter is preparing a response to Ben. Imagine two different situations where Peter has two different BATNAs.

Scenario 1:

CRM_One is Peter's first solid offer. He has calls into two other companies, Sales Fish and Market Capture, but neither of those sales representatives has returned his calls. Based on his knowledge of the market, he believes that Market Capture is going to be a more expensive solution, as this product is typically used by large companies in business-to-consumer marketing. Peter used Market Capture at his previous job, although he was not in charge of negotiating the contract. He knows very little about Sales Fish, except that the company has been around for about 18 months.

Scenario 2:

Before Peter got the offer from CRM_One, he negotiated extensively with Sales Fish, a competitor of CRM_One, which has been in business approximately 18 months. He has received the following offer from Sales Fish:

- Open-length contract

- Site license for the entire company at $18,000/year

- Free 24/7 tech support

- Web-based CRM access (no need to install software on desktops)

- Highest level of security (no insurance guarantee)

- Willingness to customize up to 10 Sales Fish dashboard screens for FoodFAST (what the user sees when logging in)

Peter feels pretty good about this offer but is a bit worried that Sales Fish is so new. CRM_One is a much more established company (>10 years). Peter has already talked to his boss, though, and the boss is comfortable with Sales Fish if Peter thinks that is the best value and will serve FoodFAST well.

Questions:

1. What is Peter's BATNA in Scenario 1?

2. What is Peter's BATNA in Scenario 2?

3. How is Peter likely to respond to CRM_One in Scenario 1 versus Scenario 2? Why? How does the relative strength of the BATNA impact Peter's likely response?

4. What would you recommend Peter do in Scenario 1?

5. What would you recommend Peter do in Scenario 2?

Discussion Questions

1. Why is the concept of BATNA so fundamental to understanding and analyzing negotiations?

2. Should *good* BATNAs always be used? In what types of contexts should BATNAs be used or not used?

3. What would be the benefit to revealing a poor BATNA to the other side in a negotiation? Would this ever be a desirable action?

4. How does having a strong BATNA impact the ability to use other negotiation levers and tactics? Which ones and why?

Concept Application

1. Negotiate using your BATNA as your main tactic. Report to the class how you improved your BATNA and how you used it. Also report whether or not it was effective and why.

2. Find a real-life negotiation where the sides each threatened to walk away. Assess whether this tactic helped either side (or both) and why. If it didn't help, speculate on why the two sides continue to use such tactics. Why do you think certain (entrenched) parties negotiate via BATNAs in this way?

Role-Play Exercise: H-Electrix Automotive

This is a negotiation between the chief financial officer (CFO) of H-Electrix Automotive and the CFO of Honyota USA. The negotiation is whether H-Electrix would like to purchase the Fremont manufacturing facility from Honyota.

H-Electrix is a startup company looking to produce hydrogen fuel cell vehicles. H-Electrix has developed (and acquired) designs and technology and is ready to begin manufacturing. This would be the first production facility for H-Electrix. Honyota is a Japanese auto manufacturer that has been making cars in the United States since the early 1980s. Honyota has often been an early adopter of technology, especially in the area of alternative fuels. The company sold the first commercially viable models of electric and hybrid gas-electric cars in the U.S. market. Honyota has considerable experience building hydrogen fuel cell electric cars and is one of the pioneers of this technology. As early as 2008, Honyota started selling its Lucidity model in California, which was the first hydrogen fuel cell car sold in the United States.

To reach agreement in this negotiation, the two CFOs must agree on three issues: purchase price, the time frame for when H-Electrix would take over the plant, and whether to retain the current workforce.

SAGE edge™ Visit study.sagepub.com/rockmann to help you accomplish your coursework goals in an easy-to-use learning environment.

RESOURCE AND TIME CONSTRAINTS

One of the problems you may face when trying to negotiate is that the resource you or the other side wishes to negotiate is *constrained* in some way. Take, for instance, a job negotiation, where you are negotiating with a human resources (HR) specialist over the amount of covered moving expenses. Both you and the HR specialist agree that you should receive a larger moving expense budget (e.g., $5,000) because you are moving a long distance. However, the specialist is constrained in his or her ability to give you that amount of money. In this sort of situation, there isn't actually conflict; rather, there is a resource constraint.

Consider another situation of a parent who desperately wants to give a child a new bike for his or her birthday. The child wants the bike, the parent wants to give the bike, but the parent simply lacks the money to pay for the bike. Again, in this situation there is not really conflict (unless the child doesn't believe the parent doesn't have money) but rather a resource constraint.

Resource constraints make the lessons you have learned about using various negotiation levers even more important, because now you and the person on the other side of the table are in essence a team trying to figure out how to overcome the resource constraint. In this situation it's pointless to take a convincing approach because they are already convinced. It's a matter of brainstorming how to find extra resources.

In the case of the moving expenses, one possibility would be to ask about *other* sources of funding that may be available, for instance, signing bonuses or travel stipends. It's possible that a different source of money could be allocated to you, which you could then use to help offset the moving expenses. In the case of the parent and the child, they must work together to uncover alternative ways to raise the funds for the bike. Perhaps the child can take on a part-time job or forgo participation in a sports team, both of which would ease the resource constraint present.

It can be a matter of simply figuring out who to talk to, that is, who *controls* the resources. If you are stuck in a negotiation with a potential supplier and they are refusing to budge on price, you might have to bypass the salesperson and speak directly to the sales manager. Or ask the salesperson if they are constrained in their ability to give a discount. This is why it is almost always better to negotiate a car purchase *directly* from the sales manager rather than a salesperson on the floor—the salesperson is always constrained in terms of the resources he or she controls.

In all of these cases, what it is important for the parties at the table is to figure out is that the resource is constrained. Without this knowledge, one party or another might assume that the person across the table from them doesn't care about their issue or is unwilling to work with them.

Time can also be a major constraint to using negotiation tactics. This is because all tactics take time and effort. Say you want to uncover someone's intangible interests (Chapter 5). That takes time. Or perhaps you want to develop a stronger BATNA (Chapter 9). That takes time. Or you want to develop a source of similarity between yourself and the other party (Chapter 6). That takes time. But what if you don't *have* time? Having a time constraint limits the number of tactics you can use to negotiate.

One way time impedes a negotiation is through deadlines. Don Moore has found in his research that negotiators think deadlines hurt their negotiation outcomes.[1] Although Moore found that this was not necessarily the case, the presence of a deadline can create anxiety and make someone feel like they are at a disadvantage. This can potentially lead to a self-fulfilling prophecy, where the deadline creates fear of losing a negotiation, which leads to rushed tactics or a less thoughtful approach or early concession, which *causes* the negotiator to sacrifice too much value.

The classic example of time as a barrier is comparing someone buying a car whose current car is in good condition and someone buying a car whose current car just died. The person whose current car is in good condition has the luxury of time. They can investigate multiple dealerships, test-drive cars, negotiate with different salespeople, and even purchase a car at a nonlocal location. Contrast this with the person whose car just died. They need a car today. Their ability to leverage their BATNA, leverage the uncertainty of the other side, or use formal power has been greatly reduced because they lack time.

You want to think about time carefully when you negotiate. Anticipate not only which tactics you are going to use but also whether you have enough time (or they have enough time) for you to use those tactics. If you want to have a meaningful discussion with your significant other regarding intangible interests on multiple issues, don't do this when he or she is running out the door. If you want to talk to your boss about your past performance evaluation and negotiate what you might do to improve in the next quarter, make sure your boss doesn't have a meeting in 5 minutes. Build this into your plan so that you have the freedom and flexibility to enact the negotiating plan you want rather than one you are forced to enact because there is simply no time.

CHAPTER 10

PERSISTENCE AND GOALS

CHAPTER EXAMPLE

Tony is an accounting major at a prestigious state school about two hours from his hometown.

When Tony first went to college he sat down with his parents and they discussed together what would be a good goal for Tony in his courses. Tony suggested, and his parents agreed, that he would not earn any grade lower than a B.

Tony is now a junior honors student and is taking an honors section of ECON 314: Advanced Microeconomic Theory with Professor Susan Wells, a prominent scholar in the field of economics. The class has only 25 students. Tony earned a B- on his first midterm and a C on the second midterm. As such, he is very concerned about his course grade. In addition to the goal he set with his parents, Tony wants to secure an internship for the following summer and a permanent job placement after he graduates.

The grade in the class, according to Professor Wells's syllabus, is broken down into the following categories:

First Midterm: 20%

Second Midterm: 20%

Final Exam: 40%

Class Participation: 20%

Tony engaged in the following e-mail conversation with Professor Wells after the second midterm.

Tuesday, 1:15 pm

Professor Wells,

Learning Objectives

1. Describe why goals are effective at increasing motivation.

2. Demonstrate the link between self-efficacy and negotiator motivation.

3. Use the characteristics of goals to delineate the types of negotiations that will generate persistence.

4. Utilize both intrinsic and extrinsic rewards to motivate yourself to be a more effective negotiator.

5. Describe why persistence is effective, including the concepts of tangible and intangible interests, opportunity costs, and relationships in your description.

6. Generate examples of why persistence can be valuable in a negotiation.

7. Illustrate the dangers of goal setting and increased motivation. Tie these dangers to the ethical considerations of being persistent.

Master the content at study
.sagepub.com/rockmann

I'm very disappointed in my grade on the second midterm. I thought I understood the main concepts, but I seemed to not perform very well. Is there anything I can do at this point to improve my grade?

Sincerely,
Tony

Tuesday, 1:32 pm

Tony,

Please focus on the remaining assignments in the class and perhaps come to office hours if you have questions.

Best,
Professor Wells

Tuesday, 7:03 pm

Professor Wells,

Are there any extra credit opportunities?

-Tony

Wednesday, 8:48 am

As per the syllabus, there is no extra credit in ECON 114.

Prof. Wells

Tony thought about this reply and decided to change course. He made sure to attend Professor Wells's office hours on Thursday and the following Tuesday, and again one additional time before the final exam. Each time he attended office hours, he went with questions about the chapters upcoming for that week, showing that he was prepared for class and was genuinely interested in the topics.

As the final exam approached, Tony again e-mailed Professor Wells.

Prof. Wells,

I just wanted to say thank you for all of the time at office hours during the last few weeks. I do enjoy the material. As I am studying for the final exam, would it be possible to rewrite two of my answers to the second midterm and get your feedback? I know this is extra work for you. I just want to make sure my knowledge is precise as I prepare for similar questions on the final. Please let me know if this is acceptable.

Sincerely,
Tony

Tony,

I'd be happy to. I've been impressed by your initiative this term after your poor performance and I'll gladly help you prepare for the final exam. Please send me the responses by 3 pm on Friday.

Best,
Prof. Wells

******

INTRODUCTION TO PERSISTENCE AND GOALS

In the past several chapters we have focused on what a negotiator might do to obtain value from another party in negotiation, including offering them intangible value, working with them on creative solutions, or forcing them into a decision by using alternatives. There is another set of negotiation tactics, however, that are focused on negotiator persistence. **Persistence** represents both the amount of effort put in at any moment as well as the capacity to sustain effort over time. Why do we study motivation in a negotiation book? Because negotiation takes a significant amount of effort![1] To better understand motivation in negotiation settings, we turn first to goals and goal-setting theory.

The Motivated Negotiator: Setting Goals

Goals are specific positions on specific issues that a negotiator is working to achieve. Goals direct action, which is why they are helpful to negotiators. As seen in Table 10.1, goals are different from interests in that a goal is a specific position set in order to satisfy one's interest. A goal is simply one of many positions that you can decide upon before the negotiation to increase your motivation. To generate effective goals you must go through the process of goal setting, that is, developing and formalizing the objectives you are attempting to reach.[2]

Characteristics of Motivating Goals

You may have heard the acronym SMART to describe effective goals. SMART stands for specific, measurable, attainable (but difficult), relevant, and time-bound. Figure 10.1 provides a summary of the goal-setting process.

Table 10.1 Interests, Issues, Goals, and Positions

Interest	Issue	Goal	Possible Positions
Be able to purchase a new house in desired community for new family	Salary	$92,000/year	$88,000/year $90,000/year $92,000/year . . . $100,000/year
Visit Europe during college	Money from parents	Parents pay at least half of travel costs	Parents pay nothing Parents pay one fourth Parents pay one half Parents pay three fourths Parents pay all costs
Eat Asian food for dinner	Which restaurant to go to?	P.F. Chang's	P.F. Chang's Panda Express Szechuan Garden Pei Wei

Figure 10.1 Goals and Effort

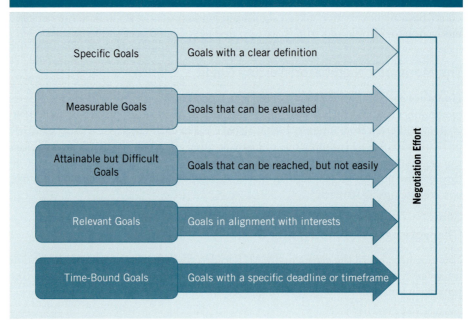

Specific Goals — Goals with a clear definition

Measurable Goals — Goals that can be evaluated

Attainable but Difficult Goals — Goals that can be reached, but not easily

Relevant Goals — Goals in alignment with interests

Time-Bound Goals — Goals with a specific deadline or timeframe

Negotiation Effort

One of the most basic reasons why you become motivated to do something is that there exists a disconnect between what the world is currently like and the way you want the world to be. In other words, you are generally not as happy when there exists a discrepancy between what you have and what you *could* have. Take the following example:

> Jalen is trying to negotiate for a raise at work. He's not sure what the raise should be, so he goes and asks his boss whether it is possible for a raise. His boss says that a raise is well overdue and that he will look into a 2% raise. Jalen leaves the office.

Should Jalen be happy with this encounter? From the outside you might say no, that Jalen should've worked harder to get a higher raise. However, without a clear goal Jalen is susceptible to the anchoring effect as discussed in Chapter 7 on uncertainty.[3] Jalen is not expecting anything; as such he is probably thrilled with the boss's offer of 2% (his boss is leveraging Jalen's uncertainty). Any concession from his boss is being compared, or contrasted, to Jalen's expectation of getting nothing. From Jalen's perspective, the boss met or exceeded Jalen's expectations, which will make Jalen feel good, at least for the moment. For Jalen this "ask" was probably a difficult thing to do, so it was probably a huge personal victory for his boss to (seemingly) agree with him. If Jalen realizes that he could have gotten much more, however, he might feel regret later on; this is known as the **winner's curse**.[4] The winner's curse is when you *agree* to something only to realize later on that you are not happy with, or regret agreeing to, the deal.

So why doesn't Jalen persist in this negotiation instead of settling for a vague promise from his boss? Because Jalen lacked a clear goal going in. Goals provide definition, guidance, and structure and help negotiators see whether they have performed at a certain level. If Jalen had a goal of getting a 5% raise, he is much more likely to be dissatisfied with what he received from this negotiation because he knew his goal was not met, so he would keep expending effort toward reaching the goal. This is the core premise of goal-setting theory: that goals, as a result of dissatisfaction, provide definition for performance, driving effort. With a goal present, for Jalen to be happy he is going to have to keep on negotiating with his boss. Without a goal present, Jalen will think he is leaving the negotiation in a good position only to feel regret later.

We can contrast Jalen's goal of a 5% raise with a "do my best" goal. With a "do my best" goal, Jalen will go into the negotiation thinking that he should "do his best." But as the word "best" has no real definition, this type of goal provides no real direction for Jalen.[5] He might think, using the previous example, that getting the boss to agree to look into the possibility for a raise was his "best," although that may have not been the case.

Specific. The first desired characteristic of goals is that they are *specific*. **Specific goals** are those that someone else can articulate—goals that are describable and understandable.

Not specific: *I want a job.*

Specific: *I want a job in the high-tech industry at one of six particular companies.*

This level of specificity directs Jalen's actions toward reaching that goal.

Measurable. **Measurability** means that there is a defined goal that can be evaluated after the negotiation.

> Not measurable: *Jalen wants a good raise.*

> Measurable: *Jalen now knows he can get a 2% raise but would really like the raise to be 5%. He also thinks there is an outside chance the new contract the company just landed could help him push his raise to 8%.*

What does "good raise" mean in the "Not measurable" line? It's unclear, and that's the problem. Without a measurable way to assess performance, the meaning of "good" may shift during the negotiation and will not drive as much motivation.

Attainable. **Attainability** captures the degree to which the individual believes they can actually reach the goal. If a negotiator believes there is no possible way to reach a certain goal, then motivation will not be increased. Likewise, the goal should not be too easy. If it's too easy, it does not increase motivation because there will be little work required to reach the goal. This is why we say that goals should be attainable but difficult.

> Not attainable: *I want a 50% raise.*

> Attainable and not difficult: *Any raise is OK with me.*

> Attainable and difficult: *I know they are offering 2%, but I believe I deserve an 8% raise and I'm going to work as hard as I can to reach that level.*

Attainability is impacted by one's self-efficacy, that is, one's belief that he or she can be successful. Believing that you can be successful is not an easy task—it can take much trial and error and positive outcomes before a sense of self-efficacy is developed. But this is critical because being more positive about your own abilities leads to better negotiation performance.[6] Self-efficacy is based in part on your personality and in part on your own experiences. Some individuals are inherently confident, regardless of the task at hand. Others may be unsure of themselves, regardless of the experience. Research has shown that training and preparation can increase self-efficacy and, consequently, the belief in one's success. This is partly why we run our students through so many negotiation exercises—to increase their belief that they can negotiate successfully and confidently.

Relevant. Goals that are clearly connected to your interests are termed to have **relevance**. If your interest in a job negotiation is financial security, your goal will likely be related to money. If your interest is making sure your roommate is satisfied with the bill-splitting arrangement, your goal should reflect his or her feelings upon exiting the negotiation. If your interests are peace of mind and getting a good value for your money, then the goal you should have when going to buy a used car should be something like "To pay a maximum of $14K for a Honda or Toyota with fewer than

50,000 miles." Once you have goals that are relevant, you can start crafting them with the other characteristics in mind.

Not relevant: *Setting a goal for a higher salary if what you really care about is flexible work and paid time off.*

Relevant: *Setting a goal for a higher salary if what you really care about is paying off loans and buying your first house.*

Time-bound. **Time-bound goals** imply that there is a specific deadline for reaching the goal.

Not time-bound: *I need to sell my car soon.*

Time-bound: *I need to sell my car by next Saturday.*

Making goals with a specific deadline or time frame drives motivation, as you will be more motivated to act to reach that goal soon.

Case Sidebar

What motivates Tony to be persistent in the chapter-opening example is that his goal is both specific and time-bound. Whereas in the beginning he was negotiating for extra credit, he realizes now that he is negotiating over how to achieve at least a B in this class. This is time-bound as Tony knows the course will end at a specific point in time. Tony's professor is ultimately influenced by the responsibility Tony takes over his actions and by satisfying the professor's interests in Tony learning the material, but it is Tony's persistence that makes that possible.

Process of Setting Goals. Another way to increase motivation is to set your own goals. When you are involved in setting goals, you are more committed to those goals because you have a sense of ownership. This goes back to the notion of consistency from Chapter 5—because you have set the goal, you are now motivated to accomplish the goal so that your beliefs and actions are consistent. This is in contrast to goals that are provided by someone else. This is why in teams it is helpful when all team members participate in the setting of team goals.[7] The increased participation in setting goals across the team motivates all team members to work toward strong team performance.

Finally, making goals public further encourages commitment to reach the goal.[8] This is why smoking cessation drugs are most effective when individuals go to treatment programs.[9] Treatment programs make the goal to quit smoking public, making it cognitively more difficult to continue smoking. If you keep smoking when in a treatment program, you will feel as if you are letting people down (or losing face - see Chapter 5). This anticipation of guilt increases commitment to the goal. Making goals public helps during the negotiation because you will continually be looking for ways to meet your goal so that you can report back to those that you've told that you were successful!

Case Sidebar

Tony's goal in the chapter-opening example is to earn nothing less than a B in all of his college courses. What makes his goal even more motivating is that he *participated* in the setting of this goal along with his parents. Because his parents know about the goal, the goal is *public*. If Tony were to fail in reaching the goal, it would cause him to lose face with his parents (Chapter 5), something that he very much wants to avoid. Not only will losing face make him feel bad in the moment, it could hinder his ability to negotiate with his parents on other issues going forward. This increases his motivation to work with his professor and find out what he needs to do to succeed in the course.

Goals and Resistance Points

Although a goal is what you hope to reach, you also need a point at which you are no longer willing to say yes. This is your resistance point, as discussed in Chapter 2. So, for example, you might rather hold on to your old drum set than sell it for less than $300; $300 in this case would be your resistance point. Or you may think that taking the new job in a different city is not worth the hassle unless they pay you at least 15% more and give you another week's vacation; in this case 15% more is your resistance point on salary and 1 week more is your resistance point on vacation time.

Although a goal *could* be the same as a resistance point (but this would leave no room for concessions), it is usually better (and never worse) than your resistance point (see Table 10.2). If your goal is something less beneficial to you than your resistance point, either (a) your resistance point is not correctly specified or (b) your goal is not difficult enough to generate effort.

Extrinsic Motivation

When you think about what motivates a negotiator, or what motivates you when you negotiate, think about the rewards at stake. What are you negotiating over? If it's a promotion at work, perhaps you are very motivated. If it is where to go out to dinner, perhaps you are less motivated. Both the promotion at work and where to go out to dinner are examples of **extrinsic motivation**, in that they are tangible and represent something that you are able to obtain or acquire as a result of negotiating. You might be thinking that persistence always comes in negotiations where the stakes are high or when someone desperately wants something, but this unfortunately is not the case.

Table 10.2 Goals and Resistance Points

Interest	Issue	Goal	Resistance Point (the point at which you are willing to say yes)
Be able to purchase a new house in desired community for new family	Salary	$95,000/year	$91,000/year
Visit Europe during college	Money from parents	Parents pay at least half of travel costs	Parents pay one quarter of travel costs
Eat Asian food for dinner	Which restaurant to go to?	P.F. Chang's	P.F. Chang's or Panda Express

Too often have we heard this story when teaching negotiation:

> Professor, I am so glad that I am taking this class because the last time
> I accepted a job I just took what they offered and didn't negotiate.

This is another example of the winner's curse, someone who takes an offer and realizes later, when it is too late, that they should've negotiated further. Job negotiations are likely the single most important thing we negotiate in our lives. Every $1,000 difference when you negotiate your first job, with modest salary growth year to year, means approximately $75,000 difference in lifetime earnings. Thus someone who is able to negotiate an additional $5,000 for their first job will expect, on average, to earn about $375,000 more during their lifetime.[10]

If extrinsic rewards are so powerful, why would this possibly happen? In addition to all of the mistakes we make when negotiating (see Chapter 1), we face an additional hurdle. Extrinsic rewards can hurt performance. The research is remarkably clear: For complex tasks (and negotiation is definitely a complex task), as the stakes are raised, performance drops.[11] Now that you have read at length about motivation, this should make sense. What prevents effective negotiation performance? Anxiety, worry, and mistrust. What increases when the stakes are raised? Anxiety, worry, and mistrust. Negotiators may want very badly to succeed but end up failing because of anxiety, worry, and mistrust. This is why planning is so critical. Planning can help calm anxiety and worry so that you do not fall into this trap.

Intrinsic Motivation

Intrinsic motivation, in contrast to extrinsic motivation, motivates people because of the fulfilling nature of the task. If someone is intrinsically motivated to negotiate, it means they derive pleasure from the exercise of negotiation. Researchers have argued that one reason this is the case is that engaging in the task makes individuals feel good about themselves.[12]

Although this may not be the case for you, you can imagine how negotiation might fulfill the need for self-esteem. After all, negotiating allows you the opportunity to obtain something for yourself. While we typically think of this in terms of tangible value (money, goods, etc.), we have already spent significant time discussing both intangible value and the intangible interests that underlie that intangible value (Chapter 7). For someone who is intrinsically motivated to negotiate, it likely means that they see negotiating as a means to not only feel good about the outcome but also enjoy the process of getting something, which makes them feel good about themselves.

Intrinsic motivation will increase persistence in the negotiation, but it can be difficult to increase your intrinsic motivation. Whether because of culture or personality, many individuals are ill at ease when negotiating, possibly out of fear of losing. Intrinsic motivation in this case is not present, because the opposite is true—instead of seeing negotiation as a means to feel *good* about oneself, negotiation is a means to feel *bad* about oneself, yet another explanation why many avoid negotiations at all costs.

Why Does Persistence Work?

The reason that persistence is effective is because *negotiation takes work*. Let's go back to our discussion of opportunity costs from Chapter 9. Opportunity cost is defined as the cost of an alternative that must be forgone in order to pursue a certain action, or the benefits you could have received by taking an alternative action.

In negotiation the opportunity cost represents the alternative (other agreement or no agreement) that you must give up in order to pursue a certain action (agreement). With every agreement we give up something, and that something represents the opportunity cost. When you are effective at being persistent, the *cost* of continuing to negotiate with you is higher than the *opportunity cost* of something else that person could be doing. This is why they say yes (see Figure 10.2).

It was an experiment. I was returning an item to the store from which I had bought it. The item was well within the return period, but there would be a 20% restocking fee. Could I evade that fee? What would I have to do or say to persuade them not to charge it to me? I thought about telling the store that my item didn't work properly or it didn't perform as expected or it didn't do what I needed—in other words, subtle ways of getting the upper-hand, of being in the right, of gaining power. But the product was fine, and lying always backfires and feels even worse than yelling. Also, trying to assert power would miss the point and violate the rules of the experiment: I was trying to see if I could get what I wanted by appealing to a powerful person's generosity. I was trying to practice. So I ruled those out.

After being turned down by the salesperson, I waited for the manager, who came out and repeated the policy. "I completely understand, and truth is, there's nothing wrong with the device; it just didn't work for me. I know you have every right to charge me the fee. And that there's no reason not to in this situation. It's just that I was really hoping you might make an exception in this case."

Now, pause for a moment and notice that I am making no attempt to exert any power in the situation—it would be absurd to try because I have no power—but I am acknowledging my powerlessness and appealing to his generosity, asking him to use his power with compassion. "I'm sorry, but, you know, we can't sell this product as new anymore. That's why we have the restocking fee policy." He was right, of course. And he made complete sense. At this point I was actually embarrassed to continue. Not only didn't I have the power, but he was using his power appropriately. Still, it was an experiment, and I was practicing and learning, which made it OK to persist. I knew I might fail but I committed to continuing.

"Yeah, that makes sense actually. I mean, you can't sell this again as new. So I would of course understand if you said no. But maybe in this situation you could make an exception? I would be really appreciative if you didn't charge me the fee." He paused for a second before responding: "We don't normally waive the fee." Did you catch that? *Normally*. Which means it *is something* they *occasionally* do. My next move was not to make a move. I just looked at him and waited in the silence. Which of course is actually a move, one that feels very awkward. But it was an experiment so I continued. He finally spoke: "Well, I'll make an exception this one time—but only this once."

I was effusive in thanking him—and I wasn't faking it. I was really so thankful that he was willing to make this exception. In fact, by our banter afterward, I think we both left the transaction feeling good about the other, a much better result than would have been accomplished by trying to force power.

Source: From Bregman, P. (2010, August 17). Live life as an experiment. *Harvard Business Review.* Retrieved from https://hbr.org/2010/08/it-was-an-experiment-i.html

Consider the hallmark example of persistence—the 3-year-old boy screaming on the airplane to get his dad's smartphone so that he can watch cartoons. Does the dad want to give the phone? No. But who is more persistent? The boy, of course. At some point the opportunity cost of continuing to negotiate (which will mean continuing to listen to his screaming) is greater than the cost of giving him the phone. The dad relents and the son gets his cartoons. This is persistence in action.

One of the ways to convince is to make the other side perceive that the cost of continuing to negotiate is higher than cost of giving you what you want. This is particularly relevant in negotiations where you care more than the other party

Figure 10.2 Persistence in Action

does about the outcome. By being motivated and persistent, the other side will say yes simply to get out of the negotiation.

Case Sidebar

Tony is not effective early in this negotiation because he is not addressing the interests of the professor, which is for her students to actually *learn!* Were Tony to simply keep asking the professor for extra credit over and over again, it probably would hurt his chances of reaching his goal of a B in the course. Tony is effective because he keeps trying to figure out the professor's interests. In this situation what the professor truly cares about is Tony showing interest in improving and learning the course material as completely as possible.

Too often students think that the solution to a poor assignment grade is extra credit, when in reality the solution is to understand the professor's interests. Tony's goal allows him to be persistent and try different tactics until he figures out what Professor Wells truly cares about, which is Tony's learning, Tony's interest in getting developmental feedback, and Tony's being respectful. This is an example of one negotiation lever (persistence) opening the door to two other negotiation levers (reciprocity and intangible interests).

The other reason motivated negotiators can obtain more value is because motivation is seen as a virtue. When others see that you care and are passionate about something, they may want to help you achieve your outcome. Going back to one of the concepts in Chapter 5, seeing someone as passionate and persistent could satisfy one's interests in principle. Consider the following example:

Felipe and Michael were trying to buy their first house, with the help of their realtor Kylie. For weeks they went to house after house, trying to find the right mixture of layout, square footage, and a yard for their two kids. Every night for months Felipe and Michael would get on the computer and look at pictures, real estate assessments, sale prices, comparable houses, prices per square foot in the neighborhoods they were looking in, school test scores, satellite imagery, and so on. They poured themselves into the task because finding the "right" place was so important to them. Kylie saw how much work they had done and how important this was to them, and it made her want to help them get their dream house. When they finally found their dream house, the price was just over their budget, and they fretted about what to do. Because Kylie had been on this journey with them and had seen their passion, she lowered her commission 1% so that they could close on the house and stay within their budget. This also helps cement Kylie as Felipe as Michael's "realtor for life."

As seen in this example, your passion and persistence may be seen as a positive trait by others involved in the negotiation, whether those others are on your side of the negotiation (e.g., agents, coalition partners) or on the other side. Even those who you negotiate against may see your passion as a positive trait and may want to actually help you achieve your goal. Consider a negotiation between a parent and a son regarding curfew on the weekends. The simple version of this negotiation is that the kid asks for a later curfew and the parent says no. It's barely a negotiation. But the kid keeps asking and asking and finally understands that what his parents are worried about is him doing his homework. This opens the door for a trade-off. For example, if the son completes his homework by Saturday afternoon, then he can stay out an extra hour on Saturday night. This is a nice example of logrolling *and* a contingent contract—the parents are making a trade-off on issues of unequal value (curfew time, homework) and they are placing a bet on the son's future action. There is something else going on here that opened the door for that agreement, and it was the son's passion and persistence in trying to get the extra hour. Further, the parents will be impressed if the son works hard all day Saturday and completes his end of the contingency. The parents are not only going to agree to their end of the contingency, but they are going to have greater respect for their son, knowing that he is willing to work hard to get what he wants. That persistence is admirable in the parents' eyes.

Finally, as seen with Tony in the chapter-opening example, persistence is valuable because it gives you more opportunities to try different tactics. Persistent negotiators are more likely to eventually try logrolling, or satisfying someone's intangible interests, or improving the BATNA, or any of the other tactics discussed in this book because they give themselves that opportunity. Tony first tries some sort of emotional appeal ("Is there anything I can do?"), then tries adding the issue of extra credit, neither of which is particularly effective at getting value from Professor Wells. His motivation keeps him going, though, as he cycles through other tactics until he finds something that works.

As seen in Table 10.3, there are three reasons why passion and persistence allow you to obtain value in negotiation.

Table 10.3 Motivation in Negotiation

Reason	Example
Having more persistence than the other side takes advantage of the fact that their opportunity costs are higher than yours and they want to end the negotiation.	Scenario: You are disputing a charge on your credit card bill and the credit card company refuses to take the charge off. Persistence: You keep asking to talk to the customer service manager and you write letter after letter and do not give up. At some point the company will cede to your request simply because they want to get rid of you.

(Continued)

Table 10.3 (Continued)

Reason	Example
Having passion is respected and valued by the other side and they work to help you get what you want.	Scenario: You are negotiating with your boss over the desire to telework more frequently. Persistence: You consistently demonstrate how hard you are willing to work when outside the office through your communications with the boss, including updates about performance. The manager respects your passion for working this way and thus helps you make this work arrangement permanent.
Being motivated allows you to keep trying various negotiation tactics.	Scenario: You are trying to get your parent to eat healthier. Persistence: You try **reciprocity** by offering rewards. You try **formal power** by saying that you will stop visiting if the parent doesn't change eating habits. You leverage **background power** by questioning what your kids think about your spouse's eating habits. Finally behavior changes when you form a **coalition**, after your spouse visits the doctor for a normal checkup, which you had arranged.

NEGOTIATION TACTICS

Being Persistent

In addition to setting goals to increase your motivation in negotiation, the main tactic in this chapter is simply to be persistent. Persistence has been shown to increase both individual negotiation performance and the achievement of joint gains.[13,14,15] When you are persistent, you keep asking questions, exploring options, and engaging the other side. Persistence has been linked to performance in activities involving many of the concepts of negotiation, such as in sales and fundraising.[16,17] Persistence helps you to try more negotiation tactics. If you reach an impasse, try to add an issue. If the person can't make a deal, find someone else who can. If you get stuck on a position, ask about interests. Remember, you are not only showing that you care, you are increasing the possibility of finding a solution that works for everyone and increasing the possibility that the other side will just agree to end the negotiation.

It's difficult to outline every type of persistence because being persistent can literally be any behavior that prolongs the discussion. Here are a few examples:

- Sitting at the car dealership and asking questions

- Asking to talk to a manager

- Continually scheduling meetings with your team to talk about difficult issues

- Going by someone's office repeatedly

- Standing at a customer service counter and waiting for them to respond

- Sending letters or e-mails repeatedly

- Delaying final agreement, signature on the contract, or shaking of hands

Each of these can be effective in various negotiations because they allow you to remain in the discussion and resist agreeing to an undesired outcome or walking away. Walking away is not being persistent. Walking away ends any process that may have been happening, typically then leading someone to use their BATNA (see Chapter 9). Persistence means you are trying to continually work with another party to get them to agree to something that you want.

Setting Goals

The first and likely most obvious tactic regarding motivation is to set goals, as outlined earlier. Set negotiation goals in line with the model of goal setting presented earlier in the chapter:

- Specific

- Measurable

- Attainable but difficult

- Relevant

- Time-bound

And as you think about the process, make sure you are participating in setting your own goals and consider telling others about your goals.

It may help to think about trade-offs regarding goals before you negotiate so that you do not fall victim to one of the dangers of goal setting, that is, getting so committed to your goal you are unable to think about alternative solutions. It is also important to diagnose your own level of belief in attaining the goal and your commitment to the goal. If you feel like you are not committed, check to see whether the goal is aligned with your interests. If you feel like you think the goal is totally unrealistic, try to figure out *why* you feel that way. Maybe the goal is unrealistic, but maybe the goal is okay and you have a confidence problem.

Using a Preference Sheet

One of the best tools to help you craft motivating goals in multiple issue negotiations is to create a preference sheet (see Chapter 3). By using a preference sheet, you can avoid crafting a goal on each possible issue. Rather, you can focus your goal on overall value gained from the negotiation.

A preference sheet is a tool you can use when planning for negotiation to outline several possible positions on several possible negotiation issues. Positions are then ranked according to importance and assigned a point value corresponding to the importance. The goal for the negotiation is then based on the total value you might seek to obtain from that negotiation. The advantage of a preference sheet is that it allows you to anticipate prior to the negotiation what trade-offs you are willing to make in order to still feel like you have satisfied your interests. This is of course preferable to a "do your best" or "salary is really important" type of goal, which will not motivate performance to the same degree.

Let's say you have a lot of issues that are not reducible or easily comparable. For example, your goal might be to get $80K, 2 weeks off, 6 months between performance reviews, and a company car. Further, let's say that you can't really use one to compensate for the other because each satisfies a different interest (e.g., the vacation is because you need downtime; the car is because you hate the hassle of car ownership). Your goals are now restricting you because in your mind you want each of these things and are motivated to get each one. However, it's possible that the company cannot provide extra vacation or a company car. What do you do? One possibility is to create a preference sheet listing the issues with artificial point values that reflect your interests. A simplified version of your preference sheet (see Chapter 3) in this situation might be the following:

Table 10.4 Preference Sheet With Position Values

Attractiveness	Salary	Vacation	Performance Review Time	Transportation
Most attractive position	$80K (60)	2 weeks or more (25)	6 months (20)	Company car (35)
	$79K (50)	1 week (10)	12 months (0)	Gas allowance (30)
	$78K (40)			Public transit card (25)
Least attractive position	$77K (0)			No Assistance (0)

The preference sheet forces you to think through the relative importance of the various issues in the negotiation. Imagine you set your goal at 100 points. Now you can see multiple paths to reach your goal. You could do this with $80K, 2 weeks vacation, 12 months until first performance review, and gas allowance (115 points); or perhaps $79K, 1 week of vacation, 6 months between performance reviews, and public transit card (105 points). You can also better evaluate trade-offs. If you find out that the company cannot give you a car (35 points), for example, but can pay for you to use the subway (25 points), you are only giving up 10 points. This is much different than moving from a salary of $80K (60 points) to a salary of $77K (0 points), a difference of 60 points. In this case, the goal of getting transportation paid for allowed you to pursue that issue but didn't impede your ability to evaluate the entire deal.

Setting Intangible Goals

You might think, given the content of this chapter, that the purpose of goals and motivation is simply to obtain more tangible value from the other side. That is definitely not the case. As discussed throughout the book, especially in Chapter 5 ("Intangible Interests"), you may have significant intangible value to obtain from the negotiation that you might forget about when setting your goals. If you are negotiating with a client over the price on a particular product, isn't one of your goals to keep a good relationship with that client going forward? After all, that client may not only buy future products from you and your company, that client might want to hire you one day!

You may similarly want process-oriented goals for your negotiation, perhaps that the negotiation is fair or that you come away with a better understanding of the other side's interests. Such goals can be quite effective. In one study related to this idea, researchers found that when negotiators were held accountable for the process of the negotiation, they were less likely to fall victim to the fixed-pie bias.[18] You can essentially have the same effect on yourself by having a goal of a fair process. This allows you a more objective view of the negotiation and thus a pathway to using more negotiation tactics.

It may not be as easy to set intangible goals that are specific, but you can definitely set intangible goals that carry the rest of the characteristics that are listed in Table 10.5. This will help shape your mindset when entering the negotiation and not only motivate persistence but help you avoid some of the mistakes detailed in Chapter 1.

Table 10.5 Setting Negotiation Goals		
Characteristic	**Poor**	**Good**
Specific	I really want to do well in this negotiation.	I'm going to get 100 points of value as defined by my preference sheet. *or* I'm not giving up until I get my boss to agree to 3 days of telework a week.

(Continued)

Table 10.5   (Continued)

Characteristic	Poor	Good
Measurable	I want to get a good deal on this car.	If I don't get 4% off MSRP, I'm walking away.
Attainable but difficult	My bosses haven't given me a raise in 4 years, so I want 60%.	I'll do the research and think about what the market is paying for my degree and for my skill set. I'll set a challenging goal but it will be a goal that I think the company will support if I can be creative in how we get there.
Relevant	I don't really care about getting to telework, but everyone else is asking for it so I guess I will, too.	What I need right now is a stipend or bonus because of some impending medical payments. If I can't get an extra source of money up front from this new job, I might have to look elsewhere.
Time-bound	I'd like to get a 3% raise at some point.	I'd like to get a 3% raise during my next performance evaluation meeting.
Participation	I'm not sure what I should ask for, so I'll ask my coworker and use that number.	I'm going to do the research myself, talk to as many people as possible, think about my interests, and then decide what my goal is going to be.
Public commitment	I'm not going to tell anyone just in case I don't get what I want.	I'm telling my friends, family, and mentor that I'm entering into this negotiation looking for a change in my work schedule so that I either no longer have to work weekends or am better compensated for such inconveniences.

BENEFITS TO LEVERAGING PERSISTENCE

Besides the simple fact that it can work, the benefit to leveraging persistence is that it is very straightforward to use. You are simply trying to get the other side to give in on some aspect of the negotiation, and to accomplish that you keep pushing. While these negotiations often involve other concepts such as formal power or alternatives or reciprocity, the use of persistence in the context of those negotiations is quite easy. You just need to keep asking. The other benefit, as noted, is that if you impress someone else with your passion, you could be seen in a more positive light—they may actually respect you for continuing to negotiate. It is a common misperception of job negotiators that if they ask for things from a prospective employer, they will be seen in a negative light. But look at the negotiation from the employer's side. The employer might think more highly of an applicant who has done his or her research and asks thoughtful questions to obtain both short-term goals like salary and bonus and long-term goals like crafting a productive, professional relationship with the organization. In this case persistence can be seen as a *positive* trait, helping you to avoid the stereotype of the "shrinking flower" who does not stand up for himself or herself.

COSTS TO LEVERAGING PERSISTENCE

As with many tactics, using motivation may not work and may even harm your ability to further the negotiation in your favor. For example, being overly persistent might be seen as *annoying* and *disrespectful* by some people, which might actually impede your ability to invoke reciprocity or leverage uncertainty. This is a problem especially for women, who can be penalized more so than men for being persistent in negotiations, something we will discuss further in Chapter 11.[19]

Persistence is more likely to work then in situations where persistence is respected. Take the following example similar to the opening of this chapter: Let's say a student wants a grade change on an exam and simply asks the professor over and over again for a grade change. With each successive request, the professor probably thinks less of the student, which makes the grade change more and more unlikely. In this case the student's behavior is actually harming his or her chances to get a grade change. Why does this fail? It fails because the professor likely sees the student's persistence as annoying, and more importantly the student's behavior is not satisfying the professor's tangible (student learning) and intangible (student being respectful) interests. Because the professor likely values student learning and being treated with respect, the student is much more likely to receive a favorable response if he or she says: "I'd really like to demonstrate to you my comprehension of the material. Is there anything else I can do?"

This echoes an overall theme for the book, which is that you always need to be focused on the perspective of the other side in order to know whether or not a tactic is likely to work. Persistence in the car dealership works because you have more power (to walk away) than they do. Persistence in the customer service interaction works because you have more power (to provide a negative rating or take away future business) than they do. With the student and professor? This is probably not the case.

Escalation of commitment is defined as the tendency for one to increasingly work toward the achievement of one or more goals.[20] What can happen in negotiation is that when a goal is made, the individual increasingly works toward that goal, even if the pursuit of that goal is ultimately harming the ability to obtain value in the negotiation. An example of this would be a company deciding to build cloud services in-house rather than sourcing another firm to provide this service. The goal in this case is the building of (rather than buying) a new cloud infrastructure. But what if things go wrong? What if the computer engineers at the company can't quite figure out how to make the in-house product work with all of the systems the company is using. The *escalation* would be pursuit toward this goal rather than realizing the need for external help. The managers of the company become blind to the reality of their predicament and focus on the initial goal rather than getting a functional cloud-based system as quickly as possible. In negotiations the pursuit of goals can have the same deleterious effects if the negotiator is so focused on the goal he or she can't see the larger picture of how the negotiation is proceeding, whether interests are being met, and how much value is being created or claimed.

Goals can restrict you as you become overly focused on the goal and lose sight of the larger negotiation package. Consider the following example:

> Danielle has three issues she is negotiating: salary, bonus, and retirement contribution. She cares about financial security, her future, and being rewarded along with her peers. In light of these interests, she sets the following goal: "I want $80K per year, a 5% bonus, and 3% retirement matching contribution [employer matches retirement contribution up to 3% of salary]." However, in the course of the negotiation she realizes that this goal is limiting her ability to be creative with her counterpart.

The problem with this goal is that it might be overspecified; there is only one way to reach it. Each of these things could be collapsed into a single "net pay" package. A better goal would be to say that she wants the equivalent of $86,400 in year 1 [80,000 + (80,000 × .05) + (80,000 × .03)]. There are lots of different ways to get to this number: lower base pay with higher bonus, no bonus but higher pay and employee contribution, or possibly even tuition reimbursement. Having the goal of $86,400 rather than the three goals on each of the issues ($85K salary, 5% bonus, 3% retirement match) gives Danielle the opportunity to be creative with her counterpart in finding the most value. This is important because she may not know on which issues the company has flexibility in negotiating.

ETHICAL CONSIDERATIONS

Goals, as noted, can motivate undesirable and potentially even unethical behaviors.[21] This happens when goals become *the only way* in which a negotiator measures himself or herself. If those goals are only tangible in nature, then the negotiator may end up losing sight of what is the "right" way to behave in the situation. For instance, if a wife determines that her goal is to convince her husband to spend $100 less a month on clothes and uses persistence to constantly pester him, will she reach her goal? Likely, but at what cost? The husband's impression of the wife might be quite negative after this "negotiation," and in some cases he might even come to fear her. Goals might cloud the wife from looking objectively at her own behavior in this situation.

In this case what has happened is that the wife's motivation has gone from being motivated to negotiate and satisfy both tangible and intangible interests to winning, which happens when individuals seek to maximize relative value even at high personal cost.[22] When individuals fall into this trap, they are worried about getting more than the other side and may even end up overbidding on items, such as in a negotiation auction.[23]

Setting goals can make people behave unethically. Maurice Schweitzer and colleagues found that "people with unmet goals were more likely to engage in unethical behavior than people attempting to do their best. This relationship held for goals both with and without economic incentives. . . . [T]he relationship between goal setting and unethical behavior was particularly strong when people fell just short of reaching their goals."[24] In negotiation parties have to be wary of the costs and benefits of reaching versus falling short of reaching the goal. If your goal is to get your significant other to let you buy a big screen TV, but the cost is that they resent you, you may have to reevaluate. Is it worth it to do everything you can to reach that goal? Probably not.

The standard here is for you to look at your options for being persistent and evaluate those options in terms of what you are comfortable with and whether you would like someone else to do those things to you. This will help you in deciphering whether your use of persistence is ethical or not. Even in the opening example of this chapter, Tony could have taken a different route that would be considered unethical. Say he decides to show up at Professor Wells's office every day asking for additional work he can do to improve his grade. At best this would be considered extremely annoying. But Professor Wells might start to fear Tony because Tony is now essentially stalking her in order to convince her to give him the grade that he wants. Is this unethical? Yes. Would Tony want someone to stalk him? No.

Ethics Discussion Questions

Consider the following scenario:

Marcela and Scott are married. Three years ago Marcela's mother moved in with them. Now that their second child is on the way, Scott has been nagging Marcela to get her mother to move out. Scott strongly dislikes his mother-in-law, as he thinks she judges everything that he does. He also feels like their house is too small to have an extra adult now that they will have two kids. Every day he harasses Marcela on this point. Marcela loves her mother and thinks to kick her out would be cruel.

"Please ask your mother what her housing plans are."

"There is not enough room in this house for all of us."

"Don't I get a say who lives in the house that I pay for?"

"Who do you love more, your mother or me?"

And on and on. Finally after 3 months, Marcela loses it and says, angrily:

"FINE! If it means THAT much to you, I'll do it, OK? Are you happy now?"

Scott achieves his goal, and Marcela's mom moves out.

1. Is this use of persistence ethical?
2. Was Scott within his rights to negotiate with Marcela in this way?

3. Was there a better way for Scott to address his underlying interests? If so, how?

4. Could Scott have been persistent without creating the negative reaction from Marcela?

CHAPTER REVIEW

Discussion Questions

Read this story and answer the first three questions that follow it.

On draft day in 2013, owner of the Boston Celtics Wyc Grousbeck and General Manager Danny Ainge had an opportunity to trade players and draft picks with the Brooklyn Nets. This story is taken from Wyc's account of how his persistence led to one of the most lopsided trades in NBA (National Basketball Association) history.

"As I recall—and Danny (Ainge) may remember slightly differently—but as I recall, he came to me with that deal on draft day (in 2013) and said, 'We're going to get two first-round picks from Brooklyn for (Garnett, Pierce, Terry, and White), and take on some contracts.'"

"And I said, 'OK, are (the picks) unprotected?' And he said, 'Yes, in fact, they are.' I said, 'Great. Let's go get a third pick.'" "And he goes, 'Whoa, whoa, whoa,' but, 'All right, I'll ask.' And he's not afraid to ask, he wasn't pushing back. But he went and asked, and he said, 'Unbelievable. We got a third pick. This is great.' And I said, 'Great. Go get a fourth pick. I think these guys have deal fever—we're going to keep going until they say no. I think they've been told by ownership to get the deal done, so let's go back.' And Danny sort of gave me a look, like I don't want to lose the deal by pushing too hard. Normally we try to play down the middle of the road with people, but I said, 'Go push aggressively for a fourth pick.'

"And so he went back, he came back to me and he said, 'OK, you've got your wish. They've said no now . . . they're not going to give us a fourth pick.'

I said fine, make that fourth pick into a [optional pick] swap [where the Celtics get the choice of swapping draft order with the Nets in the following draft]. Because swapping a pick doesn't feel like you're losing a pick. You still have a pick, and it's pretty unlikely that we would be able to swap—that would mean we were better than they are. And we think they're going to be pretty good with this trade. So just get the swap and call it a day. So we got that swap, and that swap turned into Jayson Tatum [a rookie-of-the-year candidate]."

Source: From the transcribed interview with Bill Simmons on the Bill Simmons Podcast by Schrock, J. (2018, May 13). Retrieved from https://nesn.com/2018/05/celtics-co-owner-wyc-grousbeck-details-how-2013-trade-with-nets-materialized/

1. *How did persistence help Wyc Grousbeck and the Boston Celtics in this trade?*

2. *What do you think was going on in the minds of Wyc Grousbeck, Danny Ainge, and the negotiators for the Brooklyn Nets during this negotiation?*

3. *Why do you think Wyc Grousbeck was able to get so much value via persistence in this negotiation versus Danny Ainge, who would've stopped asking for more picks much earlier?*

4. What are the dangers of goal setting? Do you think the benefits of goal setting outweigh the dangers of goal setting? Why or why not?

5. What are specific actions you can take to be persistent? What actions would you be

comfortable with, and what actions are you not comfortable with?

6. Gauge your own intrinsic motivation with negotiation. What do you think prevents you from enjoying negotiation more?

Concept Application

1. Create five goals for you to reach in the next 3 months. These can be for anything. Justify why these goals have the SMART characteristics to be motivating.

2. Create a preference sheet that can be used for evaluating job offers. Be clear how this preference sheet maps to your interests.

3. Create a preference sheet and use it to negotiate for something. Report to the class how you used it and how it could be improved.

4. Negotiate for something using *only* persistence. Report to the class on what you did and how it worked.

Role-Play Exercise: The Subaru

This is a negotiation between a buyer and seller over the car described in Figure 10.3.

Figure 10.3 2015 Subaru Outback 2.5i Limited

- Price: $14,984 ($248/mo. Est). Great Value! Under $18,000 CARFAX Value

- No accident or damage reported

- One-owner (purchased in 2014)

- Personal use – estimated mileage is 18,000/year

- Service history – last serviced at 83,727 miles

- Mileage 83,727

- Color: Blue

- Body type: wagon

- Engine: 4 cyl 2.5L

- Description: Used 2015 Subaru Outback 2.5i Limited with AWD, Air Conditioning, Alloy Wheels, Single Disc CD player, Cruise Control, Fog Lights

---

$SAGE edge™ Visit study.sagepub.com/rockmann to help you accomplish your coursework goals in an easy-to-use learning environment.

MANAGING *YOUR* NEGOTIATION

CHAPTER 11

INDIVIDUAL DIFFERENCES

Learning Objectives

1. Distinguish between gender and sex differences.

2. Elaborate on the importance of individual differences while negotiating, and be able to provide examples of how individual differences impact negotiations.

3. Discern between various personality differences, and describe the sometimes contradictory research on how personality differences can affect negotiation outcomes.

4. Detail how you might prepare for a negotiation if you knew that you would be negotiating with a very aggressive and angry person.

5. Illustrate the challenges women might face during a negotiation.

6. Describe some of the ethical challenges with negotiating when faced with individuals who may be very different from yourself.

Master the content at study .sagepub.com/rockmann

Much of this book has been focused on helping you understand how negotiations work, as well as explaining how to be more effective in getting value when negotiating. However, we also need to consider various factors that can make it either easier or more difficult for you to negotiate and that could even prevent you from reaching a deal altogether. Chapters 11 and 12 will focus on factors that fall into this category. In this chapter we will focus on individual differences among people, such as knowledge, skills or abilities, personality, emotions, and gender. In the next chapter (Chapter 12) we will focus on cultural differences. Unlike the previous chapters (4–10), which address specific negotiation levers and tactics that will help you be effective as a negotiator, Chapters 11 and 12 introduce you to important factors that can have big effects across all of the previous topics.

In addition to understanding the general principles of negotiations, you also need to have as much knowledge and information as possible about the specific negotiation you are involved in, because the application and effects of the principles in this book will often depend on some of those specific details. One of those details is the question of *who* is involved in the negotiation. There are many characteristics of individuals that can affect the process and outcome of a negotiation in significant ways. A tactic that might work really well for one person might not be effective at all for another. A behavior that might build trust with one individual might serve to make another individual suspicious or angry. Some people dislike and avoid conflict, whereas others enjoy it. The better you understand and recognize such factors, the more you can prepare yourself and ultimately be more effective and achieve better outcomes.

Although this might sound like an almost impossible task—*precisely because everyone is unique*—fortunately, researchers have identified some systematic differences and tendencies among people that can make your task a little more manageable.

GENDER AND SEX DIFFERENCES

When considering differences between people, the biological distinction of male and female is often the first one that springs to your mind. Not only is it a visible and physical difference, but it has implications throughout society (in some cultures more than others). Before we discuss its effects on negotiation processes and outcomes, however, it is important to clarify the distinction between gender and sex; **sex** is defined as the strict biological categories of male and female, whereas **gender** refers to the socially constructed characteristics distinguishing between masculinity and femininity. In other words, while sex and gender are typically aligned in individuals, they are conceptually distinct and do not have to be correlated. This distinction was introduced in the 1950s and has been widely discussed in various literatures since then.[1,2] Sex differences have been studied extensively,[3] and although an enormous amount of knowledge has been accumulated, it is useful to question whether causal effects are always from biological sex or might sometimes be from psychological gender. As such, our knowledge and understanding of this complex topic will undoubtedly grow.

The question of whether, and how, women and men may differ as negotiators has been studied since the early 1990s. Research suggests that men and women can have different perceptions of, and approaches to, negotiation. Watson and Kasten suggest that women can perceive negotiations in a different way than men, a finding echoed by other researchers.[4,5] As an example, women often are more alert to relationship issues and implications (including the emotional implications) of the conflict inherent in a negotiation, whereas men tend to focus more on outcomes.[6] Another potential difference in how men and women view negotiations is the perception and use of power, which traditionally in societies has benefitted men more than women, often giving them a subtle advantage in negotiations.

One of the best known gender differences in negotiation that has received a lot of attention in recent years is the apparent reluctance of many women in the workplace to ask for raises, promotions, opportunities, and other perks. Babcock and Laschever's book *Women Don't Ask: Negotiation and the Gender Divide* discusses this phenomenon in detail,[7] and it has been widely debated in magazines, television shows, newspapers, and other media. One interesting finding on this topic is that women often appear to be more sensitive to the threat of social backlash than men; Amanatullah and Morris found that women were actually quite comfortable claiming value for others, just not for themselves.[8] Women negotiators often have to contend with gender stereotypes that put them in a disadvantageous position, since male negotiators may expect them to be less assertive and nicer during negotiations.[9,10] Some research has even suggested that when women do ask by negotiating for higher salaries, it can sometimes harm their social position by making colleagues perceive them as less nice and too demanding and subsequently being less willing to work with them.[11] In fact, numerous researchers have explored potential downsides or negative effects of women being more assertive negotiators,[12,13,14] and the idea that there can be a downside for women to be assertive on their own behalf in negotiations had been theorized even earlier.[15] This of course creates a frustrating catch-22 for women. On the one hand, they are criticized for not being assertive enough at work, but when they are assertive at work, they run the risk of being perceived negatively.

> An interesting example which illustrates a reluctance to "ask" involves a colleague of ours. She was working at a consulting firm and was being recruited by a local university. She was quite interested, because she was sick of the long hours and extensive travel and was ready to work in academia. When she was negotiating with the dean, the topic of salary naturally came up. Preparing for the negotiation, she had accepted that the university probably could not match her consulting company salary of $160,000 and she expected that the university could probably only offer about $130,000. She had also decided that her bottom line—the least she would accept—was $120,000, because the university position provided a number of benefits over her current consulting work.
>
> When the dean asked her the question, "What is the lowest salary you would be willing to accept?" she truthfully answered that she would be willing to take the job for $120,000. Of course, revealing your bottom line is a bad idea during a negotiation, as it gives the other party very valuable information and an opportunity to take advantage of you. The rule of thumb is that if you tell the other party your bottom line, then that's all you are going to get! In this instance, our colleague was not only being completely honest, but she was also reluctant to ask for more. She obviously already knew that she was "worth" far more than $120,000 since her current employer was already paying her a lot more than that, yet she was unwilling to ask for anything even approaching that. She found out much later the dean would have been happy to match her current salary.

Researchers have also studied gender differences in terms of initiating negotiations, showing how the framing of the negotiation itself can have a substantial impact on whether or not women are more likely to initiate a negotiation.[16] If framed as an opportunity to negotiate, significant gender differences exist in terms of whether or not people would initiate a negotiation, but if merely framed as an opportunity to ask, then gender differences in initiating a negotiation disappear. This seems to be related to the personality characteristic of conflict avoidance, which we will discuss in more detail later in this chapter. A fascinating study by Eriksson and Sandberg found that the reluctance of women to initiate negotiations was much stronger when the negotiation counterpart was a woman than if it was a man,[17] demonstrating that the reluctance of women to ask is a very complex phenomenon. In their study, when women were paired with men, there was no difference between women and men in terms of initiating negotiations. Of course, the fact that this study was conducted in Sweden raises the question of how much this finding might be dependent on culture. Finally, there is also considerable research showing that women are treated differently than men in negotiations, often demonstrated in negotiations such as purchasing a car or negotiating for a salary.[18,19] For example, a car salesperson is less likely to make concessions on price when negotiating with a woman, as compared to negotiating with a man.

There are two clear practical takeaways from this research. First, women should try to internally frame the situation as a matter of *asking* about the issue and *exploring* opportunities instead of framing the situation as overtly negotiating or as demanding something. The more you can think about the negotiation as a conversation, in which you are simply looking for information and searching for ways to improve your situation, the easier it will be to avoid some of the reluctance to ask that may otherwise affect you. The more you can think of the situation as two people working together to find a better solution or outcome, the less likely you will think of it as confrontational or adversarial and react accordingly. Of course, this is easier said than done, and like many topics discussed in this book, it will require conscious effort and practice. The second takeaway is that women might also try to combine conscious assertiveness with an increased emphasis on emotional intelligence, relationship building, and engaging in behaviors related to warmth and empathy,[20,21] in order to defuse any negative perceptions and attributions that might occur.

In reading this, it is also important for you to separate the concept of being assertive from being antagonistic or adversarial. Being assertive doesn't imply any of that—quite the opposite, in fact. By being more assertive, you should have an easier time communicating your interests, asking for the other party's interests, and searching for creative and mutually beneficial solutions. You should think of assertive as being the opposite of submissive and meek, but not as the same as aggressive or adversarial.

In addition to the socially constructed stereotypes associated with masculinity, which include characteristics such as boldness, aggression, competitiveness, decisiveness, and control,[22] it is also worth noting the known biological components that can influence behavior. Hormones such as testosterone have an established (albeit complex and somewhat weak) association with aggression and other competitive behaviors, and there are clearly evolutionary differences in male and female development, with resulting differences in behavior.[23,24] In fact, the argument has been made that much of our existing human culture and behavioral norms are the result of evolutionary processes.[25] This raises the question of potential systematic sex and gender differences in personality, and it has been found that women generally tend to report somewhat higher levels of personality measures such as agreeableness, extroversion, and conscientiousness than men.[26]

Determining the explanation for these different effects of sex and gender can be difficult. Do women perhaps have a "built-in" genetic predisposition to be less demanding, and that is what drives the phenomenon that women are less likely to ask for raises, promotions, and better job assignments? Or are women less likely to ask simply because they are typically working in societies that have traditionally been male-dominated and where men have held greater power? Are women perhaps no different from men at all, and all of these effects are just the result of social norms, upbringing, and stereotyping? Conforming to societal norms and social pressures is a very common human behavior. If women are expected to be "nice" and not be demanding, then it can be very difficult for an individual woman to break that norm, and changes to societal norms tend to be slow and gradual over generations.

It is clear that, in some contexts, there are differences in how men and women approach negotiations, how they frame them, and also how they are treated by the other party. As such, you have to consider how these various differences may be affecting you, your perceptions, and your behavior. Some of them may be detrimental to your ability to be effective in a negotiation. For instance, if you are a woman, you may need to consider whether or not you have some reluctance to ask or to be more demanding in negotiation settings than you otherwise might feel is appropriate. You might have to deliberately change your behavior and be more assertive. However, by doing so, you also have to be aware of how that action will be perceived by others and what their reactions may be. The better you can be aware of, and understand, the differences discussed in this chapter, the more you can work to counteract and neutralize potential negative effects on your ability to be effective during a negotiation.

> One of our students, Wei, a small, short Chinese woman, looked young and spoke softly. When asked questions during a negotiation, she often took a long time before replying and sometimes hesitated in the middle of sentences. In reality, she was without question one of the best negotiators in the class. She could be absolutely ruthless during negotiations and, when necessary, was very skilled at manipulating the other party's perceptions. There is no doubt that many other students—when paired with her in a dyadic negotiation—underestimated her considerably, and paid the price! Her demeanor and style undoubtedly triggered multiple stereotypes, and men in particular were unprepared for her assertiveness. Because she was extremely skilled, she deliberately used the fact that people underestimated her to great advantage, and often behaved in ways that would reinforce those stereotypes.

Of course, in any discussion like this, it is important to constantly remind ourselves that the differences that researchers have observed between men and women in negotiations are typically *average* differences in a study sample. Within any sample, there is inevitably lots of variation. So these research findings certainly do not mean that *all* women are reluctant to ask or are less assertive in negotiations. There are highly assertive women, and there are men who are not assertive at all. The research findings are an illustration that, on average, there is a measurable difference when we look at a large number of people, and any random woman we may encounter is slightly less likely to be assertive than a random man is. But any one individual could fall anywhere on that distribution. Finally, our discussion here has been centered on categories of male and female because of the research to date. We know, however, that not all individuals identify with such gender labels, and we hope that research expands to include more diversity in gender identity in the future.

PERSONALITY

Although sex/gender may be the individual difference that springs to mind first for many people, personality differences may be the most commonly encountered difficulty in actual negotiations. During a negotiation, you might find some people to be pleasant and easy to negotiate with, whereas others can be difficult, frustrating, and unpleasant to interact with. In other words, different people you negotiate with can (and will) have very different responses to your behavior; these differences can depend on internal factors that are invisible to you. Some of these responses might seem quite logical and predictable, and others may be emotional and unpredictable. Unexpected emotional responses can have a substantial impact on your own perceptions of them and how you subsequently behave and negotiate. In this section of the chapter, we will explore a few possible personality traits that can substantially influence behavior in a negotiation. As you read through this section, think about how some of these traits may apply to yourself as well as how you might interact differently with other people, depending on their personality traits.

Conflict Avoidance

Many people do not like conflict and consequently have a natural inclination to avoid it. You may be one of them. Conflict avoidance refers to responding to perceived (or potential) conflict by attempting to withdraw, ignore, or suppress the conflict situation in hopes that it will go away.[27] This could be by delaying conflict resolution or simply ignoring the problem altogether. This tendency is often amplified in team or group settings, where avoidance is a common strategy for coping with intrateam conflict, particularly in self-managing teams. Conflict avoidance can be a deliberate strategy, depending on numerous factors, such as power, alternatives, who you are negotiating with, and how difficult the person might be.[28,29] The tendency to avoid conflict can also be affected by culture in that some cultures are more likely to be accepting of conflict as a natural state of affairs and consistent with assertiveness and individualism, whereas other cultures may have norms and expectations that overt conflict (especially in public) should be minimized for the greater collective good.[30,31,32] In fact, much of our understanding of how conflict avoidance affects negotiations comes from studies of cross-cultural negotiation, especially how negotiators from some cultures might be more predisposed to avoiding conflict. This is particularly the case in more collectivist cultures such as Japan or China.[33,34,35,36]

Conflict avoidance is such a ubiquitous tendency that "avoid" is included in a very common and popular framework used to describe different conflict management strategies (or styles). Typically displayed as a 2 × 2 table (see Chapter 2, Figure 2.1), "avoid" is the lose/lose category in terms of outcomes, because obviously neither party will gain any benefit from a negotiated outcome if one party simply chooses to avoid the conflict altogether.

Avoidance of something that is unpleasant to you is not a complicated psychological process but rather a very basic (almost instinctual) behavior. We all try to avoid things we do not like, and this is why avoidance is so common and why it is an "easy" strategy for people to choose. If you are an individual who scores high on conflict avoidance, you may be tempted to find a way to avoid a negotiation or a conflict entirely.[37] Of course, avoiding a negotiation entirely precludes you from any positive outcome, benefits, or resolution that might result. Even if you force yourself to engage in a negotiation, you might be more likely to make concessions or accept a lesser outcome in order to end the unpleasant experience as quickly as possible. Alternatively, you may be distracted by the unpleasantness of the experience (at both a conscious and an unconscious level), resulting in being less able to focus on the negotiation and on achieving a good outcome.

As discussed earlier in this chapter, understanding the effects of personality on negotiation doesn't just involve understanding other people or personality differences in general—it very much involves understanding your *own* personality and how it may affect your own behavior and perceptions. Conflict avoidance is a perfect example of this. If you have relatively high levels of conflict avoidance, it can seriously limit your ability to successfully engage in negotiations. If this is the case, then it is very important that you be proactive in trying to find ways to either mitigate the effect or reduce your tendency to experience conflict avoidance. Essentially, the higher your conflict avoidance is, the higher the "bar" will be that you need to overcome in order to choose to engage in negotiation to resolve disputes.

> One of us (the authors of this book) actually hates negotiating. He finds it a very unpleasant experience and would rather avoid it. However, he has also realized that this doesn't prevent him from being a very effective negotiator, and so he doesn't indulge his desire to avoid it, because he knows he can do it well. He has learned to be a very skilled negotiator, and through knowledge and experience, he is able to be very effective—but he will never enjoy it or even like it. This is often an important insight for his students when he reveals this fact to them at the end of the semester. You don't have to like it to be really good at it!

Agreeableness

One of the "Big Five" personality dimensions, **agreeableness** is defined as behavioral characteristics that are perceived as kind, sympathetic, cooperative, warm, and considerate.[38] Agreeableness is generally a very positive trait for negotiators. Research has consistently shown that higher agreeableness is associated with more cooperative or understanding approaches.[39] This tendency to be more cooperative can also result in attributions of agreeableness based on observed negotiation behavior; in other words, if someone behaves in a cooperative way during a negotiation, other parties are likely to attribute such behavior to a personality trait of agreeableness on the part of the negotiator and will subsequently view them more positively. It has also been found that individuals with high agreeableness often do better in negotiations where there is potential to create value.[40,41] Another interesting finding is that there can be a very positive effect of a match between levels of agreeableness; in other words, if two individuals with high agreeableness are paired in a negotiation, or two individuals with low agreeableness are paired, both pairs are likely to experience positive dynamics and outcomes, compared to the pairing of individual negotiators with different levels of agreeableness, where the outcomes can be more mixed.[42]

Despite the generally positive effects of agreeableness, being agreeable can have a downside. Agreeableness tends to be correlated with conflict avoidance, and so people who score high on agreeableness may sometimes also be more likely to want to avoid conflict.[43] Scoring high on agreeableness can be a potential liability because it might be easier for others to take advantage of you.[44,45] This is something you have to be conscious of and deliberately plan for.

Social Value Orientation

Individuals also differ in their **social value orientation** (SVO), defined in terms of the value people place on their own and others' outcomes.[46] If you are concerned with the outcomes of other people, you are considered more "pro-social" and if you are focused on maximizing only your own gains, you would be considered more "pro-self." As you would expect, pro-social individuals are more likely to be cooperative during a negotiation and are more likely to give the other party the benefit of the doubt in terms of positive attributions.[47] Pro-self individuals, on the other hand, are likely to be more individualist or competitive.[48] This is very important for negotiations, since the dynamics are going to be very different depending on the SVO of the person you are negotiating with. Pro-social individuals are much more likely to engage in understanding tactics, whereas pro-self individuals are more likely to engage in convincing tactics. Clearly, we all would prefer to be sitting across the table from a pro-social individual if given the choice!

When examining what we know about the effect of SVO differences on negotiations, it is important to not just assume that everything will be easy and pleasant if we end up negotiating with a pro-social individual. The effect of different levels of SVO on cooperative behavior can depend on various situational factors; for pro-social individuals the perception of trust is important for them to choose to cooperate with you, as they are concerned about the *relationship*. For pro-self individuals, however, the perception of goal alignment is more important, as they are most worried about the *outcome*.[49] This is another reason to try to understand and anticipate the interests of the other side—you will be able to strategically choose your tactics, depending on whether they are concerned about the relationship or the outcome.

Propensity to Trust

The topic of trust in negotiation has been studied for many years,[50] and the general consensus is that trust can be very helpful during a negotiation. Trust, as discussed in Chapter 6, can be thought of as the willingness of someone to make themselves vulnerable in a social interaction, typically by relying on the good intentions of the other party. Thus, higher trust between parties should facilitate communication and information sharing, as people will be more likely to reveal information about their interests and positions to you than they otherwise would. Studies as early as the 1970s and 1980s showed that higher trust can result in more cooperative behaviors and increased information sharing in negotiations[51] and that lower trust tended to result in more competitive behaviors.[52] Interestingly, there has also been considerable research demonstrating that although trust (and expectations of trust) can increase information sharing and communication, it does not necessarily appear to result in better or more efficient negotiation outcomes.[53] As mentioned earlier, there is a positive link between the propensity to trust others and the personality dimension of agreeableness,[54] which seems intuitive. The cooperative friendly people are more likely to be trusting as well.

There are a couple ways to think about trust in a negotiation setting—namely, propensity and intention. Propensity to trust describes a person's underlying tendency to trust others in general, whereas the intention to trust is a more situationally determined variable that partly depends on their perception of you.[55,56,57,58] In other words, the fact that someone might have a high inherent propensity to trust does not automatically mean that they will share information and engage in trusting behaviors with you during a negotiation. If you appear untrustworthy or engage in behaviors that undermine their trust, that can obviously reduce their intention to trust you in that specific scenario, even if they have a high propensity to trust in general.

You need to be careful when thinking about individual differences such as agreeableness and trust. Although agreeableness and the propensity (and intention) to trust can facilitate the negotiation process by making people more likely to share information, be more cooperative, and generally experience more positive emotions, it can also make them more vulnerable to opportunistic behavior and deception or lying by the other party. By its very definition, trust implies risk, and being more agreeable and trusting in a negotiation exposes you to that risk. So, if you are generally a person characterized by agreeableness and high levels of trust toward other people, it can absolutely benefit you during negotiations and make better outcomes more likely, but you also need to accept that it will make some people more likely to try to take advantage of you. So you need to be prepared to trust while realizing that in some instances the cost of trusting will be that someone takes advantage of you.

Of course, you also need to think about topics such as trust and agreeableness in terms of how their *absence* can make negotiations more difficult. Negotiating with people that have a very low propensity to trust, or have zero intention to trust, for example, will clearly be difficult, as they will be extremely reluctant to share information or communicate openly. Perhaps an ironic takeaway from this chapter is that you would ideally *prefer* the people you negotiate with to have a high propensity to trust and to be very agreeable, but you don't necessarily want to be too trusting or too agreeable yourself. Remember the power of reciprocity (Chapter 4). If you are *not* trusting, that lack of trust may easily be reciprocated by the other side, impeding your ability to build a trusting relationship, not necessarily because of the other side's low propensity to trust but because *your* low propensity to trust was reciprocated.

This of course also raises potential ethical questions. If you are negotiating with someone who is very trusting, which means that you could potentially be opportunistic and take advantage of them, should you? We will discuss this and other important ethical questions toward the end of the chapter.

Summary. When considering personality, it is important for you to look inward as well as outward. Understanding how different types of personalities you negotiate with might affect you is clearly important, but it is equally important to understand how your own personality is affecting your perceptions and behaviors and how it might be affecting their perceptions of you. Are you generally a trusting person? Are you perhaps too trusting and feel as if you often get taken advantage of in negotiations? Are you very competitive and thus a pro-self person? Do you tend to be aggressive when negotiating? Do you prefer to avoid conflict? Do you get angry or frustrated if the negotiation is not going well?

Again, everyone is different, so every reader of this book will have different answers to these questions. There are no right or wrong answers, because anything can potentially be either a strength or a weakness. The key is for you to have a good understanding of your own personality traits and how they might affect your behavior during negotiations.

Depending on your personality and the personality of the person (or people) you are negotiating with, you are likely to have emotional reactions to what happens during the negotiation. You may get frustrated or angry. You might also experience positive emotions, such as satisfaction, optimism, or trust. Many students in negotiation classes mention that they do not like to negotiate and that it makes them uneasy, uncomfortable, or anxious, and this can substantially affect their performance and behavior during the negotiation.[59] Thus, for many people, the emotional component of a negotiation begins even before the negotiation commences. In the next section we will explore how emotions, both yours and those of other parties, might affect the negotiation process and outcomes.

EMOTIONS

It is well established that emotions play an important role in negotiations; the role that they play is complex, much like emotions themselves.[60,61,62] Different studies reveal different results on the impact of expressing emotions while negotiating. These differences arise primarily out of differences in moderating factors such as power, motivation, perception of genuineness, and communication channel (face-to-face vs. online). Moreover, interpersonal and intrapersonal responses differ when emotions are expressed in a negotiation setting. Therefore, there is no overarching rule that expressing emotions while negotiating is essentially good or bad. Displaying your emotions will definitely have an effect; that is, it influences the behavior of the other party, but those effects can vary enormously.

In one company we have studied, we found that several of the senior vice presidents intensely disliked one another and were seemingly incapable of controlling their emotions. This group of individuals no longer meets. Before the decision was made to completely abandon meetings, there had been many instances of loud yelling and swearing, insults exchanged, objects literally being thrown across the room, and doors being slammed angrily as furious people stormed out of meetings. Being unable to physically meet with others certainly does not mean that negotiation is impossible, but it can definitely constrain it. Furthermore, the lack of ability (or willingness) of a small number of people to control their emotions effectively prevented many other people from participating in meetings that otherwise might have been productive and resulted in all sorts of creative decisions and outcomes.

Anger

Emotions can reveal intentions, show limits, and give rise to perceptions about toughness.[63,64,65] This information is then either consciously or unconsciously used to determine if the other party should concede or make more demands. For example, Van Kleef and colleagues demonstrated that angry opponents conveyed that their limits were high, and as a result individuals paired with such angry negotiators gave them more concessions and made fewer demands of their own.[66] In general, considerable evidence suggests that if you display or communicate anger, you can obtain more value from the other side. However, it also turns out that expressing or communicating anger can result in worse outcomes, depending on the context and the perceptions of the other party.[67,68,69] One of these outcomes is that the other party also expresses anger and becomes more willing to engage in deception.[70] This happens through the process of **emotional contagion**, where emotions spread from one person to another.[71] So, although it may be tempting for you to fake anger in order to achieve better outcomes, acting angry can easily undermine trust in the negotiation and ultimately reduce your value by increasing the other party's demands.[72]

Alex is in the process of buying a new car, and after several weeks of negotiating with multiple dealerships, she believes that she has pushed them about as far down as they will go on price, and she is ready to close the deal today. At this point, she has basically identical offers from two different dealerships (A and B), with a third dealership (C) claiming they cannot match the price of $26,800 that the other dealerships agreed to. She decides to go with Dealer A—because she liked the color of their car a little better—and schedules an appointment with the salesperson she has been working with. She tells Arnie, the salesperson, that she is ready to sign a deal tonight. Before leaving the house, she remembers to bring a discount offer that she has printed out—an $800 discount from the manufacturer for any recent college graduate. The instructions on the discount form say that you should negotiate your best deal and then apply this offer to get an additional $800 discount at the dealership. After Alex arrives and makes some small talk with the salesman, Arnie says that he is going to go get the paperwork and contract ready. Alex hands him the rebate form and tells him that she wants to apply the rebate, since she is a recent college graduate. "Of course," Arnie says and goes into the back room. When he returns about 10 minutes later with the contract and other paperwork, he offers Alex a seat to sit down and look over the contract before signing it. However, when she looks at the final price, it is still listed as $26,800. Confused, Alex looks at the contract more closely, thinking that perhaps they forgot the discount, but then she sees a line for the $800 discount further up. Even more confused, she brings this up to Arnie.

"Oh, we assumed you already qualified for the discount, so we've been incorporating it into the negotiation from the beginning" he replied.

"What?" Alex said, stunned. "I never brought up this discount, and we never talked about whether or not I was a college grad. For the past several days, you and I have been purely talking about the PRICE of the car, nothing else—no discounts or other factors!" At this point her voice was already getting louder.

"Oh, it was clear to us that you were a college grad, so of course we knew you would qualify for the discount. This is just how we do things," Arnie said, in a tone that Alex found very condescending.

"WHAT?" she responded even more loudly, and other customers in the showroom were starting to look at them. At this point she was furious.

"You are basically just trying to get another $800 from me at the last second. I never mentioned this discount before, and NOW you are suddenly saying that you are not going to honor this manufacturer's discount because you secretly and without telling me were already applying it, but never mentioned it? I am not going to fall for it. I'm leaving and going to the other dealership right now!" Alex was yelling.

At this point even more people were staring, and the manager was hurrying over.

He whisked Alex into a private office and asked her what was going on. When she angrily explained the situation, he quickly agreed to honor the discount, and she bought the car for $26,000. As she was leaving, the manager handed her coupons for some free oil changes and apologized for the misunderstanding.

In this example, Alex was genuinely angry, and it was a completely spontaneous reaction. From a principled negotiation perspective, losing control of her emotions was not a good thing to happen during a negotiation, but in this case it ended up being (unintentionally) very effective. It is unknown if the salesperson was actually trying to cheat her or if it was an honest misunderstanding. Alex was lucky that her spontaneous expression of genuine anger resulted in a positive outcome. It could easily also have resulted in the salesperson or manager getting angry in return and all of them coming to an impasse.

The practical takeaway is that *if* you want to try to obtain value by deliberately expressing anger, it is more likely to be successful if it is perceived as genuine. If the other party suspects that you are faking it, your attempt to influence them will likely backfire, undermining trust and cooperation. Furthermore, even if you do convince the other party that you are genuinely angry, there is still a chance that they will respond with anger or deception of their own, derailing the negotiation. As such, faking anger is a risky strategy and can easily have detrimental effects, harming your outcome.

Emotion Expression

Beyond just the expression of anger (a very specific negative emotion), it is also worth briefly considering the strategy of deliberately communicating emotions in general, both positive and negative. When studying this topic, Kopelman, Rosette, and Thompson found that the expression of positive emotions was more likely to result in concessions from the other party and more likely to close a deal, whereas the expression of negative emotions resulted in more extreme demands from the other party.[73] Ironically, this seems to indicate that fake negative emotions may have counterproductive effects but that fake positive emotions can help someone do better in a negotiation. So it seems that if you are going to try to get value from the other party by pretending to be emotional, the expression of positive emotions is a less risky strategy than the expression of negative emotions. Whereas pretending to be angry can result in all sorts of "backfiring" in which the other party becomes angry, suspicious, or less cooperative, there is not very much potential for negative effects if you are expressing positive emotions. If you express positive emotions, the only downside could be that the other party thinks you might be easy to take advantage of and might attempt to do so. However, if you are only faking the positive emotions, then you are not actually as susceptible to being taken advantage of. Our conclusion is that if you choose to express emotions as a deliberate strategy, you are much more likely to end up with beneficial outcomes by communicating positive emotions rather than negative ones.

An interesting finding relates to the consistency of expressed emotions during a negotiation. Naomi Rothman has studied the impact of expressing **emotional ambivalence** (two contradicting emotions) as opposed to a single discrete emotion such as anger or happiness and found that an ambivalent negotiator gets dominated by his or her opponent, apparently because partners perceive ambivalence as submissiveness. This is because ambivalence suggests greater deliberation.[74] Interestingly, conflicting results were found in another recent study, in which the authors demonstrated that an inconsistency in emotions expressed during negotiation made the opponent feel less in control and therefore more susceptible to give in to demands.[75] As a general approach, consistency in emotional expression is important as it will contribute to an understanding approach to negotiation.

Anxiety and Fear

Anxiety is another individual difference and emotion that is often associated with negotiations, especially with inexperienced negotiators. In our classes, particularly at the beginning of a course, it is very common for many students to report that they are anxious and uncomfortable in negotiation settings. Perhaps you have felt the same thing! Much like conflict avoidance, anxiety and fear can result in the avoidance of negotiations entirely, thus missing out on all the opportunities for understanding and value creation. In general, anxious negotiators tend to expect poorer outcomes in negotiations, make lower first offers, respond more quickly to offers, and exit bargaining situations sooner.[76] As a result, negotiators who are anxious tend to end up with worse outcomes. Anxiety is one emotion you need to work very hard on reducing! One approach is to try to suppress and control it,[77] and another way is to gradually reduce it over time as you gain familiarity with the negotiation context through experience and practice. Another slightly more positive "silver lining" way of thinking about anxiety in negotiations is that the increase in pulse, attention, and cognitive activity can present an opportunity for creativity and the fostering of collaborative relationships.[78] That initial anxiety, as if you were giving a performance, can provide a rush of adrenaline—what psychologists refer to as arousal—which could open new pathways for exploration between you and the person you are negotiating with.[79] Anxiety is also an illustration of how many of these individual differences can be related, in that women are more likely to experience anxiety in negotiations than are men.[80]

Emotional Intelligence

Because of the impact emotions can have on negotiations, a relatively recent area of research is on the link between emotional intelligence and negotiation process and outcomes.[81,82,83] **Emotional intelligence** is defined as the ability to monitor one's own and others' feelings and emotions, to discriminate among them, and to use this information to guide one's thinking and actions.[84] Interestingly, although higher emotional intelligence seems to be related to being able to build trust with other parties, and to enjoying the negotiation more and being less anxious, there is no strong evidence yet that higher emotional intelligence results in objectively better outcomes.[85,86] It seems intuitive that emotional intelligence should be positively related to negotiation success on multiple levels, and we expect that researchers will more clearly establish this link.

Summary. The important takeaway from thinking about emotions in negotiation is for you to do as much as you can to *control* your emotions, particularly negative ones, before and during a negotiation.[87] Ultimately, during a negotiation you need to be analytical and deliberate, not emotional. There are many skills you can develop to help manage your emotions. What you are doing right now—reading about it, and hopefully taking a class in which you get to practice negotiations—is a very valuable exercise. Developing more experience with negotiations will make you more comfortable and at ease during the negotiation and will allow you to remain calm and in control. Calming exercises and meditation help some people. Fisher, Ury, and Patton, in their popular book *Getting to Yes*, note that being able to "separate the people from the problem" is a crucial skill.[88] You may perceive the individual person you are sitting across from as rude, annoying, frustrating, inflexible, or any number of other attributes that affect you emotionally and distract you from the actual issues in the negotiation. Do not let those perceptions distract you! For all you know, it may be a deliberate and planned tactic on the part of the other person—trying to create an emotional reaction in you to prevent you from fully focusing on the negotiation itself. As we mentioned earlier, people may fake anger or other emotions during a negotiation in an attempt to create an advantage for themselves. The more you can focus on the issue in the negotiation, and not be distracted by the personality or distracting behavior of the other party, the more effective you are going to be.

DIFFERENCES IN NEGOTIATION ABILITY

Another approach toward individual differences is to consider differences in knowledge, skills, or abilities (KSAs), as opposed to demographic or dispositional differences. As mentioned earlier, there are skills that can be developed that can help you be more effective in negotiations, for example, being able to separate the people from the problem. Clearly, individuals can differ enormously in terms of the knowledge that they have (and in fact this book has repeatedly emphasized the importance of information in negotiations), as well as their skills and abilities. For example, some people are going to be better at communicating than others, and some are going to be better at controlling or regulating their emotions.[89,90] Some people may simply have better negotiation skills than others, and the cognitive ability of negotiators may also have an impact on negotiation outcomes.[91,92] As a general rule, we expect that more intelligent people will do better in negotiations that less intelligent people. Some people, by virtue of their careers or jobs or age, may have a lot more experience negotiating than you, and others may have a lot of formal training in negotiation. The critical importance of experience cannot be understated. You can be highly intelligent and have a lot of knowledge but still do poorly in a negotiation if you have no experience, especially in the particular context you find yourself in.

You need to constantly remind yourself to consider differences in KSAs in situations that may not be as obvious as the previous example. There can often be substantial differences in KSAs—related either to negotiation in general or to the specific context—which could give one party or another an advantage in the negotiation. It is your job to do everything you can to try to make sure that *you* are the person with that advantage! Although it can be virtually impossible to change your personality, and it can be difficult (and takes considerable effort) to change your experienced emotions or emotional reactions to events and other people, fortunately you *can* change and improve your KSAs. Knowledge and information can be quite easy to improve and can really help you during negotiations (as discussed in Chapters 4, 5, and 7). By the same token, you can learn to improve communication skills and listening skills, and you can obviously learn to develop and improve your negotiation skills in general—as evidenced by your reading of this book!

ETHICAL CONSIDERATIONS

Many of the topics in this chapter, such as gender and sex, personality differences, faked and/or genuine emotions, and differences in ability, raise possible ethical questions. At some level, everyone presumably agrees that faking anger so as to influence the other side to get you what you want is unethical. It could be argued that such a negotiating approach is both deceptive and manipulative—especially if it's intended to intimidate or coerce another party. You would ideally avoid engaging in such behavior, and you should be critical of (perhaps even angry at) individuals who engage in such behavior.

As discussed earlier, though, research shows that if anger is expressed (especially if it's convincing), it can sometimes help you get better outcomes. Knowing this, it could be argued that the effective negotiator *should* use this to their advantage if they judge that it would work and should strategically communicate anger to the other party, consistent with a classical utilitarianism ethical approach.[93]

In this chapter, we have discussed the importance of being in control of your emotions and actively suppressing emotions that might be detrimental to a successful negotiation. Is that deceptive? Are you hiding your honest emotions from the other party? If you have spent a lot of time learning about emotions and the psychology of negotiators, would it be unethical of you to *use* that additional knowledge to give yourself an advantage? Many people would argue that if you invested time and effort in developing your negotiation KSAs, then it is entirely appropriate and ethical for you to use your knowledge and expertise about negotiations to get a better outcome for yourself. After all, is that not the purpose of taking a class on negotiations and reading a book like this?

Another more subtle ethical question involves more subconscious effects. Some phenomena may operate at an almost subconscious level, and you might be engaging in incorrect attributions and inaccurate judgments as a result of all sorts of cognitive biases and heuristics of which you may not be consciously aware. Take, for instance, differences in personality or ability. If you *know* someone else is a conflict avoider or high on agreeableness, what is the right thing to do? Obtaining value from them quickly might provide them relief because the negotiation would be over. But if you take this route, are you treating them as you would like to be treated? This is where you have to evaluate your own knowledge and how you are leveraging that knowledge to get what you want. If you are violating your own personal standard, you should rethink how you are approaching the person and situation.

Ethics Discussion Questions

1. If you are negotiating with someone who appears to be very trusting (i.e., has a high propensity to trust), is it ethical for you to be deceptive in order to take advantage of that propensity and get a better deal for yourself?

2. If someone is mistakenly stereotyping you (e.g., if they believe you are not very educated or intelligent because of the accent you have or the way you dress), is it ethical to take advantage of them in the negotiation by letting them continue to believe their mistaken assumptions, or should you correct them?

3. If you are negotiating with someone who appears to be anxious and seems like she or he would prefer to avoid confrontation, is it ethical for you to pretend to be angry in order to get that person to agree to a deal that benefits you?

4. Where would you draw the line on using one's personal attributes to obtain value in a negotiation? For example, when is it wrong for an attractive person to be flirtatious, or a large person to be threatening, or a volatile person to be angry? Is it feasible to try to get rid of such individual advantages, for example, to have everyone negotiate via chat so such cues are filtered out? What would be the liabilities of doing so?

CHAPTER REVIEW

Discussion Questions

1. Discuss the main barriers that women, in particular, face in negotiation. After reading this chapter, what do you think are the best ways for women to negotiate when in low power positions versus when they are in neutral or high power positions?

2. Do you think the problems that women face in negotiation are unique to women? Why or why not?

3. How do you use understanding tactics on individuals who are high on conflict avoidance or agreeableness?

4. Pick a particular negotiation lever you might use during a negotiation (from Chapters 4–10). Describe a tactic you might use to invoke that particular approach. Then, describe how one or two of the individual differences would inhibit your ability to use that tactic.

Concept Application

1. You are a woman and negotiating with your male supervisor for the first time. You know that you might be expected to act in a certain way (as one who is not aggressive) but that, if you do so, you might put yourself in a disadvantageous position by not asking about important interests and issues. What do you do? How are you going to gather the information you need to be successful in this negotiation? How might you uncover what the expectations of your supervisor actually are? What do you notice about how you are treated versus others by your supervisor?

2. You are a man and negotiating with your supervisor. What do you notice about how you are treated versus others by your supervisor? Does your supervisor have different interactions with women than he/she does with you? What advantages / disadvantages do you have in negotiation that others you work with do not?

3. As you complete your next negotiation plan (see Chapter 3), describe in detail what individual differences you are likely to face in that negotiation and what it means for your plan.

$SAGE edge™ Visit study.sagepub.com/rockmann to help you accomplish your coursework goals in an easy-to-use learning environment.

CHAPTER 12

CULTURE

CULTURE AS CONTEXT

When you hear the word *culture* you might be thinking *country* or *nationality*, and certainly such categories will have cultures associated with them. But as you will learn, cultures can exist in any collective where values, beliefs, and norms are shared. As such, culture can be found in teams, organizations, towns, regions, schools, or any other social group.

Culture can sometimes be subtle and consist of many unspoken rules or norms for behavior that can be difficult to ascertain. For example, when negotiating in Venezuela, it is entirely acceptable to discuss business matters over lunch, but it is considered inappropriate and even rude to attempt to do so at dinner. Culture may affect how we communicate, the pace of the negotiation, and even what is considered ethical or unethical. When trying to negotiate for the price of a rug in a bazaar in Marrakesh, for example, the initial price asked for by the seller is likely going to be many times greater than the actual price he will be willing to accept (especially if he suspects the buyer is a "rich" Westerner looking for a bargain!), and the negotiating process will likely involve lots of fake drama, friendly lies, and outrageous exaggerations—and perhaps also some delicious tea and biscuits.

Culture allows us to interpret information, telling us what the things that are happening during (and surrounding) the negotiations mean. In one context, a negotiator getting agitated and dramatic could be a sign that you've offended and insulted the person, and the negotiation is over. In another context, the same behavior might be a sign that the negotiation is going particularly well, with the negotiator signaling that he or she is close to the bottom line and a final agreement. If you do not understand the context, you are likely to miss important information, misunderstand the meanings of events that occur, or engage in inappropriate or even offensive behavior.

Learning Objectives

1. Be able to identify systematic differences across cultures, including the dimensions of culture.

2. Articulate why the differences in culture impact negotiations.

3. Know how to effectively engage negotiators from different cultures.

4. Distinguish between national cultures, local cultures, and organizational cultures.

5. Use the differences in culture as an opportunity to create value in negotiation.

6. Demonstrate the ethical implications of negotiating across cultures, especially when faced with imperfect information about what you should do.

Master the content at study .sagepub.com/rockmann

Best case, the result will be suboptimal or poor negotiation outcomes; worst case, the result will be a failed negotiation and lost opportunities for mutual gain.

DEFINING CULTURE

A simple definition of **culture** is the character of a social group that sets it apart from other social groups.[1] There are a lot of ways that we can see and observe culture in any group. Some of these manifestations of culture include the following:

- Characteristic values stated, communicated, and shared by members of the group

- Social, legal, and economic rules and institutions that govern the group

- Unique products of the group, such as art, literature, architecture, music, theater, and so on.

Culture essentially operates by guiding interpretation of experience and providing information about actions and events. In other words, it's a sensemaking tool that provides *meaning* to events and actions that members of the group observe and experience. Culture functions by providing shared norms and rules for what is appropriate behavior in the context. One can think of culture as a type of rulebook that everyone

Figure 12.1 Culture as an Iceberg

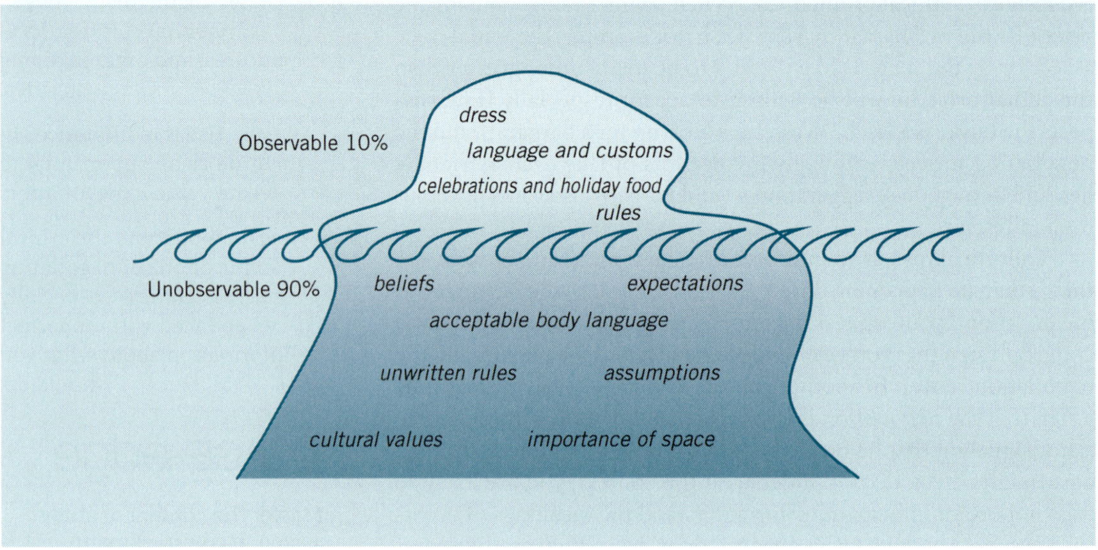

Observable 10%
dress
language and customs
celebrations and holiday food
rules

Unobservable 90%
beliefs
expectations
acceptable body language
unwritten rules
assumptions
cultural values
importance of space

in a particular context shares. They know what the rules are, how to follow the rules, and what the penalties are if rules are broken.

As shown in Figure 12.1, one common way to conceptualize culture is to think of it as an iceberg. As you probably know, the visible part that you can see above the water's surface is just a small part of the iceberg, with the vast majority of the iceberg being submerged. This is a very good analogy for culture, because the visible manifestations that you can actually observe and experience—such as the behavior of members of the group, the products and artifacts, and the structures and institutions—are ultimately just a small part of the overall culture. The challenge for you, if you are not part of the group, is to try to figure out what the underlying and invisible factors are, in order to be effective in negotiating with the members of the group. The better you can understand the values, beliefs, and norms under the surface that are driving the behaviors, products and artifacts, and structures and institutions, the more effective you will be.[2]

As an outsider to a social group, you will probably never fully understand the culture. However, the higher the stakes (i.e., the more important the negotiation), the "deeper" you should be trying to develop your understanding of the culture in question. Fortunately, these days there is an enormous amount of information available—not only in many different books and research publications, but also in a multitude of online resources. One important rule of thumb is *"When in Rome . . . be an effective foreigner!" Never* try to be the Roman in Rome. You will never be able to do it as well as the Romans themselves do, and you will merely put yourself at a disadvantage by trying to be something you are not. Instead, you want to be the foreigner that has a good understanding of the Roman culture and can be effective negotiating with Romans—accepting that there are always going to be things you do not fully understand, and there is going to be nuance that you may miss or misunderstand.

An interesting illustration of this notion comes from Japan and is summarized in the box titled "Naniwabushi."

NANIWABUSHI

A common method of negotiation or dispute resolution in Japan is referred to as *naniwabushi*—a reference to a type of historic and dramatic Japanese poem that dates to the 16th century. Negotiating in a dramatic style, based on the structure of this type of poem, is considered an acceptable method for resolving disputes or reaching agreements in business situations, particularly among older Japanese negotiators. Such a negotiation follows a specific three-part narrative. Suppose, for example, that a business owner today was falling behind on payment on a loan to the bank as a result of the global financial crisis and recession.

(Continued)

(Continued)

His attempt to renegotiate the terms of his loan with his banker, using the *naniwabushi* strategy, might look as follows:

In the opening, which is called the *kikkake*, he recounts the past relationship between himself and the bank, emphasizing how he has always made payments on time, been a good customer, and has been a good investment and risk for the bank. The *kikkake* might also summarize how he thinks the other party (the banker) feels about the relationship. The purpose is to provide the background for the drama that is to follow.

In the second part, called the *seme*, the critical events leading up to the crisis are described. The business owner might describe how demand has dropped and how customers are no longer spending like they used to. He recounts how his attempts to remedy the problem in other ways, cutting back, reducing costs, and so on, have not been successful. He might explain how his family now eats nothing but gruel and his children cannot afford shoes. This will be particularly effective if his family is there, standing ashamed and crying in the corner.

In the third and final part, the *urei*, the drama culminates when he describes how he and his family will become destitute and homeless if the loan payments are not lowered, and then he will be able to pay the bank nothing. The *urei* is all about drama and pathos and could be especially impressive if perhaps he pulled out a sword at the right moment, or a bottle of poison, suggesting a desire to kill himself because of the shame. A component of the *urei* is also the sorrow and shame on the part of the petitioner to have to ask for this, and to apologize to the banker for having put the banker in this position.

If this *naniwabushi* strategy is executed skillfully, and is dramatic and tragic, it can be very effective. Many Japanese business people would be willing to forget prior contracts or commitments and come to some new agreement. In this culture it may be considered heartless or cruel to *not* be moved to a well-executed *naniwabushi* plea.

This is an example of a type of cultural context that is so specific that it is highly unlikely that an outsider negotiating with a Japanese negotiator would even have any awareness of this type of specific strategy. Furthermore, even if an outsider were aware of it (as you now are, having just read about it), the likelihood of being able to use it, by perhaps trying to implement such an appeal, is probably very low. Part of the reason is that you would not have the background information telling you what sort of cadence and pacing to use or how dramatic or tragic to act, to be consistent with the *naniwabushi* historical poem. Another reason is that, as an outsider, you might simply be excluded from being able to attempt this at all, because the Japanese negotiator might not view it as appropriate for an outsider. Whereas in some cultures it might be seen as a compliment and accepted as a sincere attempt by the outsider to fit in, an attempt by an outsider to be Japanese by attempting this kind of strategy is fraught with risk. Finally, there's a possibility that, if attempted, it would fall flat because the person you are negotiating with is younger, does not care about "old" or "traditional" styles of negotiating like *naniwabushi*, and perhaps learned how to negotiate at a Western business school.

DIMENSIONS OF CULTURE

While such specific examples of idiosyncratic cultural characteristics are fascinating and illustrate an important point, they are less relevant than powerful and systematic differences that have been observed between cultures. Table 12.1 highlights some examples of observable behaviors that are typical for negotiators from three different cultures. The numbers in the table represent the relative frequency of the behavior in each of the three cultures when they are at the negotiating table.

Table 12.1 Cultural Differences			
Behavior	**Japanese**	**American**	**Brazilian**
Silence	5.5	3.5	0
Conversational overlaps (talking while others talk)	12.6	10.3	28.6
Staring	1.3	3.3	5.2
Touching	0	0	4.7

What you immediately notice are the profound behavioral differences. For instance, while a typical Japanese negotiator is more silent during a negotiation than the typical American counterpart, the Brazilian negotiating style is characterized by pretty much never being silent. If you imagine a negotiation between typical Brazilian and Japanese negotiators, the former will be doing the vast majority of the talking. In fact, as the "conversational overlaps" row demonstrates, the Brazilian negotiator is far more likely to talk even while other negotiators are talking as well. The table also highlights other fascinating differences, namely, that the Brazilian negotiator is far more likely to physically touch other negotiators, whereas neither the American nor the Japanese culture considers this appropriate behavior. Thus, even from a cursory examination of some simple behaviors, we can see strong differences among the styles of behavior from people representing different cultures. These differences in behavior are ultimately driven by the cultural factors "under the surface," that is, the part of the culture iceberg that we cannot readily see.

To try to understand what some of these underlying and "invisible" factors are, researchers have identified a number of dimensions of culture and have developed systems to categorize and measure them. Over the years, researchers have described a variety of such dimensions, and many are based on the original work by Geert Hofstede from the 1980s and 1990s. These have been expanded by the Global Leadership and

Organizational Behavior Effectiveness (GLOBE) research project. We will look at some of these dimensions in order to try to build a rough "snapshot" of how one might categorize different cultures and appreciate some of the underlying differences between them. Even with such a rough picture, it is immediately evident just how different some cultures are and how negotiating (and doing business) in them will vary enormously.[3]

The following list shows some additional dimensions of culture:

- **Performance orientation**: The degree to which the culture encourages and rewards individuals for performance improvement and excellence.

- **Assertiveness**: The degree to which individuals are assertive, confrontational, and aggressive in their relationships with others.

- **Future orientation**: The extent to which individuals engage in future-oriented behaviors such as delaying gratification, planning, and investing in the future. As an example, cultures that score high on this dimension are likely to have higher rates of household savings and investment, as well as a focus on education.

- **Collectivism**: The degree to which individuals express pride, loyalty, and cohesiveness in their organizations or families. A strongly collectivist society is one in which the needs and achievements of the individual are less important than the stability of the collective.

- **Gender egalitarianism**: The degree to which the culture minimizes gender inequality.

- **Power distance**: The extent to which it is accepted in a society that power is distributed unequally. The higher this number is, the more unequal the society is, the less upward mobility there is, the more stratification or caste systems exist, and the more important social status is.

- **Uncertainty avoidance**: The level of tolerance for uncertainty and ambiguity within a society. The higher this score is, the less people in the society like or tolerate uncertainty or ambiguity in society, and instead prefer rules and standards in order to make their society more regulated and predictable.

The usefulness of such dimensions is demonstrated if we look at some examples where societies are shown in terms of their scores on these dimensions. In Figure 12.2 you can see the scores for the United States, South Korea, Nigeria, and Denmark.

Just from a cursory glance at the charts, you can immediately tell that these are very different societies, and that behaviors, perceptions, and expectations are likely going to be very different. Preparing to negotiate with a typical negotiator from Denmark is clearly going to be very different from preparing to negotiate with a typical negotiator from South Korea.

Before looking in more detail at some of the differences between the cultures, it is important to remind ourselves not to fall into the trap of stereotyping. There is always going to be considerable variation within each culture around the mean score represented

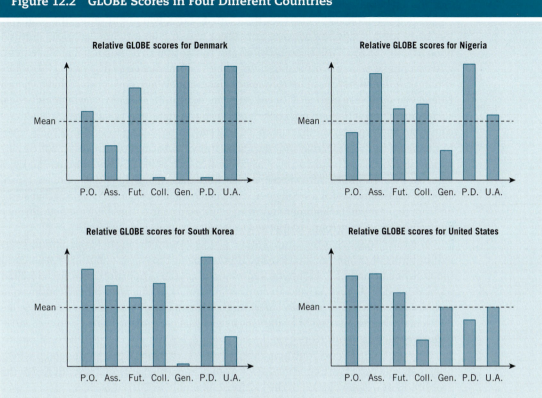

Figure 12.2 GLOBE Scores in Four Different Countries

Relative GLOBE scores for Denmark

Relative GLOBE scores for Nigeria

Relative GLOBE scores for South Korea

Relative GLOBE scores for United States

Note: P.O. = Performance Orientation; Ass. = Assertiveness; Fut. = Future Orientation; Coll. = Collectivism; Gen. = Gender Egalitarianism; P.D. = Power Distance; U.A. = Uncertainty Avoidance.

in the GLOBE assessment. It is probably not surprising to anyone that the mean height of men in South Korea (170.7 cm) is less than the mean height of men in Denmark (180.5 cm). But—at the risk of stating the obvious—there obviously are short people in Denmark, and there obviously are tall people in Korea. By the same token, we have to avoid thinking of *every* person in South Korea as scoring low on gender egalitarianism and *every* person in Denmark scoring high. There are undoubtedly many individuals in South Korea who would prefer higher gender egalitarianism in their society, and there are undoubtedly many people in Denmark who would prefer lower gender egalitarianism in Denmark. The mean scores are exactly that—the mean tendency in the society—and nothing more. It would be stereotyping to assume that every person in a country would have the exact same values, attitudes, and beliefs. As we talk about the "typical" negotiators from Denmark, Nigeria, South Korea, or the United States, you need to constantly remind yourself that these are aggregated means, and any individual you encounter in that culture will fall somewhere on a distribution around that mean. Some will be above the mean, and some will be below the mean, and occasionally you may run into an outlier.

So the mean can definitely help you prepare generally, but you still need to be alert to individual differences surrounding that mean.

When you look at the chart for the United States, you might notice the relatively low score for collectivism, which is consistent with the underlying American cultural phenomenon of the "American Dream" and the notion that individual achievement, initiative, and work are central underlying values in American culture, which is also consistent with the high score in performance orientation. When you contrast that to South Korea, you see a very high level of collectivism, indicating a society in which individual achievement and action are not considered as appropriate, and in fact there is a general consensus and expectation that the individual should be willing to subsume themselves to the needs of the collective and of society. Individual accomplishment in collectivist societies such as South Korea is not as celebrated as it is in the United States, and disagreeing with the group is frowned upon far more than in individualistic cultures. Japan, another nation known for a strong collectivist culture has a saying: "The nail that sticks up from the rest will be hammered down," reinforcing the cultural norm of conformity and being part of the group, as opposed to standing out as an individual.[4]

You can also see that the United States scores around the mean (of all nations studied) in terms of gender egalitarianism. If you look at the representation of women in the U.S. Senate and U.S. House of Representatives, the proportion of women in 2018 was 21% and 23%, respectively. In contrast, Denmark (along with other Scandinavian and Nordic countries) scores extremely high on gender egalitarianism. In a country like Sweden, the representation of women in the national parliament was over 46% in 2018. A country such as South Korea, on the other hand, has much lower gender egalitarianism than the United States, meaning that there are very strong expectations about which roles, jobs, and careers are appropriate for women and which are not. In South Korea the proportion of women elected to the National Assembly in 2018 was 16%.

If you look at the dimension of power distance, you will also see extreme differences among cultures, even among the few countries shown in Figure 12.2. Nigeria and South Korea are characterized by very high measures of power distance, meaning that power and status are very important in those cultures and that people in those societies consider it normal and even appropriate that power, resources, and wealth are divided unequally. In contrast, a country like Denmark has a culture characterized by extremely low levels of power distance, indicating that the average Dane does not care very much about power or status differences and believes that the equitable distribution of resources is very important. In fact, in Denmark there is a very strong cultural norm (called the "Jante Law") that tells Danes that it is wrong to think that you are better than anyone, and as a result it is extremely inappropriate to ever act as if you are better than others. As an example, if you joined a social club—for cross-country running or curling or playing bridge—one member of the club might be a corporate CEO and another might be a bus driver. If the CEO ever acted as if he or she was better than the bus driver, the average Dane would be horrified and would find such behavior to be extremely inappropriate. This type of equality norm is also displayed in that it is considered rude and inappropriate to ask people what they do for a living in social settings, such as at a party or when meeting someone for the first time. This is in contrast to the United States, where someone's job is often one of the first things people ask about when they meet someone new.

What perhaps makes the study of culture even more difficult is that you cannot define a culture by one characteristic. Culture involves a multitude of strategies and values,[5] a fact that makes it even more imperative that you pay close attention to what is happening in your negotiation rather than simply rely on a graphic such as Figure 12.2 to inform you how someone in another culture might behave. Again, this emphasizes the importance of trying to understand cultural values and norms both observed and hidden.

IMPLICATIONS OF CULTURAL DIFFERENCES

That these differences can have significant implications for negotiation, and how to act differently in different cultures, is pretty much self-evident. For instance, in a society that has a high level of power distance, it will be much easier for you to obtain value from the other side if they have a perception of you as having high social status, or being wealthy, or having important titles or qualifications. So, in a nation such a Nigeria or South Korea, titles and status are something to emphasize when interacting with people you hope to influence, whereas it will not have much effect (if any at all), in a nation like Denmark. Remember that effective negotiation, especially choosing an understanding approach, is based on information exchange. It is your task to understand the norms for information exchange in that culture, as well as how your attempts to share information will be interpreted.[6]

Beyond differences in behavior and expectations, another important difference between cultures is the perception of what the purpose of negotiation is and how it is supposed to work. In India it is acceptable to try to negotiate or haggle almost any purchase or business arrangement, for instance, whereas in other societies there are clear boundaries between the situations in which negotiation is accepted and those in which it is not. In the United States, it is entirely appropriate to try to negotiate the terms of a job offer, and you are expected to negotiate for the price of a car. However, if one tried to negotiate for the price of a gallon of milk in a U.S. supermarket or the price of a pair of socks in a department store, the reaction would typically be surprise and confusion, as U.S. culture generally does not expect or condone such behavior.

If you have ever observed a negotiation in a different country or between two individuals from a different culture, you may have noticed a different pattern, or *cadence*, to the conversation. British linguist Richard Lewis has done fascinating research in this regard. In the United States, for example, negotiators generally want to get down to business quickly and will provoke and confront the other side until concessions are made and the deal gets made. In Canada or the United Kingdom, however, negotiators are generally much more genteel. They start with more reasonable proposals, look carefully at the pros and cons of multiple options, and strive to reach a "win-win" agreement so that all sides are able to save face. Spanish negotiations are likely marked by emotional appeals and the desire to test the loyalty of the other side. In India negotiations may take much longer, as negotiators start with long introductions before moving into the substance of the negotiation and modifying agreements after the fact.

Source: Lewis, R. (2006). *When cultures collide* (3rd ed.). Boston, MA: Nicholas Brealey.

At a more general level, there can be different perceptions and expectations about the purpose of a meeting. Negotiators from the United States, for instance, tend to be very interested in getting down to business and typically want to start talking about the specifics of the issues to be negotiated during the first meeting. In other cultures, however, that is not necessarily the purpose of the first meeting between the two parties. A typical Mexican negotiator, in contrast, may view the purpose of the first meeting as being all about the two parties getting to know each other and developing a better understanding of whether or not an agreement is even desirable. Thus, for a first meeting, a Mexican negotiator might be much more interested in meeting at a restaurant or for drinks and would prefer to spend most of the time talking about the general relationship and getting to know the other negotiator personally as opposed to being interested in talking about specific issues. This is because the Mexican negotiator typically wants to *first* establish whether or not you (and your company) are the type of person that she believes will be able to have a successful relationship with her (and her company). If the potential for a successful relationship is not there, then it would be a waste of time to talk about the specific issues of the negotiation.

Having different expectations about the purpose of the first meeting can obviously cause considerable misunderstanding. If one negotiator believes the first meeting is for getting to know one another and the other negotiator believes the first meeting is for starting to hammer out the specifics of a deal, then such a meeting can easily result in negative perceptions and attributions about each other and ultimately a negative outcome. Imagine the American negotiator who wants to talk about specifics of the deal and is faced with a Mexican counterpart who seems evasive and unwilling to talk about those specifics and instead wants to go for drinks and talk about his family. The American negotiator might have a series of data-based arguments she wishes to make (see Chapter 7) but struggles to make those arguments as the Mexican counterpart is not really interested in negotiating (yet). If we see it from the Mexican perspective, the Mexican negotiator is trying to build a relationship and trying to get an impression about what kind of person is on the other side of the table and is instead faced with an insensitive and impatient American counterpart, who seems to have no interest in the relationship and keeps trying to move the conversation prematurely to the details that are not yet important. So even though both parties might be really interested in a deal, it is possible that both walk could away from the first meeting with the impression that the other party is not really interested or serious. That obviously is *not* a good outcome and could jeopardize future interactions between the parties. It could even derail the negotiations entirely.

A similar phenomenon can often be observed in negotiations with Japanese firms, in which a relatively high-ranking representative of a Japanese business might want to spend most of the first meeting talking about the two companies, their respective histories and values, and the possible relationship between them and may never really get down to the specifics of the negotiation. Sometimes in Japan, the "negotiation" might be more a matter of developing personal rapport and a relationship with the other negotiator, which often involves dinner and drinking later in the evening. Once the Japanese negotiator has decided that the companies and people *can* work together, then the details of the actual negotiations will be handed off to some lower level employees in the company to work out at a later date, but the important part of the negotiation—forging the future relationship—will already have been completed.[7] This notion of the timing of events in a negotiation, in other words, when it is appropriate to talk about what, and when we are expected to engage in different types of communication or different negotiating strategies,[8] can clearly vary enormously from culture to culture, and not understanding those differences can result in harmful misunderstandings. In the same way, researchers have found that the use of different types of communication (and communication channels) can have different effects in different cultures.[9]

Overall, these examples emphasize the importance of "cultural perspective taking"—in the sense that you can be much more effective in your cross-cultural negotiations if you are able to understand the other party's perspective.[10] As a result, if you know that you are going to be negotiating with parties from another culture, developing an understanding of that culture should be an integral part of your preparation for the negotiation. In the same way that you will be thinking about interests, power, uncertainty, and all of the topics we have covered in this book, you also need to be thinking about culture—because if you are unable to understand how the other party's culture might affect their perceptions and behavior, you will ultimately be at a disadvantage and will be limited in how effective you can be in the negotiation. This is a less-than-ideal solution, however, as perspective taking is difficult. This would be like expecting to perform *Naniwabushi* after just seeing it once.

CULTURE AND EMOTION

The expression of emotion can obviously be an important signal in negotiations, letting you know if the other party is pleased, annoyed, or even offended (see Chapter 11). As a result, being able to accurately recognize emotion during negotiations is an important skill.[11] However, how emotion is expressed is another factor that can differ considerably across cultures, and societal standards for how and when it is appropriate to express emotion can vary enormously. As you would probably expect, societies that have higher scores in assertiveness would generally consider it more acceptable to express emotions during a negotiation, whereas societies with higher scores in collectivism would consider it much less appropriate, and possibly even offensive. By the same token, different cultures have developed different ways to resolve emotional conflict, so what is considered helpful in one culture may be considered harmful in another.[12] As a result, it is very important for a negotiator who is entering a cross-cultural situation to have an understanding of what the rules and expectations are for the expression of emotion.

As a general rule, negotiators tend to concede more to angry opponents than to happy ones, but that partly depends on perceptions of power.[13] Sometimes this can be to your advantage; for example, the stereotype is that European American negotiators tend to be more emotionally expressive, and East Asian negotiators tend to be less emotionally expressive. It turns out that if East Asian negotiators act more emotional, they can be perceived as tougher and more aggressive and can elicit more cooperation from the other party.[14] Of course, you might sometimes find yourself in the situation where the other party or parties have also done *their* homework and have developed an understanding of the acceptability of expressing emotion according to your culture. This raises the possibility of the strategic use of emotion in negotiations,[15] especially in the cross-cultural context, where different cultures might have very different rules and expectations about emotion expression. This means that negotiators have to be very careful, precisely because responses to emotional displays will vary so much across cultures. Kopelman and Rosette found that East Asian negotiators responded more favorably to positive displays of emotion, whereas a negative (and aggressive) display of emotion could be more effective in negotiating with a European or American counterpart.[16] Furthermore, Adam, Shirako, and Maddux found that those differences in part depended on whether or not an expressed emotion such as anger was perceived as being appropriate or justified.[17] It is also important to note that there is a lot of research illustrating that people from Asian cultures in general have a higher tendency toward conflict avoidance than people from Western cultures.[18]

Summary. National culture provides an extremely powerful context, which influences the perceptions, attributions, and behaviors of members of the society. Having a sophisticated and deep understanding of the culture of your negotiating partners is extremely important—not only because having such an understanding will allow you to communicate better and discover underlying interests better but also because the absence of such understanding can easily result in misunderstandings and miscommunications that will prevent you from creating optimal outcomes and, worst case, will prevent agreement altogether.

LOCAL, ORGANIZATIONAL, AND TEAM CULTURES

Hopefully the preceding section has helped to convey the critical importance of understanding the underlying context and of the pervasive effect culture can have on your negotiations. However, thinking of culture in terms of nations or large societies exclusively is ultimately a very limiting perspective. Culture is not just about differences in nationalities, societies, or foreign locales. Culture can exist at many levels. It may not always be as salient and powerful as, say the differences between Danish negotiators and Nigerian negotiators, but it can still be very important. One example is how culture can vary considerably within nations. Even talking about the "culture" of the United States as a unified construct can be a little misleading, because the United States is obviously a large and diverse country, with many regional subcultures and groups that have unique identities within the larger society. People on the West Coast (especially California) typically see themselves as quite different from people on the East Coast (especially New England). A negotiator from San Diego might come to the negotiating table with a different perspective and have different values and expectations of social norms than a negotiator from New Jersey, for example. Negotiating with a business in a far northern state such as Massachusetts may be quite different from doing business in a southern state such as Alabama, where historical roots differ significantly.

This is not just a feature of the United States, of course. A country like the Republic of South Africa, for instance, has a variety of subcultures that have distinct identities as well. The "European" versus "African" ethnicity, which might at first seem to be the big difference, is not a sufficient way of trying to distinguish between possible cultural differences. Within the "European" heritage of South African culture, for example, there are descendants of English settlers who self-identify as different from descendants of Dutch/Boer settlers. Communication (even language), expectations, and behavior during a negotiation can be very different, depending on which subgroup you are interacting with. On the "African" heritage side of South African culture, there can be substantial difference in local customs, expectations, behavior, and norms, depending on whether individuals come from a Zulu, Xhosa, or Sotho ethnic background, for example. In addition, South Africa has a considerable population of ethnic Indians (it is a little known fact that Mahatma Gandhi lived and worked in South Africa for more than 20 years of his life), and so it is very possible for the visiting negotiator to end up across the table from someone who is neither from the "European" nor the "African" heritage side of South African culture, but another group entirely.

In addition to local variations of culture—especially in large and diverse countries such as the United States, China, or India—the cultures of organizations can also exert considerable influence on individual negotiators. Organizational cultures vary enormously within the United States. For instance, the culture at SpaceX is very different from the culture at NASA. NASA is an extremely rule-bound and bureaucratic organization, often very concerned with politics because it must secure congressional and budgetary funding. NASA is often criticized for having many "old" employees, in terms of not just actual physical age but also tenure in the organization. SpaceX, on the other hand, is a very young organization that is characterized by constantly seeking innovation and questioning the status quo and the "traditional" way of doing things; this organization prefers to hire young and energetic people. Whereas NASA employees are often afraid of risk and obsessed with routines and procedures, employees at SpaceX are encouraged to explore alternative processes and take risks. In much the same way, the culture at a startup video game software company in California is likely to be very different from the culture at a New York investment bank. Expected behavior—from how people dress to how they communicate—can be completely different between such organizations. What is acceptable and normal in the California startup technology company might be completely unacceptable and even considered unprofessional and offensive in the New York investment bank. The software startup is likely to be very informal and unstructured, whereas a New York investment bank is likely to be extremely formal and rigid, with many explicit and restrictive rules. Even within industries, there can be considerable differences. Even within companies, cultural differences can be substantial. An engineering department is going to have different expectations, rules, and assumptions than a marketing department, even within the same organization.

Some of what is shared in organizational settings is not just values, beliefs, and behaviors but also emotions. In Mandy O'Neill and Nancy Rothbard's research on emotional culture among firefighters, they found two dominant shared emotions in these organizational settings: joviality and companionate love. That is, there were many instances of these firefighters joking around with one another, as well as deep feelings of caring and support for these individuals who spent countless hours together, many of which were during serious events. One of the implications from this research was that whereas joviality on its own led to some risky behaviors among the firefighters, this effect was somewhat attenuated by a culture of companionate love.

From a negotiation perspective, this furthers the point that cultural differences can be found *anywhere*. If you need to negotiate with someone from a strong organizational culture such as firefighters, military, hospitals, and so on, you may need to view such a situation in the same light as you would view a different country. Not by trying to be one of them, but trying to understand their perspective.

Source: O'Neill, O. A., & Rothbard, N. P. (2017). Is love all you need? The effects of emotional culture, suppression, and work–family conflict on firefighter risk-taking and health. *Academy of Management Journal, 60*(1), 78–108.

This type of differentiation can even extend all the way down into work teams. Different teams within the same company, and even within the same department or unit, may have quite different norms, expectations for behavior, methods of communication, and social interactions. One team may be very focused on work and be characterized by low communication and no social interaction outside work, whereas another might be the opposite, spending lots of time socializing outside of work, even though on paper, they would be considered identical teams. One team might be far more concerned with social interaction and relationships and have a very collaborate approach to work, whereas another might be very performance oriented and have a more competitive mind-set. When trying to resolve a dispute in a team, for example, finding out the particulars of a team's unique culture should precede the beginning of a negotiation.

ADVICE FOR CROSS-CULTURAL NEGOTIATIONS

This section includes a number of points of general advice for people who are going to be negotiating in different cultures. Part of this discussion will also address possible risks and dangers of cross-cultural negotiation.

Anticipate Differences in Strategy and Tactics

As with all negotiations, you need to do your homework before you ever sit down across the table from someone. If the other party is from another culture, then you have even more homework to do. The better you understand not just the visible part of the culture iceberg but also some of the underlying values and assumptions under the surface, the better prepared you will be and the less likely you will experience misunderstandings.[19] Fortunately, in the modern world with the vast resources of the Internet, it is far easier to prepare for negotiating in another culture than it was 30 years ago.

Leverage Cultural Differences to Create Value

One path to creating value is to logroll (see Chapter 4); figure out which issues are more important to one party and trade those against issues they care less about but that are more important to the other party. Imagine this scenario:

> Anthony is an American manager of a floral distribution facility sent to Colombia to oversee a joint venture regarding cut flower production. The production facility is managed by Carlos, a long-time partner with Anthony's company. Anthony's goals are to cut production costs by 15%, secure a longer term contract, and increase the frequency of Carlos's production metric reporting to verify reduction in cost. Anthony has never met Carlos before nor has he been to Colombia.

Although Anthony can go into this negotiation without any thought as to what Carlos might want, he is better served by thinking about Carlos's culture and what Carlos's interests might be. For example, Anthony might realize that, being from a Latin American culture, Carlos might have a more flexible view of time than Anthony. This leads to a possible trade-off between Anthony and Carlos. Anthony agrees to drop the production metric reporting in exchange for Carlos's commitment to cut costs. Anthony is essence shows Carlos trust in sticking to the proposed cost reduction, and Carlos agrees to cut costs. This is logrolling because Anthony cares more about cutting costs than anything else in the long run, and Carlos is fine with cutting costs as long as he is not micromanaged.

What we see here is Anthony using some knowledge of culture to anticipate one possible way to create value. Without any knowledge of culture, Anthony might assume that Carlos thinks the same way he does (false consensus effect), which would lead to a difficult discussion, a harmed relationship, and a potential stalemate. Instead, Anthony has used cultural knowledge to find issues that can be traded off, creating value.

Avoid Attribution Errors

We talked about attribution, and the centrality of it to the perceptual and negotiation process, in Chapter 7. When it comes to negotiating with people from a different culture, we are obviously going to be much more prone to making errors of attribution.[20] A behavior that might be polite in one culture could be offensive in another, and so we have to be extremely careful about attribution, because our normal lexicon that tells us the meaning of behavior is no longer necessarily going to be accurate. As a result, we must be very cautious about jumping to conclusions when we are in cross-cultural situations.

Avoid Ethnocentrism

Related to the issue of attribution errors, ethnocentrism is essentially the belief that "our way" of doing things is inherently correct. Culture helps us define and understand what is appropriate and inappropriate behavior. Because most of us have grown up entirely within one culture, our perception is that "our way" is not only correct but also normal. Thus, it is easy to accidentally fall into the frame of thinking of "our way" as being the "right way," and it is easy to develop blind spots and not necessarily even realize we are doing it. After all, when we are at home in our own culture, we don't really think consciously about these things, because culture operates very much in the background.[21]

If we are negotiating with someone from another culture, however, they are of course also going to have the tendency to think of their cultural perspective as being the "right way" and ours as being weird and wrong.

Show Respect

In terms of learning what behaviors are appropriate and inappropriate, the starting point should be to understand how to show respect and how to avoid accidentally giving offense (satisfy their intangible interests; see Chapter 5). This can be accomplished by reading about the culture, observing the culture, and asking questions to cultural natives regarding how to behave in the culture. Showing respect for cultural practices is about giving these practices their due attention and treating them seriously. So, for example, imagine the culture is to speak formally to people of higher rank (e.g., in the military). Showing respect for this norm means not only behaving in a way that conforms to it, such as addressing those of higher rank with Mr. or Ms., but also behaving as though you, too, believe that this is the way people should behave.

Be Aware of Exceptions and Differences

A final piece of advice is to be aware that, first, there can be a lot of differences within a culture. Just because Japan and South Korea are characterized by low individualism and are generally considered collectivist societies does not mean that every Japanese or Korean person or negotiator you encounter values collectivism over individualism. It's possible to go to a collectivist culture and still encounter individuals who are focused on individual accomplishment and are more ambitious and driven toward that goal than the average person in an individualistic society. This is similarly true in organizations—just because an organization generally has a culture of innovation and exploration does not mean *every* person in that organization values innovation or is thinking about innovation on a day-to-day basis.

ETHICAL CONSIDERATIONS

Differences in culture also mean that ethical problems or dilemmas can arise easily. This may happen not only as a result of miscommunication or misunderstandings but also because the culture allows different people to perceive the same reality in very different ways. What is accepted and appropriate in one society might be considered highly inappropriate or even illegal or immoral according to another culture. The more ethnocentric the parties to the negotiation are, the more likely this will be.

One example is that of bribes. In most Western countries, bribes are considered inappropriate and are typically illegal. In other countries it can be considered simply a cost of doing business, and payments are seen as a way to facilitate things, or to "lubricate" the business process. This can create an ethical dilemma for organizations that wish to do business is such cultures but have strict internal policies or rules against paying bribes or making payments of that nature.

A fascinating example of different cultural values colliding in the business context is Africa. Historically, foreign trade in Africa has been characterized by relationships with former colonial powers (such as Great Britain, France, or other Western European countries), in which very different values and attitudes have to be managed. More recently, China has become increasingly involved in African trade, investment, and infrastructure development, and so an entirely different culture is now introduced. For instance, China funded a railway project in Kenya and is doing more than $200 billion worth of trade with Africa every year.[22] An African business that is used to negotiating with a British company, for example, would likely need to substantially change their approach and thinking if negotiating with a Chinese company.

The issue of being able to adapt to negotiating in different contexts or with different cultures also emphasizes the notion, mentioned earlier, of having a personal standard of how much you are willing to change. On the one hand, you have to accept that having completely inflexible standards of behavior will make you an ineffective negotiator in a global world filled with different cultures. On the other hand, you need to maintain clear personal standards that remain constant across different situations, both for your own moral sake and to maintain your reputation and manage perceptions of integrity and honesty. Finding that balance is something that each negotiator needs to do—and preferably *before* they are already deep inside an unfamiliar context and faced with a difficult choice. The better prepared negotiators are, and the more prepared for an unfamiliar context by having done their "homework" of studying the rules and norms of that culture, the less likely they are to end up in an ethical dilemma, or accidentally offending the other party, or causing irreparable damage to the relationship.[23]

Consider the example of buying a Persian rug in a bazaar in Istanbul. In this context, haggling and outrageous demands may not only be perfectly acceptable but may even be considered an integral part of the negotiating process. If the seller starts the negotiation by saying that $1,000 would be a fair price and that his 14 children will starve if you pay less than $800, you can be almost certain that he is not telling the truth. Given that context and those particular rules and norms, it would be perfectly acceptable for you to say that you only have $200 on you—and pull the bills out of your pocket to show him, and just not mention that you have another $300 in your other pocket. Or perhaps you might claim that your wife or husband will divorce you if you pay more than $200. Those would definitely be overt lies, but in the context of that particular situation, it will seem to be an acceptable lie to most people.

There is a broader notion here of what is right and wrong in different cultures. In America, if you give undue preference in hiring and deal making to your friends, you might get sued. In China, that is called *guanxi* and is central to the facilitation of business and negotiation. As a cross-cultural negotiator, you need flexibility. Much of what you consider to be obviously right and wrong is based on your own cultural norms. You should not simply assume that these norms are universal or universally ethical.

As mentioned in other parts of this book, you have to decide where your personal ethical "line" is. You might have a standard of *never* telling a lie or trying to deceive people. That is obviously perfectly fine and a laudable attitude. But you probably should accept that either (a) you will do poorly in some negotiation contexts or (b) you should *not* be the one to conduct negotiations with Persian rug dealers, and negotiation outcomes will be much better if someone else negotiates on your behalf. So the takeaway from this discussion is *not* that you should be ethically flexible. Rather, it is that the standards for what ethical behavior is can change from context to context and can be very different across different cultures. Ultimately, the better you understand this and can predict it, the better prepared you will be to negotiate effectively in such situations. And sometimes, the best outcome for you (and your personal ethical standards) may be to *not* negotiate.

Ethics Discussion Questions

1. You are negotiating for a sari in a Mumbai market. The price asked for is 3,000 rupees, which is approximately $40 or €35. You think this is a great price given how much you would pay for such a garment in your home country. You also know you are expected to negotiate. You respond by saying 1,500 rupees, at which point the shop owner gets very agitated and angry. What do you do? What is the right way to respond in this situation?

2. When do you think it is acceptable to lie in cross-cultural negotiations? When do you think it is acceptable to get angry in cross-cultural negotiations?

3. We have observed in many foreign locations that Americans will often be obnoxious in that they are not responding to the local culture in any way. That is, they don't attempt to understand the cultural differences or how to leverage such differences to create value. However, we've also observed that many of those same Americans get what they want. Why? Do you think this practice of ethnocentrism is acceptable? Under what conditions might it be acceptable?

4. A local "fixer" in a foreign country approaches you and says that he is willing to be your company's agent, stating that he can facilitate doing business in the country through his connections and network. He tells you he will need a substantial discretionary budget (and no questions asked) in order to do his job. How would you reply?

CHAPTER REVIEW

Discussion Questions

1. Your employer is sending you to Finland to negotiate a possible joint venture with a local technology firm there. List five questions that you really need answers to before you would feel ready to negotiate.

2. What is the difference between adopting a culture and adopting a cultural perspective?

3. Strong cultures are typically thought of as situations where there is a lot of agreement around shared values, norms, and beliefs. What are some examples of strong local, organizational, or national cultures that you know? What is it like to negotiate with individuals from strong cultures?

4. If your company really wants to do business in a country where bribery is common, but you have a corporate policy against paying bribes, what would you recommend they do?

Concept Application

1. Go to a local business (shop, restaurant, etc.) that has a different ethnic origin from your own. Try to negotiate for an item or items at that business. Reflect on what you notice. What did they do that you would not normally see if you were negotiating with someone from your own cultural background? How did it affect the negotiation? How did you change your own behavior in this unfamiliar context?

2. Ask someone from a different culture how negotiating is different in that culture. Ask about purchasing items in stores, but also ask about how conflict is solved in the home. Compare and contrast those differences with your own culture.

3. Cultures can change! What changes in terms of negotiating have you noticed in your lifetime? Are there some items that used to be negotiable that are not any longer? Why do you think that is? In what situations is negotiation still acceptable in your culture?

$SAGE edge™   Visit study.sagepub.com/rockmann to help you accomplish your coursework goals in an easy-to-use learning environment.

APPENDIX 1
Mini Cases

This appendix comprises a series of six vignettes with follow-up questions. The idea in presenting these vignettes is to demonstrate how the concepts from the book are *intertwined* or *connected*. That is, in many (if not all!) negotiations, it is not just one concept that matters; rather, it is the interplay of several concepts that determines the outcome. As Druckman has described in the context of international negotiations, countries flow back and forth from hard tactics to soft tactics and back again through various negotiation stages.[1] How can we try to understand such complexity? The goal here is for you not just to identify a negotiation lever (e.g., reciprocity, intangible interests, relationships, formal power, uncertainty, alternatives, and persistence) but to see how multiple concepts and tactics might impact one negotiation. In this way your thinking will move beyond just knowing the language of negotiation to truly understanding how negotiators think and behave.

VIGNETTE 1: PROFESSOR POE

Professor Poe recently left Upper River College for a job at a new university. However, because she was a very skilled instructor and was especially popular at teaching a particular class, one of her former students asked her if she'd be interested in teaching a course for her company, Technocorp. Technocorp would basically pay her as an independent contractor. She said yes, since she had taught classes for companies before and enjoyed it, and she knew these contracts usually paid very well.

Teaching a class requires a considerable amount of advance preparation (writing the syllabus, creating reading lists, setting up online resources, etc.), so 10 weeks before the class was scheduled to start, Professor Poe contacted her former student to find out the details of offering the class at Technocorp. Her former student told her that the course had been approved and that someone from Technocorp would get back to her with the details, probably the vice president (VP) of human resources or the chief financial officer (CFO), with the exact terms of her contract so that she could decide if she was going to do it. After all, if her estimate of how much they were going to pay her was unrealistically high and they actually paid far less, perhaps it wouldn't be worth her time to teach the class.

After receiving no answer and getting closer to when she would have to start preparing for the class, Professor Poe repeatedly contacted Technocorp, this time asking to speak to the CFO and VP of human resources directly. Six weeks before classes started, she finally got a phone call from the VP of human resources, specifying compensation of $15,000 plus expenses. Since she thought $15,000 was a lucrative sum for five classes of 4 hours each, Professor Poe immediately agreed and began preparations for the class.

After 6 weeks, the class started, and Professor Poe began teaching. Two weeks after classes began, Professor Poe started to wonder how she would be paid, whether in a single lump sum (presumably once her work teaching the class was done) or in installments. She e-mailed the person in charge of payroll and received a cryptic e-mail back saying that there was some confusion about her pay and that they didn't know what to do about it. Shortly thereafter, she received an e-mail from the VP of human resources. The e-mail stated that he was very sorry to inform her that he made a mistake when he told her $15,000 for the class and that her payment for the class would be $10,000. The e-mail went on to explain that the budget for continuing education had recently been cut and was therefore going to be $2,000 per 4-hour class, and would only allow for four classes per course (so $8,000 total). The VP went on to explain that they were going to honor the original five-class agreement, so Professor Poe should be very happy with the $10,000, because technically she should only be paid $8,000. The VP also mentioned in the e-mail that when he promised her $15,000 he was still relatively new in his position and that this rate reduction came a few weeks after he had taken the position.

Professor Poe was understandably surprised, and quite a bit annoyed, by this revelation. Her options were to either accept the new pay of $10,000, refuse and insist that the school honor the $15,000 promise, or do something else.

Discussion Questions

1. What is this negotiation about? What concepts are *central* to this upcoming negotiation?

2. What does Professor Poe have to plan for in this negotiation?

3. Should Professor Poe use a convincing or understanding approach in this negotiation? Why?

4. What tactics *could* Professor Poe use in this negotiation?

5. Does it matter that the $15,000 offer was made over the phone rather than in writing?

6. What would you do if you were Professor Poe and, more importantly, *why*?

7. What would you do if you were the VP of human resources and, more importantly, *why?*

8. Incorporating the concepts of reciprocity (Chapter 4), formal power (Chapter 8), BATNA (Chapter 9), and uncertainty (Chapter 7), what strategies might Professor Poe and/or the VP of human resources use to obtain the most *value* from this negotiation?

VIGNETTE 2: *THE PRINCESS BRIDE*

In the 1987 classic movie *The Princess Bride*, there is a conflict between Inigo Montoya and the "Man in Black," who, later to be learned, is Westley, the farmboy and love of Princess Buttercup.

The conflict is over how Inigo Montoya is going to fight the Man in Black, who is stuck hanging on the side of a cliff after Inigo's employer, Vizzini, cut most (but not all) of the rope from the top of the cliff, forcing the Man in Black to start climbing the rocks. Inigo has been told by Vizzini to kill the Man in Black. Inigo, however, wants to kill the Man in Black in a sword fight, not by letting the Man in Black fall off the side of a cliff to the ocean below. Here is the dialogue of the scene:

Man in Black:	[clinging to the rock] You could give me a tree branch or something.
Inigo:	I could do that. I've got some rope up here, but I do not think you would accept my help, since I am only waiting around to kill you.
Man in Black:	That does put a damper on our relationship.
Inigo:	But I promise I will not kill you until you reach the top.
Man in Black:	That's very comforting, but I'm afraid you'll just have to wait.
Inigo:	I hate waiting. . . . [pause] . . . I could give you my word as a Spaniard.
Man in Black:	No good. I've known too many Spaniards.
Inigo:	Isn't there any way you'd trust me?
Man in Black:	Nothing comes to mind.
Inigo:	I swear on the soul of my father Domingo Montoya, you will reach the top alive.
Man in Black:	Throw me the rope. [Inigo throws the rope and helps the Man in Black to the top of the cliff]

Discussion Questions

1. What is this negotiation about? What concepts are *central* to this upcoming negotiation?

2. Why is this a negotiation? What is negotiated here?

3. What concepts explain why Inigo decides to throw the rope down to the Man in Black?

4. What concepts explain why Westley decides to trust Inigo Montoya that he will help him up instead of cutting the rope once Westley begins to use it?

5. Why would these two characters who are bound to fight (and perhaps kill) one another be willing to trust each other first?

VIGNETTE 3: JACOB AND THE GARDEN

Jacob is a volunteer at his child's school working to improve the flower gardens in the back of the school so that the kids and teachers can have an outdoor classroom area. Jacob works with two other parents, Stephanie and Mahesh, on the gardening projects for the school.

One spring day, Jacob, Stephanie, and Mahesh get together at the school to discuss garden plans for the summer. There is conflict, as you will see, around what projects they are going to prioritize for the year. Here is how the negotiation proceeds:

Stephanie: I'd really like to build a bench for the garden this year.

Jacob: I'm not sure a bench is really part of the vision for the garden. We still have so much to do in terms of planting and weeding.

Stephanie: A bench would be great, though. It would give teachers and kids a place to sit and observe the garden.

Jacob: True, but we already have the tree stumps for the kids and having a bench will take space away from the plantings. It will also take a lot of our budget, and we need to mulch again this year, which will cost money.

Mahesh: Those are good points, but we've talked about the budget and it looks okay.

Stephanie: I actually found a bench kit in this catalog that we can buy for only $100.

Jacob: Yes, I've seen that catalog. The parts are not the best, and if we have a bench we will have to maintain and weed around it. I just worry this is going to create more maintenance work when we are all volunteers.

Mahesh: Would it be a harm to just try the bench and see how it goes this year?

Jacob: You really want to bring in concrete mix and set a bench in the garden? That seems like a lot of work on top of what we already have to do.

Stephanie: I'll be in charge of building it and making sure it looks good this year. And I know how good you are, Jacob, at helping us know what else we need to do in the garden. I'll be sure to find you enough volunteers. Okay?

Jacob: Fine.

Discussion Questions

1. What is this negotiation about? What concepts are central in this negotiation?

2. How are the following tactics used in this negotiation?

   a. BATNA

   b. Coalition

    c.   Persistence

    d.   Contingent contract

    e.   Data-based arguments

    f.   Intangible interests

3. What made Jacob say "yes" in this negotiation? That is, of all the tactics that Stephanie and Mahesh use, which is most effective and why?

4. What else could Jacob have done in this negotiation to change Stephanie's mind about having the bench in the garden?

VIGNETTE 4: JALEN AND BRIAN

Jalen and his roommate, Brian, are both dreading the upcoming negotiation. They have lived in an apartment together for 2 years, but Jalen would like to renegotiate their agreement. When they first agreed to live together, Jalen had already been living on his own in the apartment for about 8 months. His college friend, Brian, had no job and needed a cheap place to live. Jalen needed a bit of extra cash, so this seemed like a good fit. Jalen's rent at the time was $1,600/month. He offered Brian a room at $500/month, knowing that that was all Brian could really afford at the time.

    With regular increases the rent is now $1,750/month, and Brian is still only paying $500. Brian now has a full-time job and knows he is getting a good deal. Jalen is sensitive to the fact that, although Brian is now employed, Brian is not in as good of a position as Jalen is financially. Jalen cannot quite shake the sinking feeling, though, that his friend is taking advantage of his goodwill. Even Brian is worried about this and is open to renegotiating the rental terms with Jalen. Finally, one night, after sharing a pizza, Jalen asks if they can discuss the rent.

Brian: I know what you are going to say—you'd like more rent.

Jalen: I feel bad asking, but, you know, since you are doing better now . . .

Brian: I've done a lot of thinking about this, and in looking at my entry-level salary and raise I might be getting, I think I can swing another $100 a month.

Jalen: But that's still you paying $600 and me paying $1,150.

Brian: But me paying another $100 a month would mean another $1,200 a year for you. That doesn't seem too bad.

Jalen: Yeah, I know that's a lot. I was just hoping you'd be able to do more.

Brian: Do you have anyone else that wants to move in?

Jalen: No, and I'm not excited about finding someone else given that you are pretty easy to live with. What about $800?

Brian:	I'd have to run the numbers, but I might be able to swing $650. That's only because I think I might be getting that raise. What about that?
Jalen:	That's better. Any chance you could do $700?
Brian:	How about we split the difference—$675, if I get the raise. We'll start in 2 months, okay?
Jalen:	Yeah, okay.

Discussion Questions

1. What is this negotiation about? What concepts are *central* to this negotiation?

2. Why is uncertainty so important in this negotiation between Jalen and Brian?

3. What tactics do Jalen and Brian each use?

4. What tactics are most effective in this negotiation?

5. This is a one-issue negotiation. What is that one issue and how does negotiating this way limit Jalen and Brian?

VIGNETTE 5: THE MOFRED GLASS CORPORATION

Susan and Laurie are two lawyers representing a client who was injured while installing a faulty panel from the Mofred Glass Corporation in a high-rise building. They are sitting on a couch in a conference room at the Mofred Glass Corporation, waiting for the CEO of the company, Dwayne Jackson, to join them.

The administrative assistant has told them that there is a problem on the manufacturing floor, so the CEO will be slightly delayed. To pass the time, Susan and Laurie are chatting about a negotiation they were involved in the previous week.

"Can you believe how nice Rebecca turned out to be?" Laurie asks. Susan nods and smiles.

"I know. I was worried that this hot-shot executive we were supposed to meet was going to be super-competitive and difficult to negotiate with, but she was just absolutely delightful," Susan replies. "I really loved how she went out of her way to make sure we were comfortable with all the facts and data, and was willing to take as much time as we needed to explain things to us. I think that settlement really worked for everyone."

"Well, it certainly didn't hurt that the two of you realized you had not only gone to the same college but had also been in the same sorority," Laurie laughs.

"Yeah, no kidding," Susan agrees. "That certainly helped to break the ice. It really made me feel like I was talking to an old friend rather than just having an impersonal business meeting. I think she felt the same way. Plus, it was fun to reminisce about the campus and our favorite hang-out spots."

"I also love the way she dresses," Laurie adds. "That outfit was spectacular, and I think she and I not only wear the same size but have very similar taste in suits."

"I think she definitely noticed that as well," Susan agrees, "given how she recognized the brand of suit you were wearing and complimented your choice of accessories."

Laurie is about to reply, when the assistant opens the door to let them know that the CEO is on his way. Both Susan and Laurie are startled, not because of the assistant opening the door but because they can hear the CEO yelling loudly outside the door. He sounds very agitated.

"And you tell Frank that if he breaks that tool again, he's fired!" They almost expect to hear the sound of a door slamming or a chair being thrown, he sounds so angry.

Laurie glances at Susan, and gets a slightly shocked look back. They are both very surprised, and Laurie can tell from Susan's rigid body language that she is nervous.

When Dwayne shoulders his way into the room past his assistant, the other surprise is how big he is. He is at least 6 ft, 5 in and very large. He looks muscular but also has a bit of a belly, so he probably weighs over 300 pounds.

"Sorry I am late, ladies," he says, with a very loud and obviously annoyed voice that seems to echo off the walls. "I am dealing with a bunch of idiots who keep breaking equipment, and it upsets me that I have to waste time with that kind of junk. I'm tempted to just go down to the line and bust some heads! Maybe that would get everyone to straighten up their act." He smiles, but it looks more predatory than friendly. "Anyway, I'm Dwayne. Dwayne Jackson."

Susan and Laurie introduce themselves, and he gestures toward the conference table.

"Excellent! I am always happy to meet two beautiful ladies." He pauses and angrily wags a finger in their direction. "Although don't think your pretty looks will influence me. I know how ruthless your firm can be, and I'm telling you right now, you are not going to take advantage of this guy! Okay, let's get down to business and not waste any more time."

He waves his hands and practically pushes them toward the conference table.

"Now, before we get started, do either of you ladies need to use the restroom?" he asks. "I know how women can be, and I don't want to have to stop the meeting later because one of you needs to go. I swear, when my wife and I drive down to Florida, I feel like we have to stop every 30 minutes because of her!"

As he walks toward one side of the table, Susan leans over to Laurie and whispers, "I don't think this negotiation is going to be as smooth as the last one. The guy seems like a huge jerk, and doesn't seem very intelligent either."

Laurie nods nervously and replies, "Maybe we shouldn't even raise the question of who pays the legal fees if we do not reach an agreement."

"Perhaps we should just accept that cost rather than risk arguing with him about it," Susan whispers back.

Discussion Questions

1. What is this negotiation about? What concepts are *central* to this upcoming negotiation?

2. What tactics have already been used in this negotiation, which technically has not begun yet? Have any of these tactics been effective?

3. How are individual differences likely to impact the negotiation from Laurie and Susan's point of view? And from Dwayne's point of view?

4. What assumptions are being made in this example, and by whom?

5. What should Laurie and Susan do in this situation? How can they plan on the fly now that they have more information about Dwayne? Or should they change their plan at all?

6. If Dwayne's anger and aggression is an act, is it ethical? If it is not an act, is it ethical? How do you best negotiate with someone who is clearly discriminating against others?

VIGNETTE 6: MYKALEA AND INVF

Mykalea Hanson is a nurse in the Detroit area. She has been working at a fertility clinic (INVF) for the past 2 years and very much enjoys her work. During the time she has been at INVF she has finished her nursing degree and is now a registered nurse (RN). Her manager, Donna, at INVF has been very impressed with her work, noting that Mykalea has excellent customer service skills and excellent attention to detail.

Mykalea has now been offered a team leader position at INVF. Donna has told Mykalea that Donna's boss, Cheri, will make the final decision but that INVF is not interviewing anyone else and would like Mykalea to take the position. Donna has also told Mykalea that she should expect an offer letter from Cheri and that this is her opportunity to negotiate for a salary increase beyond the 2% or 3% she would get in a normal year.

The next day Mykalea receives this letter from Cheri.

Dear Ms. Hanson,

It is our pleasure at INVF to offer you the Team Leader, RN position. We have been thrilled with your work during your 2 years at INVF and would like you to remain as a valued member of the team.

In the Team Leader, RN role you will continue much of your current work but with the added responsibility of staff scheduling and evaluation. You will be freed up from some of your patient time in order for you to complete those tasks. Donna can give you more detail on how day-to-day life will change.

Given the change in level, we are prepared to offer you a salary increase of 4%, so your new salary would be $72,211. This is commensurate with other team leaders in the INVF network, and we hope it will be satisfactory to you.

Thank you very much for your consideration, and we look forward to your reply.

Sincerely,

Cheri Littleton

Mykalea, who was quite excited about the opportunity offered by INVF, is quite disappointed with the letter. A 4% increase? For taking on managerial responsibilities? Mykalea feels like they are taking advantage of her.

Before writing back, Mykalea does a few things. She researches Glassdoor.com and finds that RNs with her level of experience in the Detroit area are making between $65K and $115K. Clearly she is at the low end of that range with her new salary. She also calls several friends from nursing school and finds similar information. Once classmates received their RN license, they were making at least $75K if not more. Comparisons are somewhat difficult because some RNs are working in hospitals, some are working in more urban areas, and some have teaching/educator responsibilities. Still, though, Mykalea feels like the increase should be more substantial.

She writes a draft of a letter back to Cheri.

Dear Ms. Littleton,

Thank you so much for the offer. As you know, I have received the highest performance reviews possible during my time at INVF, despite going to school at night and on the weekends to finish my RN degree. I have also covered shifts on countless occasions to aid the office, and have stayed late many times in the office when we have gotten behind.

I have several questions about your offer. Given the managerial responsibilities, I was thinking the offer would be significantly higher. I went to Glassdoor.com and found positions in Detroit for RNs that are between $100K and $110K. While I would very much like to stay at INVF, can you help me understand the discrepancy between what I would make at INVF and what other RNs with my level of experience are making elsewhere?

I look forward to your reply.

Sincerely,

Mykalea Hanson

After sleeping on this and going back to read this book, Mykalea deleted this letter from her computer and started again.

Dear Ms. Littleton,

This is a very important transition for all of us, and I want to make sure we are all on the same page regarding the job and compensation before we say yes. Compensation is always tricky, and I do not envy your position in this regard. You have a budget to manage, you have us pain-in-the-you-know-what nurses to manage, and you have policies and procedures you have to follow. On my side I find myself desiring a significant change in compensation, not only because of the new position but also because such opportunities like these do not come along often in my career. More than anything I want to find a solution that works for both of us. If I accept a modest increase, I fear my ability to raise my compensation at a later date will be basically impossible as the Team Leader position is likely as high as I would go at INVF. I've been advised by professional colleagues to go searching for another job, but I don't want to do that. I love the work I do, and I'm committed to working out a solution so that I can stay and thrive at INVF.

Thank you for the 4% increase for compensation for the Team Leader position. I want to be completely honest, though—I'm struggling with this number. I've been searching around at Glassdoor.com just to get a sense of what the market would pay for my set of skills. Yes, this is an imperfect science, but given my research (which I am happy to share by the way), I thought the raise might be closer to 20%. While it may not seem like a major change in total compensation ($72,211 vs. $83,187), to me this is a significant difference commensurate with the change in position.

So, my question is, how can we reach a productive conclusion here? Would you like the Glassdoor research? While this is not my preference, would it help you convince your management if I were to search around for other positions so as to judge my marketability? Can we craft the job somehow so as to justify a more substantial increase? Can we plan on a partial increase now and another increase in 6 months contingent on my performance in the Team Leader role? What other ideas do you have that might help us bridge this gap?

I have other questions as well about the position that might inform this discussion. Will I have additional work on training and socialization of new staff? How do you see this position growing and/or expanding in the future? Does this proposed change of grade level change the formula, or amount, of paid time off that is earned annually? When I am working on administrative work, will there be any flexibility to work from home?

I want to be extremely clear that I am excited and very interested in the position of Team Leader. I would be very pleased to be able to grow professionally and continue to offer patients and our organization more of my time and talents in the years to come. I am very proud to be a part of INVF.

I hope we can chat in person about these issues. I look forward to your counsel and advice.

Sincerely,

Mykalea Hanson

After meeting face-to-face, Cheri and Mykalea agree on the following compensation package:

- *Base salary of $80,000*

- *One-time spot bonus of $3,000*

- *Another 5% raise possible in 12 months contingent on performance review*
- *Mykalea agrees to create new training materials for entire INVF network (on her own time)*
- *Mykalea can work from home 2 days a month*
- *Mykalea agrees to lead the search process for two more nurses*

Discussion Questions

1. What is this negotiation about? What concepts are *central* to this negotiation and agreement?

2. What tactics did Cheri use in this negotiation?

3. What tactics did Mykalea use in this negotiation?

4. Do you think it was smart that Mykalea deleted the first letter? Why? What changed in her approach between the first letter and second letter? (*Hint: Not just tactics but a broader approach to the negotiation*)

5. Was value created in this negotiation? How?

6. What are the lessons that you can take away from how Mykalea handled this negotiation?

APPENDIX 2

Elqui Terra Case

This is a case describing a negotiation between Alex, a buyer for Elqui Manufacturing (pronounced "L-Key"), and Roberto, a salesperson for Terra Mining. Alex, as a buyer for Elqui, is attempting to renegotiate a contract for raw materials with Terra that is set to expire soon. Although Alex and Roberto have negotiated before, each is finding the need to change the terms of the negotiation as both firms are facing financial challenges.

Scene I: Monday, 7 pm

As Alex drove down 5th Avenue, he wondered why Roberto had insisted that they meet at a restaurant for their meeting, instead of Roberto just coming by his office to talk when he got into town that afternoon. Then again, the Italian restaurant Roberto had wanted to meet at was known as a great place to eat. Since Roberto had offered to pay, Alex was happy to oblige. It would be good to see Roberto again, as it had been over a year since they had last met face-to-face. Given that it was time for Alex's company (Elqui Manufacturing) to renegotiate their contract with Roberto's company (Terra Mining), and both of them had been the ones to negotiate the specific terms of the contract the last two times it was up for renewal, neither of them was surprised when their respective bosses asked them to negotiate this year's contract. Alex was looking forward to negotiating with Roberto but was also a little apprehensive. Because he and Roberto had negotiated these contracts in the past, they knew each other quite well and stayed in touch during the year, mostly if issues or conflicts related to the terms of the contract came up but also sometimes just to exchange pleasantries and talk about families and unrelated topics. They also respected one another and accepted that each knew his job and brought credible expertise to the table.

   The conversation eventually turned to the important issues that needed to be agreed upon for the next contract. Both Alex and Roberto knew the issues well, and both understood very clearly how important those issues were to their companies. Terra Mining supplies crucial raw materials that were central to Elqui Manufacturing's business. Both companies had benefitted from the relationship in the past, but there clearly were issues on which they had different preferences. For example, the purity of the raw material was something that had to be agreed upon and was something that was important to both companies. The lower the purity, the more the manufacturing costs increased for Elqui, but on the other hand, the higher the purity, the more the refining costs increased for Terra. Another issue was that of delivery schedule—how much of the raw materials were delivered and how frequently. Obviously, the price of the raw material (per ton) was very important to both companies, as well as the question of how the money changed hands. As the seller, Terra clearly preferred to have all of their money paid upon delivery, whereas Elqui, as the buyer, would clearly prefer to finance payments over time. Finally, the length of the contract would also have to be determined. The longer the contract, the less cost to either party in renegotiating it, but the more possible risk due to unanticipated fluctuations in demand, energy prices, transportation costs, and other factors. There were other issues that needed to be settled as well, but these were the main ones; these were issues that could have substantial financial impact on the two companies.

Scene II: Tuesday, 9 am

Alex, as the representative of the buyer, Elqui Manufacturing, had started informal negotiations with several other suppliers—competitors of Roberto's company—not only to get a clearer idea of the best deal out there but also to possibly find an alternative to Terra, if Roberto couldn't give him a good enough deal this time around.

Thinking about the possibility of a new supplier contract with a company other than Roberto's made Alex wonder if the plans they had made for a happy family vacation together in Florida might fall apart if there was no deal. Sure, he and Roberto were "friends" to a certain extent, but they were also each trying to do what was best for their respective companies, and Alex sadly wondered if their personal relationship might end if their professional relationship ended.

The morning began easily enough. They began with the issue of the purity of the raw materials. Alex had opened the issue by asking for 92% purity, an increase of 2% over their previous deal.

Alex: "Getting 92% is really important to us because it can significantly decrease our manufacturing costs, and with other costs rising, including labor, any savings we can make on manufacturing is critical to the company."

Roberto: "There's no way we can agree to 92% purity. What you are asking for is impossible, because we cannot go above 90%. It's not that we don't want to; it's that the technology simply doesn't allow us to get higher refinement than 90%."

Alex: "Are you sure about that? The reason I ask that is that we've been talking to another possible supplier, and they've told us that they are willing to provide 91% purity. I figured you might be able to beat their offer, which is why I asked for 92%. Now I know that the technology you guys use is pretty standard in the industry, so I don't imagine they are doing anything radically different that you are. So if they can go above 90%, why can't you?"

There was a silence in the room that uncomfortably dragged on a few long moments before Roberto replied.

Roberto:	"You're right, Alex. I may have spoken too quickly. It's not that we absolutely cannot physically achieve that level of purity. I've just been told by our technical staff that it becomes prohibitively expensive for us. So, can it be done, technically? Apparently yes, it can. But can we do it without making the product so expensive that you'll refuse to buy it? I don't think so. Look, I hope you know I wasn't purposely lying to you. It's just that I have a pretty good idea what you can and cannot afford. After all, we've negotiated these deals before, and we both have a pretty good understanding of the various costs involved. I figured what would really be dishonest would be to tell you that, sure, we can do 92% no problem and then have you feel like I misled you when I then pull out a cost estimate that is way higher than you can afford."
Alex:	"So how is it that other suppliers are telling me they can provide 91% and can do so without busting my budget?"
Roberto:	"In all honesty, I am pretty sure I can guess who these 'other suppliers' are. We obviously know a thing or two about our competitors and the general industry and market conditions we are operating in. It's no secret that there are some newer overseas players that have far lower labor costs than we do, and that do not have to worry about all kinds of safety laws and regulations where they do business. Of course they can offer a lower price—their costs are lower."

Alex opened his mouth to reply, but Roberto held up his hand, and Alex waited as he continued.

Roberto:	"So, why shouldn't you go with them as your supplier? Well, I can give you several reasons why the deal may not be as good as it seems at first. First of all, there's obviously going to be more risk in terms of delivery schedules if the raw material is being shipped from China as opposed to Pennsylvania. If something goes wrong in that supply pipeline—from hurricanes to pirates to labor unrest—it can seriously impact your production schedule and jeopardize contracts that you have. Second, if something goes wrong on the production side, in terms of specs, you're going to have to spend a lot of time and money on airfare and flying to the other side of the world, as opposed to driving two states over to Pittsburgh to talk to me. Third, if you make a deal with some person you've never met from another culture, do you really know what you are agreeing to? Are the standards and expectations really going to be the ones you are used to? On the one hand, it might be a super deal and everything will work out, but on the other hand, it could end up being a nightmare of misunderstandings, corruption, missed deadlines, and poor quality. After all, along with the benefits of lack of safety rules and regulations, there might also be a corresponding lack of quality control and

consistency. Not to mention the fact that in addition to having to deal with all sorts of import and customs officials on this end, you may also have to deal with difficult government officials on the other end, which might involve payoffs or bribes, which I am pretty sure your company has a policy against. Look, I'm not telling you that you shouldn't take a deal that is better than we can offer you. Obviously, you need to do what is best for your company—we're both in that boat. I'm just telling you that you need to be sure that it's actually a better deal and not something you'd regret down the line."

Alex: "You know, those are actually some of the very issues I've been concerned about as well, and I'm just not sure that my company should take the risks involved, just for the promise of saving a few bucks up front. Also, I have to admit that the couple of times I talked on the phone to their rep, I was a bit confused. The salesperson on the phone just seemed to agree to everything I asked—whether it was about product specifications, shipping schedules, or volume—whatever it was, he'd just agree. That really made me a bit skeptical, and I couldn't really tell if he was agreeing because he was just trying to be polite, or maybe he was agreeing because he didn't really understand what I was saying—since his English wasn't perfect, and my Chinese is nonexistent—or whether he was just willing to say anything to get the contract but couldn't *really* deliver on those specs, delivery schedules, or volume. Because of this, we're not really sure about them yet."

Scene III: Tuesday, 6 pm

The reason Alex was a little apprehensive driving home was because the timing of this negotiation was somewhat important to Alex personally. Since this was a contract with Elqui's largest supplier of raw materials, it would have quite an impact on Elqui's bottom line. Consequently, if Alex did well in the negotiations, he would receive a substantial bonus. The reason for this is that bonuses for contract negotiations are based on the value to the company over the length of the contract. The minimum length contract is a year, but contracts can be lengthened up to 5 years according to company policy. This means that the longer the contract Alex can get Roberto to agree to and the better the terms, the larger the potential bonus. Alex's company likes longer contracts because they can fix raw material prices in at certain rates, thereby avoiding market fluctuations and mitigating risk. Normally, the timing of bonuses—whether smaller ones every year or a big one every 4 or 5 years—wouldn't really matter to Alex, but now it did. His daughter was getting married in 6 months, and if he could secure a large bonus, he would be able to give his daughter the perfect wedding she had always dreamed of.

Alex reminded himself that his job was to get the best deal possible for his company, and he had to be sure that he didn't let his liking for Roberto as a person get in the way of that. After all, the raw materials supply was a competitive business, and just because Terra had been a good partner in the past didn't necessarily guarantee that Terra would always be the best choice for Elqui Manufacturing. As part of making sure that his company would be getting the best deal possible, Alex had been doing his homework. He had been using the Internet and trade publications to try to get an idea of what other companies were paying for similar raw materials, and had even called some of his counterparts at other companies (he kept a stack of business cards from running into them at conventions) to see if they'd give him an idea of what kinds of terms they had negotiated with suppliers. Just before leaving, Alex and Roberto shared the following exchange:

Alex: "You know, Helena and the kids really enjoyed meeting you and your family last year at the conference. We should really get together again sometime."

Roberto: "I'm glad you brought that up. We really enjoyed the evening, too. Alejandra and I have been talking and wanted to invite you and Helena and the family to Florida this summer for a long weekend. We were given a timeshare for a week and we thought you guys might like some time on the beach. The kids could entertain each other, and you and I and our wives could play golf."

Alex: "Really? Wow, I'll have to talk to Helena about it but that sounds like a great idea. Thanks for the invitation."

Driving home, Alex spoke with his wife Helena. It turns out she was thrilled at the idea of spending some on their summer vacation in Florida with Roberto and Alejandra and their family. Alex was glad that Roberto had offered this invitation while the two were at dinner, since Roberto was a great guy and fun to hang out with. In fact, negotiating with someone like Roberto whom he liked and knew personally was so much easier than with some stranger that you couldn't necessarily trust. He felt encouraged with how the dinner had gone and looked forward to the rest of the negotiation.

Back in his hotel, Roberto, too, thought that the day had gone well. In addition to talking about all of the issues that were important to the two companies in the negotiation, his and Alex's relationship still seemed strong. In fact, it seemed his idea about Florida was well received by Alex. Alex's wife Helena and his wife Alejandra had really gotten along when they had met at a company-sponsored conference last year, and the kids were of ages that would probably get along. Roberto hoped that the personal relationship between them would make it easier to find a good deal that would work for both companies. When negotiating a deal that his job depended on, he felt much more confident sitting across the table from someone who knew and liked him than some stranger he didn't know or feel comfortable with.

Later that evening, Roberto got an e-mail. Alex must've called Helena to talk about the vacation, and Helena was e-mailing to express her thanks for the invitation to Florida.

Dear Roberto,

I just wanted to say thank you for the invitation to Florida—Alex just called with the good news. I really enjoyed hanging out with you and Alejandra last year, and I think the kids are all going to have a blast together. We were thinking about taking the family to Florida anyway to see my parents, so this way we can spend a few days with you all and a few days with them. Please send my best to Alejandra and we'll be in touch to plan soon.

All the best,

Helena

Both Roberto and his wife Alejandra wrote Helena back saying they were excited that the vacation was going to work out. A few minutes later as Roberto checked his e-mail he noticed there was a second e-mail from Alex's wife Helena. Curious if she had perhaps remembered something additional about the trip, he opened it, only to realize that she had accidentally copied him on an e-mail to Alex. As he reached for the "delete" button—not wanting to read a personal e-mail—he couldn't help but notice a particular sentence.

Just finished writing Roberto a thank-you note—the trip should be a lot of fun. Now you just have to close the deal! I so hope you manage to get that big bonus for getting a 5-year contract. Tammy would just be so thrilled if we could pay for the wedding. –H

Roberto felt conflicted and a bit betrayed when he read the e-mail from Helena. On the one hand, he had this personal relationship with Alex that was strong and they had just had a good day, which he hoped would set the stage for a positive negotiation. On the other hand, he couldn't help but question whether the vacation agreement and everything else Alex had said and done was just to set him up to get a 5-year contract. He felt there was now this huge "elephant in the room" that was going to cloud everything else that would happen during the negotiation. All of a sudden, he wasn't sure how the meeting the next morning would go.

Scene IV: Wednesday, 8:30 am

Roberto was struggling with how to deal with Alex. He knew they had this long-standing relationship, but given the information from last night it seemed as if Alex was only looking out for his own personal interests in getting a 5-year contract, which to Roberto seemed completely unreasonable. Roberto also realized that he did not have all the information—all he had was one stray e-mail from Helena, which hardly painted a complete picture of Alex's interests. He decided to proceed carefully.

Roberto: "Good morning, Alex. I'd like to hear what you think about the contract length because I'm worried we are going to have significant conflict on this issue."

Alex:	"Really, why do you think so? Of course we'd like a longer contract, but we have room to negotiate."
Roberto:	"Well, I want you to know that Helena accidentally copied me on the e-mail where she mentioned Tammy's wedding and the bonus."
Alex:	"How dare you accuse me of negotiating with my own personal interests at stake? My loyalty lies solely with the company! Who cares what any e-mail says?"

Alex had not realized that Helena had copied Roberto on that e-mail and was seemingly both embarrassed and angry. This was a shift in tone from the friendly conversation from the night before, and Roberto didn't quite know what to say. Roberto was shocked, not only at the denial but also at the anger with which Alex responded. He suspected that there was more truth in that e-mail than Alex was letting on, and Alex now knew that his cover was blown. He also knew that if he couldn't figure out a way to get Roberto negotiating again about the issues, they weren't going to have any deal at all. After a few moments Roberto replied.

Roberto:	"There's a lot to digest here. I think we should take a break. Let's meet back here in an hour."
Alex:	"Fine."

Both Alex and Roberto left the office without another word. They both went separately for a coffee break and returned to the conference room as agreed.

Roberto:	"I want to apologize for what I said this morning. My intention was only to be honest with you about what Helena did, not accuse you of putting your own interests above the company. I also wanted to tell you that I have a daughter getting married and I completely understand the tension between wanting something for your daughter yet knowing that you have to represent the company the best you can. I think this is a tension we all face when we have multiple interests."
Alex:	"I'm sorry too. Let's get back to talking about purity."

After another hour of discussion, both parties agreed to talk with their bosses and come back to the table later in the day.

Scene V: Wednesday, 3 pm

Alex's boss Cathy wanted an update regarding the progress of the negotiation, which was fine with Alex because she ultimately had to sign off on whatever Alex came up with. After exchanging pleasantries, Cathy asked Alex for an update.

Alex:	"Cathy, we're in a dogfight, and I'm not sure how it is going to turn out. We want to keep our costs the same, increase the purity of the raw

material, and have a longer contract. Terra wants a short contract, can't or won't increase the purity of the raw material, and wants to raise the costs. I feel like there might be some movement on the price, but I'm not sure about the other issues. I told Roberto about our competing offer from the Chinese firm and he admitted they cannot match that offer. He was very aware of their business model, though, and knows that if we go with them we are exposing ourselves to a great deal of risk."

Cathy: "Alex, we are in a serious budget crunch right now and I need the costs to be as low as possible this year. If that means agreeing to a shorter contract and renegotiating sooner, so be it. I would rather have the same contract for one more year while we continue to check out the Chinese firm than get locked into a high price for a long period of time. Do what you need to do on purity—you know our manufacturing costs—but don't come back to me asking for big money commitments for several years."

Alex: "Would you rather go with the Chinese firm?"

Cathy: "No, not necessarily. I agree with you that importing our raw material could throw off our production schedule, especially if any problems arise. And while that is not as important as cost, production delays will reflect badly on our department. I'd much rather have a deal we can live with buying from Terra."

Alex: "Thanks, Cathy. I appreciate the talk."

Alex left troubled by this meeting, though. He now had a clear picture of what Cathy wanted and realized that his most important issue (the 5-year contract) was not necessarily what Cathy's most important issue was. He wasn't sure how he was going to proceed with Roberto.

Meanwhile, Roberto was in discussions with Tony, his manager back at Terra.

Roberto: "So Tony, I accidentally got this message from Alex's wife, which seems to suggest that he'd do anything to get a 5-year contract."

Tony: "No way. Do you know what would happen to us if we agree to a 5-year deal and prices go up along with our costs? We'd be forgoing millions in profit, and it could mean the end of Terra."

Roberto: "I know, that's what I told him, but he has his daughter's wedding to pay for and he is angling for a big bonus."

Tony: "His daughter's wedding, huh? You need to use this against him. Tell him we WILL give him a 5-year contract IF he agrees to $5,000 per ton. No way prices would go that high, so if he's really willing to pay, he'll go for this."

Roberto:	"But Tony, isn't that likely to upset him and make him feel threatened? He might walk away."
Tony:	"Isn't he the one who is putting his personal needs first, though? Maybe he should feel threatened. You're the negotiator. Do what you think best to get us the best deal."
Roberto:	"Okay, I'll ask more questions and try to figure this out."

Scene VI: Wednesday, 5 pm

After conferring with each of their bosses, Alex and Roberto were back at the table ready to close the deal.

Roberto:	"Let's try to look at these issues another way. It feels like we are just going in circles right now. I mean, I completely understand that you guys want higher purity, and you completely understand that we want lower purity. By the same token, we both understand that my company prefers to have all payments made now, and your company prefers the payments to be spread over the life of the contract. Furthermore, we both understand that you'd like a lower cost and a longer contract while we, of course, would like a higher cost and a shorter contract."
Alex:	"Yes, we seem to be on the same page. We both understand what the other side wants, and we've got opposite preferences—in the same way that you'd like a higher price, and we'd like a lower price, obviously. It seems like we're just going to do the same dance we do every time and slowly haggle our way down to a compromise on each issue."
Roberto:	"That *is* what we usually do, isn't it? I wonder if there's a better approach—instead of just 'splitting the difference' so to speak."
Alex:	"I'm listening. What do you have in mind?"
Roberto:	"Well, here's how I see it. Obviously, on an issue like price per ton, there's not much we can do other than try to meet somewhere in the middle. After all, a difference in a dollar per ton is worth a dollar to either of us. There's nothing we can do about that."
Alex:	"Right."
Roberto:	"But what about some of these other things? Purity, for instance. Now I get that you prefer higher purity, because your manufacturing gets more expensive the lower the purity of the raw material is. And obviously you know—because I keep telling you about it—how we prefer the lower purity, because our extraction and refining gets more expensive the higher the purity is. When we were talking about the Chinese company,

you said that it saves you $400 a ton for each 1% in purity increase in the raw material, correct?"

Alex: "Yes, that's what my chief engineer says."

Roberto: "Well, I checked with our mining chief engineer and he says that it costs us $800 per ton to go from 90% to 91%. This means that if we were to agree to 91%, between both of us we'd be losing $400—we lose $800 and you gain $400 (–$800 [Terra] + $400 [Elqui] = –$400). This doesn't really make much sense because we'd really have to raise the price to a level, like $4,900 per ton, which you don't want. On the other side, though, *if we were able to go to 89% purity*, we'd GAIN $400 between both of us because we would get $800 in cost savings and you'd be paying only $400 more in increased costs ($800 [Terra] – $400 [Elqui] = +$400). If we take my proposed price of $4,100, which reflects our increase in costs, and split this $400 gain, we could offer you the following: $3,500 per ton at 89%. The $3,500 comes from our savings of $800 off the $4,100 plus the $200 split in cost savings: $4,100 – $800 + $200 = $3,500. In reality of course what that means is that you'd have to pay $3,900 per ton—$3,500 to us and $400 in increased manufacturing costs—which is actually lower than our current deal. How does that sound?"

Alex: "I think I see what you are saying. If it costs you an extra $800 per ton to increase purity by 1%, but we only save $400 per ton in our manufacturing process for that extra percent, then it's inefficient to just meet in the middle. Instead, we should be agreeing to a lower percentage, and you could share some of those cost savings with us by paying a higher price."

Roberto: "Exactly! So what about the length of contract? That seems to be our other difficult issue."

Alex: "Well, I guess the cat's out of the bag. Please don't think I was trying to take advantage of you over just to get a bigger bonus, Roberto. I was just hoping there might be a way to find a longer contract that would work for both companies. If there was a way, then I'd just rather have one large bonus now, instead of five small ones over the next 5 years. Obviously, I wouldn't want to risk your job over the wedding. If I have to put a lot of money on a credit card, I'd do that before seeing you risk your job."

Roberto: "Thanks, Alex. I appreciate that."

Alex: "I understand what you are saying about the risk in longer contracts, but don't you think there might still be a way we could go for a longer contract, if we can find a way to do it without putting your company at greater risk? After all, if times are tough for your industry and company, if you can lock in a long-term deal without some of the risk, that would be a good thing, right?"

Roberto: "That's a good point, but I'm not sure how we could avoid the risk. After all, we can't predict which way our chemical costs are going to fluctuate over time or what grade of raw material we might extract. Right now, hydrochloric acid is pretty expensive, but the material we are mining is pretty rich. Two years from now, the price of acid might be down, or the material could be a lot leaner, or nothing could change."

Alex: "Well, maybe instead of trying to predict it, we can build some variability into the contract. Maybe we can negotiate a price and then index, or link, the price in any given year to some objective measures of acid cost or your material grade or other factors that are driving your costs."

Roberto: "You know, if you're able to do that, it might actually be workable. Because in these tough times, my company absolutely would love to have a client tied up for a long-term contract, but we've just not been willing to face the risk. But this way, we could mitigate the risk and get the benefit of the long contract—not only to my company, but to you personally."

Alex: "Great. Let's talk about some numbers and see if there's a way to do this."

Roberto: "Okay, I'll need to get with my engineers and see what the costs are. If you're willing to do this, I'll get the cost information, clear it with my boss, and build it into the final contract. My guess, though, knowing what my boss cares about, is that if we can protect ourselves from rising costs, we'd be willing to go to 5 years."

Alex: "I'm really happy that we kept plugging away at this until you came up with your suggestions. Now, this seems to be a much better deal for both of us, and we can both go back to our companies with a better deal."

Roberto: "I agree. When I first thought about it, it just seemed to make more and more sense. I'm just glad that you were willing to listen. Once we both put our heads together, it became pretty clear what a good idea this was."

Alex: "That's a good point about me being willing to listen. To be honest, initially I was skeptical about going to 89%. I thought you might be trying to pull something on me. If you had been some new guy from Terra that I had never met before, I'm not sure I would have been as willing to consider this. It just sounded too strange to be workable. I knew, though, that you wouldn't have suggested a vacation and then tried to turn around and stick it to me. This is why I listened."

Roberto: "Thanks, Alex. I'll get those numbers on our raw materials to you in the morning, we can hammer out the indexing of the contract, and hopefully we'll be done with this by the end of the week."

Case Discussion Questions

General

1. Of all the concepts discussed in the book, which are the most important in this negotiation?
2. What best explains why Alex and Roberto did what they did in this negotiation?
3. Could you have predicted the outcome from the beginning of the negotiation? Why or why not?
4. What should Alex and Roberto have done differently?

From Chapter 1

1. What mistakes are made in this negotiation by Alex and Roberto?
2. What do you think is contained in the mental model of both Alex and Roberto as they enter this negotiation?

From Chapter 2

1. What are the obvious issues in this negotiation?
2. What are the potential issues in this negotiation?
3. What are the interests of Alex and Roberto in this negotiation?
4. How do Alex's and Roberto's interests differ from each of their companies' interests?
5. What are the desired positions of Alex and Roberto in this negotiation?
6. What can you guess about their resistance points? Does this present an opportunity or a challenge?
7. What behavior is ethically questionable in this negotiation?

From Chapter 3

1. What is the evidence that either Alex or Roberto had a defined negotiation plan before entering this negotiation?
2. How could both sides have benefited from additional planning in this negotiation?
3. How did the planning they likely engaged in help in the negotiation?

From Chapter 4

1. What is being reciprocated between Alex and Roberto in this negotiation?
2. What is the *role* of reciprocity in this negotiation? Is reciprocity important in explaining the outcome of this negotiation? Why or why not?

3. What tactics that leverage reciprocity are used in this negotiation by Alex and/or Roberto? Are these effective? Why or why not?

4. What tactics from Chapter 4 could've been used in this negotiation? What would be the benefits and costs of using those tactics?

From Chapter 5

1. Whose identity is more threatened in this negotiation?

2. What is the role of respect and identity in this negotiation? Are respect and identity important in explaining the outcome of this negotiation? Why or why not?

3. What tactics that manage respect and identity are used in this negotiation by Alex and/or Roberto? Are these effective? Why or why not?

4. What tactics from Chapter 5 could've been used in this negotiation? What would be the benefits and costs of using those tactics?

From Chapter 6

1. What is the role of the relationship between Alex and Roberto in this negotiation? Is uncertainty important in explaining the outcome of this negotiation? Why or why not?

2. Where does the trust between Alex and Roberto come from? How is that threatened in this negotiation? How is it restored?

3. What tactics that leverage relationships are used in this negotiation by Alex and/or Roberto? Are these effective? Why or why not?

4. What tactics from Chapter 6 could've been used in this negotiation? What would be the benefits and costs of using those tactics?

From Chapter 7

1. Who has more uncertainty in this negotiation? Why?

2. What is the role of uncertainty in this negotiation? Is uncertainty important in explaining the outcome of this negotiation? Why or why not?

3. What tactics that leverage uncertainty are used in this negotiation by Alex and/or Roberto? Are these effective? Why or why not?

4. What tactics from Chapter 7 could've been used in this negotiation? What would be the benefits and costs of using those tactics?

From Chapter 8

1. Who has more formal power in this negotiation?

2. What is the role of formal power in this negotiation? Is formal power important in explaining the outcome of this negotiation? Why or why not?

3. What tactics that leverage formal power are used in this negotiation by Alex and/or Roberto? Are these effective? Why or why not?

4. What tactics from Chapter 8 could've been used in this negotiation? What would be the benefits and costs of using those tactics?

From Chapter 9

1. What is each side's BATNA in this negotiation?

2. What is the relative strength of each BATNA in this negotiation?

3. What is the impact of those BATNAs on confidence and power in this negotiation?

4. Who has the better BATNA in this negotiation?

5. What is the role of BATNAs in this negotiation? When, specifically, are BATNAs important in explaining the behaviors within the negotiation as well as the outcome of this negotiation?

6. What tactics that leverage BATNAs are used in this negotiation by Alex and/or Roberto? Are these effective? Why or why not?

7. What tactics from Chapter 9 could've been used in this negotiation? What would be the benefits and costs of using those tactics?

From Chapter 10

1. What is the role of motivation in this negotiation? Is motivation important in explaining the outcome of this negotiation? Why or why not?

2. How does motivation affect Alex's and Roberto's stance toward the other?

3. What tactics that leverage motivation are used in this negotiation by Alex and/or Roberto? Are these effective? Why or why not?

4. What tactics from Chapter 10 could've been used in this negotiation? What would be the benefits and costs of using those tactics?

From Chapter 11

1. What are the individual barriers in this negotiation?

2. What is the role specifically of emotion in this negotiation? How does emotion impact Alex and Roberto?

3. What can we learn about Alex's and Roberto's personalities from this case? How do their personalities help or hinder their ability to negotiate with the other side?

From Chapter 12

1. Are there any potential cultural barriers in this negotiation?

2. What would Alex and Roberto have needed to do if they did not share English as a first language?

From Supplements

1. What is the role specifically of Alex and Roberto as agents in this negotiation? How does having bosses (background participants) impact their behavior?

2. What if this negotiation had been conducted over the phone or via e-mail? How would that have helped the negotiation? Hindered the negotiation?

3. How well did Alex and Roberto manage the process of the negotiation? Make a case for why each side did a better job in the moment.

4. How did Alex and Roberto benefit from breaking up the negotiation across multiple sessions?

APPENDIX 3

Job Negotiations

While there are many resources available to you if you are negotiating a job,[1] here are a few tips from us based on the material in this book that we have seen be quite effective for our students, friends, and family. Although we would not recommend using this resources *without reading the rest of this book*, hopefully it can provide a quick reminder or helpful tool in a pinch as you get ready for that big offer.

DON'T SKIP PLANNING

Most make the mistake of thinking that job negotiations are *only* about salary. They are not.

The bargaining mix in job negotiations can include all of the following issues:

Salary

Bonus

Stock options

Overtime possibilities

Moving expenses

PTO (paid time off)

Job responsibilities

Job autonomy/freedom to choose what to work on

Job rotation

Telework

Flexible work

Office location

Expected travel

Time frame for future evaluation(s)

Laptop

Mobile phone

Tablet

Car

Public transportation reimbursement

Childcare

And so on . . .

Do all of these issues have value to you? Likely not, but some of them will. And it is your job as the applicant to add these issues to the bargaining mix as these issues might just be potential issues (if not obvious issues) at the start of the negotiation.

This is one reason why planning for job negotiations is so important. You need to think through all of the potential issues that will add value to you so that you can form a preference sheet reflective of what you truly value (see Chapter 3).

Planning also helps you think through what is likely to be important on the other side, that is, the company or organization. What are they likely to care about? How big are they? How flexible are they likely to be? Planning forces you to gather information to try to answer these questions so that you know which tactics to use and which to avoid.

Complete the planning worksheet all the way through to the end so that you know *exactly* what you wish to ask about and say when you get into that room or on that phone call. Job negotiations are not the time for improvisation!

If you fail to plan for a job negotiation and leave just $5,000 on the table, this could mean hundreds of thousands of dollars in future earnings given that your next job is going to be based on the salary for this job. Don't short-change the planning process.

MOVE FROM CONVINCING TO UNDERSTANDING

You might think that it is your task in the job negotiation (or performance review) to convince the other side how great you are. Wrong! If you are negotiating, it means you have an offer and they already are convinced that you are the right person to hire! Don't make the mistake of trying to give them your résumé when no doubt they have already read your résumé again and again. The same holds true in performance reviews. Many employees think they have to convince their boss of their qualifications in order to get that raise or promotion. But the boss has likely already made up his or her mind about your qualifications or performance.

Your task, if you wish to obtain the most value from the negotiation, is to try to *understand* the other side. Here are some phrases that can help you in this regard:

"Is it okay if I ask you some questions about the offer?"

"I'd like to talk about some additional issues. Is that something you are willing to do?"

"I'm sorry for asking so many questions, but I really want to understand where you are flexible and where you are not."

"Which of the issues is most important to you?"

"For which issues might the company have flexibility?"

"Has anyone been able to successfully negotiate a signing bonus [or other issue]?"

"What are the hurdles that you face when trying to hire or promote employees?"

Yes, you want something, but to get that thing you have to show a level of understanding to the other side. This not only helps you use tactics related to intangible interests and relationships (Chapters 5 and 6), but it gives you information that you can use to facilitate reciprocity (Chapter 4).

For example, if you wish to logroll (e.g., you take a higher signing bonus, which you need to pay off debt, for slightly lower salary), you first have to figure out if those issues are valued unequally between yourself and the company. To do that, you have to ask questions to understand the interests of the employer. If you are focused on convincing the other side the entire time, you will lose out on these opportunities.

IMPROVE YOUR BATNA

Your BATNA might stink. That's okay. Perhaps it is to stay in your parents' basement another few months, or work at a grocery store, or go do volunteer work. The key is to continually work to improve your BATNA. This does not mean you need a BATNA as good as what you are currently negotiating. That might be out of reach at the moment. Even incrementally improving your BATNA, though, increases your confidence in the negotiation.

If you are interviewing for a professional job, you are in a much better position if your BATNA is to work at Starbucks than it is to be unemployed. At least you will be earning a salary with benefits. Similarly, if you are looking at an engineering position, a BATNA of working part-time with a grade-school STEM program is a better BATNA than working part-time walking dogs.

The problem occurs when the basement-dweller or the dog-walker only looks for jobs and opportunities that are seen to be ideal. This can be a dangerous cycle that is difficult to break. Just because opportunities are not ideal does not mean that they are not worthy.

Similarly, if you have an interview with your *perfect* job, do not stop interviewing elsewhere! You never know what is going to happen during an interview or a job search situation. Keep your options open (for improving your BATNA) until your negotiation is complete.

FIND A TRUTH TELLER (INSIDER)

This next point is mainly about reducing uncertainty. As discussed extensively in Chapter 7, uncertainty is everywhere in negotiations, and it can leave you quite vulnerable. In job negotiations you may not know what is or is not possible to negotiate, and you may not know what issues can be added. You also may not know *how* the company likes to negotiate. Do they set low anchoring offers? Do they ask candidates for opening offers? Do they pay all new hires the same?

All of these questions can cause you anxiety and decrease your ability to obtain value from the negotiation. So find someone on the inside. Reduce your uncertainty by reaching out to your network and talk with someone who is at the company, who used to be at the company, or who knows someone at the company. Is this always possible? No. But for many this is possible and can help you understand the context in which you will be conducting one of the most important negotiations of your life.

DON'T FORGET ABOUT CONTINGENT CONTRACTS

Contingent contracts (Chapter 4) are an incredibly valuable tool in a wide variety of job negotiations. Even if you are not a professional basketball player building in contingencies based on points scored or games played, you can still use this to your advantage. The benefit of contingencies is that they mitigate risk for all parties. Both parties essentially "get what they want" by placing a bet on some future unknown.

Here are some possible contingencies in job negotiations.

Place a bet on your performance: "If I perform at a certain level in the next 6 months, I get the added salary increase."

Place another bet on your performance: "I will get an X% bonus for each percentage point over my quota."

Place a bet on an impending job opening: "If that position comes up in the next year, I will be first in line."

Place a bet on the company: "If the company meets X sales forecast, I will get the raise."

Place a bet on a future move: "For now I agree to stay, but if you (boss) get a different position in the company, you will bring me over to the new unit."

Place a bet on unknown family circumstance: "If we have another child, you will let me telework 3 days a week."

Place a bet on others: "If you get complaints from my team, I will stop teleworking."

This can go on and on. The key is to resolve a difficult issue by placing some bet on a future unknown that can be *quantified* in some way so that all parties know the outcome of the bet. In all of these circumstances, the applicant or employee is happier in the moment because he or she understands what will happen in the future.

SEE YOUR OPPONENT AS A POSSIBLE MENTOR

This point is about leveraging intangible interests. What do people love to talk about the most? Themselves! People (generally) like telling their stories, conveying their history, talking about how they came to the company or how the organization has changed. So why does this matter?

Because you have a resource to give them—your ability to listen. Perhaps you've never heard the stories before, so you have the unique ability to give them the opportunity to tell their stories to a new audience. If you are talking the whole time about yourself, though, you waste this opportunity.

We like to give students the mental model of a mentor–mentee relationship instead of an opponent relationship when negotiating for a job. This is especially useful if the person you are negotiating with is or is going to be your future manager. You can ask them questions about themselves, about their work, about why they love it there, about how they negotiated their position, and so on.

One thing that often works well, especially if you get stuck in a job negotiation, is to ask them something like the following:

> "We seem to be at a bit of an impasse over this issue in the negotiation. Taking your manager hat off for a moment, if you were in my shoes, how would you proceed?"

This invokes perspective taking on their side and changes the nature of the conversation.

TRY TO AVOID E-MAIL

E-mail is great for keeping track of offers and complex information, but it is also much easier for an employer to say no to something over e-mail than it is to say no face-to-face. If you are getting into extended e-mail conversations with your future employer, try to schedule a phone call or, better yet, a face-to-face meeting. Plan for what you are going to say and why (Chapter 3), and try to form a positive relationship with the other person.

REMEMBER THAT "VALUE" COMES IN ALL SHAPES AND SIZES

You have crafted a great plan, you have tried to add issues to the negotiation, you had a clear goal based on salary, you asked a lot of questions, and at the end of the day you got nothing beyond the initial offer.

Does this happen? Of course! Did you "lose"? Absolutely not.

This is still a valuable negotiation because, although your offers might be the same, you have gotten so much more value than the person who didn't negotiate at all.

After going through this negotiation, you have knowledge about the following:

- The company

- Whom they pay and why

- What they are willing to negotiate

- The people you negotiated with

- That no matter what you did, they were not going to increase the offer

This knowledge is the value that you have obtained from this negotiation. With this knowledge, you can better evaluate the offer and the company. Is this a place you want to work in the short term? Is this a place you want to work in the long term? Do you like the people you are going to be working with? Do you respect the individuals you negotiated with? Now you have more confidence in your own decisions, simply because you chose to negotiate.

Happy negotiating!

GLOSSARY

Actual power: another person acknowledging a source of power and being willing to acquiesce as a result

Adding issue: adding a potential issue to the list of issues being negotiated

Agreeableness: behavioral characteristics that are perceived as kind, sympathetic, cooperative, warm, and considerate

Altruism: when one's goal is to keep another person happy at the expense of oneself

Anchor: a negotiation tactic where one party makes an opening offer to leverage the uncertainty of the other side

Apparent conflict: the people want, or seem to want, different things

Assertiveness: the degree to which individuals are assertive, confrontational, and aggressive in their relationships with others

Attainability: the degree to which the individual believes they can actually reach the goal

Availability bias: overvaluing experiences and information that one can easily recall

Background nonparticipants: people who have an interest in the negotiation but have no way to directly change its course or influence the parties at the table

Background participants: people with the capability to directly change or affect the progression of the negotiation via their influence on the parties at the table

Background power: a negotiation tactic when one party leverages the legitimate power of a background participant (e.g., manager)

Bargaining mix: the set of issues being negotiated

BATNA: best alternative to a negotiated agreement— what you will end up with if you walk away from the negotiation at hand without a deal

Bogey: a deceptive tactic by which a negotiator pretends to value an issue only to give a "concession" on that issue to get a concession on an issue that is truly valued

Claiming value: the process by which one party attempts to negotiate in such a way as to cause the other party to give up something without getting anything in return

Coalition: when more than one party align in order to negotiate collectively with another party

Coercive power: results from being able to inflict punishment on another

Cognitive dissonance: the process by which one seeks to align one's actions with one's thoughts or cognitions

Collectivism: the degree to which individuals express pride, loyalty, and cohesiveness in their organizations or families

Compromise: a negotiation tactic whereby the parties agree to "meet in the middle" or "split the difference" on a particular issue in order to reach resolution

Concession: giving some value to another party in a negotiation

Confirming evidence bias: the tendency for people to seek out and pay attention only to information that confirms their prior beliefs

Consistency: the desire for current and future actions or attitudes to align with past actions or attitudes

Contingent contract: an agreement that involves a bet on some future, unknown event

Convincing: approach to negotiation in which one attempts to alter the beliefs or actions of the other side in order to obtain something of value

Counteroffer: response to an initial offer by the other party

Creating value: the process by which negotiators find ways to increase the total value to be gained from the negotiation

Culture: the character of a social group that sets it apart from other social groups

Distributive agreement: a negotiated outcome where negotiators only claim, rather than create, value

Egocentrism: being more interested in one's own interests and needs than the interests of the other party

Emotional ambivalence: expression of two contradicting emotions

Emotional appeal: a negotiation tactic based on getting the other side to feel sorry for you or emotionally attached to the issue you are negotiating

Emotional contagion: spread of emotions from one person to another

Emotional intelligence: the ability to monitor one's own and others' feelings and emotions, to discriminate among them, and to use this information to guide one's thinking and actions

Endowment effect: the tendency to demand more for an item than one would pay for an item

Escalation of commitment: the tendency for one to increasingly work toward the achievement of one or more goals

Expert power: the extent to which individuals are seen to have relevant knowledge or expertise

Extrinsic motivation: motivation due to tangible rewards

False-consensus effect: the tendency to overestimate the degree to which one's own values, beliefs, and attitudes are normal and shared by others

Feeling of obligation: occurs when someone gives something or does something for someone else

Fixed-pie bias/zero-sum bias: thinking that anything one gets in an agreement costs the other side just as much

Framing as gains: a negotiation tactic where one party states a concession or an offer in terms of the potential gain in value to the other side

Free-riding: when a team member puts in less than his or her fair share of effort

Functional fixedness: comes from the tendency to use an object only in an intended way; the inability to adapt or change behavior to account for the situation

Future orientation: the extent to which individuals engage in future-oriented behaviors such as delaying gratification, planning, and investing in the future

Gender egalitarianism: the degree to which a culture minimizes gender inequality

Gender: the socially constructed characteristics distinguishing between masculinity and femininity

Generalized exchange: a rule of exchange describing when one person is willing to provide for another regardless of when they might be paid back

Goals: a specific outcome a party wishes to achieve in a negotiation

Group-based identity: identity derived from membership in important groups

Identity threat: when an individual perceives harm to a valued identity

Identity: how one defines oneself

Illusory conflict: assuming that there is conflict when there really is not any conflict

Impression management: a conscious management of how someone else perceives you

Inert knowledge problem: the difficulty in transferring details from one situation to the next

Influence: the degree of actual change in someone's behavior, attitudes, or values and beliefs

Information asymmetry: when one party in the negotiation has more relevant information than the other

Intangible interests: underlying wants that cannot be seen, touched, or felt (e.g., respect, love, appreciation)

Integrative agreement: a negotiated outcome where negotiators successfully create value

Interests in principle: intangible interests that originate from what individuals see as universally appropriate or ethical

Interests: fundamental reasons people want what they want

Intrinsic motivation: motivation due to the fulfilling nature of a task

Issues: items on the table being negotiated (e.g., salary, bonus, vacation time)

Joint action: the people have to deal with each other in order to get what they want

Legitimate power: determined by an individual's organization role and status

Logrolling: trading issues that have unequal value to the parties in the negotiation

Lose face: when an individual is put into a position where he or she is seen as inconsistent with a desired sense of self

Lose-lose agreement: reaching a decision that neither party really wanted

Measurability: the ability of a defined goal to be evaluated after the negotiation

Mental models: explanations or thought processes about how things work in the real world

Negotiated exchange: a rule of exchange describing when one person is willing to provide for another and expects to be paid back immediately

Negotiation potential: the degree to which a conflict situation might be resolved through a negotiation

Obvious issues: issues that both parties know must be negotiated

Opportunity costs: the benefits available from an alternative that must be forgone in order to pursue a certain action

Overspecification: specifying a precise goal for each issue

Packaging issues: making an offer with multiple issues

Paradox of reciprocity: although sharing information leads to more information from others (via reciprocity) and the opportunity to create value, negotiators don't share information because they fear they will lose value by being vulnerable

Parties at the table: those who actually perform the negotiation

Performance orientation: the degree to which the culture encourages and rewards individuals for performance improvement and excellence

Persistence: the amount of effort put in at any moment as well as the capacity to sustain effort over time

Perspective taking: a negotiator's capacity to consider the world from another individual's viewpoint

Phantom BATNA: a potential, rather than the actual, BATNA

Planning script: what you plan to actually say in the negotiation

Position: specific options within issues; negotiation offers are made up of positions on issues (e.g., $54,000 for salary, $2,000 bonus, 3 weeks of vacation)

Potential issues: issues that could be added to the bargaining mix throughout the negotiation

Potential power: power based on one's position or knowledge that *could* be influential

Power distance: the extent to which a society accepts that power is distributed unequally

Power: the capacity to produce effects on others; the ability to influence another

Preference table: tool used to determine relative importance of issues and relative importance of possible positions within issues

Reciprocal exchange: a rule of exchange describing when one person is willing to provide for another and expects to be paid back at some point in the future

Reciprocity: another's willingness to return equal goods or services to you when goods or services have been given to them

Relationship power: the potential influence an individual has as a result of relationships or personal ties with other people; also known as referent power

Relationship-based identity: identity derived from the meaningful relationships one has

Relevance: how important a particular piece of information is in a particular negotiation

Relevance: the degree to which goals are connected to interests

Resistance point: the position on a specific issue or issues at which a party is willing to walk away

Resource power: the ability to influence others as a result of control over a desired resource

Role-based identity: identity derived from central roles one holds

Rules of exchange: the standards by which one judges another's actions in a relationship

Save face: when an individual is put into a position where he or she seen as consistent with a desired sense of self

Self monitoring: the ability to know how you are being perceived by others

Self-efficacy: the extent to which you believe you are able to successfully perform a task

Self-fulfilling prophecy: when one's own actions or beliefs about a particular outcome end up being the cause of that outcome

Sensemaking: the process by which individuals seek information in the context in order to figure out, or *make sense*, of why things are happening

Sex: strict biological categories of male and female

Social value orientation: the importance people place on their own versus others' outcomes in situations of interdependence

Specific goals: goals that someone else can understand and articulate

Standard: "a practice, policy, or reference point that gives a decision legitimacy" (Diamond, 2010)

Stereotypes: a usually oversimplified image or mental model of a particular group, person, or thing

Stereotyping: the attribution of traits, values, and motives to individual members of a group, based on generalizations about the group

Sunk cost bias: engaged in future effort in order to justify past effort (e.g., "I've come so far . . . let's just get this done")

Symbol-based identity: identity derived from the things one has or the stories one tells

Tactics: the behaviors that are used in the context of a negotiation

Tangible interests: underlying wants that can be seen, touched, or felt (e.g., money, goods, time)

Time-bound goals: goals with a specific deadline

Tolerance for ambiguity: how comfortable or uncomfortable an individual is in uncertain situations

Trust: the willingness to be vulnerable to someone else

Uncertainty avoidance: the level of tolerance for uncertainty and ambiguity within a society

Understanding: approach to negotiation in which one tries to understand the other side as completely as possible in order to get value

Unilateral concessions: multiple concessions in a row without a concession from the other side

Walking away: a negotiation tactic where you get up and walk away from the table

Winner's curse: feeling regret from the realization that one could have gotten much more out of a negotiation

Zone of potential agreement (ZOPA): the distance between each party's resistance point; can be positive or negative

NOTES

PREFACE

1. Tenbrunsel, A. E., & Smith-Crowe, K. (2008). Ethical decision making: Where we've been and where we're going. *Academy of Management Annals*, *2*(1), 545–607.

CHAPTER 1

1. Kopelman, S. (2014). *Negotiating genuinely: Being yourself in business*. Stanford, CA: Stanford University Press.

2. Lax, D. A., & Sebenius, J. K. (1986). *The manager as negotiator* (p. 11). New York, NY: Free Press.

3. Johnson-Laird, P. N. (1983). *Mental models: Towards a cognitive science of language, inference, and consciousness*. Cambridge, UK: Cambridge University Press.

4. Thompson, L., Valley, K. L., & Kramer, R. M. (1995). The bittersweet feeling of success: An examination of social perception in negotiation. *Journal of Experimental Social Psychology*, *31*(6), 467–492.

5. Kurtzberg, T., & Medvec, V. H. (1999). Can we negotiate and still be friends? *Negotiation Journal*, *15*(4), 355–361.

6. Best, A., & Andreasen, A. (1977). Consumer response to unsatisfactory purchases: A survey of perceiving defects, voicing complaints, and obtaining results. *Law & Society Review*, *11*, 701–742.

7. Bacharach, S. B., & Lawler, E. J. (1981). Power and tactics in bargaining. *ILR Review*, *34*(2), 219–233.

8. Barry, B., & Friedman, R. A. (1998). Bargainer characteristics in distributive and integrative negotiation. *Journal of Personality and Social Psychology*, *74*(2), 345–359.

9. Sandy, S. V., Boardman, S. K., & Deutsch, M. (2006). Personality and conflict. In M. Deutsch, P. T. Coleman, & E. C. Marcus (Eds.), *The handbook of conflict resolution: Theory and practice* (2nd ed., pp. 331–335). New York, NY: Wiley.

10. Tyler, T. R., Lind, E. A., & Huo, Y. J. (2000). Cultural values and authority relations: The psychology of conflict resolution across cultures. *Psychology, Public Policy, and Law*, *6*(4), 1138–1163.

11. Leung, K. (1988). Some determinants of conflict avoidance. *Journal of Cross-Cultural Psychology*, *19*(1), 125–136.

12. Pinckley, R. L., & Northcraft, G. B. (2003). *Get paid what you're worth: The expert negotiator's guide to salary and compensation*. New York, NY: St. Martin's Press.

13. Fisher, R., & Ury, W. (1981). *Getting to yes* (2nd ed.). New York, NY: Penguin.

14. Bazerman, M. J., & Neale, M. A. (1983). Heuristics in negotiation: Limitations to effective dispute resolution. In M. Bazerman & R. Lewicki (Eds.), *Negotiating in organizations* (pp. 51–67). Beverly Hills, CA: Sage.

15. Thompson, L., & Hastie, R. (1990). Social perception in negotiation. *Organizational Behavior and Human Decision Processes*, *47*(1), 98–123.

16. Thompson & Hastie (1990).

17. Thompson, L. L. (1991). Information exchange in negotiation. *Journal of Experimental Social Psychology*, *27*(2), 161–179.

18. Thompson, L. (1990). The influence of experience on negotiation performance. *Journal of Experimental Social Psychology*, *26*(6), 528–544.

19. Thompson, L., & Hrebec, D. (1996). Lose–lose agreements in interdependent decision making. *Psychological Bulletin*, *120*(3), 396–409.

20. Ross, L., Greene, D., & House, P. (1977). The "false consensus effect": An egocentric bias in social perception and attribution processes. *Journal of Experimental Social Psychology*, *13*(3), 279–301.

21. Morris, M. W., Larrick, R. P., & Su, S. K. (1999). Misperceiving negotiation counterparts: When situationally determined bargaining behaviors are attributed to personality traits. *Journal of Personality and Social Psychology*, 77(1), 52–67.

22. Thaler, R. (1980). Toward a positive theory of consumer choice. *Journal of Economic Behavior and Organization*, *1*, 39–60.

23. Merton, R. K. (1948). The self-fulfilling prophecy. *Antioch Review*, *8*(2), 193–210.

24. O'Connor, K. M., Arnold, J. A., & Burris, E. R. (2005). Negotiators' bargaining histories and their effects on future negotiation performance. *Journal of Applied Psychology*, *90*(2), 350–362.

25. Whitehead, A. N. (1929). *The aims of education.* New York, NY: Macmillan.

26. Schoenfeld, A. H. (1986). On having and using geometric knowledge. In J. Hiebert (Ed.), *Conceptual and procedural knowledge: The case of mathematics* (pp. 225–264). Hillsdale, NJ: Erlbaum.

27. Renkl, A., Mandl, H., & Gruber, H. (1996). Inert knowledge: Analyses and remedies. *Educational Psychologist*, *31*(2), 115–121.

28. Loewenstein, J., Thompson, L., & Gentner, D. (1999). Analogical encoding facilitates knowledge transfer in negotiation. *Psychonomic Bulletin & Review*, *6*(4), 586–597.

29. Loewenstein, J., Thompson, L., & Gentner, D. (2003). Analogical learning in negotiation teams: Comparing cases promotes learning and transfer. *Academy of Management Learning & Education*, *2*(2), 119–127.

30. Kray, L. J., & Haselhuhn, M. P. (2007). Implicit negotiation beliefs and performance: Experimental and longitudinal evidence. *Journal of Personality and Social Psychology*, *93*, 49–64.

CHAPTER 2

1. Thomas, K. W., & Kilmann, R. H. (1974). *Thomas-Kilmann conflict mode survey.* Tuxedo Junction, NY: Xicom.

2. Lax, D. A., & Sebenius, J. K. (1986). *The managerial negotiator: Bargaining for cooperation and competitive gain.* New York, NY: Free Press.

3. Raiffa, H. (1982). *The art and science of negotiation.* Cambridge, MA: Harvard University Press.

4. Lind, E. A., & Tyler, T. R. (1988). *The social psychology of procedural justice.* New York, NY: Springer Science & Business Media; Tyler, T. R., & Lind, E. A. (1992). A relational model of authority in groups. *Advances in Experimental Social Psychology*, *25*, 115–191.

5. Brosnan, S. F., & de Waal, F. B. (2014). Evolution of responses to (un)fairness. *Science*, *346*(6207). 1251776.

6. Cohen-Charash, Y., & Spector, P. E. (2001). The role of justice in organizations: A meta-analysis. *Organizational Behavior and Human Decision Processes*, *86*(2), 278–321.

7. Elfenbein, H. A., Curhan, J. R., Eisenkraft, N., Shirako, A., & Baccaro, L. (2008). Are some negotiators better than others? Individual differences in bargaining outcomes. *Journal of Research in Personality*, *42*, 1463–1475.

8. Camerer, C., & Thaler, R. H. (1995). Anomalies: Ultimatums, dictators and manners. *Journal of Economic Perspectives*, *9*(2), 209–219.

9. Roth, A. E. (1995). Bargaining experiments. In J. H. Kagel & A. E. Roth (Eds.), *Handbook of experimental economics* (Vol. 1, pp. 253–348). Princeton, NJ: Princeton University Press.

10. Milgram, S. (1974). *Obedience to authority.* New York, NY: Harper & Row.

11. Asch, S. E. (1956). Studies of independence and conformity: I. A minority of one against a unanimous majority. *Psychological Monographs: General and Applied*, *70*(9), 1–70.

12. Zimbardo, P. G. (2007). *Lucifer effect*. New York, NY: Random House.

13. Darley, J. M., & Latané, B. (1968). Bystander intervention in emergencies: Diffusion of responsibility. *Journal of Personality and Social Psychology, 8*(4, Pt. 1), 377–383.

CHAPTER 3

1. Covey, S. R. (1992). *The seven habits of highly effective people* (p. 358). London, UK: Simon & Schuster.

2. Sullivan, B. A., O'Connor, K. M., & Burris, E. R. (2006). Negotiator confidence: The impact of self-efficacy on tactics and outcomes. *Journal of Experimental Social Psychology, 42*(5), 567–581.

3. Pruitt, D. G., & Carnevale, P. J. (1993). *Negotiation in social conflict*. Maidenhead, UK: Open University Press.

4. Ohlsson, S. (1992). Information-processing explanations of insight and related phenomena. *Advances in the Psychology of Thinking, 1*, 1–44.

5. Cronin, M. A. (2006). A strategy for improving insight at work. *Academy of Management Proceedings, 2006*(1).

6. For further reading on decision-making frameworks, see Hammond, J. S., Keeney, R. L., & Raiffa, H. (2015). *Smart choices: A practical guide to making better decisions*. Cambridge, MA: Harvard Business Review Press.

7. Kahneman, D., & Egan, P. (2011). *Thinking, fast and slow* (Vol. 1). New York NY: Farrar, Straus & Giroux.

CHAPTER 4

1. Diamond, S. (2012). *Getting more*. New York, NY: Three Rivers Press.

2. Gouldner, A. W. (1960). The norm of reciprocity: A preliminary statement. *American Sociological Review*, 161–178.

3. Cialdini, R. B. (2001). Harnessing the science of persuasion. *Harvard Business Review, 79*(9), 72–81.

4. McCabe, K. A., Rigdon, M. L., & Smith, V. L. (2003). Positive reciprocity and intentions in trust games. *Journal of Economic Behavior & Organization, 52*(2), 267–275.

5. Donohue, W. A. (1981). Development of a model of rule use in negotiation interaction. *Communication Monographs, 48*, 106–120.

6. Putnam, L. L. (1983). Small group work climates: A lag-sequential analysis of group interaction. *Small Group Behavior, 14*, 465–494.

7. Weingart, L. R., Thompson, L. L., Bazerman, M. H., & Carroll, J. S. (1990). Tactical behavior and negotiation outcomes. *International Journal of Conflict Management, 1*, 7–31.

8. Fisher, R., & Ury, W. (1981). *Getting to yes* (2nd ed.). New York, NY: Penguin.

9. Putnam, L. L., & Jones, T. S. (1982). Reciprocity in negotiations: An analysis of bargaining interaction. *Communication Monographs, 49*(3), 171–191; Weingart et al. (1990).

10. Blake, R. R., & Mouton, J. S. (1964). *The managerial grid*. Houston, TX: Gulf.

11. Folger, J. P., & Poole, M. S. (1984). *Working through conflict*. Glenview, IL: Scott, Foresman.

12. Brett, J. M., Shapiro, D. L., & Lytle, A. L. (1998). Breaking the bonds of reciprocity in negotiations. *Academy of Management Journal, 41*(4), 410–424.

13. Weingart, L. R., Prietula, M. J., Hyder, E. B., & Genovese, C. R. (1999). Knowledge and the sequential processes of negotiation: A Markov chain analysis of response-in-kind. *Journal of Experimental Social Psychology, 35*(4), 366–393.

14. Baumeister, R. F., & Leary, M. R. (1995). The need to belong: Desire for interpersonal attachments as a fundamental human motivation. *Psychological Bulletin, 117*(3), 497.

15. Giles, H., Coupland, N., & Coupland, J. (1991). Accommodation theory: Communication, context, and consequence. In H. Giles, J. Coupland, & N. Coupland (Eds.), *Contexts of accommodation:*

Developments in applied sociolinguistics. Cambridge, UK: Cambridge University Press.

16. Maddux, W. W., Mullen, E., & Galinsky, A. D. (2008). Chameleons bake bigger pies and take bigger pieces: Strategic behavioral mimicry facilitates negotiation outcomes. *Journal of Experimental Social Psychology, 44*(2), 461–468.

17. Curhan, J. R., & Pentland, A. (2007). Thin slices of negotiation: Predicting outcomes from conversational dynamics within the first 5 minutes. *Journal of Applied Psychology, 92*(3), 802.

18. Boles, T. L., Croson, R. T., & Murnighan, J. K. (2000). Deception and retribution in repeated ultimatum bargaining. *Organizational Behavior and Human Decision Processes, 83*(2), 235–259.

19. Brett, J. M., Shapiro, D. L., & Lytle, A. L. (1998). Breaking the bonds of reciprocity in negotiations. *Academy of Management Journal, 41*(4), 410–424.

20. Meyerson, D., Weick, K. E., & Kramer, R. M. (1996). Swift trust and temporary groups. In R. M. Kramer & T. R. Tyler (Eds.), *Trust in organizations: Frontiers of theory and research* (pp. 166–195). Thousand Oaks, CA: Sage.

21. Clark, M. S., & Mills, J. (1979). Interpersonal attraction in exchange and communal relationships. *Journal of Personality and Social Psychology, 37*(1), 12–24.

22. Takeuchi, R., Yun, S., & Wong, K. F. E. (2011). Social influence of a coworker: A test of the effect of employee and coworker exchange ideologies on employees' exchange qualities. *Organizational Behavior and Human Decision Processes, 115*(2), 226–237.

23. Eisenberger, R., Armeli, S., Rexwinkel, B., Lynch, P. D., & Rhoades, L. (2001). Reciprocation of perceived organizational support. *Journal of Applied Psychology, 86*(1), 42–51.

24. Schubert, M., & Lambsdorff, J. G. (2014). Negative reciprocity in an environment of violent conflict: Experimental evidence from the Occupied Palestinian Territories. *Journal of Conflict Resolution, 58*(4), 539–563.

25. Lee, H. (1960). *To kill a mockingbird*. Philadelphia, PA: Lippincott.

26. Trötschel, R., Hüffmeier, J., Loschelder, D. D., Schwartz, K., & Gollwitzer, P. M. (2011). Perspective taking as a means to overcome motivational barriers in negotiations: When putting oneself into the opponent's shoes helps to walk toward agreements. *Journal of Personality and Social Psychology, 101*(4), 773.

27. Galinsky, A. D., Maddux, W. W., Gilin, D., & White, J. B. (2008). Why it pays to get inside the head of your opponent: The differential effects of perspective taking and empathy in negotiations. *Psychological Science, 19*(4), 378–384.

28. Neale, M., & Bazerman, M. H. (1983). The role of perspective-taking ability in negotiating under different forms of arbitration. *Industrial and Labor Relations Review, 36*(3), 378–388.

29. Tajima, M., & Fraser, N. M. (2001). Logrolling procedure for multi-issue negotiation. *Group Decision and Negotiation, 10*(3), 217–235.

30. Lax, D. A., & Sebenius, J. K. (1986). *The manager as negotiator: Bargaining for cooperation and competitive gain*. New York, NY: Free Press.

31. Bazerman, M. H., & Gillespie, J. J. (1999). Betting on the future: The virtues of contingent contracts. *Harvard Business Review, 77*(5), 155–160.

32. Bazerman, M. H., & Gillespie, J. J. (1999). Betting on the future: The virtues of contingent contracts. *Harvard Business Review, 77*(5), 155–160.

33. Cialdini, R. B., Vincent, J. E., Lewis, S. K., Catalan, J., Wheeler, D., & Darby, B. L. (1975). Reciprocal concessions procedure for inducing compliance: The door-in-the-face technique. *Journal of Personality and Social Psychology, 31*(2), 206–215.

SUPPLEMENT A

1. Grandey, A. A. (2000). Emotional regulation in the workplace: A new way to conceptualize emotional labor. *Journal of Occupational Health Psychology, 5*(1), 95.

CHAPTER 5

1. Curhan, J. R., Elfenbein, H. A., & Xu, H. (2006). What do people value when they negotiate?

Mapping the domain of subjective value in negotiation. *Journal of Personality and Social Psychology, 91*(3), 493.

2. Thompson, L., Valley, K. L., & Kramer, R. M. (1995). The bittersweet feeling of success: An examination of social perception in negotiation. *Journal of Experimental Social Psychology, 31*(6), 467–492.

3. Gecas, V. (1982). The self concept. *Annual Review of Sociology, 8,* 1–33.

4. Baumeister, R. F. (1998). The self. In D. T. Gilbert, S. T. Fiske, & G. Lindzey (Eds.), *The handbook of social psychology* (Vol. 1, pp. 680–740). Oxford, UK: Oxford University Press.

5. Gray, B. (2003). Negotiation with your nemesis. *Negotiation Journal, 19*(4), 299–310.

6. Rothman, J. (1977). *Resolving identity-based conflict in nations, organizations and communities.* San Francisco, CA: Jossey-Bass.

7. Tajfel, H., & Turner, J. C. (1979). An integrative theory of intergroup conflict. *Social Psychology of Intergroup Relations, 33*(47), 74.

8. Sluss, D. M., & Ashforth, B. E. (2007). Relational identity and identification: Defining ourselves through work relationships. *Academy of Management Review, 32*(1), 9–32.

9. Ashforth, B. E. (2001). *Role transitions in organizational life: An identity-based perspective.* Mahwah, NJ: Erlbaum.

10. Stets, J. E., & Burke, P. J. (2000). Identity theory and social identity theory. *Social Psychology Quarterly, 63,* 224–237.

11. Fine, G. A. (1996). Justifying work: Occupational rhetorics as resources in restaurant kitchens. *Administrative Science Quarterly, 41,* 90–115.

12. Petriglieri, J. (2011). Under threat: Responses to and the consequences of threats to individuals' identities. *Academy of Management Review, 36*(4), 641–662.

13. Deaux, K. (1991). Social identities: Thoughts on structure and change. In R. C. Curtis (Ed.), *The relational self: Theoretical convergences in psychoanalysis and social psychology* (pp. 77–93). New York, NY: Guilford Press.

14. Fiol, C. M., Pratt, M. G., & O'Connor, E. J. (2009). Managing intractable identity conflicts. *Academy of Management Review, 34*(1), 32–55.

15. Burton, J. (1984). *Global conflict.* College Park: University of Maryland, Center for International Development.

16. Branscombe, N. R., & Wann, D. L. (1994). Collective self-esteem consequences of outgroup derogation when a valued social identity is on trial. *European Journal of Social Psychology, 24,* 641–657.

17. Miles, E. W. (2010). The role of face in the decision not to negotiate. *International Journal of Conflict Management, 21*(4), 400–414.

18. Cialdini, R. B. (2001). *Influence: Science and practice* (4th ed.). Boston, MA: Allyn & Bacon.

19. Festinger, L. (1962). *A theory of cognitive dissonance* (Vol. 2). Stanford, CA: Stanford University Press.

20. Elster, J. (1983). *Sour grapes: Essays in the subversion of rationality.* Cambridge, UK: Cambridge University Press.

21. Babcock, L., Wang, X., & Loewenstein, G. (1996). Choosing the wrong pond: Social comparisons in negotiations that reflect a self-serving bias. *Quarterly Journal of Economics, 111*(1), 1–19.

22. Lax, D. A., & Sebenius, J. K. (1986). *The manager as negotiator: Bargaining for cooperation and competitive gain.* New York, NY: Free Press.

23. Nierenberg, G. (1976). *The complete negotiator.* New York NY: Neirenberg & Zelf.

24. Lalljee, M., Laham, S. M., & Tam, T. (2007). Unconditional respect for persons: A social psychological analysis. *Gruppendynamik und Organisationsberatung, 38,* 451–464.

25. Rogers, K. M., Corley, K. G., & Ashforth, B. E. (2017). Seeing more than orange: Organizational respect and positive identity transformation in a prison context. *Administrative Science Quarterly, 62*(2), 219–269.

26. Tyler, T. R. (1999). Why people cooperate with organizations: An identity-based perspective. In R. I. Sutton & B. M. Shaw (Eds.), *Research in*

organizational behavior (Vol. 21, pp. 201–246). Stamford, CT: JAI Press.

27. White, J. B., Tynan, R., Galinsky, A. D., & Thompson, L. (2004). Face threat sensitivity in negotiation: Roadblock to agreement and joint gain. *Organizational Behavior and Human Decision Processes, 94*(2), 102–124.

28. Tjosvold, D., & Huston, T. L. (1978). Social face and resistance to compromise in bargaining. *Journal of Social Psychology, 104,* 57–68.

29. Clyman, D. R., & Tripp, T. M. (2000). Discrepant values and measures of negotiator performance. *Group Decision & Negotiation, 9*(4), 251–274.

30. Batson, C. D., & Shaw, L. L. (1991). Evidence for altruism: Toward a pluralism of prosocial motives. *Psychological Inquiry, 2,* 107–122.

31. Diamond, S. (2010). *Getting more.* New York, NY: Three Rivers Press.

32. For a further discussion on this topic, listen to https://www.wnycstudios.org/story/radiolab-apologetical.

SUPPLEMENT B

1. Lin, C. A. (2014). Communication technology and social change. In C. A. Lin & D. J. Atkin (Eds.), *Communication technology and social change* (pp. 17–30). New York, NY: Routledge.

2. Daft, R. L., & Lengel, R. H. (1986). Organizational information requirements, media richness and structural design. *Management Science, 32*(5), 554–571.

3. Rockmann, K. W., & Northcraft, G. B. (2008). To be or not to be trusted: The influence of media richness on defection and deception. *Organizational Behavior and Human Decision Processes, 107*(2), 106–122.

4. Wilson, J. M., Straus, S. G., & McEvily, B. (2006). All in due time: The development of trust in computer-mediated and face-to-face teams. *Organizational Behavior and Human Decision Processes, 99*(1), 16–33.

5. Rockmann & Northcraft (2008).

6. Santana, A. D. (2014). Virtuous or vitriolic: The effect of anonymity on civility in online newspaper reader comment boards. *Journalism Practice, 8*(1), 18–33.

7. See Edmunds.com; kbb.com.

CHAPTER 6

1. French, J. R., & Raven, B. (1959). The bases of social power. In D. P. Cartwright (Ed.), *Studies in social power* (pp. 150–167). Ann Arbor: University of Michigan, Institute for Social Research.

2. Blau, P. M. (1964). *Exchange and power in social life.* New York, NY: Wiley.

3. Cropanzano, R., & Mitchell, M. S. (2005). Social exchange theory: An interdisciplinary review. *Journal of Management, 31,* 874–900.

4. Molm, L. D., Collett, J. L., & Schaefer, D. R. (2007). Building solidarity through generalized exchange: A theory of reciprocity. *American Journal of Sociology, 113*(1), 205–242.

5. Fehr, E., & Fischbacher, U. (2003). The nature of human altruism. *Nature, 425*(6960), 785–791.

6. Ballinger, G. A., & Rockmann, K. W. (2010). Chutes versus ladders: Anchoring events and a punctuated-equilibrium perspective on social exchange relationships. *Academy of Management Review, 35*(3), 373–391.

7. Roskos-Ewoldsen, D. R., Bichsel, J., & Hoffman, K. (2002). The influence of accessibility of source likability on persuasion. *Journal of Experimental Social Psychology, 38*(2), 137–143.

8. Horai, J., Naccari, N., & Fatoullah, E. (1974). The effects of expertise and physical attractiveness upon opinion agreement and liking. *Sociometry, 37*(4), 601–606.

9. Rosenblat, T. S. (2008). The beauty premium: Physical attractiveness and gender in dictator games. *Negotiation Journal, 24*(4), 465–481.

10. Griffin, E., & Sparks, G. G. (1990). Friends forever: A longitudinal exploration of intimacy in same-sex friends and platonic pairs. *Journal of Social and Personal Relationships, 7*(1), 29–46.

11. Tajfel, H. (1970). Experiments in intergroup discrimination. *Scientific American*, *223*(5), 96–103.

12. Brewer, M. B. (1979). In-group bias in the minimal intergroup situation: A cognitive-motivational analysis. *Psychological Bulletin*, *86*(2), 307–324; Tajfel, H. (1982). Social psychology of intergroup relations. *Annual Review of Psychology*, *33*(1), 1–39.

13. Swaab, R., Postmes, T., Van Beest, I., & Spears, R. (2007). Shared cognition as a product of, and precursor to, shared identity in negotiations. *Personality and Social Psychology Bulletin*, *33*(2), 187–199.

14. Mayer, R. C., Davis, J. H., & Schoorman, F. D. (1995). An integrative model of organizational trust. *Academy of Management Review*, *20*(3), 709–734.

15. Axelrod, R. (1984). *The evolution of cooperation*. New York, NY: Basic Books.

16. Lewicki, R. J., & Bunker, B. B. (1996). Developing and maintaining trust in work relationships. In R. M. Kramer & T. R. Tyler (Eds), *Trust in organizations: Frontiers of theory and research* (pp. 114–139). Thousand Oaks, CA: Sage.

17. Bottom, W. P., Gibson, K., Daniels, S. E., & Murnighan, J. K. (2002). When talk is not cheap: Substantive penance and expression of intent in rebuilding cooperation. *Organization Science*, *13*, 497–513.

18. Leunissen, J. M., De Cremer, D., & Folmer, C. P. R. (2012). An instrumental perspective on apologizing in bargaining: The importance of forgiveness to apologize. *Journal of Economic Psychology*, *33*(1), 215–222.

19. Lind, E. A., & Tyler, T. R. (1988). *The social psychology of procedural justice*. New York, NY: Springer Science & Business Media.

20. Schweitzer, M. E., Hershey, J. C., & Bradlow, E. T. (2006). Promises and lies: Restoring violated trust. *Organizational Behavior and Human Decision Processes*, *101*(1), 1–19.

21. Lawler, E. J. (2001). An affect theory of social exchange. *American Journal of Sociology*, *107*(2), 321–352.

22. Valley, K. L., Neale, M. A., & Mannix, E. A. (1995). Friends, lovers, colleagues, strangers: The effects of relationships on the process and outcome of dyadic negotiations. *Research on Negotiation in Organizations*, *5*, 65–94.

23. Thompson, L., & DeHarpport, T. (1998). Relationships, goal incompatibility, and communal orientation in negotiations. *Basic and Applied Social Psychology*, *20*(1), 33–44.

SUPPLEMENT C

1. Brett, J. M., Friedman, R., & Behfar, K. (2009, September). How to manage your negotiating team. *Harvard Business Review*, pp. 105–109.

2. Thompson, L. (2018). *Making the team: A guide for managers* (6th ed.). New York, NY: Pearson.

3. Thompson, L., Peterson, E., & Brodt, S. E. (1996). Team negotiation: An examination of integrative and distributive bargaining. *Journal of Personality and Social Psychology*, *70*(1), 66–78.

4. McCallum, D. M., Harring, K., Gilmore, R., Drenan, S., Chase, J. P., Insko, C. A., & Thibaut, J. (1985). Competition and cooperation between groups and between individuals. *Journal of Experimental Social Psychology*, *21*(4), 301–320.

5. Klimoski, R., & Mohammed, S. (1994). Team mental model: Construct or metaphor? *Journal of Management*, *20*(2), 403–437.

6. Polzer, J. T., Mannix, E. A., & Neale, M. A. (1998). Interest alignment and coalitions in multiparty negotiation. *Academy of Management Journal*, *41*(1), 42–54.

7. Eisenhardt, K. M. (1989). Agency theory: An assessment and review. *Academy of Management Review*, *14*(1), 57–74.

8. Tjosvold, D., & Sun, H. F. (2002). Understanding conflict avoidance: Relationship, motivations, actions, and consequences. *International Journal of Conflict Management*, *13*(2), 142–164.

9. Fisher, R., & Davis, W. (1999). Authority of an agent: When is less better? In R. H. Mnookin & L. E. Susskind (Eds.), *Negotiating on behalf of others* (pp. 59–80). Thousand Oaks, CA: Sage.

CHAPTER 7

1. Lindley, D. V. (2006). *Understanding uncertainty* (p. xi). Hoboken, NJ: Wiley.

2. Johnson-Laird, P. N. (1983). *Mental models: Towards a cognitive science of language, inference, and consciousness.* Cambridge, MA: Harvard University Press.

3. Staw, B. M., Sandelands, L. E., & Dutton, J. E. (1981). Threat rigidity effects in organizational behavior: A multilevel analysis. *Administrative Science Quarterly, 26*(4), 501–524.

4. Todd, A. R., Forstmann, M., Burgmer, P., Brooks, A. W., & Galinsky, A. D. (2015). Anxious and egocentric: How specific emotions influence perspective taking. *Journal of Experimental Psychology: General, 144*(2), 374–391.

5. Weick, K. E. (1995). *Sensemaking in organizations* (Vol. 3). Thousand Oaks, CA: Sage.

6. Adapted from Davidson, A. (Producer/Director). (1990). *The lunch date* [Short film]. Available at https://www.youtube.com/watch?v=epuTZigxUY8

7. Judd, C. M., & Park, B. (1993). Definition and assessment of accuracy in social stereotypes. *Psychological Review, 100*(1), 109–128.

8. Kahneman, D., & Egan, P. (2011). *Thinking, fast and slow* (Vol. 1). New York, NY: Farrar, Straus & Giroux.

9. See Connelly, B. L., Certo, S. T., Ireland, R. D., & Reutzel, C. R. (2011). Signaling theory: A review and assessment. *Journal of Management, 37*(1), 39–67.

10. Furnham, A., & Ribchester, T. (1995). Tolerance of ambiguity: A review of the concept, its measurement and applications. *Current Psychology, 14*(3), 179–199.

11. Hofstede, G., & Bond, M. H. (1988). The Confucius connection: From cultural roots to economic growth. *Organizational Dynamics, 16*(4), 5–21.

12. Kale, S., & McIntyre, R. P. (1991). Distribution channel relationships in diverse cultures. *International Marketing Review, 8*(3), 31–45.

13. French, J. R., & Raven, B. (1959). The bases of social power. In D. P. Cartwright (Ed.), *Studies in social power* (pp. 150–167). Ann Arbor: University of Michigan, Institute for Social Research.

14. Yukl, G. (1974). Effects of the opponent's initial offer, concession magnitude and concession frequency on bargaining behavior. *Journal of Personality and Social Psychology, 30*(3), 323–335.

15. Osgood, C. E. (1962). *An alternative to war or surrender.* Urbana: University of Illinois Press.

16. Galinsky, A. D., & Mussweiler, T. (2001). First offers as anchors: The role of perspective-taking and negotiator focus. *Journal of Personality and Social Psychology, 81*(4), 657–669.

17. Cialdini, R. B. (1993). *Influence: The psychology of persuasion* (Rev. ed.). New York, NY: William Morrow.

18. Kahneman, D., & Tversky, A. (1979). Prospect theory: An analysis of decision under risk. *Econometrica: Journal of the Econometric Society, 47*(2), 263–291.

19. Tversky, A., & Kahneman, D. (1981). The framing of decisions and the psychology of choice. *Science, 211*(4481), 453–458.

20. Tversky & Kahneman (1981).

21. Cialdini, R. B. (2001). Harnessing the science of persuasion. *Harvard Business Review, 79*(9), 72–81.

22. Langer, E. J., Blank, A., & Chanowitz, B. (1978). The mindlessness of ostensibly thoughtful action: The role of "placebic" information in interpersonal interaction. *Journal of Personality and Social Psychology, 36*(6), 635–642.

SUPPLEMENT D

1. Brett, J. M., Barsness, Z. I., & Goldberg, S. B. (1996). The effectiveness of mediation: An independent analysis of cases handled by four major service providers. *Negotiation Journal, 12*(3), 259–269.

2. Greig, J. M. (2001). Moments of opportunity: Recognizing conditions of ripeness for international mediation between enduring rivals. *Journal of Conflict Resolution, 45*(6), 691–718.

3. Feuille, P. (1975). Final offer arbitration and the chilling effect. *Industrial Relations, 14*(3), 302–310.

4. Vroom, V. H., & Jago, A. G. (1988). *The new leader-ship: Managing participation in organizations*. Engle-wood Cliffs, NJ: Prentice-Hall.

CHAPTER 8

1. House, R. J. (1984). *Power in organizations: A social psychological perspective*. Unpublished manuscript, Faculty of Management, University of Toronto, Ontario, Canada.

2. Hughes, R. L., Ginnett, R. C., & Curphy, G. J. (2009). *Leadership: Enhancing the lessons of experi-ence*. New York, NY: McGraw-Hill.

3. Kim, P. H., Pinkley, R. L., & Fragale, A. R. (2005). Power dynamics in negotiation. *Academy of Man-agement Review*, *30*(4), 799–822.

4. French, J. R., & Raven, B. (1959). The bases of social power. In D. P. Cartwright (Ed.), *Studies in social power* (pp. 150–167). Ann Arbor: University of Michigan, Institute for Social Research.

5. Milgram, S. (1963). Behavioral study of obedience. *Journal of Abnormal and Social Psychology*, *67*(4), 371–378.

6. You can watch this study at https://youtu.be/fCVlI-_4GZQ or a more recent replication at https://youtube/Xxq4QtK3j0Y.

7. Hollander, M. (2015). The repertoire of resistance: Non-compliance with directives in Milgram's "obedience" experiments. *British Journal of Social Psychology*, *54*(3), 425–444.

8. Greenberg, K. J., & Dratel, J. L. (Eds.). (2005). *The torture papers: The road to Abu Ghraib*. Cambridge, UK: Cambridge University Press.

9. See https://time.com/time-person-of-the-year-2017-silence-breakers/ for more information.

10. Greer, L. L., & van Kleef, G. A. (2010). Equality versus differentiation: The effects of power disper-sion on group interaction. *Journal of Applied Psy-chology*, *95*(6), 1032.

11. Greer, L. L., Caruso, H. M., & Jehn, K. A. (2011). The bigger they are, the harder they fall: Link-ing team power, team conflict, and performance.

Organizational Behavior and Human Decision Pro-cesses, *116*(1), 116–128.

12. Layne, N. (2015, October 18). Wal-Mart puts the squeeze on suppliers to share its pain as earn-ings sag. Reuters. Retrieved from https://www.reuters.com/article/us-wal-mart-suppliers-insight/wal-mart-puts-the-squeeze-on-suppliers-to-share-its-pain-as-earn-ings-sag-idUSKCN0SD0CZ20151019

13. Polzer, J. T., Mannix, E. A., & Neale, M. A. (1998). Interest alignment and coalitions in multiparty negotiation. *Academy of Management Journal*, *41*(1), 42–54.

14. Weingart, L. R., Cronin, M. A., Houser, C. J. S., Cagan, J., & Vogel, C. M. (2005). Functional diver-sity and conflict in cross-functional product devel-opment teams: Considering representational gaps and task characteristics. *Understanding Teams*, *4*, 89–110.

15. Magee, J. C., Galinsky, A. D., & Gruenfeld, D. H. (2007). Power, propensity to negotiate, and mov-ing first in competitive interactions. *Personality and Social Psychology Bulletin*, *33*(2), 200–212.

16. Van Kleef, G. A., & Côté, S. (2007). Expressing anger in conflict: When it helps and when it hurts. *Journal of Applied Psychology*, *92*(6), 1557–1569.

17. Greer, L. L., & van Kleef, G. A. (2010). Equality versus differentiation: The effects of power disper-sion on group interaction. *Journal of Applied Psy-chology*, *95*(6), 1032–1044.

18. Greer, L. L., Caruso, H. M., & Jehn, K. A. (2011). The bigger they are, the harder they fall: Linking team power, team conflict, and performance. *Orga-nizational Behavior and Human Decision Processes*, *116*(1), 116–128.

19. Kteily, N., Saguy, T., Sidanius, J., & Taylor, D. M. (2013). Negotiating power: Agenda ordering and the willingness to negotiate in asymmetric inter-group conflicts. *Journal of Personality and Social Psy-chology*, *105*(6), 978–995.

20. Donohue, W. A., & Taylor, P. J. (2007). Role effects in negotiation: The one-down phenomenon. *Negotiation Journal*, *23*(3), 307–331.

21. Levine, T. R., & Boster, F. J. (2001). The effects of power and message variables on compliance. *Communication Monographs*, *68*, 28–48.

22. Dijkstra, M., Beersma, B., & van Leeuwen, J. (2014). Gossiping as a response to conflict with the boss: Alternative conflict management behavior? *International Journal of Conflict Management*, *25*(4), 431–454.

23. Cialdini, R. (1993). *The psychology of influence*. New York, NY: William Morrow.

SUPPLEMENT E

1. Hilty, J. A., & Carnevale, P. J. (1993). Black-hat/white-hat strategy in bilateral negotiation. *Organizational Behavior and Human Decision Processes*, *55*(3), 444–469.

2. Robinson, Robert J. (1995). Defusing the exploding offer: The farpoint gambit. *Negotiation Journal*, 11: 277–285.

CHAPTER 9

1. Von Wieser, F. (1927). *Social economics*. New York, NY: Aldephi.

2. Buchanan J. M. (1987). Opportunity cost. In J. Eatwell, M. Milgate, P. Newman (Eds.), *The new Palgrave: A dictionary of economic theory and doctrine* (Vol. 3, 718–721). London, UK: Macmillan.

3. Retrieved from https://en.wikipedia.org/wiki/Affordable_Health_Care_for_America_Act

4. Fisher, R., Ury, W., & Patton, B. (1991). *Getting to yes: Negotiating agreement without giving in*. New York, NY: Penguin.

5. Bandura, A. (1994). Self-efficacy. In V. S. Ramachaudran (Ed.), *Encyclopedia of human behavior* (Vol. 4, pp. 71–81). New York, NY: Academic Press. (Reprinted in H. Friedman [Ed.], *Encyclopedia of mental health*. San Diego, CA: Academic Press, 1998).

6. Woodman, T. I. M., & Hardy, L. E. W. (2003). The relative impact of cognitive anxiety and self-confidence upon sport performance: A meta-analysis. *Journal of Sports Sciences*, *21*(6), 443–457.

7. Stajkovic, A. D., & Luthans, F. (1998). Self-efficacy and work-related performance: A meta-analysis. *Psychological Bulletin*, *124*(2), 240–261.

8. Magee, J. C., Galinsky, A. D., & Gruenfeld, D. (2007). Power, propensity to negotiate, and moving first in competitive interactions. *Personality and Social Psychology Bulletin*, *33*(2), 200–212.

9. Pinkley, R. L., Neale, M. A., & Bennett, R. J. (1994). The impact of alternatives to settlement in dyadic negotiation. *Organizational Behavior and Human Decision Processes*, *57*(1), 97–116.

10. Pinkley, R. L., Conlon, D. E., Sawyer, J. E., Sleesman, D. J., Vandewalle, D., & Kuenzi, M. (2017). Unpacking BATNA availability: How probability can impact power in negotiation. *Academy of Management Proceedings*, *2017*(1), 16888.

11. Paese, P. W., & Gilin, D. A. (2000). When an adversary is caught telling the truth: Reciprocal cooperation versus self-interest in distributive bargaining. *Personality and Social Psychology Bulletin*, *26*(1), 79–90.

12. Staudohar, P. (2005, December). The hockey lockout of 2004-05. *Monthly Labor Review*, pp. 23–29.

13. Buelens, M., & Van Poucke, D. (2004). Determinants of a negotiator's initial opening offer. *Journal of Business and Psychology*, *19*(1), 23–35.

14. de Dreu, C. K. W., Giebels, E., & van de Vliert, E. (1998). Social motives and trust in integrative negotiations: The disruptive effects of punitive capability. *Journal of Applied Psychology*, *83*(3), 408–422.

SUPPLEMENT F

1. Moore, D. A. (2004). The unexpected benefits of final deadlines in negotiation. *Journal of Experimental Social Psychology*, *40*(1), 121–127.

CHAPTER 10

1. Ury, W. (1993). *Getting past no: Negotiating your way from confrontation to cooperation*. New York, NY: Bantam Books.

2. Locke, E. A., & Latham, G. (1990). *A theory of goal setting and task performance*. Englewood Cliffs, NJ: Prentice Hall.

3. Plous, S. (1993). *The psychology of judgment and decision making*. New York, NY: McGraw-Hill.

4. Thaler, R. (2012). *The winner's curse: Paradoxes and anomalies of economic life*. New York, NY: Simon & Schuster.

5. Thaler (2012).

6. Amantullah, E. T., Morris, M. W., & Curhan, J. R. (2008). Negotiators who give too much: Unmitigated communion, relational anxieties, and economic costs in distributive and integrative bargaining. *Journal of Personality and Social Psychology, 95*, 723–738.

7. Kirkman, B. L., & Rosen, B. (1999). Beyond self-management: Antecedents and consequences of team empowerment. *Academy of Management Journal, 42*(1), 58–74.

8. Hollenbeck, J. R., Williams, C. R., & Klein, H. J. (1989). An empirical examination of the antecedents of commitment to difficult goals. *Journal of Applied Psychology, 74*(1), 18–23.

9. Henningfield, J. E. (1995). Nicotine medications for smoking cessation. *New England Journal of Medicine, 333*(18), 1196–1203.

10. Pinkley, R. L., & Northcraft, G. B. (2000). *Get paid what you're worth: The expert negotiators guide to salary and compensation*. New York, NY: St. Martin's Press.

11. Ariely, D., Gneezy, U., Loewenstein, G., & Mazar, N. (2009). Large stakes and big mistakes. *Review of Economic Studies, 76*(2), 451–469.

12. Deci, E. L. (1980). *The psychology of self-determination*. Lexington, MA: Heath.

13. Siegel, S., & Fouraker, L. E. (1960). *Bargaining and group decision making: Experiments in bilateral monopoly*. New York, NY: McGraw-Hill.

14. Ben-Yoav, O., & Pruitt, D. G. (1984). Resistance to yielding and the expectation of cooperative future interaction in negotiation. *Journal of Experimental Social Psychology, 20*(4), 323–335.

15. Bowles, H. R., & Flynn, F. (2010). Gender and persistence in negotiation: A dyadic perspective. *Academy of Management Journal, 53*(4), 769–787.

16. Seligman, E., & Schulman, P. (1986). Explanatory style as a predictor of productivity and quitting among life insurance sales agents. *Journal of Personality and Social Psychology, 50*, 832–838.

17. Grant, A. M., Campbell, E. M., Chen, G., Cottone, K., Lapedis, D., & Lee, K. (2007). Impact and the art of motivation maintenance: The effects of contact with beneficiaries on persistence behavior. *Organizational Behavior and Human Decision Processes, 103*, 53–67.

18. De Dreu, C. W. K., Koole, S. L., & Steinel, W. (2000). Unfixing the fixed pie: A motivated information-processing approach to integrative negotiation. *Journal of Personality and Social Psychology, 79*(6), 975–987.

19. Bowles, H. R., Babcock, L., & Lai, L. (2007). Social incentives for gender differences in the propensity to initiate negotiations: Sometimes it does hurt to ask. *Organizational Behavior and Human Decision Processes, 103*(1), 84–103.

20. Staw, B. M. (1981). The escalation of commitment to a course of action. *Academy of Management Review, 6*(4), 577–587.

21. Ordóñez, L. D., Schweitzer, M. E., Galinsky, A. D., & Bazerman, M. H. (2009). Goals gone wild: The systematic side effects of overprescribing goal setting. *Academy of Management Perspectives, 23*(1), 6–16.

22. Bazerman, M. H., Loewenstein, G. F., & White, S. B. (1992). Reversals of preference in allocation decisions: Judging an alternative versus choosing among alternatives. *Administrative Science Quarterly, 37*, 220–240.

23. Malhotra, D. (2010). The desire to win: The effects of competitive arousal on motivation and behavior. *Organizational Behavior and Human Decision Processes, 111*(2), 139–146.

24. Schweitzer, M. E., Ordóñez, L., & Douma, B. (2004). Goal setting as a motivator of unethical behavior. *Academy of Management Journal, 47*(3), 422–432.

CHAPTER 11

1. Deaux, K. (1985). Sex and gender. *Annual Review of Psychology, 36*(1), 49–81.

2. Archer, J., & Lloyd, B. (2002). *Sex and gender.* Cambridge, UK: Cambridge University Press.

3. Oakley, A. (2016). *Sex, gender and society.* New York, NY: Routledge.

4. Watson, C., & Kasten, B. (1988). *Separate strengths? How women and men negotiate.* Newark, NJ: Rutgers University, Center for Negotiation and Conflict Resolution.

5. Small, D. A., Gelfand, M., Babcock, L., & Gettman, H. (2007). Who goes to the bargaining table? The influence of gender and framing on the initiation of negotiation. *Journal of Personality and Social Psychology, 93*(4), 600–613.

6. Sweeney, P. D., & McFarlin, D. B. (1997). Process and outcome: Gender differences in the assessment of justice. *Journal of Organizational Behavior, 18*(1), 83–98.

7. Babcock, L., & Laschever, S. (2003). *Women don't ask: Negotiation and the gender divide.* Princeton, NJ: Princeton University Press.

8. Amanatullah, E. T., & Morris, M. W. (2010). Negotiating gender roles: Gender differences in assertive negotiating are mediated by women's fear of backlash and attenuated when negotiating on behalf of others. *Journal of Personality and Social Psychology, 98*(2), 256–267.

9. Kray, L. J., Galinsky, A. D., & Thompson, L. (2002). Reversing the gender gap in negotiations: An exploration of stereotype regeneration. *Organizational Behavior and Human Decision Processes, 87*(2), 386–409.

10. Kray, L. J., Thompson, L., & Galinsky, A. (2001). Battle of the sexes: Gender stereotype confirmation and reactance in negotiations. *Journal of Personality and Social Psychology, 80*(6), 942–958.

11. Bowles, H. R., & Babcock, L. (2013). How can women escape the compensation negotiation dilemma? Relational accounts are one answer. *Psychology of Women Quarterly, 37*(1), 80–96.

12. Bowles, H. R., Babcock, L., & Lai, L. (2007). Social incentives for gender differences in the propensity to initiate negotiations: Sometimes it does hurt to ask. *Organizational Behavior and Human Decision Processes, 103*(1), 84–103.

13. Amanatullah, E. T., & Tinsley, C. H. (2013). Ask and ye shall receive? How gender and status moderate negotiation success. *Negotiation and Conflict Management Research, 6*(4), 253–272.

14. Kulik, C. T., & Olekalns, M. (2012). Negotiating the gender divide: Lessons from the negotiation and organizational behavior literatures. *Journal of Management, 38*(4), 1387–1415.

15. Wade, M. E. (2001). Women and salary negotiation: The costs of self-advocacy. *Psychology of Women Quarterly, 25*(1), 65–76.

16. Small et al. (2007).

17. Eriksson, K. H., & Sandberg, A. (2012). Gender differences in initiation of negotiation: Does the gender of the negotiation counterpart matter? *Negotiation Journal, 28*(4), 407–428.

18. Ayres, I., & Siegelman, P. (1995). Race and gender discrimination in bargaining for a new car. *American Economic Review, 85*(3), 304–321.

19. Gerhart, B., & Rynes, S. (1991). Determinants and consequences of salary negotiations by male and female MBA graduates. *Journal of Applied Psychology, 76*(2), 256–262.

20. Rosete, D., & Ciarrochi, J. (2005). Emotional intelligence and its relationship to workplace performance outcomes of leadership effectiveness. *Leadership & Organization Development Journal, 26*(5), 388–399.

21. Mayer, J. D., Roberts, R. D., Barsade, S. G. (2008). Human abilities: Emotional intelligence. *Annual Review of Psychology 59*, 507–536.

22. Ronk, L. L. (1993). Gender gaps within management. *Nursing Management, 24*(5), 65.

23. Book, A. S., Starzyk, K. B., & Quinsey, V. L. (2001). The relationship between testosterone and aggression: A meta-analysis. *Aggression and Violent Behavior, 6*(6), 579–599.

24. Buss, D. (2015). *Evolutionary psychology: The new science of the mind.* Hove, UK: Psychology Press.

25. Barkow, J. H., Cosmides, L., & Tooby, J. (Eds.). (1995). *The adapted mind: Evolutionary psychology and the generation of culture.* New York, NY: Oxford University Press.

26. Schmitt, D. P., Realo, A., Voracek, M., & Allik, J. (2008). Why can't a man be more like a woman? Sex differences in Big Five personality traits across 55 cultures. *Journal of Personality and Social Psychology, 94*(1), 168–182.

27. Barsky, A. E., & Wood, L. (2005). Conflict avoidance in a university context. *Higher Education Research & Development, 24*(3), 249–264.

28. Bacharach, S. B., & Lawler, E. J. (1981). Power and tactics in bargaining. *ILR Review, 34*(2), 219–233.

29. Sandy, S. V., Boardman, S. K., & Deutsch, M. (2006). Personality and conflict. In M. Deutsch, P. T. Coleman, & E. C. Marcus (Eds.), *The handbook of conflict resolution: Theory and practice* (2nd ed., pp. 331–355).

30. Tjosvold, D., & Sun, H. F. (2002). Understanding conflict avoidance: Relationship, motivations, actions, and consequences. *International Journal of Conflict Management, 13*(2), 142–164.

31. Leung, K. (1988). Some determinants of conflict avoidance. *Journal of Cross-Cultural Psychology, 19*(1), 125–136.

32. Tyler, T. R., Lind, E. A., & Huo, Y. J. (2000). Cultural values and authority relations: The psychology of conflict resolution across cultures. *Psychology, Public Policy, and Law, 6*(4), 1138–1163.

33. Tjosvold, D., & Sun, H. F. (2002). Understanding conflict avoidance: Relationship, motivations, actions, and consequences. *International Journal of Conflict Management, 13*(2), 142–164.

34. Pearson, V. M., & Stephan, W. G. (1998). Preferences for styles of negotiation: A comparison of Brazil and the US. *International Journal of Intercultural Relations, 22*(1), 67–83.

35. Morris, M. W., Williams, K. Y., Leung, K., Larrick, R., Mendoza, M. T., Bhatnagar, D., . . . & Hu, J. C. (1998). Conflict management style: Accounting for cross-national differences. *Journal of International Business Studies, 29*(4), 729–747.

36. van Oudenhoven, J. P., Mechelse, L., & De Dreu, C. K. (1998). Managerial conflict management in five European countries: The importance of power distance, uncertainty avoidance, and masculinity. *Applied Psychology, 47*(3), 439–455.

37. Bear, J. (2011). "Passing the buck": Incongruence between gender role and topic leads to avoidance of negotiation. *Negotiation and Conflict Management Research, 4*(1), 47–72.

38. Thompson, E. R. (2008). Development and validation of an International English Big-Five Mini-Markers. *Personality and Individual Differences, 45*(6), 542–548.

39. Graziano, W. G., Jensen-Campbell, L. A., & Hair, E. C. (1996). Perceiving interpersonal conflict and reacting to it: the case for agreeableness. *Journal of Personality and Social Psychology, 70*(4), 820–835.

40. Morris, M. W., Larrick, R. P., & Su, S. K. (1999). Misperceiving negotiation counterparts: When situationally determined bargaining behaviors are attributed to personality traits. *Journal of Personality and Social Psychology, 77*(1), 52–67.

41. Dimotakis, N., Conlon, D. E., & Ilies, R. (2012). The mind and heart (literally) of the negotiator: Personality and contextual determinants of experiential reactions and economic outcomes in negotiation. *Journal of Applied Psychology, 97*(1), 183–193.

42. Wilson, K. S., DeRue, D. S., Matta, F. K., Howe, M., & Conlon, D. E. (2016). Personality similarity in negotiations: Testing the dyadic effects of similarity in interpersonal traits and the use of emotional displays on negotiation outcomes. *Journal of Applied Psychology, 101*(10), 1405–1421.

43. Jensen-Campbell, L. A., & Graziano, W. G. (2001). Agreeableness as a moderator of interpersonal conflict. *Journal of Personality, 69*(2), 323–362.

44. Barry, B., & Friedman, R. A. (1998). Bargainer characteristics in distributive and integrative negotiation. *Journal of personality and social psychology, 74*(2), 345–359.

45. Dimotakis et al. (2012).

46. Balliet, D., Parks, C., & Joireman, J. (2009). Social value orientation and cooperation in social dilemmas: A meta-analysis. *Group Processes & Intergroup Relations, 12*(4), 533–547.

47. De Dreu, C. K., & Van Lange, P. A. (1995). The impact of social value orientations on negotiator cognition and behavior. *Personality and Social Psychology Bulletin, 21*(11), 1178–1188.

48. Van Lange, P. A. (1999). The pursuit of joint outcomes and equality in outcomes: An integrative model of social value orientation. *Journal of Personality and Social Psychology, 77*(2), 337–349.

49. Bogaert, S., Boone, C., & Declerck, C. (2008). Social value orientation and cooperation in social dilemmas: A review and conceptual model. *British Journal of Social Psychology, 47*(3), 453–480.

50. Kramer, R. M., & Carnevale, P. J. (2003). Trust and intergroup negotiation. In R. Brown & S. L. Gaertner (Eds.), *Blackwell handbook of social psychology: Intergroup processes* (pp. 431–450).

51. Pruitt, D. G., & Lewis, S. A. (1975). Development of integrative solutions in bilateral negotiation. *Journal of Personality and Social Psychology, 31*(4), 621–633.

52. Kimmel, M. J., Pruitt, D. G., Magenau, J. M., Konar-Goldband, E., & Carnevale, P. J. (1980). Effects of trust, aspiration, and gender on negotiation tactics. *Journal of Personality and Social Psychology, 38*(1), 9–22.

53. Butler, J. K., Jr. (1999). Trust expectations, information sharing, climate of trust, and negotiation effectiveness and efficiency. *Group & Organization Management, 24*(2), 217–238.

54. Mooradian, T., Renzl, B., & Matzler, K. (2006). Who trusts? Personality, trust and knowledge sharing. *Management Learning, 37*(4), 523–540.

55. Rotter, J. B. (1971). Generalized expectancies for interpersonal trust. *American Psychologist, 26*(5), 443–452.

56. Mayer, R. C., Davis, J. H., & Schoorman, F. D. (1995). An integrative model of organizational trust. *Academy of Management Review, 20*(3), 709–734.

57. Mooradian et al. (2006).

58. Gill, H., Boies, K., Finegan, J. E., & McNally, J. (2005). Antecedents of trust: Establishing a boundary condition for the relation between propensity to trust and intention to trust. *Journal of Business and Psychology, 19*(3), 287–302.

59. Rosette, A. S., Kopelman, S., & Abbott, J. L. (2014). Good grief! Anxiety sours the economic benefits of first offers. *Group Decision and Negotiation, 23*(3), 629–647.

60. Olekalns, M., & Druckman, D. (2014). With feeling: How emotions shape negotiation. *Negotiation Journal, 30*(4), 455–478.

61. Overbeck, J. R., Neale, M. A., & Govan, C. L. (2010). I feel, therefore you act: Intrapersonal and interpersonal effects of emotion on negotiation as a function of social power. *Organizational Behavior and Human Decision Processes, 112*(2), 126–139.

62. Steinel, W., Van Kleef, G. A., & Harinck, F. (2008). Are you talking to me?! Separating the people from the problem when expressing emotions in negotiation. *Journal of Experimental Social Psychology, 44*(2), 362–369.

63. Fridlund, A. J. (1997). The new ethology of human facial expressions. In J. A. Russell & J. M. Fernández (Eds.), *The psychology of facial expression* (pp. 103–129). Cambridge, UK: Cambridge University Press.

64. Van Kleef, G. A., De Dreu, C. K., & Manstead, A. S. (2004). The interpersonal effects of emotions in negotiations: A motivated information processing approach. *Journal of Personality and Social Psychology, 87*(4), 510–528.

65. Sinaceur, M., & Tiedens, L. Z. (2006). Get mad and get more than even: When and why anger expression is effective in negotiations. *Journal of Experimental Social Psychology, 42*(3), 314–322.

66. Van Kleef, G. A., De Dreu, C. K., & Manstead, A. S. (2004). The interpersonal effects of anger and happiness in negotiations. *Journal of Personality and Social Psychology, 86*(1), 57–76.

67. Sinaceur & Tiedens (2006).

68. Van Kleef, G. A., van Dijk, E., Steinel, W., Harinck, F., & Van Beest, I. (2008). Anger in social conflict: Cross-situational comparisons and suggestions for the future. *Group Decision and Negotiation, 17*(1), 13–30.

69. Wang, L., Northcraft, G. B., & Van Kleef, G. A. (2012). Beyond negotiated outcomes: The hidden costs of anger expression in dyadic negotiation. *Organizational Behavior and Human Decision Processes, 119*(1), 54–63.

70. Van Dijk, E., Van Kleef, G. A., Steinel, W., & Van Beest, I. (2008). A social functional approach to emotions in bargaining: When communicating anger pays and when it backfires. *Journal of Personality and Social Psychology*, *94*(4), 600–614.

71. Hatfield, E., Cacioppo, J. T., & Rapson, R. L. (1993). Emotional contagion. *Current Directions in Psychological Science*, *2*(3), 96–100.

72. Côté, S., Hideg, I., & van Kleef, G. A. (2013). The consequences of faking anger in negotiations. *Journal of Experimental Social Psychology*, *49*(3), 453–463.

73. Kopelman, S., Rosette, A. S., & Thompson, L. (2006). The three faces of Eve: Strategic displays of positive, negative, and neutral emotions in negotiations. *Organizational Behavior and Human Decision Processes*, *99*(1), 81–101.

74. Rothman, N. B. (2011). Steering sheep: How expressed emotional ambivalence elicits dominance in interdependent decision making contexts. *Organizational Behavior and Human Decision Processes*, *116*(1), 66–82.

75. Sinaceur, M., Adam, H., Van Kleef, G. A., & Galinsky, A. D. (2013). The advantages of being unpredictable: How emotional inconsistency extracts concessions in negotiation. *Journal of Experimental Social Psychology*, *49*(3), 498–508.

76. Brooks, A. W., & Schweitzer, M. E. (2011). Can Nervous Nelly negotiate? How anxiety causes negotiators to make low first offers, exit early, and earn less profit. *Organizational Behavior and Human Decision Processes*, *115*(1), 43–54.

77. Adler, R. S., Rosen, B., & Silverstein, E. M. (1998). Emotions in negotiation: How to manage fear and anger. *Negotiation Journal*, *14*(2), 161–179.

78. Wheeler, M. (2004). Anxious moments: Openings in negotiation. *Negotiation Journal*, *20*(2), 153–169.

79. Martindale, C. (1999). Biological bases of creativity. In R. J. Sternberg (Ed.), *Handbook of creativity* (pp. 137–152). Cambridge, UK: Cambridge University Press.

80. Babcock, L., & Laschever, S. (2009). *Women don't ask: Negotiation and the gender divide*. Princeton, NJ: Princeton University Press.

81. Ogilvie, J. R., & Carsky, M. L. (2002). Building emotional intelligence in negotiations. *International Journal of Conflict Management*, *13*(4), 381–400.

82. Smithey Fulmer, I., & Barry, B. (2004). The smart negotiator: Cognitive ability and emotional intelligence in negotiation. *International Journal of Conflict Management*, *15*(3), 245–272.

83. Druckman, D., & Olekalns, M. (2008). Emotions in negotiation. *Group Decision and Negotiation*, *17*(1), 1–11.

84. Salovey, P., & Mayer, J. D. (1990). Emotional intelligence. *Imagination, Cognition and Personality*, *9*(3), 185–211.

85. Kim, K., Cundiff, N. L., & Choi, S. B. (2014). The influence of emotional intelligence on negotiation outcomes and the mediating effect of rapport: A structural equation modeling approach. *Negotiation Journal*, *30*(1), 49–68.

86. Der Foo, M., Anger Elfenbein, H., Hoon Tan, H., & Chuan Aik, V. (2004). Emotional intelligence and negotiation: The tension between creating and claiming value. *International Journal of Conflict Management*, *15*(4), 411–429.

87. Adler, R. S., Rosen, B., & Silverstein, E. M. (1998). Emotions in negotiation: How to manage fear and anger. *Negotiation Journal*, *14*(2), 161–179.

88. Fisher, R., Ury, W. L., & Patton, B. (2011). *Getting to yes: Negotiating agreement without giving in*. New York, NY: Penguin.

89. Putnam, L. L., & Roloff, M. E. (Eds.). (1992). *Communication and negotiation*. Newbury Park, CA: Sage.

90. Tamir, M., & Ford, B. Q. (2012). When feeling bad is expected to be good: Emotion regulation and outcome expectancies in social conflicts. *Emotion*, *12*(4), 807–816.

91. Elfenbein, H. A., Curhan, J. R., Eisenkraft, N., Shirako, A., & Baccaro, L. (2008). Are some negotiators better than others? Individual differences in bargaining outcomes. *Journal of Research in Personality*, *42*(6), 1463–1475.

92. Smithey Fulmer & Barry (2004).

93. Habibi, D. (2001). Mill's moral philosophy. In *John Stuart Mill and the ethic of human growth* (pp. 89–90, 112). Dordrecht, Netherlands: Springer.

CHAPTER 12

1. Adair, W., Brett, J., Lempereur, A., Okumura, T., Shikhirev, P., Tinsley, C., & Lytle, A. (2004). Culture and negotiation strategy. *Negotiation Journal, 20*(1), 87–111.

2. Gelfand, M. J., & Brett, J. M. (2004). *The handbook of negotiation and culture*. Stanford, CA: Stanford University Press.

3. Hofstede, G. J., Jonker, C. M., & Verwaart, T. (2012). Cultural differentiation of negotiating agents. *Group Decision and Negotiation, 21*(1), 79–98.

4. Oetzel, J. G., & Ting-Toomey, S. (2003). Face concerns in interpersonal conflict: A cross-cultural empirical test of the face negotiation theory. *Communication Research, 30*(6), 599–624.

5. Tinsley, C. H. (2001). How negotiators get to yes: Predicting the constellation of conflict management strategies used across cultures. *Journal of Applied Psychology, 86*(4), 583–593.

6. Adair et al. (2004).

7. Adair, W. L., Weingart, L., & Brett, J. (2007). The timing and function of offers in U.S. and Japanese negotiations. *Journal of Applied Psychology, 92*(4), 1056–1068.

8. Adair, W. L., & Brett, J. M. (2005). The negotiation dance: Time, culture, and behavioral sequences in negotiation. *Organization Science, 16*(1), 33–51.

9. Swaab, R. I., Galinsky, A. D., Medvec, V., & Diermeier, D. A. (2012). The communication orientation model: Explaining the diverse effects of sight, sound, and synchronicity on negotiation and group decision-making outcomes. *Personality and Social Psychology Review, 16*(1), 25–53.

10. Lee, S., Adair, W. L., & Seo, S.-J. (2013). Cultural perspective taking in cross-cultural negotiation. *Group Decision and Negotiation, 22*(3), 389–405.

11. Elfenbein, H. A., Der Foo, M., White, J., Tan, H. H., & Aik, V. C. (2007). Reading your counterpart: The benefit of emotion recognition accuracy for effectiveness in negotiation. *Journal of Nonverbal Behavior, 31*(4), 205–223.

12. Brett, J. M. (2000). Culture and negotiation. *International Journal of Psychology, 35*(2), 97–104.

13. Van Kleef, G. A., De Dreu, C. K., Pietroni, D., & Manstead, A. S. (2006). Power and emotion in negotiation: Power moderates the interpersonal effects of anger and happiness on concession making. *European Journal of Social Psychology, 36*(4), 557–581.

14. Adam, H., & Shirako, A. (2013). Not all anger is created equal: The impact of the expresser's culture on the social effects of anger in negotiations. *Journal of Applied Psychology, 98*(5), 785–798.

15. Druckman, D., & Olekalns, M. (2008). Emotions in negotiation. *Group Decision and Negotiation, 17*(1), 1–11.

16. Kopelman, S., & Rosette, A. S. (2008). Cultural variation in response to strategic emotions in negotiations. *Group Decision and Negotiation, 17*(1), 65–77.

17. Adam, H., Shirako, A., & Maddux, W. W. (2010). Cultural variance in the interpersonal effects of anger in negotiations. *Psychological Science, 21*(6), 882–889.

18. Brett, J. (2010). Clueless about culture and indirect confrontation of conflict. *Negotiation and Conflict Management Research, 3*(3), 169–178.

19. Liu, L. A., Friedman, R., Barry, B., Gelfand, M. J., & Zhang, Z. X. (2012). The dynamics of consensus building in intracultural and intercultural negotiations. *Administrative Science Quarterly, 57*(2), 269–304.

20. Valenzuela, A., Srivastava, J., & Lee, S. (2005). The role of cultural orientation in bargaining under incomplete information: Differences in causal attributions. *Organizational Behavior and Human Decision Processes, 96*(1), 72–88.

21. Adair, W. L., Okumura, T., & Brett, J. M. (2001). Negotiation behavior when cultures collide: The

United States and Japan. *Journal of Applied Psychology, 86*(3), 371.

22. Marsh, J. (2019, May 21). A legacy of lunacy haunts Kenya's old railway. Will China's $3.6B line be different? CNN. Retrieved from https://www.cnn.com/2019/05/20/china/china-kenya-sgr-rail-africa-intl/index.html

23. Imai, L., & Gelfand, M. J. (2010). The culturally intelligent negotiator: The impact of cultural intelligence (CQ) on negotiation sequences and outcomes. *Organizational Behavior and Human Decision Processes, 112*(2), 83–98.

APPENDIX 1

1. Druckman, D. (1986). Stages, turning points, and crises: Negotiating military base rights, Spain and the United States. *Journal of Conflict Resolution, 30*(2), 327–360.

APPENDIX 3

1. See Pinkley, R. L., & Northcraft, G. B. (2000). *Get paid what you're worth*. New York, NY: St. Martin's Press.

INDEX

future orientation and, 292

gender egalitarianism, 292, 293, 294

gender, initiating negotiation and, 272

GLOBE research project and, 291–292, 293, 293 (figure)

hard vs. soft tactics and, 306

individualistic cultures and, 294

information, interpretation of, 287–288

leveraged differences, value creation and, 301

local culture/subcultures and, 298–299

multiple values/norms and, 295, 304

naniwabushi negotiation process example and, 289–290, 297

negotiation behaviors and, 291, 291 (table), 295–297

negotiation planning process and, 66–67, 66 (table)

nuance, appreciation for, 289, 298

organizational culture and, 299–300

performance orientation and, 292

perspective taking capacity and, 297

power distance and, 292, 294, 295

purpose/workings of negotiation, perspectives on, 295–297, 298

respectful behaviors/attitudes and, 302

sensemaking imperative and, 288–289

stereotyping, trap of, 292–294

team culture and, 300

trust, violation of, 145

uncertainty avoidance and, 292

understanding, development of, 289, 297–298, 302

See also Individual differences; Negotiation management

Curhan, J. R., 111

Darley, J. M., 45

Distributive agreement, 41

Druckman, D., 306

Egocentrism, 10, 16, 166

Elfenbein, H. A., 111

Emotional ambivalence, 282

Emotional appeal tactic, 126–127

Emotional contagion, 280

Emotional intelligence (EI), 273, 282–283

Emotions, 279

anger and, 279–281, 297

anxiety/fear and, 282

control over, 283

cultural differences and, 297–298

emotional ambivalence and, 282

emotional contagion and, 280

emotional intelligence and, 273, 282–283

expression of, 281–282, 297–298

faking emotions and, 280, 281, 283

genuine expression of, 281, 298

meditation/calming exercises and, 283

negotiation process and, 279–283, 297–298

strategic use of, 298

See also Individual differences; Personality traits

Endowment effect, 16

Eppers, M., 107

Escalation of commitment, 263–264

Ethics of negotiation, 41–42

alternatives in negotiation/BATNA and, 238–240

bad people vs. bad behaviors and, 45–46

billboard test and, 46

bluffing and, 44

bogey tactic and, 101

bribing practice and, 45–46, 303

contextual factors and, 43–46

cultural contexts/differences and, 44, 45–46, 302–304

deception and, 44

dilemmas and, 45–46

door-in-the-face technique and, 100–101

ethics, definition of, 42

fairness/justice concerns and, 42–43

formal power, leveraging of, 209–211

goal setting/persistence/motivation and, 264–266

individual differences, consideration of, 284–285

influence, practice of, 42

intangible interests, genuine understanding of, 129–130

intangible interests, leveraging of, 128

integrity and, 44–45

lying, unethical nature of, 43–44

negotiation planning and, 46, 77–78, 303

perception manipulation/management and, 43

personal ethics standards and, 43–45, 77, 101, 303, 304

planning negotiation strategies and, 46

reciprocity issues and, 100–102

relationship management and, 153

social network members, preferential treatment of, 44

trust dynamics and, 278

ultimatum/dictator game, resource allocation and, 43

goal setting, motivated negotiators and, 247, 248 (figure, table), 249

goal-setting process, motivation and, 251–252

goal-setting theory and, 249

intangible goal setting tactic and, 261, 261–262 (table)

intrinsic motivation and, 253–254

measurable goals and, 247, 248 (figure), 250, 262 (table)

motivating goals, characteristics of, 247, 249

negotiation effort and, 248 (figure)

negotiation motivation, impact on, 65, 247, 249

negotiation tactics and, 258–262

overspecification danger and, 65, 264

participation goals and, 262 (table)

personality traits, effect of, 250

preference sheet use tactic, 260–261, 260 (table)

public commitment goals and, 262 (table)

relevant goals, 247, 248 (figure), 250–251, 262 (table)

resistance points and, 252, 253 (table)

restrictive/overspecified goals and, 264

self-efficacy, role of, 250

setting goals tactic and, 259

SMART goals and, 247, 248 (figure), 249–251, 261, 261–262 (table)

specific goals, 247, 248 (figure), 249, 251, 261 (table)

time-bound goals, 247, 248 (figure), 251, 262 (table)

winner's curse and, 249, 253

See also Motivation; Persistence

Group-based identity, 112–113, 113 (figure)

Gruber, H., 19

Hardball tactics, 10, 213

artificial focal points and, 217

authority, limitations of, 214

bogey/phony issues and, 215–216

Boulwarism and, 218–219

emotions/play acting and, 218

extreme demands, highball/lowball offers and, 215

good cop/bad cop situation and, 213–214

nibble deal and, 216

playing chicken and, 216–217

response to, 213

slicing/small requests and, 219

snow job and, 219–220

See also Formal power; Negotiation; Power; Tactics

Hershey, J. C., 264

Heuristics, 12–13

Hitler, A., 194

Hofstede, G., 291

Iceberg metaphor, 288–289, 288 (figure)

Identity, 10, 111–112

apologies and, 146

belongingness and, 112

consistency, cognitive dissonance and, 117–119

definition/function of, 112

group-based identity, 112–113, 113 (figure)

identity threats and, 116–117, 119, 146

in-group bias and, 112

interests in principle and, 120

losing face and, 117–118

multiple facets/layers of, 115–116

relationship-based identity, 113 (figure), 114

role-based identity, 113–114, 113 (figure), 121

saving face and, 118

self-worth/self-esteem and, 112

sources of, 112–115, 113 (figure)

symbol-based identity, 113 (figure), 115

See also Intangible interests; Relationships

Identity threats, 116–117, 119, 146

Illusory conflict, 14

Impression management, 148, 206–207

In-group effects, 143–144, 150

Individual differences, 270

agreeableness and, 276–277, 278

conflict avoidance and, 275–276

cultural factors and, 272, 273, 275

emotions/emotional responses and, 279–283

gender/sex differences and, 271–274

knowledge/skills/abilities and, 283–284

loss sensitivity, prospect theory and, 178

luck of the draw and, 127

negotiation ability, differences in, 283–284

negotiation planning and, 66–67, 66 (table)

personality traits and, 10–11, 66 (table), 127, 250, 274–279

pro-social/pro-self individuals and, 277

social value orientation and, 277

taking advantage, tendency toward, 276, 277, 278

trust, degree of, 144, 277–278

See also Cultural factors; Negotiation management

Individualistic cultures, 294

Inert knowledge problem, 19–20

Influence, 7, 42, 193–194

Information, 51
  creative negotiation and, 54–55
  false-consensus effect and, 51–52
  filters on, 53
  negotiation tactics, anticipation of, 54
  packaging issues and, 96
  reciprocity, information exchange and, 83
  relevance of, 52–53
  sensemaking imperative and, 167–169
  signaling theory and, 170
  sources of, 172, 173 (table)
  technology resources and, 135–136
  trust, information sharing and, 2–3, 86–87,
      87 (figure), 144, 145, 277
  truth, evaluation of, 51–52, 53
  types of, 51, 52 (table)
  uncertainty, leveraging of, 180–181
  value creation, planning for, 54–55
  See also Negotiation planning
Information asymmetry, 169–170
Information sharing, 2–3, 86–87, 87 (figure),
    144, 145, 277
Intangible interests, 36–39, 108
  consistency, cognitive dissonance and, 117–119, 122,
      127, 128
  definition of, 111
  discourse vs. outcome of negotiation and, 112
  emotional appeal tactic and, 126–127
  ethical considerations and, 129–130
  example of, 108–110
  face concerns and, 117–118, 121, 122
  face saving tactics and, 122
  framing positions tactic and, 122–123
  identity/self considerations and, 111–119,
      113 (figure)
  intangible goal setting tactic and,
      261, 261–262 (table)
  intangible resources utilization tactic and, 123–126
  interests in principle and, 119–120, 121
  leveraging intangible interests, benefits to, 127–128
  leveraging intangible interests, costs of, 128–129
  losing/saving face and, 117–118, 121, 122
  negotiation tactics and, 122–127
  respect and, 120–121
  standards application tactic and, 127
  tangible vs. intangible interests and,
      111, 111 (Table)
  technology resources and, 134–136

  trading of, 111–112, 126
  See also Interests; Negotiation levers;
      Tangible interests
Integrative agreement, 41, 201
Integrative tactic, xv
  See also Adding issues tactic; Creating value
Integrity, 44–45
Interdependence, 4–5, 6 (table)
Interests, 32–33
  identification of, 90–91
  interest-based questions, posing of, 92–93
  negotiation process and, 26, 32–33, 36, 88–89, 90–91
  positions and, 34–35, 34 (table), 35 (figure), 39,
      92–93, 93 (figure)
  reciprocity and, 83, 88
  tangible interests, 36–39, 111 (table)
  uncertainty, diminishment of, 164
  universal interests and, 33
  See also Intangible interests; Negotiation approaches
Interests in principle, 119–120, 121
Intrinsic motivation, 253–254
Issues, 2, 32
  adding issues tactic and, xv, 41
  interests vs. positions and, 34–35, 34 (table)
  logrolling tactic and, 63–64
  multiple-issue negotiation and, 39–40
  negotiation planning and, 57–58
  obvious issues, 32, 33 (table), 57
  overspecification and, 65, 264
  packaging issues tactic and, 96, 96 (table)
  potential issues, 32, 33 (table), 57
  preference tables and, 58–65, 59–64 (tables)
  resistance points and, 39–40, 40 (figure)
  single-issue negotiation and, 39
  See also Negotiation; Negotiation approaches;
      Negotiation planning

Jante Law, 294
Job negotiations, 332
  BATNA improvement tactic and, 334
  contingent contract tactic and, 335–336
  convincing-to-understanding movement and,
      333–334
  e-mail communication, avoidance of, 336
  inside knowledge, access to, 335
  issues for negotiation and, 332–333
  mentor-mentee relationship and, 336
  negotiation planning and, 332–333

opponent-as-mentor perspective and, 336
planning worksheet, completion of, 333
proactive questioning and, 333–334
uncertainty, reduction of, 335
value, recognition of, 336–337
Joint action, 4, 5, 7

Kahneman, D., 169, 181
Kasten, B., 271
King, P., 188
Knowledge/skills/abilities (KSAs), 283–284
Kopelman, S., 3, 281, 298

Labor-management negotiations, 189–190
Larimar, S., 120
Laschever, S., 271
Latané, B., 45
Legitimate power, 195 (table), 196, 197, 202 (table)
Levers. *See* Negotiation levers
Lewicki, R. J., 144
Lewis, R., 295
Loewenstein, J., 19
Logrolling tactic, 63–64, 80–81, 85, 89, 95, 96, 126, 231, 257, 301
Lose-Lose agreement, 14
Losing face, 117–118

Maddux, W. W., 298
Major League Soccer Player's Union, 187–188
Management. *See* Negotiation management
Mandl, H., 19
Meaning. *See* Sensemaking process
Measurable goals, 247, 248 (figure), 250, 262 (table)
Media richness theory, 134–135
Mediation, 186–189, 187 (table)
Mental models, 7–8, 82, 87, 91
Milgram, S., 45, 196, 197
Mimicry, 84
Mini cases. *See* Case vignettes
Mistakes in negotiation, 7, 9 (figure)
    assumptions, mistaken beliefs and, 14–16
    availability bias and, 16–17
    commonalities, recognition of, 20–21
    compartmentalized knowledge and, 19, 20
    compromise, flawed negotiation and, 10
    confirming evidence bias and, 17
    conflict avoidance strategy and, 10–11, 11 (figure)
    egocentrism and, 16

endowment effect and, 16
expectation of attitudinal/behavioral consistency and, 15
false-consensus effect and, 14–15, 51–52, 56, 91
fixed-pie bias, succumbing to, 12–14, 13 (table)
fold wisdom, use of, 10
functional fixedness bias and, 17–18
hardball tactics and, 10
heuristics, information misinterpretation and, 12–13
illusory conflict and, 14
inert knowledge problem and, 19–20
knowledge transfer, barriers to, 18–20
lose-lose agreements and, 14
mental models, role of, 7–8
negotiation planning, neglect of, 11–12
organizational change, dangerous assumptions and, 15–16
outcomes-based interest, beliefs about, 111
poor negotiation behaviors, struggle to change and, 17–18
self-fulfilling prophecy and, 17
self-serving motivations and, 16–17, 111
successful negotiation, preconceived notions of, 9–10
tactics, selection criteria for, 17–18
threatening behaviors and, 10
See also Alternatives in negotiation; Negotiation
Moore, D. A., 244
Morris, M. W., 271
Motivation, 247
    ethics considerations and, 264–266
    extrinsic motivation, 252–253
    goal-setting process and, 251–252
    goals, impact of, 65, 247, 249
    intrinsic motivation, 253–254
    negotiation process, persistence in, 254–257, 257–258 (table)
    preference sheet use tactic and, 260–261, 260 (table)
    reciprocity motivation and, 82–83
    virtue of, 256–257
    See also Goals; Persistence
Multiparty negotiations, 158–159

Naniwabushi negotiation process, 289–290, 297
Negotiated exchange, 141, 142 (table)
Negotiation:
    adding an issue and, xv
    art/science of, 2

SMART (specific/measurable/attainable/relevant/
time-bound) goals, 247, 248 (figure), 249–251
Social exchange, 140
altruism and, 140
experiences, sharing of, 150
generalized exchange and, 140, 141, 142 (table)
negotiated exchange and, 141, 142 (table)
reciprocal exchange and, 140, 142 (table)
rules of exchange and, 139–141, 142 (table)
See also Relationship power
Social norms, 84, 273
Social value orientation (SVO), 277
Specific goals, 247, 248 (figure), 249, 251, 261 (table)
Standards:
fairness principle and, 127
personal ethics standards and, 43–45, 77, 101, 303, 304
standards application tactic and, 127
Stanford Prison Experiment, 45
Stereotypes, 169, 271, 273
Stereotyping, 11, 169, 274, 292–294
Sunk cost bias, 66
Symbol-based identity, 113 (figure), 115

Tactics, 17, 67
adding issues tactic, 41, 94–95, 99–100
aggressive tactics, 10
anchor tactic, 105, 176–177
bogey tactic, 101
coalition building tactic, 198, 205, 231
common ground/similarities focus tactic, 150
communication modality and, 135
compromise tactic, 2, 10, 93–94
concession planning tactic, 175, 176 (table)
consistency tactic, 148–149
contingent contract tactic, 96–98, 106, 335–336
data-based arguments tactic, 173–175, 174 (figure)
dependability tactic, 149
disclosing BATNA tactic, 235–237
emotional appeal tactic, 126–127
experience sharing tactic, 150
exposing another's BATNA tactic, 237
face saving tactics, 122
formal power and, 202 (table), 203–207
framing as gains tactic, 178–179
framing positions tactic, 122–123
friendliness/openness tactic, 148
hard vs. soft tactics, 306
impression management tactic, 206–207

improving BATNA tactic, 234–235, 234 (table),
257, 334
intangible interests and, 122–127
integrative tactic, xv
interest-based questions, posing of, 92–93, 93 (figure)
interests, identification of, 90–91
legitimacy leveraging tactic, 204
logrolling tactic, 63–64, 80–81, 85, 89, 95, 96, 126, 231
negotiation tactics, anticipation of, 54
opening offer/anchor tactic, 176–177
packaging issues tactic, 96, 96 (table)
persistence tactic, 258–259
perspective taking and, 91
preference sheet use tactic, 260–261, 260 (table)
professional appearance tactic, 148
reciprocity tactic and, 83, 149
relationships and, 148–150
research/information gathering tactic, 172, 173 (table)
resource leveraging tactic, 203–204
selection criteria for, 17–18
self-monitoring tactic, 148
uncertainty and, 172–179
walking away tactic, 237, 259
See also Hardball tactics; Intangible interests;
Negotiation levers
Tangible interests, 36–39, 111 (table)
See also Intangible interests; Interests
Team negotiations, 157
Technology resources, 67, 134
alternatives, understanding of, 135–136
communication technology, use of, 134, 135
e-mail communication and, 336
face-to-face communication, benefits of, 134–135
information, availability of, 135–136
media richness theory and, 134–135
negotiation documentation and, 135
negotiation tactics, communication modality and, 135
See also Negotiation levers
Thompson, L. L., 19, 83, 281
Threatening behavior, 10
See also Identity threats
Time-bound goals, 247, 248 (figure), 251, 262 (table)
Time constraints, 67, 243–244
Tolerance for ambiguity, 170–171
Trade-offs, 57, 63–64, 85, 89, 95, 260
Trust:
agreeableness and, 277, 278
anger and, 280